From the Absurd to Revolt

Dynamics in Albert Camus's Thought

De l'absurde à la révolte

Dynamique de la pensée
d'Albert Camus

From the Absurd to Revolt

Dynamics in Albert Camus's Thought

De l'absurde à la révolte

Dynamique de la pensée d'Albert Camus

Editors

Maciej Kałuża, Piotr Mróz

Jagiellonian University Press

REVIEWER
dr hab. Izabela Trzcińska

COVER DESIGN
Jadwiga Burek

This project was financed by the Nation Science Centre,
granted on basis of decision number DEC-2013/09/D/HS1/00873

Publikacja została sfinansowana ze środków Narodowego Centrum Nauki
przyznanych na podstawie decyzji numer DEC-2013/09/D/HS1/00873

First edition, Kraków 2017

ISBN 978-83-233-4253-3
ISBN 978-83-233-9606-2 (e-book)

JAGIELLONIAN UNIVERSITY PRESS
www.wuj.pl

Jagiellonian University Press
Editorial Offices: ul. Michałowskiego 9/2, 31-126 Krakow
Phone: +48 12 663 23 80, +48 12 663 23 82, Fax: +48 12 663 23 83
Distribution: Phone: +48 12 631 01 97, Fax: +48 12 631 01 98
Cell Phone: +48 506 006 674, e-mail: sprzedaz@wuj.pl
Bank: PEKAO SA, IBAN PL80 1240 4722 1111 0000 4856 3325

Table of Contents

Part Two: Camus's Revolt in Contemporary Analysis

Part Three: Camus's Revolt in Comparatistic Studies

Introduction

The book which we present today came into being, like many other books, with a single sentence and a simple idea, written down in 2013 in a research project, stating our wish to organize a conference in Cracow dedicated to the notions of the absurd and revolt in Albert Camus's thought. Like many other books, it is a proof that it is always better to be solidary than solitary, especially with all the support one can get from the people, dedicated to Camus's *œuvre.* The idea developed slowly but gradually and was patiently consulted with Agnès Spiquel, the President of Société des Études Camusiennes, who gave us great encouragement and support to the idea of the conference and the present publication. We also received a great aid from Sophie Bastien and David Sprintzen, as well as members of Albert Camus Society US/UK. Much support came from Polish scholars, Czesława Piecuch, Ignacy S. Fiut and Joanna Hańderek. These wonderful people did not only help in making the 2016 Cracow conference come true – but they also added significantly by helping in the difficult, yet necessary decision-making process of evaluating research proposals, arriving by droves after the announcement of our conference. Our meeting in February was unique by all accounts. The conference, inaugurated by the Dean of Faculty of Philosophy at the Jagiellonian University, Jarosław Górniak, and the wonderful greeting letter from Agnès Spiquel, was – as I see it today – a proof of timeliness of Camus's ideas and a fascinating example of a continuing interest in his profound reflection on modern human condition. The principal aim of our conference was to discuss the philosophical aspects of the two main concepts prevalent in Camus's philosophy: the absurd and revolt, debating on the dynamics of Camus's philosophical journey. Our analysis of the progression of his thought, from the individualized experience and consciousness of the absurd to understanding human revolt through solidarity seems to me, even after more than 65 years since the publication of Camus's second major philosophical essay, a fertile ground for discussion and finding new answers to questions, evoked by philosophical dilemmas found in Camus's writings.

Our discussions and considerations resulted in this book, which, we have decided to divide into three major parts. The first part of our study harks back at the origins and sources of the Camusian progression from absurd-oriented reflection to his analysis of revolt. Simon Lea in the first chapter goes back to Camus's understanding of indifference in relation to Camusian notion of revolt. In chapter two, Virginie Lupo reaches for *Caligula*, a work signifying the development of Camusian reflection. Chapters three and four both focus on *La Peste* from varying angles, offering, in the study of Marie-Thérèse Blondeau, a profound analysis of engagement, an important aspect of revolt. Eric Berg offers a study of theological aspects of Camus's novel, giving an insightful perspective of Bonhoeffer's conclusions to the dilemmas of Father Paneloux. In chapter five, Christian Chevandier offers an exhaustive account of Camus's intellectual preparation for writing his study of rebellion. Chapter six goes back to the conclusions from Camus's reflection on absurdity and revolt in two essays, *La liberté absurde* and *L'absurde et le meurtre*, and may be considered a brief evaluation of my recent research carried out at the Jagiellonian University.

Part two, dedicated to a contemporary perspective for studies of Camus's thought, opens with the intriguing chapter by Sophie Bastien and Emmanuel Habimana, who present the philosopher's influence by reference to the concept of resilience. In chapter eight, Théodore Caponis offers a fine example of an analytic approach, presenting the role of the notion of "murder" in *L'Homme révolté* by means of the method of semantic fields. Chapter nine, by Tomasso Visone, introduces the contemporary debate on Camus's view on modernity in reference to the famous debate on secularisation thesis. In Chapter ten, Ignacy S. Fiut considers the thought of Camus from the perspective of European universalism. Chapter eleven, by Ewa Średnicka, is a thought-provoking analysis of the idea of justice in Camus's editorials from *Combat,* seen from the complex perspective of his changing attitude during *L'épuration*.

The last part of our study is dedicated to the comparative perspective. Giovanni Gaetani opens this section with his remarkable and well carried out idea to confront Camus's idea of revolt with the presentation of Irish revolutionaries, as presented by Ken Loach in the movie *The Wind That Shakes the Barley*. Chapter thirteen by Raphael Luiz de Araújo offers a convincing study of similarities and differences between Marxist critique, Leszek Kołakowski, and Camus's idea of revolt. Chapter fourteen by Barbara Zauli is an original attempt at perspective on Camus's Nietzschean sources, whereas in chapter fifteen Marcin Urbaniak presents Colin Wilson's interpretation of Camusian revolt. Chapter sixteen by Justyna Gambert reaches to *La Chute* in an exhaustive study of Iwaszkiewicz's work from 1957, *Wzlot*. The final, concluding chapter by Piotr Mróz and Remigiusz Król presents the "strange spiritual affinity" of Camus and Dostoevsky.

During our editing work for this book, we have received the sorrowful information that late Michel Henri Kowalewicz, a dedicated scholar to the history of ideas, who eagerly contributed to our February discussions in Cracow, had died. It is our deepest regret that He would not be acquainted with the result of our discussions he in so many diverse ways had inspired.

Wishing that our readers find inspiration in this rich and diverse selection of attempts at rethinking Camus's philosophical and literary achievement we would like to thank all our friends and colleagues for their support, help, comments, understanding and kindness. We sincerely hope that the reading of this book will be for you as enriching as it was for us.

Maciej Kałuża, Piotr Mróz
Cracow, October 2016

Part One:
From the Absurd to Revolt,
Analysis of Sources for Camusian Concept of Revolt

Profound Indifference: The Source of Revolt in the Early Writings of Camus

SIMON LEA

INTRODUCTION

I have considered the "early writings" of Albert Camus as: the five essays collected in *The Wrong Side and the Right Side*; the four of *Nuptials*; the abandoned novella *A Happy Death*; *The Stranger*; and the long essay *The Myth of Sisyphus*. For brevity, I have omitted all but the briefest reference to Camus's plays, *The Misunderstanding* and *Caligula*, as discussion of these works would neither add nor subtract greatly from my argument. Finally, because I am interested in Camus's philosophical response to indifference, and in particular his conception of profound indifference, I will not be looking at his journalistic work. *The Plague* represents a strong shift in Camus's attitude to indifference; the introduction of the social question adds an entirely new dimension to his concept of revolt. Since I am interested here in indifference as the origin of revolt, I stop short before this novel.

VARIETIES OF INDIFFERENCE

There are many ways of being indifferent and almost limitless objects to which one can be indifferent. Indifference can be a vice; in the common usage of the label it most often is, but there are forms of indifference that are virtuous. And it is possible for an individual to live a life that is indifferent to some object in a way that is contemptible while at the same time exhibiting indifference to some other object in a way that is commendable. When we say of a person that they *are* indifferent contra indifferent *to* some object, what we usually mean is they are apathetically indifferent to some aspect of life in a way damaging to character. However, as we shall see, it is possible to be indifferent in a way that is character building. In my discussion of Camus's different uses of indifference, I will be drawing heavily on Lillehammer's work on varieties of indifference in which he identifies eight kinds divided equally into virtues and vices. I will give a brief overview of these indifferences with one or two examples of each taken from Camus's work. My intention here is to lay the ground for discussion of indifference later in this article. For example, to understand, say, Meursault's indifference in *The Stranger* we need to be able to say in this instance what kind of indifference we mean, and to what he is indifferent, and where applicable, why he is so. In addition, familiarity with the many ways it is possible to be indifferent is necessary before we can understand what Camus means when he says, "... real nobility (that of the heart) is based on scorn, courage and profound indifference."[1]

What Lillehammer calls "virtuous apathy" occurs when a person fails to cultivate "a caring orientation towards some feature of the world" where this failure does not express a negative judgement of the object.[2] This virtue can be contrasted with "apathetic indifference," which involves "a state of not caring about certain features of the world that are of genuine ethical significance."[3] In *Death in the Soul*, referring to the teeming early morning commuters, Camus writes: "Around me were a million human beings who had been alive all this time whose existence had never concerned me."[4] His indifference to these existences can not be an expression of a negative judgement because Camus until now has not thought about these people. Thus, using Lillehammer's terminology we can say Camus here displays virtuous apathy. In *The Plague* we have a good example of apathetic indifference. Dr. Rieux observes a "steady growth of strange indifference in himself and his friends."[5] Their indifference is brought about by the stress of their task, the mental and physical exhaustion. They simply stop bothering to take the necessary precautions before

1 A. Camus, *Notebook III, Notebooks 1935–1942*, trans. P. Thody, Chicago, Ivan R. Dee, 2010, p. 140.

2 H. Lillehammer, *Minding Your own Business? Understanding Indifference as a Virtue* [pdf], "Philosophical Perspectives" 2014, vol. 28, no. 01. Available at http://www.hallvardlillehammer.com/online-papers.html [access: June 2016], p. 3.

3 H. Lillehammer, *Who is My Neighbour? Understanding Indifference as Vice* [pdf], "Philosophy" 2014, vol. 89, no. 04. Available at http://www.hallvardlillehammer.com/online-papers.html [access: June 2016], p. 6.

4 A. Camus, *Albert Camus: Lyrical and Critical Essays*, trans. C. Kennedy, ed. P. Thody, New York, Random House, 1970, p. 40.

5 A. Camus, *The Plague*, trans. R. Buss, Penguin Books Ltd, 2001, p. 147.

dealing with the sick; basic hygiene is neglected and if the effort of getting fresh inoculations is required they simply go without. The townspeople of Oran "suffered a kind of spiritual and physical emaciation."[6] They no longer see the point of making value-judgements: "no one cared any longer about the quality of their clothes or the food they bought."[7] Lillehammer's next two varieties are indifference as "virtuous rejection" and its corresponding vice "blinkered indifference." The first is a failure to care about something judged to be unworthy of concern because time is better spent on other pursuits. Don Juan, as depicted in *The Myth of Sisyphus*, moves on from woman to woman, indifferent to all but his current conquest. He rejects love as an illusion of the eternal and forgets each woman as he moves on to the next.[8] In this way Don Juan is not a "collector" of sexual experiences; thoughts of the past, especially regret, and the notion of love are subjects deemed unworthy of concern. Camus uses the fictional libertine as an example of the absurd man and the kind of indifference he seeks; however the same legend could be used by others to demonstrate blinkered indifference. In that case, the Don Juan myth could be used to illustrate indifference to moral concerns in the pursuit of selfish ends. Unlike the apathetic indifferences discussed above, both virtuous rejection and blinkered indifference, and the others to follow, are active rather than passive.

When particular groups are singled out as unworthy of moral consideration we have what Lillehammer terms "negating indifference." If Meursault, or the white Europeans of Algiers, or Camus himself, is indifferent to the loss of the Arab's life (or the sexual assault on his sister) *because* he is an Arab and therefore considered to be unworthy of moral consideration, then we have a clear-cut example of negating indifference. When two or more social groups live side by side in the same communities, the attitude that one group is unworthy of consideration is almost certainly going to lead to hostility and violence. The more apparent the differences between members of opposing groups, the more likely a disruptive outcome. "Indifference as civility," involves a deliberate lack of interest in pursuing subjects that could, if probed, lead to otherwise avoidable hostilities: a live-and-let-live attitude to cultural differences within communities. Another example of this kind of indifference is the general prohibition on discussing religion and politics at dinner parties. We can also include the simple minding of

---

6 *Ibidem*, p. 139.

7 *Ibidem*, p. 142.

8 A. Camus, *The Myth of Sisyphus*, trans. J. O'Brien, London, Penguin Books Ltd, 2000, p. 69–70.

one's own business when appropriate among friends. In *The Misunderstanding* Martha's policy of "amiable indifference" towards guests is an example of this kind of civil indifference.[9] On the other hand, her indifference to human life when she murders rich guests is a blending of most of the vices described above.

"Controlled indifference" occurs when a thing, possibly of ethical significance, is deliberately met with indifference in order to give appropriate attention to competing objects. This would include an indifference to temptation. Examples include an institution's policy of indifference to race and gender when handing out benefits; and the appropriate indifference to the demands or expectations of friendship expected of government officials when carrying out their duties. The temptations here are of acting on prejudice and nepotism. We see in *The Stranger* the indifference to Meursault's crime displayed after his arrest by the officials of the State. The police, examining magistrate, lawyers and prison warders all display indifference to the criminal act that brought Meursault into their hands. While we would not expect officials to be on friendly terms with prisoners, we can expect them, in carrying out their duties, to display indifference to feelings of contempt or disgust they may have, however tempting. The corresponding vice is "exclusionary indifference." The opposite of ethically appropriate indifference to friends and members of one's own social group, exclusionary indifference is a failure to care about those outside of the group because priority is given to members. It could be argued that Meursault fails to see why he should not write Raymond's letter for him because he is indifferent to the interests of Arabs or women.

PROFOUND INDIFFERENCE

The indifference that lies at the core of Camus's revolt is to the temptation of hope. In what way will be discussed below in the section on hope. It is a kind of controlled indifference. It is profound in three ways:

1. It is all-consuming passion, a revolt that "challenges the world anew every second."[10]
2. The cultivation and maintenance of this attitude is of great importance.
3. It is an intense experience.

---

9 A. Camus, *The Misunderstanding, Caligula and Three Other Plays*, trans. S. Gilbert, New York, Random House, 1962, p. 96.

10 A. Camus, *The Myth...*, p. 53.

Now that we have a sense of what profound indifference is for Camus we turn to the cause of his indifference: a reflection on time in relation to death and the necessity of lucid thinking.

DEATH, TIME AND LUCIDITY

"The present and the succession of presents before a constantly conscious soul is the ideal of the absurd man."[11] Camus, as Dunwoodie observes, places "exceptional stress on the unique value of the present."[12] He sees in the essays of *The Wrong Side and the Right Side* the need to "control" the tension caused by a love of life and the presence of death.[13] Hanna, referring to *Nuptials*, identifies Camus's recurring conviction that the reality of death must be faced, that our lives and actions must be "adjusted" to this inescapable destiny.[14] This control, the ability to adjust, comes from indifference. "Everything," Camus claims in *The Myth of Sisyphus*, "begins with lucid indifference."[15] In the long essay Camus argues that the struggle (for indifference) repeats itself daily. Constant vigilance is required; the confrontation with the absurd must be "unceasing,"[16] and one must be constantly aware, "ever revived, ever alert."[17] Revolt, he says, "challenges the world anew every second."[18] To understand Camus's notion of indifference we need to see how it relates to time, death and lucidity.

Awareness of death is an awareness that life is subject to a time-limit with the consequent realisation that time is precious. It appears puzzling, at first blush, that for Camus death is the foundation of indifference.[19] How can something we are required to attend to also be a matter of indifference? Camus expends a great deal of energy writing essays, novels and plays that ask the question: how can a life subject to time, in other words living "condemned to death," hold value? Given this attention, it cannot be death, or more accurately the question of what we ought to do faced with the inevitability of death, that leaves him indifferent. He hardly displays a lack of concern; as Bespaloff

---

11 *Ibidem*, p. 62.

12 P. Dunwoodie, *L'Envers et L'endroit and L'Exil et le Royaume*, London, Grant & Cutler, 1985, p. 28.

13 *Ibidem*, p. 9–10.

14 T. Hanna, *The Thought and Art of Albert Camus*, Chicago, Henry Regnery Company, 1958, p. 6.

15 A. Camus, *The Myth…*, p. 87.

16 *Ibidem*, p. 34.

17 *Ibidem*, p. 52.

18 *Ibidem*, p. 53.

19 T. Hanna, *op.cit.*, p. 61.

puts it, "Camus refuses to take his mind off this question."[20] In *The Myth of Sisyphus* he refers to the achievement and maintenance of indifference as an "ascesis," success requires therefore rigorous mental self-discipline; an activity seemingly the opposite of indifference.[21] To find what we are looking for we must look not at death itself but the horror of death.

For Camus this horror comes from the "mathematical aspect of the event."[22] It is time, he says, that frightens us.[23] More accurately, it is our lack thereof that is the problem. Time, not death itself, is identified as the enemy in *The Myth of Sisyphus*, and realisation of our antagonistic relationship with time triggers revolt.[24] We note our age one day and realise our place on a timeline. For Camus, dreams of the future, living for a life to come rather than in the present, is time squandered; wasted "longing for tomorrow" when everything in us should have "rejected it."[25] We all know we will die, yet, says Camus, "one will never be sufficiently surprised that everyone lives as if no one 'knew'."[26] Here we have an indifference of which Camus disapproves: indifference towards a diminishing resource. Realising our place on a timeline is shocking because most of the time we act as if we were unaware of our mortality; what shocks is our previous indifference to this fact. Camus is being ironic when he talks of "sufficient surprise;" he understands the temptation to avoid facing the reality of the future; it is the temptation of hope for an alternative. The effort to meet hope with indifference requires constant, rigorous mental self-discipline; the struggle against time's destructive power is severe and the necessity bitter.[27]

INDIFFERENCE TO HOPE

The indifference that Camus struggles to achieve is to a particular way of thinking about the future that involves hope. This is a particular kind of hope, one he sees as an evil.[28] "From the mass of human evils swarming in Pandora's

---

20 R. Bespaloff, *The World of the Man Condemned to Death* [in:] *Camus: A Collection of Critical Essays*, ed. G. Brée, New Jersey, Prentice–Hall, 1962, p. 92.

21 A. Camus, *The Myth…*, p. 104.

22 *Ibidem*, p. 20.

23 *Ibidem*.

24 *Ibidem*.

25 *Ibidem*.

26 *Ibidem*, p. 21.

27 J. Cruickshank, *Albert Camus and the Literature of Revolt*, London–New York, Oxford University Press, 1960, p. 29.

28 Peyre claims that Camus's "most original revolt is against hope." In: *Camus: A Collection of Critical Essays…*, p. 68.

box, the Greeks brought out hope at the very last, as the most terrible of all. I don't know any symbol more moving. For hope, contrary to popular belief, is tantamount to resignation. And to live is not to be resigned."[29] Camus is repeating an idea found in Nietzsche, that hope is the worst evil because it prolongs suffering.[30] To be resigned is to calmly accept an inevitable, unpleasant fate. The kind of hope Camus opposes then is an attitude that allows a person to be calm about their fate. Like Stendhal's Cardinal Carrafa, Camus wants to face death not calmly but with silent scorn. From the epigraph to *Nuptials*: "The Cardinal looked at the hangman without deigning to utter a word."[31] For Camus, freedom from hope is the source of human freedom. "A man devoid of hope and conscious of being so has ceased to *belong* to the future"[32] (my emphasis). To hope is to belong not to oneself but to the future; it is not to be free but to suffer enslavement to an idea.[33]

Camus is not indifferent to all kinds of hope. From the trivial to the profound, he has no problem with wanting something to happen or be the case; Patrice Mersault can hope his lentils are not too dry, Rieux can hope the plague will take no more lives, and Camus can hope for the right kind of indifference. The hope towards which Camus cultivates indifference is for consolation to the finality of death; he wants to "live *without appeal*."[34] This consolation is most often in the form of something to come, for example the promise of life after death. In this case hope and the future are entwined and inseparable. Most of the time Camus's focus is on this kind of hope, however it is possible to be indifferent to hope, in what Camus would consider the right way, whilst being indifferent to the future in the wrong way.[35] For example: Camus demands constant, lucid attention to the reality of time (death) therefore he rejects any claim that death is an event not worth thinking about. That is, against the idea that there are better things on which to spend our mental energy, what Lillehammer would call indifference as "virtuous rejection," (and Camus would consider "blinkered indifference"). The temptations

29 A. Camus, *Albert Camus: Lyrical and Critical...*, p. 92.

30 F. Nietzsche, *Human All Too Human*, trans. M. Faber and S. Lehmann, London, Penguin Books Ltd, 2004, p. 58.

31 A. Camus, *Albert Camus: Lyrical and Critical...*, p. 63.

32 A. Camus, *The Myth...*, p. 35.

33 In the opening pages of *The Myth of Sisyphus* Camus refers to the trickery of those who evade the question of death by living "not for life itself, but some great idea that will transcend it, refine it, give it meaning, and betray it." Trans. J. O'Brien, London, Penguin Books Ltd, 2000, p. 15.

34 A. Camus, *The Myth...*, p. 53.

35 Camus does not talk of "right" and "wrong" indifference; however the distinction is clear.

then, that Camus wants to meet with indifference, are: (1) hope for another life, and (2) refusal to confront the fact of death. As we have just seen, for Camus, someone given in to (1) would also give in to (2) but it is possible to be tempted by (2) but indifferent to (1).

A wrong kind of indifference to time is the subject of *Irony*. In the essay Camus illustrates both of the temptations discussed above. The young people of Algiers are indifferent not only to the present suffering of the elderly (a kind of exclusionary indifference) but also the future suffering they themselves will have to endure. Camus's interest lies not in championing the plight of the elderly but in the lack of concern he sees in the general attitude towards the future. Rather than face up to the reality of time, most people prefer comforting fantasies of a future peaceful withdrawal from society. "They want to become foremen so they can retire to a little house in the country."[36] In *The Myth of Sisyphus* Camus offers a similar scenario: "A man wants to earn money in order to be happy and his whole effort and the best of life are devoted to the earning of that money. Happiness is forgotten; the means are taken for the end."[37] The goal, happy retirement, is forgotten, yet the man toils away in service of his future. He is a Sisyphus, indifferent to the top of his mountain and without the pleasure of the walk back down; the best of life for him is spent entirely "cheek to stone." Meursault rejects careerism and Patrice Mersault kills to avoid the financial necessity of work. Returning to *Irony*; for the average person dreams of wiling away their remaining days in peace become nightmares in reality. When the time comes it is not experienced by hazily conceived future selves but by present selves in a reality of hopeless solitude. However, anyone returning to society looking for the protection of other people will only meet indifference.[38] To protect their vague fantasies of the future, an indifference to the reality of time, the young must avoid thinking lucidly about their fate; the elderly, demonstrable evidence of the reality of temporal life, cannot become objects of concern. Accordingly, the presence of an old man is tolerated if his antics are amusing, and ignored once he starts to bore. It is indifference without enmity; to hate is to care. Camus sums up the attitude of the young: "What do an old man's sufferings matter when life absorbs you completely?"[39] We have to be careful: absorption in life is what Camus is hoping to achieve, however in this instance he refers to absorption

36 A. Camus, *Albert Camus: Lyrical and Critical* ..., p. 26.
37 A. Camus, *The Myth*..., p. 94.
38 A. Camus, *Albert Camus: Lyrical and Critical*..., p. 26.
39 *Ibidem*, p. 24.

in mind-numbing activities designed as a distraction from "the imbecility of everyday work."[40] Just as the careerist becomes absorbed in work, the young men described above are absorbed in palliatives to work.[41] In this essay we have examples of both temptations discussed above: those given into the hope of another life, focusing their energies on becoming foremen in order to retire to the country; and those turning away from the elderly to preserve the illusion they are immune to time. For both, death holds no fear. The former believe they can meet the enemy gently in a country garden while the latter do not think of it at all. They seek to eliminate the passion and intensity of the reality of death but in so doing reduce the passion and intensity of life. In their different ways they fail to cultivate a proper concern and this indifference is, as we have seen, the wrong kind. Hiding from the true nature of death is a false consciousness for Camus: "To a conscious man old age and what it portends are not a surprise. Indeed, he is conscious only in so far as he does not conceal the horror from himself."[42]

When I introduced the profound indifference I said merely that it was to hope; now we can see a clearer picture. Camus's profound indifference is an ascesis that demands a constant lucid awareness of the reality of time with a continual focus on death. Without death there would be no need for indifference. Hence, Hanna's observation that for Camus, the foundation of indifference is death. The indifference Camus hopes to achieve is to the twin temptations: of consoling hope of another life lived in the future; and the temptation to block out the true reality of the future. However, there is more to profound indifference than a revolt against hope. In his early work Camus has an obsession with matching his indifference to that he perceives in nature. It is to this we now turn with a look first at the "face" of indifference.

STASIS AND THE INDIFFERENCE OF THE WORLD

The face of indifference for Camus is expressionless. Upon this unmoving face he fancies he can see a smile. Referring to his mother in *Between Yes and No*, he says: "... though her lips do not move her face lights up in a beautiful

---

40 *Ibidem.*

41 This kind of indifference, the desire for a numbness in lieu of a solution to a particular problem, is shown to fail for Clamence in *The Fall*, and Jonas in *The Artist at Work*.

42 A. Camus, *The Myth...*, p. 71.

smile."[43] He thinks he can detect an *inner* smile on the face of St. Francis in Giotto's paintings.[44] Claire and the students in *A Happy Death* have "grave and smiling faces."[45] To show that Eliane, a visitor to the House above the World, has only pretensions of indifference, Camus says: "she thinks she looks like *The Man with a Glove*, though no-one else does."[46] Meursault, although he claims he is smiling, notices that his reflection is grave.[47] Sisyphus, in "silent joy," has a face that is turned to stone."[48] One final example: "As he emerges from the tomb, the risen Christ of Piero della Francesca has no human expression on his face – only a fierce and soulless grandeur that I cannot help taking for a resolve to live."[49] Substitute profound indifference for the Lord God, and Camus is expressing Isaiah 50:7: "... therefore have I set my face like a flint, and I know that I shall not be ashamed."

Camus's interest in Florentine art is more than as illustrations of the face of profound indifference. Artists work in the present; a painting freezes a single moment in time that lasts an eternity. In Francesco's *Flagellation of Christ*, for example, we see the expressionless grandeur of a man frozen in time, without a past or a future, suffering without hope.[50] "Why," Camus asks, "should a man who expects no tomorrow feel emotion?"[51] These images provide a focal point that allow Camus to himself withdraw into stasis. Such moments are lived focused on the present, indifferent to both future and past. The only use Camus has for the future is an invigoration of the present achieved by lucid thinking about death. As for the time between now and that point, events to come have no meaning. "The absurd enlightens me on this point: there is no future."[52] Memories have a similar limited value in that thoughts of things past can help invigorate the reality of the present.

Between Yes and No is a meditation on suspended time. Sat in a Moorish café one evening, Camus contemplates the wind that blows across the bay bringing with it the "peace and indifference of immortal things."[53] Memory

---

43 A. Camus, *Albert Camus: Lyrical and Critical...*, p. 37.

44 *Ibidem*, p. 100.

45 A. Camus, *A Happy Death*, trans. R. Howard, Middlesex, Penguin Books Ltd, 1974, p. 65.

46 *Ibidem*, p. 68.

47 A. Camus, *The Stranger*, trans. M. Ward, New York, Random House, 1989, p. 81.

48 A. Camus, *The Myth...*, p. 108.

49 A. Camus, *Albert Camus: Lyrical and Critical...*, p. 104.

50 T. Hanna, *op.cit.*, p. 5.

51 A. Camus, *Albert Camus: Lyrical and Critical...*, p. 94.

52 A. Camus, *The Myth ...*, p. 57.

53 A. Camus, *Albert Camus: Lyrical and Critical...*, p. 32.

intrudes the reverie; suddenly he is "home again."[54] Camus sees himself as a young boy silently approaching his mother. He is afraid, and her silence makes him want to "cry with pain." But he also feels pity for his mother and wonders if this is the same as loving her. "She has never hugged or kissed him, for she wouldn't know how."[55] Back in the café, Camus reflects on this mental intrusion and brings together his feelings for the woman who bore him and the world he was born into: "The indifference of this strange mother! Only the immense solitude of the world can be the measure of it."[56] "The whole of life," for Camus "can be summed up in an image;"[57] this image is his mother. He uses it as a focus point allowing withdrawal into stasis.[58] This memory proves useful as an aid to understanding his emotional response to the world; he rediscovers his experience of his mother's indifference and finds it a match to the indifference of the world. He is between yes and no because he suspends judgement; Camus *feels* the two sensations are the same and, for the moment, he is satisfied limiting himself to this. The essays in *Nuptials* are concerned with the physical experience of the world; only later in the *The Myth of Sisyphus* he will intellectualize this experience.[59] Camus's memory allows him to make an analogy between his feelings for his mother and mother nature. Rizzuto wonders if mother and nature are in Camus's mind two distinct realities or can be considered interchangeable.[60] In other words, whether the pain caused by the indifference of his mother is the same as the one caused by the indifference of the world. What Camus seeks in the early essays is a union of oneness with the world: "When am I truer than when I am the world?"[61] Later in *The Myth of Sisyphus* he refers to his relationship with the world as a divorce and the need to maintain the tension; he is united with the world as enemies. Between these two is *The Stranger*, in which Meursault experiences the indifferent world as fraternal.[62] From *Irony* to *Sisyphus*, Camus's attitude undergoes a change, from love to hate, but the indifference of the world remains unchanged. What changes is not the indifference of the world but Camus's attitude to this indifference. Our

54 *Ibidem*.

55 *Ibidem*, p. 33.

56 *Ibidem*, p. 34.

57 *Ibidem*, p. 37.

58 P. Dunwoodie, *op.cit.*, p. 16.

59 J. Cruickshank, *op.cit.*, p. 43.

60 A. Rizutto, *Camus' Imperial Vision*, Carbondale, Southern Illinois University Press, 1981, p. 38.

61 A. Camus, *Albert Camus: Lyrical and Critical…*, p. 60.

62 A. Camus, *The Myth…*, p. 123.

focus is not his relationship with his natural mother but with mother nature and Camus's desire to match her indifference.

MOTHER NATURE

Camus gives the world a face: a mouth that can smile or bite, lips that can kiss and arms that can caress. The "heavens smiled their foolish, indifferent smile"[63] and the sun "clothes everything in an eternal smile"[64]. In *Nuptials at Tipasa*, we read that the sea sucks and kisses; smiles with its "glittering teeth"[65] and that it meets the sun "lips to lips."[66] We saw above how Camus sees smiles where there are none. In addition to a face the world also has body parts. He finds himself "confusing the throbbing of [his] own heart with the great sonorous beating of [the world's] omnipresent natural heart."[67] The union Camus describes between man and the earth in *Summer in Algiers* is highly sexualised. For instance, when he smells carob trees and fancies he can detect the scent of semen; this "fragrance," he says, "consecrates the nuptials of man and earth."[68] This idea is repeated in *A Happy Death*: "it is as if the entire earth were resting, after having given itself to the sun, its womb drenched with a sperm smelling of bitter almonds." For Camus, Nature is mythologised as a female and in the early essays it is with her that Camus consummates his love.[69] Rizzuto argues that mother-son incest is the central and controlling theme in *Nuptials*;[70] this however has nothing to do with Camus's feelings for his own mother. What Camus has in mind is a kind of palingenetic fantasy, a rebirth in which the earth is his mother and he is his own father.

Nicodemus asked Christ how it was possible to enter the mother's womb a second time and he replied: "Very truly I tell you, no-one can enter the kingdom of God unless they are born of water and the spirit." [John 3: 3–5] In the Myth of Sisyphus we read that for the absurd man: "This hell of the present is his Kingdom at last."[71] In both *A Happy Death* and *The Stranger*

---

63 A. Camus, *Albert Camus: Lyrical and Critical...*, p. 26.

64 *Ibidem*, p. 60.

65 Ibidem, p. 66.

66 *Ibidem*, p. 68.

67 *Ibidem*.

68 *Ibidem*, p. 92.

69 *Ibidem*, p. 68.

70 A. Rizutto, *Camus' Imperial...*, p. 20.

71 *Ibidem*, p. 52.

we see a rebirth made possible by a life lived in the present and a succession of presents: borne of the earth/water in the spirit of indifference.

In *A Happy Death*, Patrice Mersault's metaphorical rebirth is clearly illustrated. After achieving the indifference he sought, a self-abandonment in the face of the world that denied him without anger, he strips naked and enters the sea, "warm as a mouth and as soft, ready to yield beneath a man's weight."[72] He swims out so that land is far away, to be alone in the heart of the world. In the dark, with neither land nor horizon in sight, in warm water, the experience is overtly womb-like. He feels an immense urge drawing him to his death down beneath the surface but resists the temptation.[73] Like Camus in Tipasa, he consummates his love with the world in water and here, in the salty womb, Mersault is the product of his shared love. He is his own father and he chooses to live.

After his confrontation with the chaplain, Meursault wakes to thoughts of his mother and the brotherly indifference of the world. It is more than a literal awakening but a spiritual one, what Sherman terms a "psychic rebirth."[74] His first insight as a new man is to why his mother chose to begin her life again, to be reborn, so close to death. His outburst to the chaplain is a kind of baptism: "As if that blind rage had *washed me clean*, rid me of hope; for the first time, in that night alive with signs and stars, I opened myself to the gentle indifference of the world"[75] (my emphasis). Camus is offering an inversion of Psalm 51; of particular interest are verses 2, 5, and 17: "Wash away all my iniquity, and cleanse me from my sin; Surely I was sinful from birth, sinful from the time my mother conceived me; My sacrifice, O God, is a broken spirit." Sin, for Camus, is hoping for another life.[76] Meursault too resolutely rejects the idea. Camus, similarly, totally rejects the notion of original sin.[77] Rather than a broken spirit, Meursault sacrifices himself with a vitalized spirit of profound indifference.[78]

---

72 A. Camus, *A Happy Death...*, p. 98–99.

73 *Ibidem*, p. 99.

74 D. Sherman, *Camus*, Chichester, Wiley–Blackwell, 2009, p. 78. For Meursault's spiritual awakening see: T. Hanna, *op.cit.*, p. 51; J. Cruickshank, *op.cit.*, p. 159; R. Champigny, *A Pagan Hero: An Interpretation of Camus' The Stranger*, trans. R. Portis, Philadelphia, University of Pennsylvania Press, 1969, 83; Sprintzen, 33.

75 A. Camus, *The Stranger...*, p. 122.

76 A. Camus, *Albert Camus: Lyrical and Critical...*, p. 91.

77 A. Camus, *Unbeliever and the Christians* [in:] *Resistance, Rebellion, and Death*, trans. J. O'Brien, New York, Random House, 1988, p. 72–73.

78 Here we see a fundamental difference between *The Stranger* and *The Myth of Sisyphus*. Meursault refuses to lie and accepts the consequence: death. In the essay, Camus writes: "There will never be any substitute for twenty years of life and experience," p. 61.

Meursault's profound indifference has puzzled many commentators. For Hanna, the character is a paradox because although he shows "the absolute indifference of the absurd hero" he does not have the lucid awareness required for the revolt.[79] "His 'extreme indifference' however continues to puzzle...," comments Longstaffe, because he seems to have "zero awareness."[80] Sartre suggests that Meursault's indifference is "given to him" by his creator.[81] However, things become less puzzling if we look closely at the kinds of indifference Meursault experiences. In the first half of the book, Meursault lives a life of apathetic indifference, one we can imagine that is almost identical to that of Patrice Mersault. For both men, the death of their mothers brings about a severe deepening of their indifference. From *The Happy Death*: "[After his mother's death] Things that in other circumstances would have excited him left him unmoved now, for they were simply part of his life, until the moment he was back in his room using all his strength and care to smother the flame of life in him."[82] We see from the second chapters of the books that both men live identical lives back in their rooms. The first book tells the story of the hero's quest for profound indifference, often repeating passages from Camus's own quest detailed in the early essays. The hero of *The Stranger* does not undergo such a quest; Camus uses time to help Meursault achieve profound indifference.[83] When Meursault realises in his cell that he had always been right, what he means is that his apathetic indifference in the first half of the book involved a lack of concern for things that he now realises truly are indifferent. Due to a prison life in which time is experienced as a succession of the same day over and over, lived in continual anticipation of death, he comes to his awakening without realising that it was something he was looking for. In this way Camus helps Meursault achieve profound indifference unlike Patrice who does the work himself. The results however are the same – both men revolt against hope in the face of death based on a profound indifference to this hope.

---

[79] T. Hanna, *op.cit.*, p. 51.

[80] M. Longstaffe, *The Fiction of Albert Camus: A Complex Simplicity*, Bern, Peter Lang Academic Publishers, 2007, p. 81.

[81] J.P. Sartre, *An Explication of The Stranger* [in:] *Camus: A Collection of Critical Essays*, trans. A. Michelson, ed. G. Brée, New Jersey, Prentice–Hall, 1962, p. 114.

[82] A. Camus, *A Happy Death*..., p. 14.

[83] J. Cruickshank, *op.cit.*, p. 159.

PROFOUND INDIFFERENCE AS THE SOURCE OF REVOLT

For Camus profound indifference is the starting point of conscious life. It is a difficult state to achieve, born of the unceasing struggle that is life lived in lucid awareness of the absurd. In itself, it is a refusal to be led into the temptation of hope for a life different to the only one we have. What is revolt but a sustained refusal? The rebel is someone who says "no." In the works we have been looking at, what we have seen is profound indifference as the mere starting point of revolt. Camus in his notebooks referred to *The Stranger* and *The Myth of Sisyphus* as "the zero point" from which *The Plague* will progress.[84] In his later works, he will address revolt as unity with other people rather than with the world alone, but he could not have reached this point without first locating the origin of revolt.

BIBLIOGRAPHY

Bespaloff, R., *The World of the Man Condemned to Death* [in:] *Camus: A Collection of Critical Essays*, ed. G. Brée, New Jersey, Prentice–Hall, 1962.

Camus, A., *A Happy Death*, trans. R. Howard, Middlesex, Penguin Books Ltd, 1974.

Camus, A., *Albert Camus: Lyrical and Critical Essays*, trans. C. Kennedy, ed. P. Thody, New York, Random House, 1970.

Camus, A., *Exile and the Kingdom*, trans. J. O'Brien, London, Penguin Books Ltd, 2002.

Camus, A., *The Fall*, trans. J. O'Brien, London, Penguin Books Ltd, 2000.

Camus, A., *Notebook III, Notebooks 1935–1942*, trans. P. Thody, Chicago, Ivan R. Dee, 2010.

Camus, A., *Notebook IV, Notebooks 1942–1951*, trans. J. O'Brien, New York, Paragon, 1991.

Camus, A., *The Misunderstanding, Caligula and Three other Plays*, trans. S. Gilbert, New York, Random House, 1962.

Camus, A., *The Myth of Sisyphus*, trans. J. O'Brien, London, Penguin Books Ltd, 2000.

Camus, A., *The Plague*, trans. R. Buss, London, Penguin Books Ltd, 2001.

Camus, A., *Resistance, Rebellion, and Death*, trans. J. O'Brien, New York, Random House, 1988.

Camus A., *Unbeliever and the Christians* [in:] *Resistance, Rebellion, and Death*, trans. J. O'Brien, New York, Random House, 1988.

Camus, A., *The Stranger*, trans. M. Ward, New York, Random House, 1989.

Champigny, R., *A Pagan Hero: An Interpretation of Camus' The Stranger*, trans. R. Portis, Philadelphia, University of Pennsylvania Press, 1969.

---

[84] A. Camus, *Notebook IV, Notebooks 1942–1951*, trans. J. O'Brien, New York, Paragon, 1991, p. 20.

Cruickshank, J., *Albert Camus and the Literature of Revolt*, London–New York, Oxford University Press, 1960.

Dunwoodie, P., *L'Envers et L'endroit and L'Exil et le Royaume*, London, Grant & Cutler, 1985.

Hanna, T., *The Thought and Art of Albert Camus*, Chicago, Henry Regnery Company, 1958.

Lillehammer, H., *Minding Your own Business? Understanding Indifference as a Virtue* [pdf], "Philosophical Perspectives" 2014, vol. 28, no. 01. Available at http://www.hallvardlillehammer.com/online-papers.html [access: June 2016].

Lillehammer, H., *Who is my Neighbour? Understanding Indifference as Vice* [pdf], "Philosophy" 2014, vol. 89, no. 04. Available at http://www.hallvardlillehammer.com/online-papers.html [access: June 2016].

Longstaffe, M., *The Fiction of Albert Camus: A Complex Simplicity*, Bern, Peter Lang Academic Publishers, 2007.

Nietzsche, F., *Human All Too Human*, trans. M. Faber and S. Lehmann, London, Penguin Books Ltd, 2004.

Peyre, H., *Camus the Pagan* [in:] *Camus: A Collection of Critical Essays*, ed. G. Brée, New Jersey, Prentice–Hall, 1962.

Rizutto, A., *Camus' Imperial Vision*, Carbondale, Southern Illinois University Press, 1981.

Rizutto, A., *Camus: Love and Sexuality*, Gainesville, University Press Florida, 1998.

Sartre, J.P., *An Explication of The Stranger* [in:] *Camus: A Collection of Critical Essays*, trans. A. Michelson, ed. G. Brée, New Jersey, Prentice–Hall, 1962.

Sherman, D., *Camus*, Chichester, Wiley–Blackwell, 2009.

Sprintzen, D., *Camus: A Critical Examination*, Philadelphia: Temple U, 1988.

Un personnage emblématique : *Caligula*, ou la pensée en action de l'absurde à la révolte

VIRGINIE LUPO

13 février 1936.
Je demande aux êtres plus qu'ils ne peuvent m'apporter. Vanité de prétendre le contraire. Mais quelle erreur et quelle désespérance. Et moi-même peut-être.

Carnets I, II, p. 801.

Je crois que notre fraternité – sur tous les plans – va encore plus loin que nous l'envisageons.

René Char à Albert Camus, 3 novembre 1951.

« L'œuvre est le miroir de l'auteur, il y prend conscience de soi »[1]. « [...] Ce que l'art se doit à lui-même [c'est] d'être cette tâche de mise en question de soi, qui d'ailleurs n'aura pas de fin »[2]. C'est Yves Bonnefoy qui s'exprime ici dans ces deux citations extraites de *L'Inachevable, Entretiens sur la poésie 1990–2010.*

Il pourrait paraître surprenant d'ouvrir une réflexion sur le théâtre de Camus par les citations d'un poète. Pourtant, invoquer Yves Bonnefoy nous permettra ici de mettre en lumière la partie poétique de *Caligula*. En effet, pour comprendre parfaitement la pièce et ses remaniements nombreux, la poésie nous est nécessaire... Ainsi, en jouant sur le titre de l'ouvrage de Yves Bonnefoy, *L'Inachevable* donc, nous allons nous interroger sur cette question : *Caligula* est-elle une pièce « inachevable » ?

---

1 Y. Bonnefoy, *L'Inachevable, Entretiens sur la poésie 1990–2010*, Paris, Albin Michel, Réédition Le Livre de poche, 2012, p. 58

2 *Ibidem*, p. 61.

On peut quasiment dire que *Caligula* est la pièce qui ouvre et qui clôt – par la force des choses bien entendu – l'œuvre (théâtrale) de Camus puisqu'il y travaille de 1937 à 1958. Camus la présentera d'ailleurs toujours comme sa première pièce, conçue en 1938, et ce, malgré ses nombreux remaniements. Cette précision sur la date de conception joue deux rôles : d'une part, elle lui permet de réduire les possibles rapprochements avec la figure d'Hitler, mais d'autre part, elle écarte également toute identification trop appuyée avec l'existentialisme. Le personnage de Caligula fut toutefois souvent assimilé à la figure d'Hitler comme le montre notamment la correspondance entre Francis Ponge et Camus. Dès l'été 1943 une nouvelle version de la pièce prend forme. Le 11 juillet, l'auteur de *L'Étranger* écrit au poète : « […] je ne travaille pratiquement pas, après avoir cependant réécrit un acte de *Caligula*[3] ». Puis, le dimanche 14 novembre 1943, dans une nouvelle lettre au poète, on peut lire : « La Compagnie des Sept [une troupe fondée par Jean Vilar à l'automne 1943] veut jouer Le Malentendu. Je n'ai pas encore donné ma réponse. Elle est tentée aussi par Caligula, mais hésite devant le scandale. Elle a bien raison » : la pièce, pouvant être comprise comme évoquant Hitler était en effet difficile à monter dans le Paris occupé de 1943.

Rares sont les œuvres qui furent réécrites ainsi. Certes, les auteurs ont coutume de reprendre leurs ouvrages pour une nouvelle édition, ou pour une publication différente. Par exemple, on sait que Balzac supprima l'organisation en chapitres du roman qui s'intitulait au départ *La Transaction* et qui porte désormais le nom du *Colonel Chabert*, ou qu'Apollinaire supprima toute la ponctuation d'*Alcools* en 1913. On sait également que *La Mort heureuse* constitue une sorte de première version de *L'Étranger* et que Camus avait coutume de réécrire ses textes. Celle qui fut sa secrétaire pendant les treize dernières années de sa vie, Suzanne Agnely, raconte que Camus lui fournissait un premier jet qu'il était impatient de lire dactylographié et que parfois il réécrivait jusqu'à sept fois son œuvre – « ce fut le cas de **La Peste** », dit-elle dans un film de 1974[4]. Il faisait de multiples corrections mais la première version devait toujours être dactylographiée immédiatement. Suzanne Agnely dit encore qu' « il y avait quatre ou cinq versions de la totalité de ses œuvres ». Toutefois, une même œuvre reprise et retravaillée ainsi, après sa publication, et ce, pendant près de 20 ans, est une expérience assez rare.

---

[3] A. Camus, F. Ponge, *Correspondance, 1941–1957*, Paris, Gallimard, p. 55.

[4] Film de Cécile Clairval-Milhaud (1974) (Ina.fr) intitulé *Albert Camus.*

Notons que dès le mois de mai 1937, Camus évoque cette pratique de la réécriture dans ses *Carnets* puisqu'il écrit : « Écrire, c'est se désintéresser. Un certain renoncement en art. Réécrire. L'effort qui apporte toujours un gain, quel qu'il soit. Question de paresse pour ceux qui ne réussissent pas »[5] ; il revient sur cette question le 30 septembre de la même année en notant : « C'est pour briller plus vite qu'on ne consent pas à réécrire. Méprisable. A recommencer »[6].

Nous aimerions nous arrêter un instant sur ces deux remarques qui nous semblent importantes : en effet, cette pratique de la réécriture a trait pour Camus avec une certaine dose d'humilité, d'honnêteté. L'écriture ne doit en aucun cas servir l'auteur pour sa propre gloire, « pour briller » donc, mais elle doit être une nécessité de l'être.

Même s'il est évident que Camus pensait à *Caligula* dès 1936, la première mention de la pièce apparaît en janvier 1937 dans les *Carnets* ; voilà comment Camus l'imagine : « Caligula ou le sens de la mort. 4 actes ». Il faut bien soupeser l'importance de ce titre : « le sens de la mort ». Camus connaît dès le mois de décembre 1930 les premières atteintes de la tuberculose : cela fait donc sept ans qu'il vit avec sa maladie, qu'il lutte pour sa santé. Quelques semaines auparavant, Camus écrivait en effet, toujours dans ses *Carnets* : « [...] Je ne dirai pas autre chose que mon amour de vivre. Mais je le dirai à ma façon... [...] moi c'est de mes bonheurs que sortiront mes écrits. Même dans ce qu'ils auront de cruel. Il me faut écrire comme il me faut nager, parce que mon corps l'exige »[7] : on retrouve ici l'idée de la nécessité de l'écriture dont nous parlions plus haut, mais aussi le fait que la maladie, la tuberculose contre laquelle il doit lutter, l'occupe entièrement : « Cette fièvre qui bat aux tempes, l'abandon singulier et soudain du monde et des hommes. Lutter contre son corps. Sur mon banc, dans le vent, vidé et creusé par l'intérieur, je pensais tout le temps à K. Mansfield, à cette longue histoire tendre et douloureuse d'une lutte avec la maladie. Ce qui m'attend dans les Alpes c'est, avec la solitude et l'idée que je serai là pour me soigner, la ‘ conscience' de ma maladie »[8]. On le voit avec ces différentes mentions, *Caligula* naît sous la plume de Camus au moment-même où l'auteur prend véritablement conscience de sa finitude. En janvier 1937, Camus précise aussi quelques scènes de l'acte I et II :

---

5 OC II, p. 816.

6 *Ibidem*, p. 838.

7 *Ibidem*, p. 811.

8 *Ibidem*, p. 822.

« I a) Son accession. Joie. Discours vertueux (Cf. Suétone)
b) Miroir
II a) Ses sœurs et Drusilla
b) Mépris des grands
c) Mort de Drusilla. Fuite de Caligula » ; l'acte III, reste encore indéterminé. Mais, ce qui me semble intéressant est le fait que la fin soit déjà en germe puisque le dramaturge écrit : « Fin : Caligula apparaît en ouvrant le rideau :

> Non, Caligula n'est pas mort. Il est là, et là. Il est en chacun de vous. Si le pouvoir vous était donné, si vous aviez du cœur, si vous aimiez la vie, vous le verriez se déchaîner, ce monstre ou cet ange que vous portez en vous. Notre époque meurt d'avoir cru aux valeurs et que les choses pouvaient être belles et cesser d'être absurdes. Adieu, je rentre dans l'histoire où me tiennent enfermé depuis si longtemps ceux qui craignent de trop aimer[9] ».

Les *Carnets*, au moment de l'écriture de *Caligula*, ne cessent de retentir d'un chant d'amour à la vie. Camus revient sur un thème constant, l'amour de la vie et son corollaire, la tentation de la mort. Tous ses projets littéraires flirtent avec cela. D'ailleurs, *La Mort heureuse* et la genèse de la création de son personnage principal, Mersault, ne disent pas autre chose :

> On m'aide à faire mes besoins. On me lave. On m'essuie. Je suis à peu près sourd. Eh bien, je ne ferai jamais un geste pour abréger une vie à laquelle je crois tant. J'accepterais pire encore. D'être aveugle et sans aucune sensibilité – d'être muet et sans contact avec l'extérieur – pourvu seulement que je sente en moi cette flamme sombre et ardente qui est moi et moi vivant – remerciant encore la vie pour m'avoir permis de brûler[10].

Caligula, ainsi que *L'Étranger* et *Le Mythe de Sisyphe*, ce que Camus nomme dans ses *Carnets* les « trois Absurdes », sont terminés le 21 février 1941. En réalité, si le roman et l'essai le sont réellement, la pièce, elle, va continuer à profiter de la réflexion de Camus sur ses nouveaux écrits.

Car cette pièce possède véritablement un statut à part dans l'œuvre de Camus. Si elle est « classée » dans le cycle de l'Absurde, si elle aborde en effet des thèmes communs à *L'Étranger* et au *Mythe de Sisyphe*, elle n'incarne pas les idées des deux autres « Absurdes ». Ainsi, lorsqu'en 1951, on demande

---

9 *Ibidem*, p. 812.
10 *Ibidem*, p. 842.

à Camus si ses idées ont évolué depuis la publication du *Mythe de Sisyphe*, il répond : « J'en ai peur »[11], façon à la fois élégante et quelque peu provocatrice d'insister sur l'évidence du propos. Puis, lorsque, avec une certaine perfidie, on lui demande encore si ses pièces et ses romans postérieurs ne reprennent et n'incarnent pas ces mêmes idées « sans rien y changer », il répond encore : « Incarner une idée, c'est y changer forcément quelque chose ». Cette réponse est intéressante car Camus, sans doute agacé par le ton du journaliste, réaffirme toutefois la spécificité du théâtre, de son théâtre. Il ne souhaite pas représenter sur scène les idées qu'il a d'abord développées dans ses textes : il est un homme de scène et à ce titre-là, il pense en metteur en scène.

D'ailleurs, certains remaniements de *Caligula* vont intervenir pour des raisons inhérentes à l'espace scénique. En effet, en 1957, *Caligula* est reprise pour le Festival d'Angers[12], appelé désormais le Festival Marcel Herrand. Le festival a lieu en plein air, au mois de juin, et le plein air est un endroit qui nécessite quelques transformations, une « difficile transposition ». Cette difficulté s'adresse en premier lieu aux acteurs qui doivent ajuster leur jeu à ces espaces « où leur voix doit peupler le vent et la nuit »[13]. La difficulté pour les comédiens est alors double puisqu'ils doivent chercher à transmettre la vérité de leur personnage tout en en soulignant la grandeur.

En plein air, le jeu du comédien doit atteindre ce quelque chose de mystérieux, cette « vérité » « secrète » puisque « l'acteur doit réaliser l'union contradictoire d'un jeu large, ' théâtral ', au beau sens du mot, et d'un sentiment profond »[14].

> Rester vrai tout en jouant large, voilà ce qu'est l'art suprême du comédien de théâtre et qui le mettra toujours, pour moi du moins, au-dessus du comédien de cinéma. Mais cet art devient plus périlleux en plein air, où le jeu doit encore s'élargir au risque de déraciner le sentiment lui-même, à moins que le sentiment à son tour ne croisse proportionnellement en profondeur, et n'ajoute ainsi la force à la vérité[15],

---

11 OC III, « Vos projets et travaux en cours ? » (1951), p. 1092.

12 Dans la *Correspondance*, Camus écrit à René Char en juin 1957 que les « répétitions [du Festival d'Angers où il s'assure de la mise en scène de son adaptation du Chevalier d'Olmedo et de Caligula] ne [lui] ont laissé aucun répit » et il précise les dates des représentations de *Caligula* : samedi 22, mardi 25, jeudi 27, dimanche 30.

13 OC III, p. 909.

14 *Ibidem*.

15 *Ibidem*, p. 910.

expliquera Camus lors de la présentation du Festival. Mais l'écueil n'est pas moins grand pour le metteur en scène qui doit également ajuster le décor, la lumière, le son, l'espace de la scène et celui du plein air. La conception d'un spectacle en plein air diffère radicalement de celle d'un spectacle en salle : les proportions et les effets changent résolument :

> Après expérience, il me semble incontestable que le plein air peut faire beaucoup de peu. A la seule condition que la mise en scène ait fixé solidement les places et les parcours (ce que j'appellerais la géométrie de l'action), installé enfin les fondations du drame, tout, sauf les catastrophes atmosphériques (et encore concourt à grandir et à transformer l'œuvre présentée. Le décor naturel, le vent, les nuages ou les étoiles donnent au drame une sorte de corps astral, et le contre-chant incessant de ces mouvements du ciel fournit à l'action une étrange et insaisissable unité qui n'est le fait ni du créateur, ni de ses serviteurs. Une parole humaine, sous le ciel de nuit, et, soudain familière, la grandeur s'installe sans bruit autour de nous[16].

Camus, qui avait travaillé souvent à des mises en scène en plein air, que ce soit en Algérie ou aux Festivals d'Angers – notamment en 1953 – connaît précisément ces difficultés auxquelles il fait face en modifiant certains points de *Caligula* ; ainsi, Camus simplifie le décor qui ne comporte plus de palais, mais uniquement trois portes, une tour, des plans de remparts et deux escaliers. Camus permettait ainsi de laisser « la grandeur » s'installer sur la scène en toute discrétion.

Revenons cependant au lien de la pièce avec les deux autres « Absurdes ». Nous avons vu que *Caligula* « n'illustre pas » les idées philosophiques du *Mythe de Sisyphe* car ce serait, en quelque sorte, reconnaître qu'il ne s'agit que d'un théâtre d'idées – reproche que l'on a souvent et à tort fait à Camus. Or, *Caligula* est une pièce de metteur en scène – Camus l'a d'ailleurs souvent répété[17] – nous venons de le voir, mais également une pièce d'acteur. Lorsqu'il se met à penser au personnage de l'empereur romain, Camus lit Suétone et surtout, il semble comme habité par l'homme ; Christiane Galindo en

---

16 *Ibidem.*

17 « Caligula a été écrit en 1938. J'avais 25 ans. Notre troupe, qui s'appelait l'Équipe, avait déjà plusieurs années d'âge. Elle s'était proposé jusque-là des entreprises considérables : Eschyle ; les élisabéthains, Dostoïevski, Malraux, Gide. ' Caligula n'était qu'un essai ', et par certains côtés ' une pièce de metteur en scène '. Je devais jouer le rôle de Caligula. Et puis les circonstances furent contraires. La guerre est venue et avec elle une certaine vie, qui était belle, a pris fin », « Douze auteurs en quête de personnages », Émission de Renée Saurel, OC I, p. 444.

témoigne : « Il était fasciné par le personnage. Il en parlait constamment et surtout le ' jouait '. Maison Fichu [la fameuse Maison devant le Monde où Camus aimait se retirer pour écrire], dans la vie courante, il répondait en Caligula »[18]. Témoignage troublant et amusant, corroboré par Camus lui-même quelques années après, puisqu'il écrit dans sa Préface à l'édition américaine de « *Caligula* and Three others Plays » : « Je destinais cette pièce au petit théâtre que j'avais créé à Alger et mon intention, en toute simplicité, était de créer le rôle de Caligula. Les acteurs débutants ont de ces ingénuités. Et puis j'avais 25 ans, âge où l'on doute de tout, sauf de soi »[19]. Car faut-il rappeler qu'à cette époque-là Camus est comédien dans la troupe théâtrale de Radio-Alger et qu'en février 1937, ils partent en tournée.

Parce qu'il faut bien avoir à l'esprit que le théâtre est pour Camus une occupation, un questionnement constants, une présence quotidienne : chacun de ses regards sur ce qui l'entoure le ramène à « la mise en scène ». Ainsi, lors de son voyage en Italie en septembre 1937, il est frappé par l'art des « Primitifs siennois et florentins ». Il constate en effet une différence de proportions qui lui semble intéressante à appliquer au théâtre : « Leur obstination à faire les monuments plus petits que les hommes ne vient pas d'une ignorance à l'égard de la perspective, mais de la persévérance dans le crédit qu'ils font à l'homme et aux saints qu'ils mettent en scène. S'en inspirer pour décor de théâtre »[20], conclut-il. Remarque doublement intéressante pour *Caligula* puisque Camus souhaitait justement mettre en valeur le personnage. Ceci nous amène justement au cœur de notre propos : le personnage de Caligula.

Si *Caligula* s'inscrit bien dans le Cycle de l'Absurde, si Camus y aborde bien ses préoccupations majeures à ce moment-là, ce qu'il souhaite faire avant tout, c'est s'appuyer sur le personnage : il a surtout l'ambition de peindre « un caractère tel qu'il convient au théâtre : simplifié et poussé à bout' »[21], comme Camus l'explique dans l'émission de Renée Saurel en 1945 ou 1946. C'est la passion de l'impossible, mais également les erreurs de Caligula pour s'en accommoder, qui intéressent le jeune dramaturge. Ainsi, on l'a vu, en janvier 1937, la mort de Drusilla et la fuite de Caligula sont au centre de la pièce, à ce qu'il note à cette date le c) de l'acte II, alors qu'à partir de 1939, ces deux événements ont lieu avant le début de la pièce : désormais, on ne « voit » plus sur scène l'accession au pouvoir de l'empereur avec ses discours et la

---

18 OC I, p. 1305.

19 *Ibidem*, p. 1304.

20 OC II, p. 831.

21 OC I, p. 445.

joie, tout cela n'importe plus ; la pièce s'ouvre sur le vide laissé à la fois par la mort de Drusilla et par la fuite du jeune homme. Ce sont les conséquences de la mort de Drusilla qui intéressent désormais Camus. Les patriciens, livrés à eux-mêmes, montrent, par leurs remarques acerbes, leur désappointement mais aussi leur mesquinerie et leur incompréhension de la situation. Et parmi celles-ci, une est importante et c'est Cherea qui la lance : « Ce garçon aimait trop la littérature. [...] ce n'est pas de son rang. Un empereur artiste, cela n'est pas convenable »[22].

Car, l'empereur écrit et mis en scène par Camus est un Poète et un comédien. Et au fil des différents remaniements, le lien avec la poésie est de plus en plus patent. C'est pourquoi, la version de 1941, version que l'on a coutume de qualifier de « poétique », apparaît comme essentielle : d'une part, Camus y ajoute l'acte III et surtout, il y accorde une place primordiale au personnage d'Hélicon.

La version de 1941 comporte une présence plus grande de Drusilla : à la scène 10 de l'acte I en effet, Caligula mime une sorte de dialogue avec sa sœur disparue devant une Caesonia médusée. Cette scène, assez faible d'un point de vue dramaturgique d'ailleurs, sera supprimée des autres versions, notamment parce qu'elle insiste trop sur le lien entre la prise de conscience de l'absurde du jeune empereur et la mort de sa sœur.

En revanche, l'ajout de l'acte III va orienter la pièce vers la volonté de Caligula de remplacer les dieux : il apparaît en effet costumé en une « Vénus grotesque sur un piédestal » et se fait adorer par les patriciens. Cette mascarade est la mise en scène de ce qu'il a clamé quelques scènes plus tôt à Caesonia : « Je prends en charge un royaume où l'impossible est roi ». Dans une sorte d'exaltation nietzschéenne, il démontre que désormais plus rien n'a de sens après la découverte de la mort. De plus, il incarne ainsi véritablement l'homme absurde en la personne du comédien, ce « mime du périssable » comme il l'est qualifié dans *Le Mythe de Sisyphe*. Cette scène blasphématoire, comme le lui fait remarquer Scipion, tend au contraire à montrer la possibilité de la mise en scène de l'impossible. En se faisant dramaturge, Caligula remplace les dieux : « Non, Scipion – répond-il au jeune poète – c'est de l'art dramatique ! L'erreur de tous ces hommes, c'est de ne pas croire assez au théâtre. Ils sauraient sans cela qu'il est permis à tout homme de jouer les tragédies célestes et de devenir dieu. Il suffit de se durcir le cœur »[23]. Caligula, homme

[22] *Ibidem*, p. 329.

[23] *Ibidem*, p. 363.

absurde, comédien, est frappé par la découverte de la mort : il va alors chercher dans la comédie la réponse à son interrogation.

Mais l'acte III, est aussi celui dans lequel Caligula demande à Hélicon s'il continue sa quête de la lune comme il le lui a demandé dès son retour au Palais. Or cette quête n'est autre que l'aspiration poétique à l'impossible de Caligula. Face à sa découverte de l'absurde, devant la conscience de la difficulté d'exister – « Qu'il est dur, qu'il est amer de devenir un homme ! », clame-t-il douloureusement – il va se faire poète. Parce que la poésie a pour but de changer le monde et les hommes qui entourent l'empereur. C'est en cela qu'il va apparaître comme un révolté. Il se révolte et son geste passe par la poésie. Cherea ne dit pas autre chose dans la version de 1941 : « Par Caligula et pour la première fois dans l'histoire, la poésie agit et le rêve rejoint l'action »[24] (II, 2). Là aussi, il mettra en scène ses idées en terrorisant et en faisant périr les faux poètes à la scène 12 de l'acte IV.

UNE ŒUVRE POÉTIQUE...

Mais la poésie ne trouve pas uniquement son importance du point de vue du motif ou de l'idée. Pour Camus, la poésie est intrinsèquement liée au théâtre. Dans un texte assez peu connu dans lequel il évoque le mime Marceau, le dramaturge réaffirme la place centrale que le théâtre doit allouer au corps. On se souvient de sa belle formule définissant le théâtre comme « une histoire de grandeur racontée par des corps », mais dans ce texte, il dit simplement ceci : « Sur cette scène, le corps est roi. A vrai dire, on l'avait un peu oublié, et [...] le théâtre n'est rien sans lui »[25]. Ainsi, la force du mime Marceau est-elle de nous rappeler ce qu'est le vrai théâtre, ce que doit être le théâtre, à savoir une mise en lumière des corps. On pense alors immédiatement aux scènes muettes qui apparaissent dans *Caligula* et notamment l'entrée sur scène de l'empereur, à la scène 3 de l'acte I :

> La scène reste vide quelques secondes. Caligula entre furtivement par la gauche. Il a l'air égaré, il est sale, il a les cheveux pleins d'eau et les jambes souillées. Il porte plusieurs fois la main à sa bouche. Il avance vers le miroir et s'arrête dès qu'il aperçoit sa propre image. Il grommelle des paroles indistinctes, puis va s'asseoir, à droite, les bras pendants entre les genoux écartés. Hélicon entre

---

24 A.J. Arnold, *Caligula*, version de 1941, Cahiers Albert Camus, Paris, Gallimard, 1984, p. 44.

25 OC III, p. 1138.

> à gauche. Apercevant Caligula, il s'arrête à l'extrémité de la scène et l'observe en silence. Caligula se retourne et le voit. Un temps[26].

Ce passage, qui constitue l'intégralité de la scène 3 de l'acte I est extrêmement émouvant puisqu'il marque le retour de l'empereur au palais, la naissance du nouvel empereur ; le fait qu'il soit accueilli sans un mot d'abord, par Hélicon, n'est pas anodin : Hélicon sera là du début à la fin, fidèle, sorte de double respectueux du jeune homme.

Mais dans le texte sur le mime Marceau, il y a un autre élément primordial : c'est l'affirmation par Camus de la nécessaire présence de la Poésie au théâtre : « [...] deux ou trois gestes suffisent à faire un monde. Mais il y faut l'humour, **la poésie** et la patience »[27].

Que veut dire Camus ici ? De quelle poésie veut-il parler ? Ceci pourrait étonner chez un auteur qui n'a pas écrit de poésie, hormis les très beaux textes de *La Postérité du Soleil*. On connaît également ses relations intimes avec des poètes, Françis Ponge et surtout René Char dont Camus écrivait :

> De nos jours c'est le poète qui en France élève le plus haut son chant et qui communique la plus grande richesse humaine. Et quand on parle de poésie, on est près de l'amour, cette grande force que l'on ne peut remplacer par l'argent qui est vil, ni par cette malheureuse chose qu'on appelle la morale[28].

Leur amitié, profonde, indéfectible, faite de tendresse, d'admiration et de fraternité lumineuse éclate dans cet extrait d'une lettre de Camus à Char, datée du vendredi 18 mai 1956 :

> [...] Qu'allons-nous devenir est une question qui n'a pas de sens. Nous sommes devenus. Je le sais en vous lisant. Nous avons seulement à fructifier, de nos propres fruits, quoique dans l'hiver. La question est seulement de savoir ce que la vie, ou du moins ce qu'il y a en elle d'adorable, va devenir. Cela seul suffit à faire souffrir. Mais si nous sommes malheureux, du moins nous ne sommes pas privés de vérité. Cela, je ne le saurais pas tout seul. Simplement, je le sais avec vous[29].

---

26 OC I, p. 330.

27 OC III, p. 1138.

28 *Ibidem*, p. 867.

29 A. Camus, R. Char, *Correspondance, 1946–1959*, Paris, Gallimard, 2007, p. 144.

René Char appréciait énormément la pièce de Camus ; il le lui écrit d'ailleurs dans une lettre datée du 1er mars 1946 dans laquelle il lui propose une prochaine rencontre et il conclut : « J'aurais plaisir à vous dire mon accord total avec **Caligula** outre la sympathie que j'éprouve pour vous »[30].

Si Char montre ainsi son adhésion totale à la pièce, c'est sans doute parce qu'il a compris la place centrale que la poésie y tenait. Et selon nous, c'est cette place qui innerve la vérité même de la pièce et qui explique le fait que Camus y soit revenu si souvent.

Revenons de nouveau à l'œuvre d'Yves Bonnefoy pour illustrer notre propos. En effet, pour le poète, l'art serait une « vision, [une] question sur ce qui est, [une] querelle faite à l'énigme de l'être »[31] (« Paysages de Raymond Masson », dans *Sur un sculpteur et des peintres*). La création est pour lui une quête profonde, existentielle. Il refuse résolument l'idée d'un art qui ne serait que « la beauté comme expérience autonome, sans rapport à la vérité »[32]. Le poète attend de l'art « qu'il soit la cause efficiente d'un rapport du je et de l'autre aussi étroit et transparent que possible : ce qu'en effet on pourrait dire l'avènement de la vérité dans les illusions de l'image ». L'écriture permettrait une sorte d'accès direct à l'Homme par le biais de l'évocation des sentiments impossibles à réduire à de simples systèmes, de simples concepts, car, « pour accéder véritablement à [autrui] il faut autre chose que des concepts, mais de la sympathie, ou de l'affection, ou de l'amour : ces sentiments qui ne se laissent pas enfermer dans des définitions et des déductions »[33].

Ainsi, pour Bonnefoy, celui qui écrit peut « vivre directement son rapport à la finitude »[34].

L'écriture constitue alors la quête absolue de l'être, de la connaissance de soi :

> Je ne considère donc pas la poésie comme l'expression d'une pensée consciente et présente mais comme la recherche de ce qui a lieu dans la profondeur de la vie psychique. Et je n'écris pas à partir d'une idée de ce que je vais dire, au contraire je m'intéresse à des phrases, à des images qui se forment en moi sans que je sache encore leur sens, afin de les questionner, d'y découvrir un besoin ou une pensée qui s'y cachent[35].

---

30 *Ibidem*, p. 21

31 Y. Bonnefoy, *op.cit.*, p. 52.

32 *Ibidem*, p. 56.

33 *Ibidem*, p. 57.

34 *Ibidem*, p. 63.

35 OC I, p. 422.

Or, *Caligula* n'est pas autre chose que cela, « un essai »[36], dira Camus à plusieurs reprises. La pièce est en effet une tentative, une sorte d'expérience, de « work in progress » : que fait un homme confronté à la découverte de l'absurde se demande Camus ? Comment réagit-il ? Quels sont ses doutes, ses souffrances, ses erreurs ? Et si Camus souhaitait incarner Caligula, c'est qu'il sentait combien il lui ressemblait. Et si la pièce nous touche toujours autant, c'est que les paroles de l'empereur résonnent douloureusement en chacun de nous. Et là encore, c'est Yves Bonnefoy qui nous donne la clef de ce mystère :

> Ma conviction : c'est qu'en descendant ainsi en soi-même on se fait plus universel, on retrouve les grands soucis de la condition humaine. Et la genèse de mes poèmes : c'est commencer d'écrire au hasard, retenir ce qui affleure en moi de cette façon, laisser se former ainsi des pages dont je ne sais rien ou très peu, puis questionner ce matériau de pensée, en mettant en rapport ceci ou cela dans ces bribes de parole, y reconnaissant aussi, quelquefois, des préoccupations déjà formulées, dans le passé, et comprises. Écrire, c'est en somme un dialogue entre le conscient et l'inconscient,

conclut-il.

On peut alors dire qu'« écrire c'est découvrir ». Et en effet, celui qui se trouve face à une œuvre, entre en dialogue avec son auteur, avec son créateur : « L'œuvre étudiée n'est pas devant l'écriture mais dans ses plis. [...] L'une et l'autre, écriture de l'artiste, écriture de son observateur, se mêlent, elles peuvent, dirais-je même, se parler »[37]. Ainsi, comme Caligula cherchant à faire des patriciens des Poètes, Camus, par sa pièce, nous change, nous lecteurs, nous spectateurs, en « artistes ». Nous pouvons alors nous créer, voire nous (re)créer. « A l'histoire, Caligula », hurle l'empereur à la toute fin de la pièce car Caligula vit et vivra éternellement en chacun de nous...

BIBLIOGRAPHIE

Arnold, A-J., *Caligula, version de 1941*, Cahiers Albert Camus, Paris, Gallimard, 1984.

Bonnefoy, Y., *L'Inachevable, Entretiens sur la poésie 1990–2010*, Paris, Albin Michel, 2010.

Camus, A., *Œuvres complètes*, Paris, Gallimard, Nouvelle édition de la Pléiade, 4 tomes, 2006 pour les deux premiers tomes, 2008 pour les deux suivants.

[36] *Ibidem*, « *Caligula n'était qu'un essai* », dit Camus.

[37] Y. Bonnefoy, *op.cit.*, p. 63.

Camus, A., *Carnets I,* Paris, Gallimard, 1962.

Camus, A., *Carnets II,* Paris, Gallimard, 1964.

Camus, A., *Carnets III,* Paris, Gallimard, 1989.

Camus, A., Char, R., *Correspondance, 1946–1959,* Paris, Gallimard, 2007.

Camus, A., Ponge, F., *Correspondance, 1941–1957,* Paris, Gallimard, 2013.

Lupo, V., *Le Théâtre de Camus : un théâtre classique ?, Lille,* Presses universitaires du Septentrion, 2002.

La Peste, de l'absurde à la révolte : les limites de l'engagement

MARIE-THÉRÈSE BLONDEAU

Par sa place et la longueur de sa rédaction (1942–1946), *La Peste* (1947) occupe dans l'œuvre de Camus une place intermédiaire entre deux mythes, celui de Sisyphe et celui de Prométhée. Cette chronique, rigoureusement construite en cinq parties qui rappellent les cinq actes de la tragédie classique, montre bien que les cycles, chez Camus, ne sont ni rigides, ni étanches : ils se chevauchent. Dans le récit de 1947, Sisyphe, héros de l'absurde, et Prométhée représentent les deux temps de la révolte. Le premier, au niveau individuel, refuse la condition que lui font les dieux, le second affirme la cause de l'homme et veut son affranchissement. Le thème de l'engagement est donc au centre de cette chronique fortement ancrée dans l'époque et la vie de son auteur. En confrontant les deux versions on peut suivre son évolution. C'est qu'entre décembre 1942, fin de la première version, et le 27 décembre 1946, remise du manuscrit à Gallimard, Camus a vécu une époque « intéressante », celle de la guerre et de l'immédiat après-guerre qui va lui apporter son lot d'espoir mais aussi bien des désillusions. La guerre, c'est le temps de la révolte et de l'engagement, surtout quand Camus se retrouve en France, coupé des siens et de sa terre natale par l'invasion de la zone libre par les Allemands le 11 novembre 1942. Le récit va être remanié en profondeur, les thèmes de l'exil et de la séparation prenant de l'ampleur. Mais après les journées de liesse de la libération de Paris en août 1944, viendra bien vite le temps du désenchantement. Que sont devenus les idéaux de la Résistance ? Nous nous proposons d'examiner les positions de Camus dans cette époque troublée et de voir de quelle manière elles transparaissent dans *La Peste*.

I. CAMUS ENTRE 1939 ET 1944 : DU PACIFISME À LA RÉSISTANCE

À la veille de la déclaration de guerre, Camus n'a pas une conscience très claire de la situation et ne sent pas l'imminence de la catastrophe : il n'a pas perçu la montée des périls depuis 1933. Politiquement, il est désenchanté. En juillet 1939, il fait des projets de voyage et en août il écrit à Jean Grenier: « Je pars dans dix jours pour la Grèce »[1]. La guerre qui éclate le 1 septembre 1939, le trouve désorienté, car même d'Alger, il perçoit bien le caractère surprenant de cette « drôle de guerre »[2], une guerre qui n'a pas son visage familier :

> La guerre a éclaté. Où est la guerre ? En dehors des nouvelles qu'il faut croire et des affiches qu'il faut lire, où trouver les signes de l'absurde événement ? Elle n'est pas dans ce ciel bleu sur la mer bleue, dans ces crissements de cigales, dans les cyprès des collines. Ce n'est pas ce jeune bondissement de lumière dans les rues d'Alger (OC II, p. 884)[3].

Il reprendra dans le contexte du roman cette expression : « La drôle de peste ? » (OC II, p. 977) dans les *Carnets* début 1943 alors qu'il travaille à la deuxième version de sa chronique. Pour lui, rien n'est pire que la guerre comme le montrent ses articles de 1939, dans *Le Soir républicain*[4]. Ses *Carnets*, à la même époque, insistent sur le caractère bestial de la guerre et des hommes :

> Cette haine et cette violence qu'on sent déjà monter chez les êtres. Plus rien de pur en eux. Plus rien d'inappréciable. Ils pensent ensemble. On ne rencontre que des bêtes, des faces bestiales d'Européens. Ce monde est écœurant et cette montée universelle de lâcheté, cette dérision du courage, cette contrefaçon de la grandeur, ce dépérissement de l'honneur (OC II, p. 887).

Cette haine de la guerre est chez lui viscérale : il n'avait pas un an quand son père est mort dans les premiers jours de la Grande Guerre. Pacifiste mais non défaitiste, il a conscience, après coup, de s'être fourvoyé quand il se rend

---

1 A. Camus, J. Grenier, *Correspondance 1932–1960*, Paris, Gallimard, 1981, p. 36–37.

2 Selon le mot de Dorgelès dans *Gringoire* en octobre 1939.

3 Les citations de Camus sont données dans *Œuvres complètes*, Paris, Gallimard, Bibliothèque de La Pléiade, Tomes I et II, 2006, tomes III et IV, 2008, en abrégé, OC I, OC II, etc.

4 Journal algérois né de la transformation d'*Alger-Républicain* en septembre 1939.

compte que c'est le pacifisme qui a fait signer les accords de Munich en 1938. Il note, début septembre 1939 : « Tous ont trahi, ceux qui poussaient à la résistance et ceux qui parlaient de la paix. Ils sont là, aussi dociles et plus coupables que les autres. Et jamais l'individu n'a été plus seul devant la machine à fabriquer le mensonge » (OC II, p. 886).

Rapidement il comprend que, « si ignoble que soit cette guerre, il n'est pas permis d'être en dehors » (OC II, p. 885). Il note dans ses *Carnets* en septembre 1939 :

> Il est toujours vain de vouloir se désolidariser, serait-ce de la bêtise et de la cruauté des autres. On ne peut dire « Je l'ignore ». On collabore ou on la combat. Rien n'est moins excusable que la guerre et l'appel aux haines nationales. Mais une fois la guerre survenue, il est vain et lâche de vouloir s'en écarter sous le prétexte qu'on n'en est pas responsable. Les tours d'ivoire sont tombées. La complaisance est interdite pour soi-même et pour les autres (OC II, p. 888).

Il essaie à deux reprises de s'engager. Il sera exempté pour raison de santé. Il s'en explique dans une lettre à Jean Grenier, au printemps 1940 :

> Je me suis engagé le 3 septembre, non parce que j' « adhérais », mais parce que je ne voulais pas que ma maladie me servît de paravent dans cette histoire et aussi parce que je me sentais solidaire de tous les malheureux qui partaient sans trop savoir pourquoi. La commission de réforme qui m'a examiné m'a cependant jugé inapte et m'a maintenu exempté. Depuis, une autre commission qui m'a appelé avec les réformés de ma classe m'a encore exempté[5].

Le Soir républicain, dont Camus assumait seul la responsabilité depuis le retour en France de son directeur Pascal Pia, est interdit le 10 janvier 1940. Déclaré *persona non grata* en Algérie, sans possibilité de travail, Camus arrive à Paris le 16 mars 1940, embauché à *Paris Soir* par Pia. Début juin, il connaît l'exode et gagne Clermont-Ferrand avec le journal. Le 18 juin, de Londres, de Gaulle appelle à la résistance ; le 22, Pétain signe l'armistice, la France se retrouve coupée en deux, occupée au nord de la Loire. Début janvier 1941, Camus et Francine Faure, qu'il a épousée en décembre 1940 à Lyon, regagnent Oran. En mai 1942, Camus est victime d'une nouvelle

---

5 A. Camus, J. Grenier, *op.cit.*, p. 38.

attaque de tuberculose. Fin août, Francine et lui arrivent en France, au Panelier, dans le Vivarais. Elle regagne fin septembre l'Algérie : ils seront séparés jusqu'à la Libération. C'est au Panelier que le pacifiste de 1939 va devenir résistant[6].

Si Camus a travaillé à *Paris-Soir* en 1940[7], il n'y a jamais écrit, le jugeant trop médiocre. En revanche, il participe à *Combat* clandestin, né de la fusion de deux journaux : *Vérités* et *Liberté*. Pour lui, l'engagement est un impératif moral, tout comme pour les héros de sa chronique. C'est ce que nous allons voir maintenant.

II. L'ENGAGEMENT DANS *LA PESTE*

D'une version l'autre, la résistance va s'organiser, tout comme elle s'est organisée dans la réalité. D'embryonnaire dans la première version, elle sera dirigée dans la version définitive par Tarrou ; Camus substitue aux « services sanitaires » initiaux trop officiels parce que trop liés à une administration incompétente, (comme le montre le conseil médical à la préfecture), les « formations sanitaires » : ce nouvel intitulé indique bien l'indépendance et le caractère individuel du recrutement. Cette nouvelle orientation du roman doit sans doute autant aux circonstances individuelles qu'historiques. Le 11 novembre 1942, Camus se trouve séparé des siens et de l'Algérie lorsque les Allemands envahissent la zone libre. « Comme des rats! » (OC II, p. 966), note-t-il à cette date dans ses *Carnets* qui nous révèlent que, peu après, il engrange des notes pour la « deuxième version » de *La Peste*. Le thème de la résistance se développe parallèlement à celui de la séparation et Camus note en septembre 1943 dans ses *Carnets* la nécessité de la lutte : « Peste. Tous luttent – et chacun à sa façon. La seule lâcheté est de se mettre à genoux… » (OC II, p. 1004). Tous les cas de figures sont présents dans *La Peste* : ceux qui vivent en marge, ceux qui collaborent, ceux qui s'engagent.

---

6 Sans doute en rencontrant Pierre et Marianne Fayol qui deviendront ses amis. Le 20 mai 1943, on lui délivre une fausse carte d'identité au nom d'Albert Mathé ; son pseudonyme dans la Résistance était Bauchard.

7 Il avait été embauché comme secrétaire de rédaction à 3000 francs par mois et s'occupait de la mise en page, autant dire un travail technique.

1. De l'absence d'engagement à son refus

Les êtres « mécaniques » : le petit vieux qui crachait sur les chats et le vieil asthmatique

Début 1943, alors qu'il travaille à la deuxième version de *La Peste*, Camus envisage d'écrire une « Anthologie de l'insignifiance », terme qu'il définit ainsi : « [...] l'insignifiance s'identifie presque toujours avec l'aspect mécanique des choses et des êtres – avec l'habitude le plus souvent »[8] (OC II, p. 989). Pour ces deux êtres « mécaniques », le petit vieux aux chats et le vieil asthmatique, la question de l'engagement ne se pose pas, tout occupés qu'ils sont par leur manie : cracher sur les chats du haut de son balcon pour le premier, transvaser des pois d'une marmite à l'autre pour le second. La disparition des chats au début de l'épidémie décontenance le petit vieux qui finit par vivre une véritable tragédie quand la municipalité décide de faire abattre chiens et chats. Après le 25 janvier, alors que l'épidémie semble s'éloigner, Tarrou se poste « au coin de la petite rue ». Les chats sont revenus, mais le petit vieux a disparu, vexé ou mort de la peste, on ne le saura jamais. Les deux personnages sont rapprochés par Tarrou à la fin de la chronique. Car la vie du vieil Espagnol est tout aussi mécanique : il

> avait jugé à cinquante ans qu'il en avait assez fait. Il s'était couché et ne s'était plus relevé depuis [...]. Il ne pouvait souffrir la vue d'une montre [...]. Il évaluait le temps, et surtout l'heure des repas qui était la seule qui lui importât, avec ses deux marmites dont l'une était pleine de pois à son réveil. Il remplissait l'autre, pois par pois, du même mouvement appliqué et régulier. Il trouvait ainsi ses repères dans une journée mesurée à la marmite. « Toutes les quinze minutes, disait-il, il me faut mon casse-croûte. C'est simple » (OC II, p. 114).

Aux premiers signes de l'épidémie, il se réjouit à la vue des rats ; il se frotte les mains et répète avec une voix sénile : « [...] ils sortent, vous avez vu ? » (OC II, p. 39). De son lit, au gré des visites de Rieux ou de Tarrou, il commente la peste et en tirera une leçon ; nous y reviendrons. C'est Tarrou qui

---

[8] Cette anthologie, esquissée dans les *Carnets*, fera l'objet, en 1945, d'une « Préface à une anthologie de l'insignifiance » (OC IV, p. 1323–1327) publiée dans *Saisons. Almanach des Lettres et des Arts*, no1, été 1945, p. 75–80. Cette phrase est légèrement modifiée en 1945 : « [...] les actions insignifiantes trahissent toujours l'aspect mécanique des choses et des êtres, l'habitude de ce qu'ils sont » (OC IV, p. 1326).

insiste surtout dans ses carnets sur ces deux personnages et l'on peut se demander s'il ne faudrait pas voir dans cette attirance pour l'insignifiance que lui a transmise Camus, une tentation de non engagement après une vie passée sur tous les fronts.

Refus de l'engagement : Cottard le collabo(rateur)

À travers le personnage de Cottard, Camus nous montre que la peste n'a pas que des inconvénients pour certains. Ce personnage de collabo est présent dès le début et sa silhouette variera assez peu d'une version à l'autre. Voisin de Stephan en 1942, il fait une entrée fracassante dans le récit en 1947 en tentant de se pendre. Il en réchappe, contrairement au professeur de Lettres de 1942. Il est à son aise dans la peste, content

> d'échanger ses soucis d'homme traqué contre la condition commune et partant plus confortable d'assiégé. Bien entendu, il n'était plus question d'enquêtes secrètes, de dossiers, de fiches, d'instructions mystérieuses et d'arrestation imminente. La police avait d'autres chats à fouetter, Cottard en était sûr[9].

Le Cottard de la première version qui « respirait avec légèreté l'air épais qui pesait sur la ville » est celui qui, dans la version définitive, répond « sur un ton de bravade » à Tarrou lui demandant de rejoindre les formations sanitaires : « [...] je m'y trouve bien moi, dans la peste, et je ne vois pas pourquoi je me mêlerais de la faire cesser » (OC II, p. 143). Il est persuadé que les lesdites formations sont vouées à l'échec, parce que « la peste est trop forte » (OC II, p. 143) et d'ailleurs, « il n'avait pas voulu la peste, [. . .] elle était arrivée comme ça et [. . .] ce n'était pas sa faute si elle arrangeait ses affaires pour le moment » (OC II, p. 144). Dans la version définitive, c'est lui qui met Rambert en relation avec les filières d'évasion et l'on apprend qu'il s'adonne aussi au marché noir. Camus a dû croiser plus d'un Cottard pendant l'Occupation et son arrestation, dans la version de 1947, doit sans doute beaucoup à la Libération[10] et à l'Épuration. Dans la première version, il disparaissait simplement dans la nuit, encadré par deux hommes dont on ne précisait pas s'il s'agissait de policiers.

---

9 Cette citation et la suivante sont extraites de la première version de *La Peste*.

10 Voir Ch. Chevandier, *Été 44 L'insurrection des policiers de Paris*, Paris, Vendémiaire, 2014, p. 250–253.

2. Les différents moments de l'engagement

Engagement « naturel » : les médecins : Rieux, Castel, – et les autres : Grand et Tarrou

Il est naturel pour un médecin de lutter contre la maladie ; c'est ce que fait Rieux, sans se poser de question. Pour lui, « la certitude [est] dans le travail de tous les jours [...]. L'essentiel était de bien faire son métier » (OC II, p. 62). Il approfondit sa réflexion face à Rambert : « [...] il ne s'agit pas d'héroïsme dans tout cela. Il s'agit d'honnêteté. C'est une idée qui peut faire rire, mais la seule façon de lutter contre la peste, c'est l'honnêteté ». Et au journaliste qui lui demande : « Qu'est-ce que l'honnêteté ? », il répond : « Je ne sais pas ce qu'elle est en général. Mais dans mon cas, je sais qu'elle consiste à faire mon métier » (OC II, p. 147).

Le vieux docteur Castel, qui a fait une partie de sa carrière en Chine, sait reconnaître les premiers symptômes de la maladie. Il travaille à la fabrication d'un sérum sur place :

> C'est pourquoi il était naturel que le vieux Castel mît toute sa confiance et son énergie à fabriquer des sérums sur place, avec du matériel de fortune. Rieux et lui espéraient qu'un sérum fabriqué avec les cultures du microbe même qui infestait la ville aurait une efficacité plus directe que les sérums venus de l'extérieur, puisque le microbe différait légèrement du bacille de la peste, tel qu'il était classiquement défini (OC II, p. 125).

Après son échec sur l'enfant Othon, le « nouveau sérum de Castel [connaît] quelques succès inattendus » et le vieux médecin continue « à préparer son sérum aussi soigneusement qu'il le pouvait » (OC II, p. 197).

Dès le début, il est rejoint par Grand, modeste employé de mairie dont le naturel serviable apparaît lorsqu'il propose à Rieux de surveiller Cottard après sa tentative de suicide : « il faut bien s'entraider » (OC II, p. 47) dit-il. Son travail « au service des statistiques, à l'état civil » l'amène « à faire les additions des décès. Et, de naturel obligeant, il avait consenti à apporter lui-même chez Rieux une copie de ses résultats » (OC II, p. 62). Il va rapidement sembler tout naturel au narrateur « que Grand, qui n'avait rien d'un héros, assurât maintenant une sorte de secrétariat des formations sanitaires » (OC II, p. 125). Et le narrateur juge ainsi le rôle de Grand qui n'est pas sans rappeler tous les anonymes qui luttèrent contre l'occupant : « Grand était le représentant réel de cette vertu tranquille qui animait les formations sanitaires. Il avait dit oui sans hésitation, avec la bonne volonté qui était la sienne » (OC II,

p. 126). Et s'il faut absolument qu'il y ait un héros « dans cette histoire, le narrateur propose justement ce héros insignifiant et effacé qui n'avait pour lui qu'un peu de bonté au cœur et un idéal apparemment ridicule » (OC II, p. 128). On se souvient que son idéal consiste à polir indéfiniment la première phrase de son roman mais, lorsqu'il rejoint Rieux à l'hôpital après son travail, pour « faire les additions et les statistiques dont avaient besoin les formations sanitaires [...]. Il essayait honnêtement alors de ne plus penser à son amazone et de faire seulement ce qu'il fallait » (OC II, p. 128).

De par son métier, Rieux se trouve naturellement au centre d'un réseau, même si ce n'est pas dit explicitement, et c'est à lui que s'adresse Tarrou dès la première version, dans sa hâte de rejoindre la lutte :

> Je voudrais dit Tarrou entrer dans les services sanitaires.
> Rieux eut l'air surpris
> Oui je sais il y a des bureaux qui s'occupent de ça dit Tarrou. Ms je voudrais commencer demain. On m'a parlé de vous. J'ai pensé que vous comprendriez (ms1).

Dans la version définitive, Tarrou fait preuve de plus d'initiative, il n'est plus simplement demandeur :

> J'ai appris que la préfecture envisage une sorte de service civil pour obliger les hommes valides à participer au sauvetage général [...]. Pourquoi ne pas demander des volontaires ? [...] J'ai un plan d'organisation pour les formations sanitaires volontaires. Autorisez-moi à m'en occuper et laissons l'administration de côté. Du reste, elle est débordée. J'ai des amis un peu partout et ils feront le premier noyau. Et **naturellement**[11], j'y participerai (OC II, p. 119).

Dans la version de 1942, il précise à Rieux qu'il n'est pas poussé par le dilettantisme et le docteur accepte, lui indiquant en quoi consistera son rôle : « Vous pouvez vous joindre à moi comme inspecteur sanitaire. Il s'agit de veiller aux isolements et bien d'autres choses. Si le mot ne vous choque pas, il y a une sorte de secrétariat à assurer. J'arrangerai les choses avec l'administration » (ms1). A Rieux qui lui demande ce qu'il espère trouver, Tarrou répond : « La paix intérieure ». Mais cette réponse est immédiatement rayée par Camus qui la remplacera en 1947 par la « morale de la compréhension ». « Dès le lendemain, Tarrou se mit au travail et réunit une première équipe

11 C'est nous qui soulignons.

qui devait être suivie de beaucoup d'autres » (OC II, p. 123 et 124). Et il va seconder le docteur jusqu'à sa mort.

Engagement « différé » : Paneloux, Rambert, Gonzalès, Othon

Dans les deux versions, à la fin du premier mois de peste, les autorités religieuses organisent une semaine de prières pour lutter contre le fléau. À cette occasion le père Paneloux monte en chaire pour prononcer son premier prêche. Il assène d'entrée aux Oranais cette « phrase véhémente et martelée : ‘ Mes frères, vous êtes dans le malheur, mes frères vous l'avez mérité ' » (OC II, p. 98). Il ne leur prêche pas l'action mais plutôt le consentement, l'acceptation de leur destin. La peste, pour lui, a une valeur salvatrice, « Elle manifeste la volonté divine qui sans défaillance transforme le mal en bien » (ms1). Cependant, dès la première version, l'attitude du père n'est pas en accord avec ses paroles puisque son acceptation du fléau débouche paradoxalement sur la lutte à laquelle il va prendre une part active: « Depuis son prêche au début de l'épidémie, il n'avait pas quitté les hôpitaux et s'était placé parmi les sauveteurs au rang qui lui paraissait devoir être le sien, le premier » (ms1). Dans la version définitive, il rejoint aussi les formations sanitaires après son premier prêche. Il s'agit d'un ajout manuscrit au tapuscrit :

> Tarrou arriva très animé :
> – Savez-vous dit-il que je viens de demander à Paneloux de se joindre à nous.
> – Eh ! bien lui demanda le docteur ?
> – Il a réfléchi et il a dit oui.
> – J'en suis content dit le docteur. Je suis content de le savoir meilleur que son prêche[12].

Il acceptera même de « remplacer Rambert à la maison de quarantaine », ce qui entraîne la remarque de Tarrou : « Il a déjà beaucoup fait » (OC II, p. 177).

Rambert, personnage absent de la première version, sera plus long à s'engager. Dès, la fermeture des portes, il essaie de fuir la ville empestée, poussé par le désir de retrouver la femme qu'il aime et de « fuir cette atmosphère de panique naissante » (OC II, p. 106). Le narrateur parle des « longs efforts désespérés et monotones que les derniers individus, comme Rambert, faisaient pour retrouver leur bonheur et ôter à la peste cette part d'eux-mêmes qu'ils défendaient contre toute atteinte. C'était là leur manière de refuser

---

12 On retrouve cet ajout peu modifié dans la version de 1947.

l'asservissement » (OC II, p. 129). On pense ici à Camus essayant de rejoindre l'Algérie après l'invasion de la zone libre par les Allemands le 11 novembre 1942.

Le journaliste ne répond pas à une première offre de Tarrou de rejoindre les formations sanitaires, même si ces dernières lui paraissent « très utiles » (OC II, p. 141). Il s'en expliquera un peu plus tard à Rieux : « Vous savez, docteur [...], j'ai beaucoup pensé à votre organisation. Si je ne suis pas avec vous, c'est que j'ai mes raisons. Pour le reste, je crois que je saurais encore payer de ma personne, j'ai fait la guerre d'Espagne [...] Du côté des vaincus » (OC II, p. 146). Le refus de la peste (et la préservation de son bonheur) le pousse à fuir mais sa reconnaissance le mène finalement à un engagement d'abord temporaire puis indiscutable. En apprenant que « la femme de Rieux se trouve dans une maison de santé à quelques centaines de kilomètres » (OC II, p. 147) d'Oran et que le docteur partage donc avec lui la condition de séparé, Rambert décide de rejoindre momentanément les formations sanitaires jusqu'à ce qu'il ait trouvé un moyen de quitter la ville. Mais après avoir vu ce qu'il a vu, il renonce finalement au dernier moment à partir parce que, dit-il, « Cette histoire nous concerne tous » et « il peut y avoir de la honte à être heureux tout seul » (OC II, p. 178). Comme Camus avant lui, il a compris l'inéluctabilité de l'engagement quand les circonstances le requièrent ou même l'imposent, sans pour autant oublier le goût du bonheur.

Rambert visite avec Tarrou le « camp installé sur le stade municipal » ; ils y rencontrent « Gonzalès, le joueur de football, [qui dirige] par roulement la surveillance du stade » (OC II, p. 199). Il est entré dans la résistance pour des raisons proprement humaines : il s'ennuyait du stade le week-end parce qu'il n'y avait plus de match ! Ce qui montre bien la complexité des formes d'engagement !

Le dernier à rejoindre les formations sanitaires sera le juge Othon. Après la mort de son fils et sa deuxième quarantaine, il va voir Rieux et lui annonce qu'il veut retourner au camp comme volontaire de l'administration. « Vous comprenez, j'aurais une occupation. Et puis, c'est stupide à dire, je me sentirais moins séparé de mon petit garçon » (OC II, p. 214).

3. Limites de l'engagement ou l'ère du désenchantement

Dans la vie pour Camus : désenchantement de l'après-guerre

Comme les résistants de *La Peste*, Camus a lutté pour la liberté, la justice et la dignité de l'homme. Mais l'après-guerre n'est pas plus facile pour lui que pour beaucoup de Français confrontés d'abord aux problèmes matériels, et qui va aussi apporter son lot de désillusions.

Sa première déception vient de l'épuration dont il écrit dans son éditorial du 30 août 1945 : « Le mot d'épuration était déjà assez pénible en lui-même. La chose est devenue odieuse »[13]. Camus avait abordé cette question très tôt, dans son article du 30 août 1944. (Rappelons que la libération de Paris a eu lieu le 21). Pour lui, elle est nécessaire et doit être rigoureuse. Il s'agit d'écarter ceux qui ont collaboré : industriels, fonctionnaires, journalistes ou écrivains par exemple. La première à en faire les frais est la presse, dès l'insurrection de Paris. Les journaux qui ont paru pendant l'Occupation ou à partir de novembre 1942 pour la zone libre sont interdits. S'ensuit une polémique avec Mauriac, résistant comme lui. Alors que Mauriac, dans *Le Figaro* du 13 octobre 1944 plaide pour l'apaisement et l'indulgence envers ceux qui se seraient trompés, Camus lui réplique le 18 que dans certaines situations « l'erreur n'est qu'un crime ». L'éditorialiste de *Combat* soutient l'idée d'une justice rapide et efficace, celui du *Figaro* accuse son jeune confrère « de partager les Français entre les hommes de la résistance et les hommes de la trahison et de l'injustice », tout en reconnaissant que ces derniers doivent être jugés. Il relance la polémique en opposant justice et charité : « Chaque fois qu'à propos de l'épuration, j'ai parlé de justice, M. Mauriac a parlé de charité » (OC II, 403). Dans son article du 5 janvier 1945, Camus admet que l'Épuration est en passe d'être manquée ; en août, il est persuadé que c'est un échec :

> [...] il est certain désormais que l'épuration en France est non seulement manquée, mais encore déconsidérée [...]. Elle n'avait qu'une chance de ne point le devenir qui était d'être entreprise sans esprit de vengeance ou de légèreté. Il faut croire que le chemin de la simple justice n'est pas facile à trouver entre les clameurs de la haine d'une part et les plaidoyers de la mauvaise conscience d'autre part. L'échec en tout cas est complet[14].

Il reconnaîtra, fin 1946, devant les Dominicains du couvent de Latour-Maubourg, que Mauriac avait raison contre lui. Cette polémique permet à Camus de revoir sa conception de la justice révolutionnaire. Il se méfie désormais de toute justice qui active les pulsions meurtrières de l'homme. C'est ainsi qu'il note dans ses *Carnets* en 1948: « Déchirement d'avoir accru l'injustice en croyant servir la justice » (OC II, p. 1117). Tarrou ne disait pas autre

13 J. Lévi-Valensi, *Camus à* Combat, Paris, Gallimard, Cahiers Albert Camus 8, 2002, p. 594.

14 *Ibidem*, p. 594–595.

chose dans sa confession : aucune des idées pour lesquelles on tue ne peut justifier cet acte ; les bonnes intentions elles-mêmes ne sont pas une excuse. Nous y reviendrons.

Une autre déception vient de *Combat*. Le journal clandestin avait appelé les Français à la lutte armée et tout naturellement, quand il paraît au grand jour à la Libération, il se veut libre, non affilié à un parti politique. Camus voulait « libérer les journaux de l'argent et [...] donner un ton et une vérité qui mettent le public à la hauteur de ce qu'il y a de meilleur en lui ». Mais il constate déjà, dans le même éditorial du 31 août 1944, l'échec d'une certaine presse qu'il appelle de ses vœux, « claire et virile, au langage respectable »[15]. Dès fin 1945, il ne se reconnaît plus dans les positions du journal et s'en éloigne. Il quitte définitivement la direction du quotidien le 3 juin 1947, conscient d'avoir échoué dans sa tentative de maintenir le journal dans une indépendance parfaite à l'égard du pouvoir, des partis et de l'argent. Il confie au typographe Touratier, le 28 août 1947: « [...] nous étions désarmés puisque nous étions honnêtes. Cette presse que nous voulions digne et fière, elle est aujourd'hui la honte de ce malheureux pays »[16]. À l'enthousiasme de la Libération succède le désenchantement.

Sur le plan de l'écriture, il a bien du mal à terminer sa chronique commencée en septembre 1942 au Panelier. *La Peste* paraît enfin le 6 juin 1947, et reçoit presque immédiatement le Prix des Critiques, mais Camus ne goûte pas ce succès. Il estime en effet que le roman a paru trop tard par rapport aux « événements » qu'il évoque pour un lecteur de l'époque. Il note le 25 juin dans ses *Carnets* : « Tristesse du succès. L'opposition est nécessaire. Si tout m'était plus difficile comme avant, j'aurais bien plus de droits à dire ce que je dis. Il reste que je puis aider beaucoup de gens – en attendant » (OC II, p. 1085).

Il nous reste à voir maintenant comment ce désenchantement de l'après-guerre se traduit dans *La Peste* puisque Camus n'a remis son manuscrit à Gallimard que le 27 décembre 1946 et qu'il le corrigera encore sur épreuves début 1947.

La Peste ou les limites de l'engagement

La leçon délivrée par le vieil asthmatique, observateur de l'épidémie, est pleine de bon sens mais aussi en demi teinte : « Les autres disent : ' C'est la peste, on a eu la peste '. Pour un peu, ils demanderaient à être décorés. Mais qu'est-ce

---

15 *Ibidem*, p. 169–170.

16 *À Albert Camus, ses amis du Livre*, Paris, Gallimard, 1962, p. 21–22.

que ça veut dire, la peste ? C'est la vie, voilà tout » (OC II, p. 247). Et à l'idée de « construire un monument aux morts de la peste », le vieux s'esclaffe : « Je les entends d'ici : ' Nos morts... ', et ils iront casser la croûte » (OC II, p. 247). Ce que Rieux approuve : « Le vieux avait raison, les hommes étaient toujours les mêmes » (OC II, p. 248).

La réaction de Rambert à l'ouverture des portes est tout aussi mitigée. « Impatience et désarroi » l'animent sur le quai de la gare : « Car cet amour ou cette tendresse que les mois de peste avaient réduits à l'abstraction, Rambert attendait, dans un tremblement, de les confronter avec l'être de chair qui en avait été le support » (OC II, p. 238). Mais peut-être a-t-il eu le soupçon, comme beaucoup de révoltés, que la victoire est illusoire et qu'il faudra toujours recommencer la lutte.

La confession de Tarrou, ajout manuscrit au tapuscrit (sans doute fin novembre 1946[17]), intitulée « confession d'un pestiféré », est à mettre en relation avec les 8 articles publiés dans *Combat* du 19 au 30 novembre 1946 (ce seront les derniers qu'il donnera au journal) : « Ni victimes ni bourreaux ». Elle reflète les préoccupations de Camus journaliste, donne à la chronique un arrière-plan historico-politique, et montre bien les limites de l'engagement. Celui de Tarrou vient directement de son horreur de la peine de mort réclamée par son père, avocat général :

> J'ai cru que la société où je vivais était celle qui reposait sur la condamnation à mort et qu'en la combattant, je combattrais l'assassinat. Je l'ai cru, d'autres me l'ont dit et, pour finir, c'était vrai en grande partie [...] il n'est pas de pays en Europe dont je n'aie partagé les luttes (OC II, p. 207).

Mais confronté directement à une exécution, il refuse d'être un « salaud », un « pestiféré » et entend ne plus légitimer aucun homicide. L'engagement débouche sur l'écœurement :

> J'ai compris [...] que je n'avais pas cessé d'être un pestiféré pendant toutes ces longues années où pourtant, de toute mon âme, je croyais lutter justement contre la peste. J'ai appris que j'avais indirectement souscrit à la mort de milliers d'hommes, que j'avais même provoqué cette mort en trouvant bons les actions et les principes qui l'avaient fatalement entraînée [...]. Il me semble que l'histoire m'a donné raison, aujourd'hui c'est à qui tuera le plus. Ils sont tous dans la fureur du meurtre, et ils ne peuvent pas faire autrement (OC II, p. 208).

---

17 Comme le montre sa correspondance avec Louis Guilloux.

Pour lui, la fin ne justifie pas les moyens et il refuse « de jamais donner une seule raison, une seule, […] à cette dégoûtante boucherie » qu'est une exécution. Il a donc décidé « de refuser tout ce qui, de près ou de loin, pour de bonnes ou de mauvaises raisons, fait mourir ou justifie qu'on fasse mourir » (OC II, p. 209).

Mais ce faisant, il avoue avoir perdu la paix. C'est la raison qu'il donnait dès la première version à Rieux pour expliquer son engagement. Il disait rechercher « La paix intérieure ». Même si Camus a biffé cette déclaration sur le premier manuscrit, il y revient au moment d'achever son roman. Écoutons plutôt Tarrou :

> […] j'ai appris cela, que nous étions tous dans la peste, et j'ai perdu la paix. Je la cherche encore aujourd'hui, essayant de les comprendre tous et de n'être l'ennemi mortel de personne. Je sais seulement qu'il faut faire ce qu'il faut pour ne plus être un pestiféré et que c'est là ce qui peut, seul, nous faire espérer la paix, ou une bonne mort à son défaut. C'est cela qui peut soulager les hommes et, sinon les sauver, du moins leur faire le moins de mal possible et même parfois un peu de bien. Et c'est pourquoi j'ai décidé de refuser tout ce qui, de près ou de loin, pour de bonnes ou de mauvaises raisons, fait mourir ou justifie qu'on fasse mourir (OC II, p. 209).

Dans « Ni victimes ni bourreaux », réflexion sans illusions sur les déchirements de l'Europe en général et de la France en particulier, Camus pousse un cri d'alarme contre le règne de la terreur et la légitimation du meurtre. Le premier article s'intitule d'ailleurs « Le siècle de la peur ». Voici ce qu'il écrit :

> Entre la peur très générale d'une guerre que tout le monde prépare et la peur toute particulière des idéologies meurtrières, il est donc bien vrai que nous vivons dans la terreur. Nous vivons dans la terreur parce que la persuasion n'est plus possible, parce que l'homme a été livré tout entier à l'histoire et qu'il ne peut plus se tourner vers cette part de lui-même, aussi vraie que la part historique, et qu'il retrouve devant la beauté du monde et des visages; parce que nous vivons dans le monde de l'abstraction, celui des bureaux et des machines, des idées absolues et du messianisme sans nuances (OC II, p. 437).

Deux ans plus tard, on est donc bien loin de l'enthousiasme de la Libération et l'« l'esprit de résistance » a été oublié ; l'après-guerre voit les relations avec les communistes devenir conflictuelles et les oppositions partisanes se faire de plus en plus violentes. Bientôt, ce sera la guerre froide : le temps de l'« abstraction » est revenu.

À la fin du récit, le jugement en demi teinte du narrateur sur les formations sanitaires n'est pas sans renvoyer à la réalité de l'époque: « Ceux qui se dévouèrent aux formations sanitaires n'eurent pas si grand mérite à le faire, en effet, car ils savaient que c'était la seule chose à faire et c'est de ne pas s'y décider qui alors eût été incroyable » (OC II, p. 124). Mais on sent aussi poindre son amertume : « L'intention du narrateur n'est cependant pas de donner à ces formations sanitaires plus d'importance qu'elles n'en eurent. A sa place, il est vrai que beaucoup de nos concitoyens cèderaient aujourd'hui à la tentation d'en exagérer le rôle » (OC II, p. 124). Car si Rieux combat tout naturellement la peste, il n'en est pas moins lucide quant à son engagement. À Tarrou venu lui proposer ses services et lui faisant remarquer « Vos victoires seront toujours provisoires », il répond : « Toujours, je le sais. Ce n'est pas une raison pour cesser de lutter » et il reconnaît que la peste est pour lui « une interminable défaite » (OC II, p. 122). Dès le début, le docteur est sans illusion : demain, tout sera à refaire. Et l'on songe ici à la définition que Rambert donne du fléau : « La peste [...] ça consiste à recommencer » (OC II, p. 146). Au plus fort de l'épidémie, accablé de fatigue, le médecin est sans illusions « Car il savait que, pour une période dont il n'apercevait pas le terme, son rôle n'était plus de guérir. Son rôle était de diagnostiquer. Découvrir, voir, décrire, enregistrer, puis condamner, c'était sa tâche » (OC II, p. 165). Contrairement aux couples enlacés qu'il croise dans les rues d'Oran libérée et qui croient « que la peste est finie et que la terreur avait fait son temps » (OC II, p. 240), Rieux sait que toute victoire est provisoire, quelles que soient les forces mises en œuvre pour combattre le fléau. C'est peut-être en cela que résident les limites de l'engagement. Les hommes n'ont pas de mémoire et la réaction des Oranais doit être étendue à tous :

> Ils niaient tranquillement, contre toute évidence, que nous ayons jamais connu ce monde insensé où le meurtre d'un homme était aussi quotidien que celui des mouches, cette sauvagerie bien définie, ce délire calculé, cet emprisonnement qui apportait avec lui une affreuse liberté à l'égard de tout ce qui n'était pas le présent, cette odeur de mort qui stupéfiait tous ceux qu'elle ne tuait pas, ils niaient enfin que nous ayons été ce peuple abasourdi dont tous les jours une partie, entassée dans la gueule d'un four, s'évaporaient en fumées grasses, tandis que l'autre, chargée des chaînes de l'impuissance et de la peur, attendait son tour (OC II, p. 240).

Rieux n'oublie pas que bonheur et victoire sont précaires. Il sait que

> cette chronique ne pouvait pas être celle de la victoire définitive. Elle ne pouvait être que le témoignage de ce qu'il avait fallu accomplir et que, sans doute, devraient accomplir encore, contre la terreur et son arme inlassable, malgré leurs déchirements personnels, tous les hommes qui, ne pouvant être des saints et refusant d'admettre les fléaux, s'efforcent cependant d'être des médecins (OC II, p. 248).

Car, contrairement à la foule en liesse, il sait

> [...] que le bacille de la peste ne meurt ni ne disparaît jamais, qu'il peut rester pendant des dizaines d'années endormi dans les meubles et le linge, qu'il attend patiemment dans les chambres, les caves, les malles, les mouchoirs et les paperasses, et que, peut-être, le jour viendrait où, pour le malheur et l'enseignement des hommes, la peste réveillerait ses rats et les enverrait mourir dans une cité heureuse (OC II, p. 248).

La genèse de *La Peste* montre bien l'évolution de Camus, vers une réflexion et une pensée approfondie, en fonction des circonstances. Dès septembre 1945, il s'est trouvé confronté à un dilemme dont héritera Tarrou. Il note dans ses *Carnets* : « Nous sommes dans un monde où il faut choisir d'être victime ou bourreau – et rien d'autre. Ce choix n'est pas facile » (OC II, p. 1026). Son personnage refusera de choisir, essaiera d'être « un meurtrier innocent » et imaginera « une troisième catégorie, celle des vrais médecins, mais c'est un fait qu'on n'en rencontre pas beaucoup et que ce doit être difficile » (OC II, p. 210). Tout naturellement, il mourra de la peste, tant sa position est intenable. Camus, lui, juge, non sans ironie, en 1949, dans « Le Temps des meurtriers », son époque :

> Les hommes de mon âge en France et en Europe, par exemple, sont nés juste avant ou pendant la première grande guerre, sont arrivés à l'adolescence au moment de la crise économique mondiale et ont eu 20 ans l'année de la prise de pouvoir par Hitler. Pour compléter leur éducation, on leur a offert ensuite la guerre d'Espagne, Munich, la guerre de 1939, la défaite et quatre années d'occupation et de luttes clandestines. Pour finir, on leur promet le feu d'artifice atomique. Je suppose donc que c'est ce qu'on appelle une génération intéressante (OC III, p. 353).

Il a bien conscience, un peu seul à vrai dire, dans son éditorial du 8 août 1945, que « la civilisation mécanique vient de parvenir à son dernier degré de sauvagerie » (OC II, p. 409). Le 6 les Américains ont largué la première bombe atomique sur Hiroshima ; le 9, ils recommenceront à Nagasaki. Il conclut ainsi son article :

> Devant les perspectives terrifiantes qui s'ouvrent à l'humanité, nous apercevons encore mieux que la paix est le seul combat qui vaille d'être mené. Ce n'est plus une prière, mais un ordre qui doit monter des peuples vers les gouvernements, l'ordre de choisir définitivement entre l'enfer et la raison (OC II, p. 410).

Mais les hommes oublient que l'allégresse des jours de victoire est toujours menacée ; un jour viendra où ils laisseront à nouveau s'installer la peste.

BIBLIOGRAPHIE

À Albert Camus, ses amis du Livre, Paris, Gallimard, 1962.

Camus, A., *Œuvres complètes*, Bibliothèque de La Pléiade, Paris, Gallimard, tomes I et II, 2006, tomes III et IV, 2008.

Camus, A., Grenier, J., *Correspondance 1932–1960*, Paris, Gallimard, 1981.

Chevandier, Ch., *Été 44 L'insurrection des policiers de Paris*, Paris, Vendémiaire, 2014.

Lévi-Valensi, J., *Camus à* Combat, Cahiers Albert Camus 8, Paris, Gallimard, 2002.

Camus' Religious Revolt in *The Plague*

ERIC B. BERG

"No plan ever withstands first contact with the enemy."[1]

Colonel John Cox, USAF Retired

INTRODUCTION

In Camus' *The Plague*, Father Paneloux delivers two sermons to the population of Oran. Neither sermon practically helps the people and each has a different theological foundation. Camus uses a theodicy dilemma[2] to illuminate the limits and dangers of theology (and all disciplines that can linger only in the theoretical, philosophy and science included). In this paper, I will briefly describe both sermons and the event that triggers a change in theology for Father Paneloux. From this, I will develop a "metaphysical flow chart" that will track the rise of the Absurd, the Father's reaction, and his attempt to deal with it. After illuminating the absurd and the resulting revolt against it, I will offer several possible theological foundations that Camus may have been comfortable with, or even pointed to as actually being helpful. This also helps the reader understand Camus' rather difficult statements about not believing in God and not being an atheist.[3]

---

1 Attributed to multiple sources – thus I give credit where I first heard it and saw it in action.

2 Theodicy, Greek: *theos* + *dikē* = God and Justice. God is all powerful, God always desires the good – yet evil exists. This is a problem, as if God has all the power, and wants all good, why is there evil?

3 A. Camus, *Notebooks 1935–1942*, transl. J. O'Brien, New York, Alfred A. Knopf, 1965, p. 112 (November 1, 1954).

PART I

After delivering several short sermons of instructions – these sermons appear to be essentially public service announcements – Father Paneloux crafts a theological response to the plague based in Augustine and justice. After witnessing the suffering and death of a child, he retools and crafts a second sermon based in Tertullian and the mystery of God with an "all or nothing" demand. In the end, in one of Camus' most brilliant word uses, Paneloux dies "a doubtful case." It is both possible that he died of plague and that he died a heretic in the eyes of Rome.

First, who was Father Paneloux? We know quite a bit about him from Camus. He was: Roman Catholic, Jesuit, well-informed on Augustine, *Pied-Noir*, "militant" (which I read as orthodox), a large man built to preach, intelligent, meticulous, introverted, and deeply devoted to his faith and humanity.

As the central religious character in *The Plague*, he is no strawman. Situated in North Africa, he is a fine representative of French Catholicism and Camus is well-equipped to use him in the narrative. With a Jesuit education and North African in the tradition of Augustine, Paneloux is a solid representation of the Christian response to the plague (and all it stands for in the novel: the absurd, fascism, Nazism, literal plague). He is used to represent the Christian response on all the levels of this wonderful text that works so well. One cannot dismiss the Father as a weak representation of Christianity.

It seems to me that the basic character of Father Paneloux is derived from Bossuet and possibly a certain Father Pain who was residing in Oran, Algeria, when Camus' second wife, Francine Faure, was also residing there during their separation during the war. Jacques-Bénigne Bossuet (1627–1704) is an interesting study and I am quite convinced he is the model for Father Paneloux. Bossuet was primarily known for his oratory skills, both in the construction of sermons and their delivery. He was Jesuit-educated and theologically aligned with St. Augustine; especially in his political discourse in *City of God*. From what we are given about Father Paneloux, I feel it is safe to assume Bossuet is the rough model.

The basics of sermon #1

It is delivered to the congregation at large and is well attended, in fact it is standing room only, and highly anticipated. The delivery is described as "fiery" and "powerful." Paneloux is in command of the situation. The weather is dramatic as the thunderstorm acts as an accompaniment to the powerful sermon and, like an epiphany, the sun breaks forth at the end of it. I do not have to call attention to the obvious and intentional use of the sun in Camus' works to emphasize the power of this first sermon. The plague is on the rise; the theological foundation of the sermon is Augustine and Paneloux is secure in his theology.

The basics of sermon #2

It is delivered to men only at a Mass for Men, and the Father is now competing with St. Roch, the patron saint of plague victims, for religious attention. This sermon is not well attended and the congregation is slipping. It is delivered in a much less confident way; it is described by Camus as a "performance" and lacks the confidence of the first sermon grounded in Augustine. The weather fights with Paneloux for attention, and the plague has plateaued but not abated. The theological foundation is Tertullian, which is a new territory for the Father and not near as solid in the eyes of the Roman Church. After all, Augustine is a saint and Tertullian is not.

I argue that Camus uses Father Paneloux to illuminate a religious response to the absurd and leads us to the philosophical conclusion that theology has limits to what it can understand and clearly communicate, and if theology remains in the theoretical and does not respect this limit, it is useless, and more than that, it is dangerous. When the Father searches for an intellectual foundation to understand the suffering and deathof the innocent child at a cost of actually helping others, this is the danger. There is a metaphysic that is revealed by Camus that demands attention and action.

PART II

This is the metaphysic.

The absurd waits. It is embedded in ontology. It is uncovered by our human expectations on reality not matching reality. The uncovering comes from one of two human experiences: death or Kierkegaardian anxiety.

Is the absurd a part of nature? No, it is of human construction in relationship to nature. In *The Plague*, we can see anxiety occur when human construction confronts the object it does not fit. The suffering and death of the child illuminates this, it confronts and destroys our human, constructed sense of justice. An adult, a nasty adult, suffers and dies – this we can accept. An innocent child suffers and dies, with no utilitarian benefit – this we cannot accept. It is very much like Kant's manifolds of perception. Briefly, and from Kant's pen:

> Experience is an empirical cognition, i.e., a cognition that determines an object through perceptions. Hence experience is a synthesis of perceptions that itself is not contained in perception but contains the synthetic unity of the manifold of perceptions in one consciousness. This unity amounts to what is essential for a cognition of objects of the senses, i.e., for experience (rather than merely intuition or sensation of the senses).[4] (B218–219)

Manifolds of perception allow us to make sense and order the world. The notions of time and relative position ground us; if one is taken away, we lose the ability to perceive the world around us. Human confrontation with the absurd is much like this, but scaled down. It is scaled down because we **create** these manifolds of perception individually. Time and relative position come first; we construct things after. From Camus' pen in his *Notebooks*: "The whole problem of the absurd ought to be able to be centered on a critique of the value judgment and the factual judgment."[5] The relationship between the two is critical, it is "centered" in his mind. How we create and place value on the world, and how it actually is, is the problem of the absurd.

For example, we have expectations and an understating of death that are human constructions. One may understand death via religion, and when the universe does not feel or comply with this, a manifold does not fit. We construct these manifolds after the fact. For example, if we are Lutheran (clearly a human construction), we construct a Lutheran understanding of death from a human manifold like religion. Religion, in this sense, is a manifold of perception. The clash is inevitable. Human mortality was established immediately upon humans being humans, and we construct a very well-defined understanding of death from a religion created between 1517 and 2016, specific to how we understand it as Lutherans. When one cannot account for the death of an innocent child, using all the Lutheran resources available, the world as we perceive it (in a weak sense) has lost grounding, hence

---

4 I. Kant, *Critique of Pure Reason*, transl. P. Guyer, A.W. Wood, Cambridge, Cambridge University Press, 1998, p. 67.

5 A. Camus, *Notebooks 1942–1951*, transl. J. O'Brien, New York, Alfred A. Knopf, 1965, p. 57.

Kierkegaard's description of us becoming "dizzy." This produces Kierkegaardian anxiety; the other possible "trigger" event.

And what precisely is Kierkegaardian anxiety? From Kierkegaard's pen:

> [Anxiety] is altogether different from fear and similar concepts that refer to something definite, whereas anxiety is freedom's actuality as the possibility of possibility... Anxiety may be compared with dizziness... anxiety is the dizziness of freedom, which emerges when the spirit wants to posit the synthesis and freedom looks down into its own possibility, laying hold of finiteness to support itself. Freedom succumbs to dizziness.[6] (C/A pg 42 Hong)

The first thing to recognize that anxiety as Kierkegaard sees it is different than fear, the two need to be distinguished from each other. Fear has an object, and it can be "targeted," so to speak. Anxiety has no object, it is the unlimited possibility ahead of us, and the ending of those possibilities in death. It is objectless, thus much harder to deal with. Furthermore, it is a human condition; we understand our possibilities and the end of our possibilities. It triggers a feeling of dizziness in us. Camus notes when writing about death: "...the mere sight of a handkerchief filled with blood is being plunged suddenly and effortlessly into time in a dizzying way: it is the fear of what's ahead."[7]

Paneloux is the first to connect rats and the plague, and the plague is an object that causes fear – it is biology. However, it ends our possibilities with death, and this triggers anxiety. Paneloux (and the other main characters in *The Plague*) are confronted with the transition from fear of plague to anxiety over the end of possibilities. Camus skillfully explores multiple reactions to this and here, in this paper, we look closely at Father Paneloux and the religious reaction to both fear of plague and anxiety over what it may bring. The death of the child sharpens the point, as many have illuminated, including Camus himself in reflecting on Dostoyevsky. The child is innocent. His possibilities are ended early and not due to his own agency. It is one thing to see a life-long smoker die of lung cancer, and quite another to see an innocent child die of plague. It is all biology in the end, but the smoker has agency and, most likely, a cause and effect relationship with

---

6 S. Kierkegaard, *The Concept of Anxiety*, transl. R. Thomte, Princeton, Princeton University Press, 1980, p. 42.

7 A. Camus, *Notebooks 1942–1951*, transl. J. O'Brien , New York, Alfred A. Knopf, 1965, p. 67.

the cancer, and the child has none. Our expectations on the world, justice in this case, are shattered. Plague is just biology, it attacks without concern for the victim – this is anxiety-inducing. Plague is an excellent example to use because it encompasses both fear and anxiety. Plague is biology, chemistry, and mathematics, and the scientific community attacks it as an object using biology, chemistry, and mathematics. Dr Rieux attacks the plague as an object – it is fear. However, the mathematical efficiency and indifference of the plague produces anxiety, as it has no sense of fair-play or justice. Biology, chemistry, and mathematics determined that the child would suffer and die of plague. No court or justice system did.

The created world is indifferent to our expectations; death and Kierkegaardian anxiety reveal the absurd to us, and it is how we react to it that Camus becomes a master at illuminating. Anxiety can break us, force us to reconfigure our theoretical base assumptions, force us to action, even consider suicide. This is not a once-occurring event, it repeats itself. One does not pass through this crisis and become immune to it afterwards. The obvious trigger for anxiety is the death of another, the indifference the universe shows towards this death, and our overwhelming care for the death of another forces us to react. Or, it is the sublime anxiety described so well by Kierkegaard above and known to Camus that may come by simple philosophical reflection. These two produce a metaphysical flow chart well laid out in many of the works of Camus, and *The Plague* is where he illuminates it best.[8]

This is the experience of Father Paneloux: his Augustinian grounding is destroyed by the death of the innocent, he moves to Tertullian and finds no sense of stability in him either, he undergoes a process of spiritual death. It is important to note his faith is not destroyed, only the theological construction established by Augustine and employed by Paneloux, but not his Christianity. Theology has reached its limits and overreached them at this point. To continue to apply Augustine or Tertullian to the situation is foolhardy, and anxiety-producing. Something has to give. Camus observes in his *Notebooks* from April 1939: "The Plague: abolishes all systems."[9]

8 I am interested to explore the possibility of Meursault in *The Stranger* as a study in revolt to this anxiety.

9 A. Camus, *Notebooks 1935–1942*, *op. cit.*, p. 193.

PART III

If I can make a chart, it looks something like this: The metaphysics or ontology of Father Paneloux in *The Plague*

Absurd – Plague Arrives

↓

Theoretical Revolt – Augustine: Fail

↓

Absurd Trigger Event – Death of the Child

↓

Theoretical Revolt – Tertullian: Fail

↓

Absurd – Plague Remains – Anxiety

↓

Abandon Theoretical Grounding (Theology) → Death of Spirit

The above schema gives a visual flowchart to the process Father Paneloux goes through in *The Plague* from my reading of the text. First, the absurd is set in motion for the novel with the arrival of the plague in Oran. This will be the event in nature that will encompass both fear and anxiety and the resulting anxiety will cause the Father to reconsider his theological grounding (his unifying principle or system), not once but twice, and the result will be the Father dying a "doubtful case" at the end of the novel.

The first stop on the schema illustrates how the plague triggers a theological revolt from the Father, and he stands his ground with his most trusted manifold of perception (his unifying principle), St. Augustine. This revolt ends in failure, as Augustine does not provide an adequate response for plague, especially with the death of the child. The move with Augustine is to blame the population of Oran and their sins for the coming of plague. With the death of the child, Paneloux abandons Augustine as the unifying principle or this manifold breaks with this event. Camus does a masterful job of describing the death of the child in great detail and as this process unfolds, Paneloux's theology unravels. Anxiety shatters the ability of Augustinian theology to explain this death; evil works in reality with complete indifference. The next stop on the schema shows Paneloux moving to another theologian, Tertullian, and the mystery of God, the absurdity of belief. This manifold of perception or unifying principle does not provide a solution to the anxiety; the plague remains a constant and is unmoved by theology that operates in the abstract, while the plague continues to operate in the concrete. Paneloux does change the pronoun in the text from the exclusive "you" to the inclusive "we" with this foundational theological shift from Augustine to Tertullian. At this point, Camus is illuminating just one stock reaction to plague (and all it stands for in the text), that of religion. Religion has no resolution for anxiety for the character of Paneloux. The result is the last stop on the schema; he abandons his theological grounding and drifts. Camus tells us the Father is working on a book or series of works that the Church may consider heresy, he is adrift; not grounded in Augustine or even a borderline theologian like Tertullian anymore. His manifolds of perception (Augustine, Tertullian, and the particular form of Roman Catholicism) have not provided any answer to plague, he suffers a death of spirit; the last stop on the schema. Paneloux is a study on the religious reaction to the absurd and he wonderfully illuminates Camus' view of the failure of religion when used in the way Paneloux did. The abstraction of religion and the dangerous application of it at a time of crisis like plague is the point of Paneloux's character in the text.

Camus makes this observation when working on *The Plague* in his *Notebooks* from the period when he is writing the novel. In an entry from November 1942, Camus sketches a schema for his plague:

> Development of the absurd:
> 1. If the basic concern is for unity;
> 2. If the world (or God) cannot suffice.
> It is up to man to forge a unity for himself, either by turning away from the world, or within the world. Thus are restored a morality and an austerity that remain to be defined.[10]

Camus' notes are remarkably similar to the schema I have illuminated above and were part of the inspiration for my thoughts on this question. We desire unity, a central theme in his notes on *The Plague*. Like Kant says, unity is critical. Unity in Kant is a given, imbedded in ontology, but for this "second level" in Camus, it can be created. What we see in the world does not give us this unifying principle, we must create it, and the most obvious entity to look to is – God – may "not suffice." It is up to us to "forge" this. We move forward with this manifold of perception we create, and it is connected to morality, thus action. Now, a look at what I believe Camus desires the schema to look like from a religious perspective.

---

10 A. Camus, *Notebooks 1942–1951, op.cit.*, p. 41.

Camus would have it look like this:

Absurd Arrives – Plague
↓
Establish Theoretical Foundation of Revolt
↓
Absurd Trigger Event – Often Death or Kierkegaardian Anxiety
↓
Revolt – Action Grounded in Theoretical Foundation

Religious Example: Dietrich Bonhoeffer

The above schema drives the reader to a different conclusion, and stronger one than just a reaction – to action. The same event arrives: the plague. This established the absurd in Oran and the text takes a look at the reaction from various characters, including Paneloux. It is acceptable to establish revolt by way of religion, or theological revolt, as the first stop in the schema indicates. Surprisingly to Camus' readers, one can revolt using the unifying principle of theology. The trigger event of the dramatic death of the child has the same effect; his death triggers anxiety. It is the reaction to this event that is critical. If the reaction remains in the abstraction of speculative theology, it fails to do anything, for anyone, much less Paneloux. However, if it manifests itself in action, we have something of value. The prototype is Grand, the civil-servant that keeps to his daily tasks of civil service, and the sanitation squads that risk their own lives to help the population of Oran, the common good. If theology breaks out of the abstract alone, and demands action for the common good, it is of value and can, in fact, provide an answer for anxiety.

Paneloux's problem is that he remains in the theoretical, in the abstract, where he encounters the absurd first. He operates in his comfort zone of Augustine and distances himself from the population. This fails miserably when confronted with the death of the child. However, it is not too late. He still has time to change, to act. Instead of a full change, he makes a half-measure move to Tertullian. In the end, this cannot explain the death of the child and, in an attempt at another theoretical resolution, he ponders the question raised in 1527 by another theologian well versed in St. Augustine, Martin Luther: *Whether one may Flee from a Deadly Plague*. Paneloux has drafted a work on this topic and apparently has drifted further from the orthodox fold by doing so. However, he is no closer to resolving the anxiety through theology.

The above schema leads me in the direction of the 20th century theologian Dietrich Bonhoeffer. The key change from schema #1 to #2 is that theological revolt leads to action.

What could Paneloux have done? Theology must bring forth action that helps the neighbor. And that takes courage. Contrasted with Dr. Rieux, science brings forth action from the Doctor. However, this is not to say Camus is the champion of science over religion. Science can remain quiet, theoretical, and non-active. Dr. Rieux takes his work into the population that has plague and works to help them. Theology can do this also, but in the case of Paneloux (and all he stands for in the text) it does not, it remains in the theoretical, looking for answers and not acting for the neighbor. Furthermore, there is no real need for a complicated, well-defined theoretical foundation (science or religion) – action can come forth from a simple sense of duty.[11] For example, Grand is wholly concerned with action, carrying out his daily deeds for the population of Oran. Theology can bring forth action, but it can also stagnate in the theoretical. It can give us quietism like the world witnessed in WWII as Jews were loaded into trains bound for death within sight of the Vatican.

Camus sees this metaphysic and responses that are limited to theory, and takes it one step beyond description – he moves to the prescriptive mode. What is to be done? Action. Help thy neighbor. Rebel against the indifference and the shattered manifold of perception, revolt. Revolt is action. One can do something in the face of benign indifference, one can care for the other.

In the text, Camus begins with Augustine and moves to Tertullian. I propose, using theologians that Camus either knew or who were his contemporaries, a path for theology that Camus may have been comfortable with. From Augustine to Tertullian to Kierkegaard to Simone Weil, and finally ending with Dietrich Bonhoeffer.

St. Augustine has very obvious and strong connections to Camus as his advanced degree thesis titled *Christian Metaphysics and Neoplatonism* devotes many pages to Augustine. Furthermore, Augustine is a North African theologian and he shows up in many of Camus' works, especially in *The Fall* by way of references, and the narrative style of a confession makes him an obvious choice for Camus. Augustine's ability to at least see limits to theology with his *si comprehendis non est Deus* argument is appealing to Camus and gets us pointed in the right direction by limiting the range and scope of

---

11 I use the phrase "simple sense of duty" here to contrast it with the rather complex use of duty by Kant.

theology. This first step is a legitimate pathway for Christianity (or religion) to move when confronted with the absurd that generates anxiety. Limiting theology as Augustine does theology, and this is a proper first step – the recognition of limits, that trying to answer the classic theodicy set up in *The Plague* is going to be a challenge. The imposition of limits is a necessary first step that will be included in each of the following theologians I chart out on this possible trajectory starting with Augustine. Each theologian contributes a small necessary element toward a possible answer to the absurd from the perspective of religion. Not limited to Christianity, but following Camus' lead, I take it in this direction. It is quite possible that any type of religious thinker may follow the same path. However, the problems found within Paneloux's (Camus') reading of Augustine do not hold, and that leads us to Tertullian in the text.

Tertullian pushes Father Paneloux to change the pronoun from "you" to "we" in his second sermon and drop the notion of God's justice delivered on a deserving population from his view. This is a positive step and starts to set a trajectory for Camus and religion on this question. Augustine sets limits, Tertullian moves the Father to the other or the neighbor. It is an important contribution because it drives the reader to the other, to the neighbor, when considering this question as readers of the text.

Tertullian is much less orthodox, as reflected in their ultimate disposition from the Roman Church; Augustine is a saint and Tertullian is not. Tertullian shares Augustine's limits as Tertullian was never one for metaphysical speculation, almost to a fault. In his text *Ad Nationes* Tertullian argues that it is ridiculous to blame earthquakes, floods, famine, and natural disasters on the Christian population (contra Nero's claim). Tertullian then moves into an eloquent testimony about the beauty of the Christian community, the care and giving for each other and the heathen. Tertullian states: "We are accused of every calamity. Yet we live with you."[12] This gives Paneloux the impetus to change his view of the judgment of God from Augustine to the community aspect of Tertullian, which is clearly reflected in the second sermon.

Tertullian is a very interesting choice; on the negative side of the ledger, there is the threat that his use of the word "absurd" can get confused with the highly developed meaning Camus gives it, but on the positive side, his unorthodox position and standing in the Church (or lack of it) gives him

12 Tertullian, *Ad Nationes* I, trans. Q. Howe, http://www.tertullian.org/articles/howe_adnationes1.htm, 2007.

some freedom and flexibility to take on the challenge of the absurd and anxiety from his position. Belief, because it is absurd, allows the Kierkegaardian leap of faith to become part of the equation, and furthers his position from the scientist Rieux. The Christian response put forth by Paneloux in the second sermon gives us a shift toward the trajectory of active theology that I end with; while incorporating Augustine's notion of limits, combined with Tertullian's framework for belief, sets us on a course for the next stop, Kierkegaard.

Kierkegaard is another theologian familiar to Camus and the choice of him sets us drifting further from Roman orthodoxy, very far away: from being grounded in the orthodoxy of Augustine, to the semi-orthodoxy of Tertullian, to the Protestant Kierkegaard. Retaining the limits of Augustine, building upon the demand to look to the neighbor in Tertullian, Kierkegaard is a step out of the text of *The Plague*, but a logical step with the trajectory established in *The Plague* and the evidence marshalled from other works by Camus. We know that Camus was very familiar with Kierkegaard and was, in fact, reading Kierkegaard's work in the 1940s. Kierkegaard's wonderful illumination of the relationship between faith and reason extends the trajectory of Camus' thought from Augustine to Tertullian laid out in the text and hinted at in The Father's next publication.

Kierkegaard argues that to know is not faith; precisely because I cannot know, I must have faith. This, coupled with the distinction between fear and anxiety that works so well in the text lead us from the purely theoretical to a position that will launch action. Building on what is present in the text, and especially Camus' remarks to the Jesuits (co-extensive with writing *The Plague*), Kierkegaard has two attributes that make him a successful next step towards an adequate theological response to the challenge presented in *The Plague*. By adequate, I mean one that will not be frozen by anxiety and yet stay true to the significant challenge presented to the reader by Camus. Kierkegaard breaks the mold of being trapped in a rational response to plague and anxiety, and specifically the death of the child. He identifies what it is with his sophisticated understanding of the distinction between fear and anxiety. By distinguishing the two, the response is different also. Rationality can respond to fear and plague in one sense, and anxiety can be understood as being generated from plague, but a different category all together. Something, many things, can be done about the plague and this follows the line of Rieux, for example. The serum is a potential fix to the plague, lessening fear. But the serum is no cure for anxiety. Kierkegaard offers this vision of a distinction between the two. Following Augustine, we understand the limits of the theological answer, not the why of it, but what we can do. Following Tertullian, it is to look toward the neighbor, not to search for blame. Extending to Kierkegaard, it is to distinguish between the fear caused by plague, and the anxiety caused by plague, and the resulting confrontation of the absurd. By this extension we reach Simone Weil.

Simone Weil is well known to Camus as he edited her works for Galimard and called her "the one great spirit of our time." The connection they shared through tuberculosis must have been very important for Camus as she too was limited from action in the world; in the same way Camus was against the same enemy (Hitler and company). In fact, in another paper, I argue that the father of the child who dies in *The Plague*, Othon, is modeled in part on Simone Weil.

Weil is a perfect extension from Augustine, Tertullian, and Kierkegaard. Weil is a mystic, a bit of a Catholic, and very spiritual. The key to linking Weil into this chain is her life-long need to commiserate with those who suffer. It is well documented in her biographies, as it started when she was a child not wanting to eat more than the workers around her apartment, working in auto factories to identify with the labor movements she supported, culminating in her self-denial of enough nutrients to sustain her own life as she died in England in 1943. She did not want to exceed the caloric intake of those in occupied France while she was safe in England – thus the identification and commiseration with those who suffer. Retaining the limits of Augustine, the extension to the neighbor of Tertullian, the identification of the root cause of anxiety in Kierkegaard, Weil adds commiseration with the suffering. However, Weil comes up just a bit short with commiseration. Working in auto factories to understand the plight of labor, trying to replicate the conditions in occupied France while she was in exile in the UK to the detriment of her own health moves her in the right direction, but it is not a call for action. Commiseration to understand continues the trajectory established in the text and leads us to the final desired result of theology when facing this problem: Bonhoeffer and action.

Dietrich Bonhoeffer – the Lutheran pastor that intellectually debated the question of whether it is right to actively take a role in assassinating Hitler – and decided "yes." This is not the place to debate the question if

Camus would have agreed with his decision. It is the place to show a trajectory that could end in Bonhoeffer.

Retaining the limits of Augustine, always looking toward the neighbor via Tertullian, understanding human anxiety with Kierkegaard, and commiserating with those who suffer like Weil, Bonhoeffer adds the necessary element: action. Bonhoeffer, somewhat like a Lutheran Paneloux, has a very solid, intellectually grounded world view, and from this world view, confronts absurdity, lands on revolt, and jumps into action. It is the action that Father Paneloux is missing. Bonhoeffer does not abandon his faith; furthermore, he does not even abandon his highly structured world view of Lutheranism. He is led to action. Dietrich Bonhoeffer exemplifies a response to plague that is grounded in a Christian world view that is neither naive nor too rigidly orthodox. Bonhoeffer contemplated the absurd as he saw it and acted on behalf of the neighbor, deciding to actively engage in the plot to assassinate Hitler; all while retaining his faith and credentials as a Lutheran pastor. Bonhoeffer, as a Christian response to the absurd raised by plague, leads to action on behalf of the neighbor. This, I argue, is the response Camus is looking for from Christians or religious thinkers.

In the end, there is more to admire in Bonhoeffer than the other theologians. The trajectory of theology must move from recognition of the absurd, to revolt, to action. It must "do" in reality, and must do with complete compassion.

Conclusion: to restate the thesis statement that opens this piece: theology understands conceptually. However, evil works in reality, and it works with complete indifference. Theology must move out of the conceptual state and into action. This is the failure of Paneloux, and it is in Bonhoeffer that we can find one theologian that makes this move.

Father Paneloux attempts to understand plague conceptually through Augustine's notion of Holy Justice. This fails when he observes the death of the innocent child. He then switches to another conceptually grounded theology from Tertullian – that of the mystery of God and an "all or nothing approach to faith." This slowly fails because evil is not solved conceptually, without action. As in France, the Roman Church fought to understand the genocide conceptually and as an organization, but did not fight it with action. Paneloux has no plan of action and dies a doubtful case. We can point to two or three theologians that are also European contemporaries of Camus, Simone Weil and Dietrich Bonhoeffer, that may satisfy this demand of action grounded in solid theology.

BIBLIOGRAPHY

Camus, A., *Notebooks 1935–1942*, transl. J. O'Brien, New York, Alfred A. Knopf, 1965.

Camus, A., *Notebooks 1942–1951*, transl. J. O'Brien, New York, Alfred A. Knopf, 1965.

Kant, I., *Critique of Pure Reason*, transl. P. Guyer, A.W. Wood, Cambridge, Cambridge University Press, 1998.

Kierkegaard, S., *The Concept of Anxiety*, transl. R. Thomte, Princeton, Princeton University Press, 1980.

Tertullian, *Ad Nationes* I, transl. Q. Howe, http://www.tertullian.org/articles/howe_adnationes1.htm, 2007.

Lire et écouter pour écrire *L'Homme révolté*

CHRISTIAN CHEVANDIER

« Cette montagne que vous élevez, édifiez tout à coup, refuge et arsenal à la fois, support et tremplin d'action et de pensée, nous serons nombreux, croyez-le, sans possessif exagéré, à en faire *notre montagne* » écrivait René Char à son ami Camus à propos de *L'Homme révolté*[1]. Six ans plus tôt, lors du discours de clôture du VIIème congrès du Parti communiste chinois, Mao donnait en exemple un vieillard, Yukong, qui pouvait déplacer des montagnes avec la seule aide de ses fils, singulièr éloge d'une entreprise sinon individuelle, du moins familiale. La montagne de Camus, il serait fallacieux de la percevoir comme œuvre individuelle, tant les lectures et les échanges ont permis à l'auteur de l'édifier et c'est bien Char qui avait raison en mettant en avant, « sans possessif exagéré » mais en connaissance de cause, la première personne du pluriel.

Pour Camus, le fait de mener à bien ce projet était essentiel, à tel point qu'alors que ses jumeaux avaient cinq ans, il évoqua à au moins trois reprises la fin de son écriture en des termes qui relèvent de l'obstétrique[2]. Mais, conscience prise de cet intérêt pour ce texte, le risque est grand d'anachronisme lorsque l'on lit deux tiers de siècle plus tard l'ouvrage publié par les éditions Gallimard le 18 octobre 1951. D'abord parce que sa perception est fortement biaisée par ce que l'on a lu à son propos, notamment la polémique avec *Les Temps modernes.* Francis Jeanson lui reprocha, entre autres, de n'avoir étudié les travaux d'Hegel et de Marx qu'à la lecture d'autres auteurs[3]. Mais

---

[1] A. Camus, R. Char, *Correspondance 1945–1959*, Paris, Gallimard, 2007, Char à Camus, 16 juillet 1951, p. 86–87.

[2] « Travail » peut prêter à confusion, mais « accouchement », « enfant » et « délivrance » sont sans équivoque, *ibidem*, Camus à Char, 25 février 1951, p. 79–81.

[3] F. Jeanson, *Albert Camus ou l'âme révoltée*, « Les Temps Modernes » 1952, Mai, p. 2070–2090.

écrire, c'est d'abord lire et écouter. Ce sera donc l'influence des lectures et des fréquentations de Camus que l'on étudiera ici.

I) AVEC LES AMIS

a) Char et les autres

Une des premières entrées que j'ai cherchée, en vain, lorsque j'ai pris connaissance du *Dictionnaire René Char*, paru en 2015[4], fut celle qui aurait été consacrée à *L'Homme révolté*. Car ce livre, c'est aussi, un peu, celui de Char, qui en a relu et annoté le manuscrit initial à tel point que Camus lui en a offert le dactylographe avec une longue dédicace sur leur communauté de pensée et la part qu'y a eue de son ami et dont la première page se termine par : « Une pierre blanche de plus sur le beau et étroit chemin de notre amitié ». Dans la deuxième page, il précise : « A vous, cher René, le premier état de ce livre dont je voulais qu'il soit LE NOTRE et qui, sans vous, n'aurait jamais pu être un livre d'espoir »[5], allusion probable à la collection dans laquelle Camus a publié les *Feuillets d'Hypnos*, première étape de l'amitié entre les deux hommes. Mais il ne sera pas ici question du poète, dont la part dans la genèse de l'essai mériterait à elle seule une communication, quand bien même l'on ne peut s'empêcher d'y penser lorsque l'on lit les pages consacrées au surréalisme et que l'on connaît sa position face au groupe de Breton après la publication.

Les années qui suivirent la Libération virent des amis de Camus dans les allées du pouvoir, ce qui ne pouvait le laisser indifférent. Il y avait là ceux croisés dans la Résistance, mais aussi les amis d'Alger du temps du Théâtre du Travail, de la Maison de la Culture et de la cellule communiste dite « des intellectuels » du Plateau-Saulière : Marguerite Dobrenn, Georges Dayan, Jeanne-Paul Sicard tandis qu'Yves Dechezelles fut même un temps chef de cabinet d'Adrien Tixier à l'Intérieur[6]. Tous influencés par le Front populaire, ils appartenaient à une génération marquée par la guerre d'Espagne et l'antifascisme. Les petits partis marginaux et inventifs, comme l'UDSR ou le RDR, accueillaient également des amis de l'écrivain. N'oublions pas non plus les rapports encore excellents qu'entretinrent jusqu'au printemps 1951

---

[4] Editions Classiques Garnier.

[5] Note 1 p. 86 de F. Planeille in *Correspondance 1945-1959...*, *op.cit.*

[6] Beaucoup de personnes évoquées dans ce texte ont été l'objet d'une notice dans le *Dictionnaire biographique du mouvement ouvrier français*.

Camus et Sartre. Quand bien même ils ne se gênaient pas pour s'adresser des piques réciproques, ils n'étaient pas encore si éloignés et, pour ne prendre que cet exemple, Camus et Sartre (et bien d'autres : Raymond Aron, Jean Paulhan, François Mauriac, André Breton…) ont signé en avril 1947 l'appel « Défense de Paul Nizan »[7]. Camus avait même écrit sur un exemplaire de *L'Homme révolté* la dédicace : « Au Castor,/ A Sartre/ leur ami/ A. Camus »[8]. Les échanges passaient aussi par toutes les correspondances qu'il entretint, parfois avec de jeunes gens comme Jean Daniel dont il critiqua en février 1950 une critique des *Justes* : « Le problème n'est pas de savoir si l'on doit tuer le gardien alors qu'il a des enfants et pour s'évader soi-même mais si l'on doit tuer aussi les enfants pour libérer tous les détenus »[9]. Longtemps avant de devenir président du Conseil constitutionnel, Pierre Mazeaud, étudiant en droit et militant de Jeunesse libertaire, était en cette année 1950 parmi ces correspondants[10]. Et puis il y a l'aide de tous ceux que l'on sollicite[11], souvent oralement, et qui ne laisse généralement pas de trace.

b) Syndicalistes révolutionnaires et libertaires

Pour Albert Camus, « un copain » selon le titre l'auteur d'un article du journal syndicaliste révolutionnaire *La Révolution* prolétarienne en 1957, l'amitié était presque constitutive des relations qui le liait à un milieu anarchiste pourtant prompt à se déchirer. Ne sont développés ici ni les rapports entre Camus et les libertaires, que les Actes d'une rencontres méditerranéenne de Lourmarin et le livre de Lou Marin permettent d'appréhender, ni son attrait pour le syndicalisme révolutionnaire, abordé lors d'une autre rencontre de Lourmarin[12]. Il n'y consacre dans cet ouvrage qu'une part très limitée, une rapide allusion

---

7 B. Demonsais, *Gavroche. Un hebdomadaire culturel socialiste de la Résistance à la Guerre froide*, Paris, L'Harmattan, 2006, p. 209–210.

8 L'exemplaire (conservé dans la collection du bibliophile Pierre Leroy) fut finalement envoyé à Steco Redef.

9 A. Camus, J. Daniel, extraits de la correspondance, 1949–1959 [dans :] *Camus*, dir. R. Gay-Crosier, A. Spiquel-Courdille,Cahiers de l'Herne, Paris, Herne, 2013, p. 283.

10 D. Perken [il s'agit d'un pseudonyme], *Sartre et surtout Camus s'intéressent à notre mouvement*, « Combat » 1951, 12 avril.

11 Pour le présent texte, l'aide m'a été précieuse d'Alexandre Alajbegovic, Frédéric Cépède, Patrick Eveno, Roger Grenier, Eugène Kouchkine, Jean-Clément Martin, Gilles Morin, Loïc Philip, Jean-Louis Robert, Agnès Spiquel, Philippe Vanney, Gilles Vergnon et Elie Wajeman.

12 L. Marin, *Albert Camus, écrits libertaires (1948–1960)*, Montpellier, Indigène éditions, 2016 ; *Le Don de la liberté : les relations d'Albert Camus avec les libertaires*, Lourmarin, Rencontres méditerranéennes Albert Camus, 2009 ; C. Chevandier, *Le syndicalisme révolutionnaire, une indéniable pensée de midi*, « Albert Camus et la pensée de midi », Avignon, éditions A. Barthélémy, 2016.

dans « La Révolte historique » pour remarquer que, seul, il s'est engagé dans la voie de « créer, par l'éducation et la culture, les cadres neufs qu'appelait et qu'appelle encore un monde sans honneur » (p. 248[13]) et, surtout, sa mise en avant avec la Commune de Paris comme concrétisation de la pensée de midi. Mais il l'estime essentiel :

> Je ne crois pas en tout cas que ma cause soit déjà perdue, ni celle du syndicalisme révolutionnaire. Elle est la seule vivante comme est vivante la souffrance des millions d'hommes qui appartiennent par leur malheur même à cette cause. Ce qui m'est le plus précieux pour finir dans l'ouvrage dont vous venez de parler c'est justement cet effort pour donner une forme à notre espoir commun et cette annonce de notre renaissance[14].

En réfutant le meurtre pour choisir le syndicalisme révolutionnaire, Camus fait suivre à sa pensée dans *L'Homme révolté* le parcours des anarchistes français qui, sur le constat d'échec de la « propagande par le fait » et des attentats meurtriers de Paris dans les années 1890, s'engagèrent dans le syndicalisme en construction et furent en France les premiers animateurs de la jeune CGT, une démarche que l'on trouve dans d'autres pays où l'anarchisme a joué un rôle important, l'Espagne mais aussi les États-Unis d'Amérique[15]. En 1907, une fois l'expérience terroriste inaboutie et perçue comme telle, les anarchistes russes se sont investis dans le mouvement syndical[16].

Les relations amicales qu'il entretint avec des anarchistes ou des syndicalistes révolutionnaires étaient partie prenante d'une fraternité d'idées. Il n'hésita pas à faire appel à eux, à les interroger sur leur expérience. Rirette Maîtrejean témoigne ainsi après la mort de l'écrivain :

> Je ne sais comment un jour il fut question, entre Albert Camus et moi, d'un livre de Victor Serge, mon ancien compagnon. Il me dit combien il aimait l'œuvre de Victor Serge. Il me posa des questions sur lui, longuement. Il savait très bien écouter, beaucoup mieux que de parler de lui-même. C'est ainsi que nous devînmes des amis. [...] Son amitié me fut précieuse. Quand on avait

---

13 L'indication d'un numéro de page sans plus de précision renvoie au tome III des œuvres complètes d'Albert Camus paru à la Bibliothèque de la Pléiade en 2008.

14 A. Camus, *Le goût des livres*, 29 décembre 1951, ina.fr.

15 Il utilise le terme « martyrs de Chicago » à propos des militants anarchistes américains condamnés à mort en 1886 (p. 202).

16 P. Avrich, *Les anarchistes russes*, Paris, Maspero, 1967.

bavardé un quart d'heure avec lui, il semblait que la vie fut plus légère. On s'en allait avec un réconfort, on s'accommodait mieux de l'humanité[17].

La perception des problèmes des travailleurs, notamment dans le cadre des métiers de correcteur et de typographe qu'il connaissait bien (« On pouvait le considérer comme un ouvrier du livre. Il avait adopté nos méthodes particulières, notre vocabulaire, nos qualités et nos défauts » explique Georges Roy, typographe à France-Soir[18]), se faisait en cette empathie étayée par une perception libertaire de l'humanité.

Cette proximité, implicite dans un premier temps, est passée aussi par les fréquentations du temps du Front populaire. Vincent Solera, « Camarade anarchiste » comme on l'appelait alors, jouait de l'accordéon dans la troupe du Théâtre du travail et appréciait beaucoup « Révolte dans les Asturies » à la représentation de laquelle il participa à Alger en avril 1936. Il y avait aussi l'instituteur socialiste Jean Preziosi, membre courant pédagogico-syndical l'École émancipée, chargé de mission au cabinet du ministre du Travail à la Libération, qui comme Camus publia ensuite dans *La Révolution prolétarienne* et continuait au moment de l'écriture de *L'Homme révolté* à se réclamer de la Charte d'Amiens. Mais celui qui fit découvrir le syndicalisme révolutionnaire à Camus a été présenté à tort comme militant du PC[19]. Très proche du couple qu'il formait alors avec Simone Huée, Yves Bourgeois, professeur de Lettres au lycée Bugeaud, se disait « anarcho-syndicaliste » et a fait connaître le Comité de vigilance des intellectuels antifascistes à Camus. Proche des libertaires, grand lecteur de Dostoïevski, il avait fréquenté des syndicalistes révolutionnaires à Paris puis à Lyon (notamment dans ce dernier cas un syndicat du bâtiment) et à Alger des militants de la CGT en donnant des cours à des travailleurs, une des fonctions initiales des Bourses du travail. Soutenant Camus lorsqu'il a installé le Théâtre de l'Équipe, à ses côtés au Collège du Travail, il a aidé le jeune dramaturge à monter *Révolte dans les Asturies*. Parmi les amis de Camus, le correcteur libertaire Nicolas Lazarévitch, fils de deux militants en exil de *Narodnaïa Volia*, l'a aidé à comprendre le terrorisme russe et à préparer *Les Justes*. Camus lui a confié ainsi qu'à l'aide-comptable et poète anarchiste Lucien Feuillade la publication en 1950 de l'anthologie

---

17 *A Albert Camus, ses amis du Livre*, Paris, Gallimard, 1962, p. 13–15.

18 *Ibidem*, p. 17.

19 H.R. Lottman, *Albert Camus, a Biography*, Madera, Gingko Press, 1997, p. 95–111. En 1994, Yves Bourgeois s'est inscrit en faux contre la présentation de son activité militante donnée dans cet ouvrage.

critique *Tu peux tuer cet homme, scènes de la vie révolutionnaire russe*. Ce qui ne l'empêchait pas d'être lucide sur la naïveté de l'écrivain : « Il s'en faisait encore des illusions, Camus, sur les syndicats [...], il nous voyait meilleurs que nous sommes »[20].

La curiosité de Camus sur cet aspect du socialisme russe recoupe voire anticipe l'intérêt des historiens et des politistes[21]. Certes, une certaine confusion pouvait se manifester et il existait de 1923 à 1991 une rue Kaliaïev à Leningrad tandis que le musée Lénine de Moscou consacrait un panneau à Alexandre, frère aîné du leader bolchévique, lui aussi de *Narodnaïa Volia* et pendu en 1887, mais faire connaître ces hommes était, au début des années 1950, ne pas accepter le fait accompli des historiens soviétiques qui, au temps de Staline, avaient gommé tout ce qui ne correspondait pas à une hagiographie du bolchevisme et proscrivaient toute référence positive aux socialistes-révolutionnaires.

c) Et avoir vécu

Tout autant que les amis, l'expérience nourrit la réflexion. Certains passages ne peuvent qu'évoquer la biographie de l'auteur : « Après tout, la douleur, l'exil, la claustration, sont quelquefois acceptées quand la médecine ou le bon sens nous en persuadent (p. 146) ». L'on sait à quel point le football et le théâtre l'ont marqué comme vecteur du rapport à autrui, mais il pouvait aussi passer par l'organisation de la société. Lorsque certains ouvriers de l'équipe de *Combat* clandestin proposèrent au moment de la Libération la constitution d'une coopérative ouvrière, Camus fit part à l'un d'entre eux de « son entier accord »[22].

Rares cependant sont les références à l'épreuve que venait de traverser l'humanité : il est bien question du « Führerprinzip » (p. 311) et de « camps de concentration », le terme devant être appréhendé à un moment où ils n'étaient pas distingués de celui de « camps d'extermination » et où le procès Kravchenko avait marqué la vie politique. Lorsque, dans l'introduction, il écrit que l'« on peut tisonner les crématoires », il renvoie à l'horreur du système concentrationnaire et génocidaire nazi telle qu'elle était perçue alors tandis que, un demi-siècle plus tard, ce sont les chambres à gaz homicides qui sont devenues la spécificité et le symbole de la mort industrielle. Notons d'ailleurs

---

20 *A Albert Camus...*, p. 55.

21 R. Cannac, *Netchaïev. Du nihilisme au terrorisme*, Paris, Payot, 1961 ; F. Venturi, *Les intellectuels, le peuple et la révolution. Histoire du populisme russe au XIXe siècle*, Paris, Gallimard, deux tomes, 1972.

22 *A Albert Camus...*, p. 26.

que Camus n'hésite pas à assimiler les atrocités nazies (ici la destruction de Lidice, le massacre et les déportations de ses habitants en 1942) et les crimes de la colonisation, la répression de la révolte des Cipayes en 1857 et les massacres d'Algérie à la fin de la guerre (note de la p. 219). Mais l'absence de mention de la Résistance et même des réformes de la Libération renvoie à la discrétion de Camus sur cette époque. Peut-être peut-on y voir également l'influence de l'ami Char, qui déjà dans le 195ème feuillet d'Hypnos prévenait : « Si j'en réchappe, je sais que je devrai rompre avec l'arôme des années essentielles, rejeter (non refouler) silencieusement de moi mon trésor ».

II) A TRAVERS LES LIVRES

a) Lire sans cesse

Il a fallu une bibliothèque pour écrire l'ouvrage. Et si le premier livre cité, dès l'introduction, est le Code pénal, si Hugo, Vallès, Balzac, Faulkner, Mme de La Fayette ou Bernardin de Saint-Pierre sont parmi les nombreux écrivains dont il aborde l'œuvre, les différents genres sont mis à contribution et les auteurs évoqués, d'Emilie Brontë à Chateaubriand, sont légion, dont bien sûr les philosophes : Nietzche, Scheler, Tertullien, Bentham, Rousseau, Platon. Il est fort malaisé de savoir précisément quels livres a lu un auteur. Même l'inventaire de sa bibliothèque exclut ceux qu'il a empruntés et rendus, ceux qui lui ont été empruntés et ne furent pas rendus. Il faut, parfois, avoir en main le livre poinçonné de l'ex-libris pour se rendre compte que ses pages n'ont pas été coupées. L'idéal, rarissime, est une liste des lectures, agrémentée d'un avis pour chacune d'entre elles comme en a tenue l'écrivain Georges Valero[23].

Il ne s'agira pas de se demander quelle approche a eu ici Camus des auteurs qu'il étudie longuement (Dostoïevski, Sade, Nietzsche, Stirner...), quel que soit l'intérêt de l'édition ou de la traduction qu'il utilise, mais de comprendre ce que pouvaient être pour lui, au temps de l'écriture de *L'Homme révolté*, les phénomènes évoqués. Il met en perspective différents ouvrages, critique certaines œuvres, parle des « banalités laborieuses » des *Poésies*, voire des « chants de Maldoror [qui] sont le livre d'un collégien presque génial » (p. 130). Pas question ici de commentaire de commentaires (« Ce chapitre peut être considéré comme un commentaire de *La Volonté de puissance* » explique l'auteur

[23] C. Chevandier, *La Fabrique d'une génération. Georges Valero, postier, militant et écrivain*, Paris, Editions Les Belles Lettres, 2009, p. 303–321.

en note de « Nietzche et le nihilisme », p. 117), mais une mise en situation permet de ne pas se tromper de décennie (voire de siècle) lorsque l'on tente de comprendre ce dont parlait Camus. Ainsi, la principale œuvre de Max Stirner à laquelle il consacre quatre pages (p. 113–116), si elle a eu rapidement un réel succès, est vite tombée en désuétude et n'a pas eu à la grande époque de l'anarchiste individualiste français (1890–1891) l'influence qu'on lui a prêtée[24]. Cependant, la diffusion de traductions de *L'Unique et sa propriété* dès le début du XXème siècle l'a fait connaître et Albert Camus en a lu dans les années 1930 un exemplaire prêté par un ami[25].

L'on sait que Camus n'a jamais lu Elisée Reclus « alors que les convergences entre les individus sont si grandes »[26]. Il prend en compte les livres qu'il a édité dans sa collection « Espoir », *Tu peux tuer cet homme* mais aussi *La Condition ouvrière* qu'il présente et cite (p. 247). Les notes infrapaginales sont de l'auteur et correspondent à des remarques ou indications assez tardives. Ainsi, après avoir évoqué Pierre Klossovski (frère aîné de Balthus qui de longue date fréquentait Char), il cite en note son ouvrage et l'éditeur (p. 93), rajout sans doute lorsqu'il s'est dit que le livre, paru en 1947, n'avait pas encore la notoriété de la plupart de ceux qu'il évoque. Objet également d'une note quelques pages plus loin, le livre de Maurice Blanchot, *Lautréamont et Sade*, était encore plus récent.

Indiquée en note *La Tragédie de Spartacus (Cahiers Spartacus)* (p. 153), qu'il attribue à un militant libertaire qu'il fréquente, André Prudhommeaux – en oubliant sa compagne Dori – est en réalité la conclusion d'un ouvrage plus large, *Spartacus et la Commune de Berlin 1918–1918*, réédition en 1949 d'un livre de 1934, qui mettait en perspective « les deux combats spartakistes » et se terminait par « le prolétariat est le Christ », évocation de la mise à mort des esclaves révoltés crucifiés sur la Via Appia. C'est d'ailleurs sur ce martyre que revient Camus peu après : « La croix est aussi le supplice du Christ. On peut imaginer que ce dernier ne choisit quelques années plus tard[27] le châtiment de l'esclave que pour réduire cette terrible distance qui sépare désormais la créature humiliée de la face implacable du Maître (p. 355) ». Cet intérêt pour l'esclave révolté, qui prolonge celui qui a été manifesté plusieurs décennies

---

24 G. Manfredonia, *L'individualisme anarchiste en France, 1880–1914*, thèse d'histoire, Institut d'études politiques de Paris, 1984.

25 P. Pelletier, *Albert Camus, Elisée Reclus et l'Algérie : les « indigènes de l'univers »*, Paris, Le Cavalier bleu, 2015, p. 122.

26 *Ibidem*, p. 121.

27 Un siècle sépare la répression de la révolte des esclaves et le moment présumé de la Passion.

plus tôt par certains sociaux-démocrates allemands, n'était pas une exception et donna lieu lors de la décennie suivante à deux grands films.

b) Écrire aussi

Parmi les écrits, n'oublions surtout pas ceux de Camus lui-même, la publication en 1945 de l'étude « Remarques sur la Révolte » et la part des *Justes* dans la réflexion sur le terrorisme russe[28]. Dès l'introduction, il démarque sa démarche de celle qui fut la sienne au temps du *Mythe de Sisyphe.* Avec ces livres préparatoires à *L'Homme révolté*, il y eut les articles, ceux de *Combat* notamment, tel celui du 21 octobre 1944 (« Nous nous méfions des juges qui ne doutent jamais ou des héros qui n'ont jamais tremblé »), écrit entre les deux versions de *La Peste* mais dont nous trouvons aussi un développement dans l'essai de 1951.

Ses livres, c'est aussi un style. Et si le début de la partie « L'Homme révolté » (« Qu'est-ce qu'un homme révolté ? Un homme qui dit non », p. 71) reprend celui du texte préparatoire de 1945 (« Qu'est-ce qu'un homme révolté ? C'est d'abord un homme qui dit *non* », p. 325), l'on ne peut que penser à l'éditorial de *Combat* du 23 août 1944, écrit alors que les Alliés étaient à 200 km de Paris : « Qu'est-ce qu'une insurrection ? C'est le peuple en armes. Qu'est-ce que le peuple ? C'est ce qui, dans une nation, ne veut jamais s'agenouiller ». La deuxième réponse ressemble à une des premières phrases de « La révolte historique » : « L'esprit révolutionnaire prend ainsi la défense de cette part de l'homme qui ne veut pas s'incliner (p. 150) ». Se lancer dans un texte par une question est coutumier à Camus, qui en 1946 commence « Prométhée aux enfers » par : « Que signifie Prométhée pour l'homme d'aujourd'hui ? (p. 589) ». L'écrivain Camus a su se nourrir de son œuvre d'écrivain et de ses écrits de journaliste.

c) Les révolutions françaises

Les livres, ce sont aussi les travaux des historiens lorsqu'il s'agit de réfléchir sur le passé. Le passage sur la Révolution française pourrait être imprégné d'une recherche historique qui compte de grands noms. Rien pourtant dans *L'Homme révolté* qui semble devoir aux travaux de l'historien Georges Lefebvre, que Camus avait rencontré en mars 1945 et dont Sartre s'est beaucoup inspiré, auteur notamment de *La Grande Peur de 1789* publiée près de

28 Voir notamment la notice et les notes par E. Kouchkine dans OC III, p. 1177–1212.

vingt ans plus tôt. Rien non plus des apports essentiels d'Ernest Labrousse[29], assez actif dans les milieux que Camus fréquente et qu'il a eu l'occasion de croiser, lui aussi professeur à la Sorbonne où il a succédé à Marc Bloch à la chaire d'histoire économique et sociale, auteur notamment de l'*Esquisse du mouvement des prix et des revenus au XVIIIe siècle* parue aussi dans la première moitié des années 1930 et qui avait eu le temps d'imprégner l'historiographie. Comment savoir s'il connaît Jean Varlet (p. 151) grâce au livre de Proudhon, *De la justice dans la Révolution et dans l'Eglise*[30], ou s'il s'est inspiré des ouvrages d'historiens plus récents, notamment celui de Daniel Guérin, *La lutte des classes sous la Première République, 1793–1797* paru en 1946 chez Gallimard et qui insiste sur la trahison de la Révolution par les montagnards et Robespierre ? Il avait toutes les raisons de connaître l'un et l'autre livres, et il a bien pu consulter les nombreux petits textes autobiographiques de Varlet conservés à la Bibliothèque nationale.

La Commune de Paris, si elle est présentée comme un modèle, n'est abordée qu'à deux reprises. Il convient de prendre garde à l'anachronisme, car la connaissance de la Commune était bien moindre à la fin des années 1940. Deux livres y sont essentiels, celui de 1876 du communard Prosper-Olivier de Lissagaray, et celui de Marx qu'il a inspiré. Rares sont ensuite, à l'exception des comptes rendus complets et commentés des séances de la Commune par le chartiste Georges Bourgin, les ouvrages vraiment historiques qui permettent de bien la comprendre. Deux livres d'un grand intérêt (ceux d'Edward Mason et surtout de Frank Jellinek) n'étaient disponibles qu'en anglais mais nombre de textes de souvenirs de contemporains, partisans ou adversaire de la Commune, étaient encore diffusés. Le livre d'Albert Ollivier, essai plus qu'œuvre d'historien, *La Commune*, paru en 1939, est connu de Camus qui fréquentait son auteur, autre éditorialiste de *Combat*. En une lecture proudhonienne de l'événement, Ollivier insiste sur son caractère fédéraliste et antiétatique et se termine par une attaque violente contre le parlementarisme et les partis, à l'opposé des approches des communistes (tel le livre de Maurice Lacoste préfacé par Trotsky paru en 1924 sous le pseudonyme de C. Talès) qui insistait sur la nécessité d'un parti révolutionnaire. La conclusion d'Ollivier semble d'ailleurs pour le moins camusienne : « Le véritable révolutionnaire doit avoir le courage de s'éloigner de la place publique, plus encore qu'on ne le fit sous le Second Empire, il doit résister à cette tentation

29 Aucun ouvrage de Lefebvre ni de Labrousse ne se trouvait dans la bibliothèque de Camus.

30 Paru en 1858, mais réédité dans la première moitié des années 1930 dans les œuvres complètes de Proudhon.

de l'action immédiate, si forte soit-elle, et pour cela, on accordera qu'il lui faut beaucoup d'humilité et beaucoup d'orgueil ». Peut-être cette indigence explique-t-elle qu'il n'est, somme toute, que deux références à la révolution parisienne de 1871 et que Camus y insiste sur la répression (« La destruction physique d'une élite de révoltés », p. 318). Ce refus de l'anachronisme, il faut aussi l'affirmer lorsque Camus évoque la trilogie eschyléenne et la littérature grecque antique qui sont pour nous bien différentes : Jean-Pierre Vernant venait d'entrer au CNRS, Paul Vidal-Naquet et Paul Veyne étaient en khâgne et Ariane Mnouchkine était encore une enfant.

III) AUTOUR D'ABSENCES

a) Le rêve européen et la social-démocratie

Il y a les amis qu'il croisait régulièrement, et toutes les personnes qu'il a pu rencontrer lors de conférences ou de diverses manifestations, avec lesquels il a discuté à l'occasion de signatures communes de pétitions. Parmi ses thèmes d'intérêt et, un temps, d'engagement, le fédéralisme européen l'a conduit à jouer un rôle de premier plan en juin 1944 dans la création du Comité français pour la fédération européenne. « Vous le voyez, c'est toujours la même idée, nous revenons de loin » a-t-il écrit à propos de l'Europe[31]. Les repères chronologiques à La Pléiade ne le signalent pas, mais ceux du *Dictionnaire Albert Camus*, quoique plus réduits, mentionnent : « 22–25 mars 1945 : préside une réunion de fédéralistes européens à Paris ». Il préside en effet au moins une séance de ce congrès, dont le principal organisateur est Altierro Spinelli, qui se tient devant une cinquantaine de participants, dont plus des deux tiers sont français. Si Vincent Auriol et Henri Frenay se sont désistés, Camus y croise Ernest Labrousse, Georges Lefebvre, Joseph Ours, André Ferrat, Yvon Morandat alors directeur d'*Esprit*, Jacques Baumel, André Malraux, Pascal Pia et Robert Lacoste[32]. Mais il est fort difficile de savoir véritablement ce qui s'y est dit et fait. Les archives d'André Ferrat[33] conservent le compte rendu de la journée du samedi 24 mars, présidée par Maurice Guérin, syndicaliste de

---

31 OC, II, p. 652

32 B. Vayssière, *Vers une Europe fédérale : Les espoirs et les actions fédéralistes au sortir de la Seconde Guerre mondiale*, Bruxelles, Peter Lang, 2007, p. 86–89, et A. Bresolin, *La même idée qui revient de loin* , Rencontres méditerranéennes Albert Camus, *L'Europe selon Camus*, Avignon, Éditions A. Barthélemy, 2011, p. 41–69.

33 Consultables à l'Office universitaire de recherche socialiste.

la CFTC, résistant à Combat et délégué à l'Assemblée consultative. La presse, alors contingentée en papier, ni les mémoires de participants, comme Robert Verdier et Daniel Mayer, n'en ont rien retenu. Même la police n'a accordé que peu d'intérêt à cette conférence, qu'elle n'a sans doute pas surveillée. Il n'y a dans les archives des Renseignements généraux pas le moindre rapport sur cette réunion et les dossiers de Camus et de Pascal Pia ne l'évoquent pas. Il est vrai que, alors que la guerre n'est pas terminée, la police a d'autres soucis et qu'elle s'intéressera très vite à Camus à l'occasion d'une conférence sur l'Algérie[34] et même au Comité international pour la fédération européenne, constitué le 30 juin 1945, dont elle nous apprend que son siège se situe dans les locaux du journal *Combat* et que ses responsables sont, outre Camus (« marié et père de famille »), Baumel, Kaksas, Verdier, Guérin[35].

Robert Verdier et Daniel Mayer au premier rang, les socialistes étaient nombreux parmi les participants à la réunion fédéraliste du printemps 1945. Car Camus a associé, notamment dans *L'Homme révolté*, l'attachement à l'espoir libertaire à l'intérêt pour la social-démocratie, particulièrement à l'expérience suédoise. L'historien Gilles Vergnon peut donc souligner : « Sur ce point comme sur d'autres, c'est toute la singularité d'Albert Camus que de pointer, dans une note de *L'Homme révolté*, l'intérêt des sociétés scandinaves »[36]. Au moment où Camus l'écrit, rares sont les publications permettant une approche de la social-démocratie suédoise, tout au plus un article de 1947 de la *Revue socialiste* et un texte d'un ami du temps de Combat, Emmanuel Mounier, une trentaine de pages dans *Esprit* de février 1950[37]. Mais le premier ouvrage de référence, *Le Parti socialiste suédois, son organisation,* de Raymond Fusilier, ne paraît qu'en 1954, ébauché deux ans plus tôt dans *Revue socialiste*. Il n'empêche que cette simple phrase demeure dans les esprits et, lorsqu'il a lancé en 1971 la collection « Suède en question » aux éditions Seghers, Jacques Arnault lui donnait un objectif : « Albert Camus avait-il raison d'y voir l'approximation d'une société juste ? C'est à quoi cette collection voudrait répondre »[38].

---

34 C. Chevandier, *Les Renseignements généraux à l'écoute d'Albert Camus*, « Vingtième siècle, revue d'histoire » 2016, no 129, janvier–mars, p. 163–166.

35 Archives de la Préfecture de police de Paris, dossier 291.656, note blanche du 28 février 1946, « A. S. du Comité International pour la Fédération Européenne ».

36 G. Vergnon, *Le « modèle » suédois. Les gauches françaises et l'impossible social-démocratie*, Rennes, Presses universitaires de Rennes, 2015, p. 83.

37 A. Nemo, *Perspectives du socialisme suédois*, « Revue socialiste », décembre 1947, p. 588–596, et E. Mounier, *Notes scandinaves et du Bonheur*, « Esprit », février 1950, p. 253–286.

38 J. Arnault, *Une société mixte*, Paris, Seghers, 1971, p. 9.

b) André Philip

En octobre 2010, lors des rencontres de Lourmarin, Jeanyves Guérin suggérait : « Camus a peut-être été en relations indirectes avec André Philip »[39]. Herbert R. Lottman insiste quant à lui dans sa biographie de Camus sur la présence au Chambon du député socialiste André Philip, passé lui aussi du pacifisme à la Résistance, qui avait voté contre les pleins pouvoirs à Pétain et d'un de ses proches, Paul Ricoeur[40]. Venu d'Algérie, Camus s'est installé au Panelier à la mi-août 1942 alors qu'André Philip était à Londres depuis le 25 juillet, auprès du général de Gaulle qui venait de le nommer à la tête du commissariat national à l'Intérieur et au Travail. Il était déjà depuis quelque mois dans une clandestinité qui lui avait fait quitter le Chambon, mais il s'en est fallu de peu que les deux hommes ne se croisent à ce moment crucial de l'été 1942 quand bien même il n'est pas impossible qu'ils furent en rapport dans les mois qui suivirent. La première vraie rencontre entre les deux figures de presse, alors que l'un a dirigé *Combat* jusqu'en juin 1947 et l'autre *Cité-Soir* jusqu'en juillet 1946, n'eut sans doute lieu qu'aux lendemains de la Libération[41]. Deux années donc pendant lesquelles, en dépit des charges de parlementaire, de constituant et de ministre de Philip, les deux patrons de journaux se sont croisés dans le quartier si vivant de la presse.

La bibliothèque de Camus ne recèle aucun ouvrage de Philip, mais il a surtout travaillé à Paris pour l'écriture de *L'Homme révolté*, et il était aisé d'y consulter les livres de cet homme politique alors très connu[42]. Il est cependant difficile d'en percevoir avec précision l'influence, par exemple pour les allusions aux castes hindous (p. 77) qui renvoient à l'actualité tragique de la péninsule indienne et ont pu être en partie alimentées par la lecture de *L'Inde moderne : le problème social et politique*, ouvrage paru en 1930 dans lequel le jeune professeur d'économie politique qui avait rencontré Gandhi pendant son séjour dans l'Ashram de Sabarmati soulignait les risques de conflit entre hindous et musulmans tout en manifestant son intérêt pour la non-violence. Camus participe alors à la mobilisation pour un statut d'objecteur de conscience aux côtés de l'Abbé Pierre qui a déposé en 1949 avec d'autres

---

39 J. Guérin, *Albert Camus et la construction européenne*, Rencontres méditerranéennes Albert Camus, *L'Europe selon Camus*..., 2011, p. 11–29 [note 6 p. 14].

40 Dans son dixième chapitre, *op.cit.*, p. 288.

41 Mais les archives de la Fédération nationale de la presse, déposées à l'Institut Mémoires de l'édition contemporaine, sont très lacunaires pour cette période fort agitée.

42 *André Philip, socialiste, patriote, chrétien*, dir. C. Chevandier, G. Morin, Paris, Comité pour l'histoire économique et financière de la France, 2005.

députés, dont André Philip (qui s'était inscrit au barreau pour défendre des objecteurs), un projet de loi visant à sa reconnaissance légale[43]. Et lorsque l'on lit que « l'empire idéologique [...] détruit la plupart des conquêtes du syndicalisme » (p. 316), l'on ne peut penser qu'à André Philip, invité en 1956 à prendre la parole devant le personnel d'une usine en URSS et se livrant à un exposé sur le droit de grève.

Bien des points unissaient ces personnalités proches par leur humanisme et leur intégrité. Ainsi, Philip approuvait la critique que faisait Camus de l'existentialisme sartrien et tous deux savaient quel prix accorder à la pensée de Proudhon, ce qui n'était pas exceptionnel au sein de la SFIO et qui explique notamment la réception de Camus par les socialistes[44]. Je n'ai trouvé dans les archives aucune trace de rapports entre les deux hommes mais Loïc Philip, avec la rigueur du juriste et de l'universitaire, se souvient :

> Mon père et Albert Camus se sont rencontrés à plusieurs reprises et ont échangé plusieurs correspondances. Leurs rapports ont toujours été très cordiaux et positifs. [...] Enfin, au sujet de la politique de G Mollet en Algérie, je me souviens d'une lettre de Camus à mon père lors de son exclusion du parti socialiste en 1958. Malheureusement mon père ne conservait pas sa correspondance. Il m'arrivait de récupérer des lettres de certaines personnalités dans la corbeille à papier mais ce ne fut pas le cas pour celles de Camus[45].

c) George Orwell

Nous savons tout ce que partageaient Camus et George Orwell, et il aurait été impensable qu'ils ne se soient pas lus. Associés par les contemporain dès 1947[46], les deux hommes sont si forts, leur éthique si prégnante, leurs leçons si justes que nous leur en voudrions de ne pas s'être rencontrés. Jeanyves Guérin, qui cite Orwell dans 16 pages de *Albert Camus. Littérature et politique*[47], n'évoque pas la moindre rencontre. Car il n'est jamais question d'une entrevue entre les deux hommes alors qu'Orwell était à Paris en mars 1945, logé dans un hôtel non loin du siège de *Combat*, et qu'il est parfois mentionné

---

43 Journée d'étude « Les objecteurs de conscience, entre associations et pouvoirs publics. Au « service » de qui ? », Créteil, 29 janvier 2005.

44 S. Boulouque, *Réception socialiste* [dans :] *Dictionnaire Albert Camus*, dir. J. Guérin, Paris, Robert Laffont, p. 757–759.

45 Courriel du 28 décembre 2015.

46 A. Patri, *Le Yogi et le Commissaire par Arthur Koestler*, « *Paru* » 1947, no 26, p. 67–69.

47 Paris, Honoré Champion, 2013.

parmi les personnes qui assistèrent à la conférence fédéraliste. Il n'y était sans doute plus dès le 24, jour où il envoya un article de Cologne. Il est possible qu'il ait assisté, ne serait-ce que comme correspondant du *Tribune*, à la séance inaugurale, mais son journal est lacunaire entre novembre 1942 et mai 1946 tandis que ses biographes, notamment Bernard Crick (1980) et D.J. Taylor (2003), ne le mentionnent pas. Les *Carnets* de Camus nous montrent qu'il a lu Orwell et qu'il l'apprécie, ce que notent ses biographes[48]. Plusieurs textes, y compris des travaux universitaires, mentionnent une rencontre prévue dans un café de Saint-Germain-des-Prés lors du passage à Paris de l'écrivain anglais en mars 1945, lorsqu'il rencontra Hemingway. Mais il n'est nulle trace dans les archives ou dans tout autre document contemporain d'une rencontre ni même de ce rendez-vous manqué. Mais rien ne nous empêche de croire à la belle histoire de la tuberculose de Camus qui l'empêche de se rendre au Deux Magots, ce café réservé par la cartographie de Sartre aux « vieux littérateurs », où l'attend Orwell, emporté cinq ans plus tard par la terrible maladie que l'on commence à traiter efficacement.

L'influence de Camus a perduré et la période américaine de l'œuvre d'Hanna Arendt en témoigne[49]. Sans doute les textes de 1957 et 1960 sur la Révolution française de Sartre, qui a lu Lefebvre, se situent-ils par rapport au livre de Daniel Guérin qui ravive la tradition « antirobespierriste de gauche »[50], mais il n'a pas pu ignorer les passages de Camus. Et il est impossible aujourd'hui d'écrire une histoire du terrorisme russe sans le mentionner[51]. Nombre d'essais ou d'œuvre ultérieures doivent une part de leur pertinence aux livres du cycle de la révolte : pour ne prendre qu'un exemple, le réalisateur Elie Wajeman, qui a eu l'idée de ce film qui se situe à Paris à la fin du XIXème siècle en voyant « Les Possédés »[52], fait évoquer par un des personnages des « Anarchistes » (2015) le risque qu'un enfant soit touché par l'attentat qu'ils commettent.

Dans l'introduction, Camus explique que l'ouvrage « est un effort pour comprendre [s]on temps » et insiste sur la nécessité d'« accepter la réalité du moment ». Le lecteur doit semblable effort et faire preuve de pragmatisme

---

48 O. Todd, *Albert Camus, une vie*, Paris, Gallimard, 1996, p. 421 et H.R. Lottman, *op.cit.*, p. 435.

49 J.C. Isaac, *Arendt, Camus, and Modern Rebellion*, New Haven, Yale University Press, 1994.

50 J.-N. Ducange, *La Révolution française et l'histoire du monde. Deux siècles de débats historiques et politiques 1815–1991*, Paris, Armand Colin, 2014, p. 176–181.

51 C'est le cas à quatre reprises [dans :] Y. Ternon, *Le terrorisme russe (1878–1908)* [dans :] *Histoire du terrorisme de l'Antiquité à Daesch*, dir. G. Chaliand, A. Blin, Paris, Fayard, 2015, p. 175–228. Un extrait des *Justes* est également proposé en fin d'ouvrage dans une sous-partie « Littérature et terrorisme ».

52 Mais ce n'était dans une mise en scène inspirée de celle de Camus.

épistémologique par la prise en compte de l'état des connaissances en 1951 ainsi que de la réalité politique du moment, qui n'est pas simplement la Guerre froide mais aussi la relative proximité, ne serait-ce que dans les itinéraires biographiques, de branches du mouvement ouvrier, les libertaires et les sociaux-démocrates notamment. De telles précautions permettent de supposer l'actualité plutôt que l'intemporalité de *L'Homme révolté*.

BIBLIOGRAPHIE

A Albert Camus, ses amis du Livre, Paris, Gallimard, 1962.

André Philip, socialiste, patriote, chrétien, dir. C. Chevandier, G. Morin, Paris, Comité pour l'histoire économique et financière de la France, 2005.

Arnault, J., *Une société mixte*, Paris, Seghers, 1971.

Avrich, P., *Les anarchistes russes*, Paris, Maspero, 1967.

Boulouque, S., *Réception socialiste* [dans :] *Dictionnaire Albert Camus*, dir. J. Guérin, Paris, Robert Laffont.

Bresolin, A., *La même idée qui revient de loin*, Rencontres méditerranéennes Albert Camus, *L'Europe selon Camus*, Avignon, Éditions A. Barthélemy, 2011.

Camus, A., *Le goût des livres*, 29 décembre 1951, ina.fr.

Camus, A., *Œuvres complètes*, vol. III, Paris, Gallimard, 2008.

Camus, A., Char, R., *Correspondance 1945–1959*, Paris, Gallimard, 2007.

Camus, A., Daniel, J., extraits de la correspondance, 1949–1959 [dans :] *Camus*, dir. R. Gay-Crosier, A. Spiquel-Courdille, Cahiers de l'Herne, Paris, Herne, 2013.

Cannac, R., *Netchaïev. Du nihilisme au terrorisme*, Paris, Payot, 1961.

Chevandier, C., *La Fabrique d'une génération. Georges Valero, postier, militant et écrivain*, Paris, Éditions Les Belles Lettres, 2009.

Chevandier, C., *Le syndicalisme révolutionnaire, une indéniable pensée de midi.* « Albert Camus et la pensée de midi », Avignon, éditions A. Barthélémy, 2016.

Chevandier, C., *Les Renseignements généraux à l'écoute d'Albert Camus.* « Vingtième siècle, revue d'histoire » 2016, no 129, janvier–mars.

Demonsais, B., *Gavroche. Un hebdomadaire culturel socialiste de la Résistance à la Guerre froide*, Paris, L'Harmattan, 2006.

Le Don de la liberté : les relations d'Albert Camus avec les libertaires, Lourmarin, Rencontres méditerranéennes Albert Camus, 2009.

Ducange, J.-N., *La Révolution française et l'histoire du monde. Deux siècles de débats historiques et politiques 1815–1991*, Paris, Armand Colin, 2014.

Guérin, J., *Albert Camus et la construction européenne*, Rencontres méditerranéennes Albert Camus, *L'Europe selon Camus*, Avignon, Éditions A. Barthélemy, 2011.

Isaac, J.C., *Arendt, Camus, and Modern Rebellion*, New Haven, Yale University Press, 1994.

Jeanson, F., *Albert Camus ou l'âme révoltée* , « Les Temps Modernes » 1952, Mai.

Lottman, H.R., *Albert Camus, a Biography*, Madera, Gingko Press, 1997.

Maitron, J., Pennetier, C., *Dictionnaire biographique du mouvement ouvrier français*, Paris, Éditions ouvrières–Éditions de l'Atelier, en cours de publication.

Manfredonia, G., *L'individualisme anarchiste en France, 1880–1914*, thèse d'histoire, Institut d'études politiques de Paris, 1984.

Marin, L., *Albert Camus, écrits libertaires (1948–1960)*, Montpellier, Indigène éditions, 2016.

Mounier, E., *Notes scandinaves et du Bonheur* , « Esprit » 1950, février.

Nemo, A., *Perspectives du socialisme suédois*, « Revue socialiste », décembre 1947.

Patri, A., Le Yogi et le Commissaire *par Arthur Koestler*, « Paru » 1947, no 26.

Pelletier P., *Albert Camus, Élisée Reclus et l'Algérie : Les « indigènes de l'univers »*, Paris, Le Cavalier bleu, 2015.

Perken, D., *Sartre et surtout Camus s'intéressent à notre mouvement*, « Combat » 1951, 12 avril.

Ternon, Y., *Le terrorisme russe (1878–1908)* [dans :] *Histoire du terrorisme de l'Antiquité à Daesch*, dir. G. Chaliand, A. Blin, Paris, Fayard, 2015.

Todd, O., *Albert Camus, une vie*, Paris, Gallimard, 1996.

Vayssière, B., *Vers une Europe fédérale : Les espoirs et les actions fédéralistes au sortir de la Seconde Guerre mondiale*, Bruxelles, Peter Lang, 2007.

Venturi F., *Les intellectuels, le peuple et la révolution. Histoire du populisme russe au XIXe siècle*, Paris, Gallimard, deux tomes, 1972.

Vergnon, G., *Le « modèle » suédois. Les gauches françaises et l'impossible social-démocratie*, Rennes, Presses universitaires de Rennes, 2015.

The Dynamics in Meaning of Absurdity and Revolt: between *La liberté absurde* and *L'absurde et le meurtre*

MACIEJ KAŁUŻA[1]

INTRODUCTION

Both major philosophical works of Albert Camus, *Le mythe de Sisyphe* (1942; *Myth of Sisyphus*; hereafter MS) and *L'homme Révolté* (1951; *The Rebel*; hereafter HR), relate to the themes of absurdity and revolt. In this paper, I focus on the absurd–revolt relation in two crucial moments of Camus's argumentation, showing the initial influence of the experience of absurdity on his concept of rebellion, as presented in *La liberté absurde* (1942; *Absurd freedom*), part of his first essay. Consequently, I relate to the undertaking of these exact notions as presented in *L'absurde et le meurtre* (1949; *Murder and the absurd*), which consequently became the introduction to HR. I also try to address the issue of the development of Camus's ideas that occurred in the meantime. This reference to the sources that appeared between these two philosophical texts is, I believe, necessary in order to understand the origin and direction of the absurd–revolt dynamics. In the philosophical scholarship on Camus, it is common to see a tendency to omit almost everything that led him to write the introduction of 1949, making his analysis of the absurd in the context of murder, which introduces the problem of revolt, seem to be a direct continuation (or departure from) of his thought from 1942. As I am convinced of the importance of some remarks that Camus made in the intervening

1 This chapter was written to realize research project 2013/09/D/HS1/00873, and funded by the National Science Centre in Poland.

period, my analysis cannot be complete without at least a brief mention of several texts that appeared between the publication of MS and HR. My preference – applied in this paper – for understanding the progression of Camus's thinking in a broader context of his works, essays, correspondence and notes (which I try to develop in my book, of which this paper may be considered a brief summary) is based on my strong preference for a hermeneutical and developmental approach.

THE ABSURD AND REVOLT IN *LA LIBERTÉ ABSURDE*

In the concluding section of his famous essay *La liberté absurde* in MS, Camus describes his proposition for living, given the problem of absurdity, as defined and understood in previous parts of the essay. This stance, according to Camus, is based on the acceptance of the human desire for meaning, which is in constant tension with the lack of confirmation of the existence of objective meaning in human experience:

> Je ne sais pas si ce monde a un sens qui le dépasse. Mais je sais que je ne connais pas ce sens et qu'il m'est impossible pour le moment de le connaître. Que signifie pour moi une signification hors de ma condition?[2]

Camus's essay presents the problem of suicide as a consequence of the loss of conviction that life is bearable without a clear relation to objective meaning as a possibility with which one is contemporarily confronted. We should also consider the context regarding the relation of the author himself to the ideas as presented in the essay. For Camus, the idea of the study focusing on the absurd had two important methodological limitations. First, as the introduction to the essay shows,[3] the author's aim was not to propose a philosophy of the absurd: a systematic thought process with a universally valid, concluding statement. Second, Camus intentionally avoids recourse to values in the development of his reasoning, trying to reach, in a phenomenological manner, the pure concept of human relation with the world in the context of the search for meaning, before making any moral judgement concerning its outcome and

[2] All quotes by A. Camus in this chapter come from *Œuvres complètes*, Gallimard, Bibliothèque de La Pléiade, Paris, toms I, II and III, 2006–2008, hereafter: OC I, OC II, OC III. See: OC I, p. 254.

[3] See: OC I, p. 219, especially Camus's statement: "l'absurde, pris jusqu'ici comme conclusion, est consideré dans cet essai comme un point de départ."

its relation to human activity.[4] Concluding the reasoning founded on these limitations, in *La liberté absurde* Camus addresses the grounds for making a decision to continue living even after the experience of the absurd, facing the tension between the human desire for unity and meaning and the lack of a certain, accessible and objective meaning in human experience:

> Je puis aborder maintenant la notion de suicide. [...] Il s'agissait précédemment de savoir si la vie devait avoir un sens pour être vécue. Il apparaît ici au contraire qu'elle sera d'autant mieux vécue qu'elle n'aura pas de sens. Vivre une expérience, un destin, c'est l'accepter pleinement. Or on ne vivra pas ce destin, le sachant absurde, si on ne fait pas tout pour maintenir devant soi cet absurde mis à jour par la conscience. Nier l'un des termes de l'opposition dont il vit, c'est lui échapper. Abolir la révolte consciente, c'est éluder le problème. Le thème de la révolution permanente se transporte ainsi dans l'expérience individuelle. Vivre, c'est faire vivre l'absurde, **Le faire vivre, cest avant tout le regarder**. [...] L'une des seules positions philosophiques cohérentes, c'est ainsi la révolte.[5]

This famous paragraph is founded on a claim that it is possible to live, to find a meaningful life, even in a world in which such meaning is not objectively given nor can be proven. Ever since the publication of Camus's first philosophical essay, scholars have focused on the significance of the act of maintaining (fr. *maintenir*) that allows the subject to make a lucid and conscious decision to accept life with its burden, founded on the experience of the absurd. However, the paragraph quoted above clearly shows that there is also an important relation between this new human stance and revolt. Intuitively, there is something unclear, even paradoxical in the concept of combining the necessity of maintaining a tension (between the human demand for meaning and living in the world with the experience of the absurd) with the notion of revolt. To maintain, to preserve, on a semantic level, is to do exactly the opposite to the consequence of a revolt, which aims at questioning, challenging or even destroying the experienced tension.

---

4 See: OCI, p. 260: "Une fois pour toutes, les jugements de valeur sont écartés ici au profit des jugements de fait." We may also add that, even when Camus confirms the importance of revolt in life, which requires continuation even in the face of the experience of the absurd, he does not write about the value (*valeur*) of life in revolt but the price: "Cette révolte donne son prix à la vie," OC I, p. 256.

5 See: OC I, p. 255–256.

However, as I read the proposition by Camus, the human subject, endangered by the question of suicide – in effect of the loss of belief in the possibility of reaching the objective (or transcendental) meaning – must rely, in order to continue, on some substitutive meaning, aware of the impossibility of the permanent elimination of doubt, which is cast by the feeling of the absurd. Camus also tries to explain the nature of revolt in relation to the absurd experience, making the seemingly paradoxical nature of the position more understandable:

> Elle [la révolte; M.K.] est un confrontement perpétuel de l'homme et de sa propre obscurité. Elle est exigence d'une impossible transparence. Elle remet le monde en question à chacune de ses secondes. De même que le danger fournit à l'homme l'irremplaçable occasion de la saisir, de même la révolte métaphysique étend la conscience tout le long de l'expérience. Elle est cette présence constante de l'homme à lui-même. Elle n'est pas aspiration, elle est sans espoir. Cette révolte n'est que l'assurance d'un destin écrasant, moins la résignation qui devrait l'accompagner.[6]

We may observe that the nature of this revolt, as proposed here, relies firmly on a set of attitudes of negative connotation. Revolt is confrontation; it is the consciousness of being deprived of aspiration and hope. Its positive aspect is in the refusal of resignation and despair, caused by the certainty and obscurity of death. The revolt also brings a denial of self-destruction as a consequence of its demand for constant confrontation. Rejecting despair leads to acceptance of the continuation of existence even in spite of perceived limitations. Camus reflects on the possibility of suicide in consequence of the absurd experience, seen as a solution to the conflict between the human desire for meaning and the lack of absolute certainty of its existence. In these considerations, suicide is the acceptance of the absurd without revolt; it is a sublimation of the human desire for meaning to the experience of lack of meaning, not a lucid confrontation with meaninglessness. If any human enterprise will ultimately fail, if there is no absolute possibility of knowing whether this life is objectively meaningful, one may surrender to the very nature of the relation between the human and the world. Physical suicide is a definitive acceptance of the absurd condition, which is its most radical and extreme consequence:[7]

---

6 See: OC I, p. 256.

7 In the broader perspective of the essay, Camus distinguishes another form of suicide which, according to the young philosopher, demands critique. Considering what Camus calls "existential philosophy," focusing especially on religious thinkers such as Søren Kierkegaard, Lev Shestov

> Le suicide, comme le saut, est l'acceptation à sa limite. Tout est consommé, l'homme rentre dans son histoire essentielle. Son avenir, son seul et terrible avenir, il le discerne et s'y précipite. A sa manière, le suicide résout l'absurde. Il l'entraîne dans la même mort.[8]

It may be observed that it is exactly the aforementioned revolt which makes confrontation with the experienced absurdity essentially impregnable to suicide in both forms (physical and philosophical) which are considered in Camus's essay. Revolt restores, within the human being, the possibility of the fulfilment of the desire for meaning in spite of the experienced absurdity.

The difficulty, which has led to long-lasting discussions concerning the problem of maintaining the absurd, relates, I believe, to another statement by Camus, which, in its imprecision may be interpreted in various ways:

> Mais je sais que pour se maintenir, l'absurde ne peut se résoudre. Il échappe au suicide, dans la mesure où il est en même temps conscience et refus[9] de la mort. Il est, à l'extrême pointe de la dernière pensée du condamné à mort, ce cordon de soulier qu'en dépit de tout il aperçoit à quelques mètres, au bord même de sa chute vertigineuse.[10]

It would be beneficial here to reflect on the meaning of the first sentence: what does it mean to maintain the absurd? Camus understands the absurd as a relation between the human being and the world; it is the intrinsic desire of the living being for unity and the lack of correspondence between the desire and the experienced reality. If that is the case, it certainly does not require from the human being an act, an effort in order to maintain the absurd, which is understood as the experience of separation. An act leading to resolution (fr. *se résoudre*) of the absurd situation is achievable through the elimination of one of the parts of the relation (physical suicide) or acceptance of the absurd without

---

and a specific interpretation of Edmund Husserl's phenomenology, the author confronts absurd thought with "philosophical suicide." According to Camus, the existential philosophers recognize and *accept* the absurd, whereas the position, as described in the essay, should recognize, but not accept, the experienced absurdity (see: OC I, p. 238–239, 316).

8 See: OC I, p. 256.

9 We may observe here that the fundamental difference in 1942 between Camus's reasoning and his critique of existential philosophy is based on the distinction between recognition and acceptance of the absurd of religious thinkers and recognition and refusal (in revolt). The latter would be summed up by Camus in his famous phrase: "L'absurde n'a de sens que dans la mesure où l'on n'y consent pas" (OC I, p. 240).

10 See: OC I, p. 256.

revolt (philosophical suicide), which is a resignation of the human desire for unity founded on rational (philosophical) premises. According to Camus, as long as I live and in my life I am conscious and aware of the situation, the absurd is maintained, and within the limits of human existence, cannot be permanently overcome (resolved). What demands action, though, albeit on an intellectual level, is the attitude one presents toward this situation. It is exactly here, I believe, that revolt, as discussed by Camus, seems significant. It is not the only possible reaction to the absurd, nor is it necessary in order to maintain the absurd condition, as the faith-oriented "philosophical suicides" (considered in MS) and their conclusions have shown. But for Camus, revolt becomes an essential attitude in the face of the absurd. It is the human refusal to accept the absurd situation that may eventually render individual life meaningful:

> Cette révolte donne son prix à la vie. Etendue sur toute la longueur d'une existence, elle lui restitue sa grandeur. Pour un homme sans œillères, il n'est pas de plus beau spectacle que celui de l'intelligence aux prises avec une réalité qui le dépasse. Le spectacle de l'orgueil humain est inégalable. Toutes les dépréciations n'y feront rien. Cette discipline que l'esprit se dicte à lui-même, cette volonté forgée de toutes pièces, ce face à face, ont quelque chose de puissant et de singulier.[11]

In his known *Explication de L'Étranger* (1943; *An Explication of the Stranger*), Jean-Paul Sartre noted that Camus's novel is best understood as a picture of a theory, as presented in the essay on Sisyphus. However, as far as I am concerned, it is exactly when Camus considers revolt that the reasoning of MS becomes clearer when read through the description of revolt in *L'Étranger* (1942; *The Stranger*). In the final pages of the novel, in the scene of Meursault's rejection of a priest's consolation, we are given a profound explanation of the absurd-provoked revolt. It is presented as a recognition and constant refusal of the absurd condition, without faith in overcoming the situation, performed by the human being in demand of lucidity, which is a necessary element of living (meaningfully) on. It is formed, contrary to Caligula's demands (symbolized by the desire to reach the Moon in Camus's drama *Caligula* written and corrected between 1938 and 1945), on the basis of a this-worldly experience, restoring individual significance without appeal to any suprarational order.

As this short analysis of Camus's *La liberté absurde* shows, the author finds revolt a possible stance for the human being, which permits a confrontation

---

11 See: *ibidem*.

with the absurd condition without the pretension that such an attitude will eliminate the initial discrepancy. The important question in this reasoning, however, according to many authors,[12] is whether this early combination of the absurd and revolt is not founded on an implicit and problematic shift from the epistemic to the ethical. If the whole argument concerning the absurd condition of man or woman is of a descriptive nature, the proposition of an attitude founded on revolt seems to lead to an *is-ought* problem.[13] Commentators have either criticized this moment of Camus's reasoning or tried to find a bridge between the factual and the ethical in Camus's understanding of the absurd. According to Herbert Hochberg,[14] there is a possibility of understanding Camus's considerations in regard to the shift from factual description to the normative sphere once the absurd situation is considered as not only a description of facts but also an essential truth, and as such it should be preserved by the subject who has recognized its importance. The only way of preserving the truth is by making life valuable, as only by living on is the preservation of the perceived truth achieved. We should emphasize that it is the **individual** life of the subject that finds value here, and the possibility of transcending this value, in my opinion, is at this point debatable when one considers Camus's point of view without reference to his later essays and works that appeared after the publication of MS. The proposition of considering the absurd situation as a truth has been, we may add, strongly criticized recently by M. Bowker, who claimed that such a truth, which arrives after the experience of absurdity, must be founded on the premise that "everything

12 The debate that considered the ethical consequences of Camus's essay started as early as 1943 with Maurice Blanchot's essay from his collection *Faux Pas,* Paris, Gallimard. The first analytic commentary on the problem in English was offered by J. Cruickshank, in his well-known *Albert Camus and the Literature of Revolt*, London, Oxford University Press, 1959.

13 In this regard, interesting reasoning was proposed quite recently by Matthew Bowker, who focused on the existential and emotional aspect of the problem of absurdity in his 2008 PhD thesis. Bowker's focus on an emotional element, understood in relation to ambivalence, is in my opinion understandable, as it should be remembered that the whole argument developed by Camus is actually a study of suicide in relation to the absurd, not solely a philosophical study of the absurd. Bowker's analysis does not aim at solving the problem of the relation between the factual and the ethical but rather aims at reinterpreting the problem of absurdity using a psychologically focused attitude. See: M.H. Bowker, *Albert Camus and the Political Philosophy of the Absurd*, Lanham, Lexington Books, 2013.

14 H. Hochberg, *Albert Camus and the Ethics of Absurdity*, "Ethics" 1965, vol. 75, no. 2. For further debate on the issue, see also: R.A. Duff, S.E. Marshall, *Camus and Rebellion: From Solipsism to Morality*, "Philosophical Investigations" 1982, vol. 5, no. 2, and A. Sagi, *Albert Camus and the Philosophy of Absurd*, Amsterdam – New York, Rodopi, 2002.

is equivalent." It is difficult, according to the commentator, to find common ground for the statement that "everything is equivalent" and the proposition for the initiation of revolt. To quote:

> Why should one rebel if all events, all things, and all values are equivalent? Don't rebels need to believe in values, in better and worse, maybe even in best and worst, in order to motivate and justify their rebellion? And if the absurd is "true," what does one rebel against? Should one rebel against the absurd or preserve the absurd as a truth?[15]

Many authors did indeed find difficulty in relation to the statement about absurdity (and its primarily epistemic nature, relating to knowledge and meaning in relation to existence), with its "shift" to ethics at the moment of proposing the stance of revolt. Without pretending to have the ability to resolve all the questions raised by my excellent predecessors, I would like to address here, more humbly, the exact textual reference from MS regarding the issue of the relation between absurdity and revolt. I find this necessary, since it is difficult for me to accept the statement that the proposed understanding of the truth about absurdity is simply founded on the claim that "everything is equivalent" in human revolt. Specifically, Camus makes a point about the nature of equivalence twice in MS:

> Pour l'homme absurde, il y avait une vérité en même temps qu'une **amertume** dans cette opinion purement psychologique que tous les visages du monde sont privilégiés. Que tout soit privilégié revient à dire que tout est équivalent. Mais l'aspect métaphysique de cette vérité le mène si loin que par une réaction élémentaire, il se sent plus près peut-être de Platon.[16]

> L'absurde ne délivre pas, il lie. Il n'autorise pas tous les actes. Tout est permis ne signifie pas que rien n'est défendu. L'absurde rend seulement leur équivalence aux conséquences de ces actes. Il ne recommande pas le crime, ce serait puéril, mais il restitue au remords son inutilité. De même, si toutes les expériences sont indifférentes, celle du devoir est aussi légitime qu'une autre. On peut être vertueux par caprice.[17]

---

15 See: M. Bowker, *op.cit.*, p. 88.

16 See: OC I, p. 250.

17 See: OC I, p. 266.

In the first quoted passage, which relates to the epistemological aspect of absurdity, Camus makes the point in his critique of Husserl,[18] and the author's conviction is that phenomenology leads to the equivalence of all acts of observation of the world, not an ethical equivalence of all actions. It is, however, clear, as the argument is carried out, that for Camus the claim that "everything is equivalent" in his understanding of Husserl's phenomenology is problematic and leads to a rationalization he finds untenable with absurd reasoning. What I find important here is that, even while Camus acknowledges the truth related to absurdity, he simultaneously mentions the negative reaction of the human being toward this truth: "avait une vérité en même temps qu'une amertume." Similarly, when – relating to the moral consequences of absurd freedom – Camus describes the equivalence of the consequences of actions in the second quotation, it should be remembered that his recognition of freedom in the absurd condition is instantly described as dangerous, leading him to an initial objection to relating action and the knowledge of absurdity without hesitation:

> "Tout est permis" s'écrie Ivan Karamazov. Cela aussi sent son absurde. Mais à condition de ne pas l'entendre vulgairement. Je ne sais si on l'a bien remarqué: il ne s'agit pas d'un cri de délivrance et de joie, mais d'une constatation **amère**.[19]

The truth concerning absurdity is for Camus a burden, both on an epistemic (an unresolvable paradox) and moral (a dilemma regarding human action) level. Undoubtedly, the argument as presented in MS is not very precise, but, given the author's conviction about the irreducibility of the demand for unity and meaning, it may be understandable to a certain extent why on both levels the arrival at the recognition of absurdity is not only a truth to be acknowledged but also a moral burden for the human being. The revolt does not, I believe, originate simply from the fact of recognizing the absurd but also from its fundamental inconsistency with the human desire for unity

---

[18] In regard to Camus's knowledge of Husserl's phenomenology, I highly recommend the recent work of G. Heffernan, *Absurdity, Creativity, and Constitution: Critical Observations on Camus's Critique of Husserl's Phenomenology in The Myth of Sisyphus*, "Journal of Camus Studies" 2014, vol. 4, p. 73–116. We may add here, that the primary source of Camus's knowledge of the philosophy of Husserl (and Heidegger), at the time of preparation of MS was: M. Guvritch, *Les tendances actuelles de la philosophie allemande. E. Husserl – M. Scheler – E. Lask – M. Heidegger*, Paris, Vrin, 1930.

[19] See: OC I, p. 265–266.

and meaning. In effect, the subject accepts the fact of the relation with the world as being absurd. But according to Camus, for a continuation of life as such, the subject cannot simply affirm living in the absurd world as it constantly challenges his or her desire for meaning, making him or her both accept the absurd condition and revolt against it, which causes great interpretative difficulty.[20] However paradoxical it may sound, Camus wants the absurd relation to be preserved, as one of its elements is a conscious, reflecting human being.[21] It is only by living on that the human being may relate to the absurd or consider this continuation of living on in terms of value. The truth about absurdity influencing the human condition is essential in order for the human being to act freely, without hope of finding a universal, objective meaning and against despair, leading to the surrendering of the human desire for unity and meaning. In my opinion, revolt has an essential role here: the human protest makes living with the absurd truth bearable as it confirms and maintains that the essential desire for meaning in the human being is not fully dispensable for the benefit of the recognized truth about absurdity. Without revolt, as the description of Sisyphus's effort in the concluding image of the essay shows, the consent to the truth about absurdity would be unanimous with the consent to constant suffering, leading nowhere. It is, however, the constant protest against this truth that makes for the possibility of a potentially meaningful life. But, in Camus's first philosophical essay, as I am convinced, this protest aims only at the preservation of the rebel; it allows one to continue to live in consciousness of one's own limitations. In constant relation to the experienced, lived absurdity, revolt aims at allowing

---

20 The difficulty in reading this aspect of MS may be explained as based on the combination of several statements of the author. Camus, on the one hand, clearly confirms the irreducibility of the human demand for meaning: "Je peux tout nier de cette partie de moi qui vit de nostalgies incertaines, sauf ce désir d'unité, cet appétit de résoudre, cette exigence de clarté et de cohésion" (OCI, p. 254) and clearly finds the position of the man or woman who has revolted valuable: "Tout ce qui détruit, escamote ou subtilise ces exigences (et en premier lieu le consentement qui détruit le divorce) ruine l'absurde et *dévalorise* l'attitude qu'on peut alors proposer" (OC I, p. 240). On the other hand, Camus remarks that the constant struggle of the human being is founded on the constant rejection of meaning: "Il s'agissait précédemment de savoir si la vie devait avoir un sens pour être vécue. Il apparaît ici au contraire qu'elle sera d'autant mieux vécue qu'elle n'aura pas de sens" (OC I, p. 255).

21 A very interesting and insightful proposition for resolving the inconsistency in Camus's early philosophy has been proposed by Thomas Pölzler who, after considering the simultaneous lack of possibility for values and the necessity of values, proposed considering the emergence of revolt from a different perspective, relating the protest with a self-help stance of the human being. See: T. Pölzler, *Absurdism as Self-Help: Resolving an Essential Inconsistency in Camus's Early Philosophy*, "Journal of Camus Studies" 2014, vol. 4.

the human being to endure the situation without appeal to God or to the transcendent, universal rule of life.

In developing the idea of revolt that Camus found essential while studying absurdity, we may observe that in the case of each separate presentation of absurd men and women in his works – Sisyphus, Don Juan, the actor, the conqueror, Caligula, Martha and Meursault – the rebels act for themselves. They protest against their own experience of absurdity. As we see in the next section, it is exactly this solitary aspect of revolt in reaction to the absurd that is especially important for understanding the development of these notions as they were presented in 1949.

THE TRANSITION: THE VALUE AND REVOLT

If one considers the work of Camus in the order of creation of his consequent philosophical essays and literary works, we may observe that the development of the idea of revolt – the consequence of the engagement with the absurd – was formed by Camus prior to the development of his most important work, describing the transition from the absurd position to the idea of man in revolt. This means that not only was rebellion seen as a developmental idea, which he had already remarked upon in the essay on absurdity, but also that the explanation of the process that leads from one to another was formed after both ideas, that is, the absurd and revolt, had assumed their advanced form in Camus's thought. We may, however, note that the description of the transition from the absurd to revolt, as described by Camus in 1949 (and published later, after modifications, in HR in 1951), is not a bridge which was added later to already shaped ideas, but rather a synthesis of Camus's remarks, observations and experiences that reached back to many notes and comments in his correspondence and that he had formed while working on his first essay on revolt between 1943 and 1945. Before considering the change in meaning and dynamics between the absurd and revolt in Camus's 1949 essay *L'absurde et le meurtre*, I would like to point out several, essential in my view, milestones that allow us to understand more thoroughly Camus's final recourse to value in his depiction of revolt and in his progression.

It may well be, as J. Cruickshank perceptively noted, that it was already when Camus published the essay on revolt that he found a need to support the human desire for meaning and value with a recourse to something that would bind human beings together, rather than develop themselves in solitary revolt. This concern for value was already expressed by Camus in a letter to Pierre Bonnel, dated 18 March 1943,[22] in which Camus notes, relating to his prior methodological limitations in the 1942 essay:

> L'effort de la pensée absurde (et gratuite), c'est expulsion de tous les jugements de valeur au profit des jugements de fait. Or, nous savons, vous et moi, qu'il y a des jugements de valeur inévitables.[23]

Also in 1943, Camus makes two important remarks, which together with the development of his ideas for *La Peste* (1947; *The Plague*), clearly show the direction of his thought from solitary revolt to a revolt that would allow the transgression of solitude:

> L'absurde, c'est l'homme tragique devant un miroir (Caligula).[24] Il n'est donc pas seul. Il y a le germe d'une satisfaction ou d'une complaisance. Maintenant, il faut supprimer le miroir.[25]
> Absurde. Restituer morale par le Tu. Je ne crois pas qu'il y ait un autre monde où nous devrions « rendre compte ». Mais nous avons déjà nos comptes à rendre dans ce monde-ci – à tous ceux que nous aimons.[26]

---

22 Any insightful reader will notice that many observations from this letter appear in the 1949 essay on the absurd–revolt transition, especially the entire part concerning the absurd contradiction and the necessity of silence in a state of perfect absurdity. See: OC I, p. 321, and OC III, p. 348–349. We may add that the idea of the relation between absurdity and silence was pursued by Camus in his unfinished project *Anthologie de l'insignifiance*, see: OC II, p. 987–989. Camus also mentions the motive in a letter to J. Grenier (1943): "I don't think my essay sums up everything. It seemed to me that we were living in the dark – and at the same time benefiting from – the logical consequences of a philosophy of non-signification. I made this effort coherent. But no one more than I, perhaps, senses the contradiction of such attitude. This amounts, in reality, to eliminating all value judgements and that is impossible because every act in our life is a value judgement. Everything is permitted, of course, but I know there are things I won't do, words and loyalties I won't disavow [...] There is an absurd myth, there is no absurd thought." A. Camus, J. Grenier, *Correspondence, 1932–1960*, University of Nebraska Press, Lincoln, 2003, p. 73.

23 See: OC I, p. 322. This breach between firm commitment and the methodological limitations of the essay on the absurd (OC I, p. 260: "Une fois pour toutes, les jugements de valeur sont écartés ici au profit des jugements de fait.") is, however, balanced in the letter by Camus's remark: "Mais je me refuse seulement à croire que dans l'ordre métaphysique le besoin d'un principe nécessite l'existence de ce principe" (OC I, p. 322). This statement not only shows that Camus was in search of his moral position but it is also in conflict with his later comment in *Letters to a German friend* (1943–1944): "Je continue à croire que ce monde n'a pas de sens supérieur. Mais je sais que quelque chose en lui a du sens et c'est l'homme, parce qu'il est le seul être à exiger d'en avoir." See: OC II, p. 26.

24 A person facing the mirror, we might add, is another metaphor to which Camus referred when describing the transition from the absurd to revolt in 1949. See: OC III, p. 69, 350.

25 See: OC II, p. 995.

26 See: OC II, p. 996.

Without going into the detail of this topic in regard to *La Peste*, we may add that simultaneously Camus tries to relate revolt with value, given the observed nihilistic consequences of living in the absurd situation. His *Lettres à un ami allemand* (1944; *Letters to a German friend*) show not only the necessity of finding a source of value to add a positive and super-individual content to revolt but also that the Nazi conquest may be seen as a direct consequence of nihilism, formed through accepting the absurdity of the human condition, in which revolt becomes a purely negative and destructive quest for unrestrained freedom and power. It is in these essays that Camus binds the conviction that everything is equivalent with the dangerous form of the direction of human action, founded on the absurd experience, leading to murder.[27]

Camus's ideas on simultaneous affirmation and negation in revolt that would be fully expressed in his introduction to HR were formed, in his *Remarque sur la revolte* (1945; *Remarks on revolt*). This essay contains reflection on the development between absurd position (MS) and later thought, as also presented simultaneously in *La Peste*:[28]

> Dans l'expérience absurde, la tragédie est individuelle. À partir du mouvement de révolte, elle a conscience d'être collective. Elle est l'aventure de tous. Le premier progrès d'un esprit saisi d'étrangeté est de reconnaître qu'il partage cette étrangeté avec tous les hommes et que la réalité humaine dans sa totalité souffre de cette distance par rapport à soi et au monde.[29]

It was also in 1945 that Camus referred openly to the problem of contradiction in the absurd position in regard to ethics. Camus stated at that time that absurd stance excludes value judgements, which is a paradox in regard to experience, clearly confirming the existence of value judgments and the impossibility of human beings to refrain from them.[30] In

---

27 See: OC II, p. 26–27.

28 The description of the progression from solitary to solidary experience was repeated by Camus in his well-known polemic with Roland Barthes. In a reply to Barthes's critical remarks on *The Plague*, Camus wrote: "If there is an evolution from *The Outsider* to *The Plague*, it is in the direction of solidarity and participation." A. Camus, *Letter to Roland Barthes on The Plague* [in:] *Lyrical and Critical Essays*, New York, Vintage Books, 1970, p. 338.

29 See: OC III, p. 327

30 "Car l'absurde est contradictoire en existence. Il exclut en fait les jugements de valeur et les jugements de valeur sont. Ils sont parce qu'ils sont liés au fait même d'exister. Il faut donc déplacer le raisonnement de l'absurde dans son équivalent en existence qui est la révolte. Par elle, on trouve à affirmer en même temps une certaine part de l'homme placée au-dessus de tout et une condition humaine qui lui donne à la fois son évidence et sa relativité. Car le révolté trouve ainsi en

the early essay on revolt, Camus reflects on this paradox and admits that there must be an essential link between the attitude of revolt and values. However, the emergence of values, as Camus highlights in 1945, does not mean that such a reference instantly reduces or eliminates the absurdity of human existence:

> La révolte ne nous apprendra donc rien de plus quant à la solution dernière que l'analyse absurde. Le monde est toujours fermé. Nous sommes toujours dans le cercle, avec ceci de plus, toutefois, qu'il nous est possible de répondre affirmativement à la seule question qui nous paraisse de quelque importance: l'homme peut-il, à lui seul et sans le secours de l'éternel, créer ses propres valeurs?[31]

The 1945 essay ties value, founded on revolt, to the concept of the human condition and clearly states that the act of revolt leads to the creation of value,[32] which will consequently guide the human being and allow for the transgression of solitude and overcome the possibility that the continuation of living in the face of the absurd experience will lead to a nihilistic solution. Having considered these elements, which in my view shaped Camus's attitude toward the transition, we may now conclude, while referring to the final text of this analysis, on the dynamics between the absurd and revolt in his 1949 essay *L'absurde et le meurtre*.

---

lui la valeur qui l'autorise (et qui le force) à parler et agir. Cette part de lui-même qui lui donne désormais ses raisons dénonce seulement son origine absurde dans la mesure où elle est faite a la fois pour tout le monde et pour personne.", OC III, p. 337.

31 See: OC III, p. 336. Concluding this early analysis, however, Camus notes that there is significant progress of the reflection based on the problem of revolt when compared to the analysis of absurd. His suggestion is to replace the absurd reasoning with "son équivalent en existence qui est la révolte" (p. 337). I find this statement rather difficult to understand, but the way I think it may be interpreted is that at the moment of writing, Camus would see the absurd position as a reflective stance, not leading necessarily to action, causing a paradox situation, whereas the replacement and focus on revolt contains an inherent element of change, opening the human being to a possibility of resolving the paradox of the absurd in regard to limits of human activity.

32 See: OC III, p. 329: "Dans l'ordre de l'expérience humaine, la révolte a le même sens que le cogito dans l'ordre de la pensée. Elle est la première vérité et elle crée la première valeur." We may find, however, in Camus's essay from 1945 a statement that the man in revolt finds in himself, does not create, a value that will allow him to transgress absurdity: "Car le révolté trouve ainsi en lui la valeur qui l'autorise (et qui le force) à parler et agir. Cette part de lui-même qui lui donne désormais ses raisons dénonce seulement son origine absurde dans la mesure où elle est faite à la fois pour tout le monde et pour personne" (p. 337).

THE ABSURD AND REVOLT BETWEEN 1949 AND 1951

Any serious attempt to understand the transition and statements made by Camus in 1949 must refer to the historical context that influenced him to change his focus from the analysis of solitary revolt in relation to the intellectual pessimism of the 1930s (directed against suicide) to the value-oriented solidary revolt (directed against ideology and the legitimization of murder).[33] The shift of focus from the phenomenon of absurdity toward a deeper understanding of revolt may be seen as a consequence of not only the personal, philosophical deliberations of the author but also his deepening knowledge of historical events and their correlation with the ideological roots of contemporary totalitarianisms (especially Nazism and communism, but also an openly stated, firm commitment against the colonial violence of the Western world). It would be, I believe, difficult to estimate the importance of these events in the process of shaping Camus's critical thought; however, it becomes clear that as early as 1946 (with the cycle of essays *Ni victimes ni bourreaux, Neither victims nor executioners*), the theme of the introductory essay of HR (which would become the introduction to Camus's second philosophical essay) captures the essential problem of Camus in the late 1940s: the problem of the legitimization of violence and murder in philosophically supported ideologies that resulted in the genocide that took place in German and Soviet concentration camps.[34] It is within the context of the horrible experiences of mass murder, performed on an individual as well as the state level by descendants of European culture and civilization, that Camus's idea of revolt (within the context of the absurd) decisively reaches beyond the limits of nihilism.

---

33 I have covered this aspect of development in Camus's thought, especially regarding the political orientation of post-war France, in my article "The Shaping of Revolt: Camus's Neither Victims nor Executioners in Relation to the Origins of the Author's Position, Merleau-Ponty's Humanism and Terror and the Later Political Debate Concerning Camus's Critique of the Legitimization of Violence."

34 Camus openly links the legitimization of murder with European philosophy in the analyzed essay stating that philosophy changes murderers into judges (OC III, p. 344). (For Camus's 1946 position against legitimate violence, see: OC II, p. 436–441.) The theme of the Soviet concentration camps, aside from Camus's reading notes from his lectures on David Rousset or Józef Czapski in his *Carnets*, was (as far as my knowledge goes) publicly expressed by Camus in 1948, the year of the publication of his *State of Siege*. In his second response to Emmanuel d'Astier de La Vigerie, Camus openly connected his criticism of legitimate violence with the knowledge of the existence of German and Soviet concentration camps. He also remarked (and this thought would be developed in his analysis of historical revolt in the third part of HR) that the existence of the Soviet camps was justified by historical necessity (see: OC II, p. 466–467).

The essential question regarding the development of Camus's thought, concerning the role of the 1949 essay is, I believe, not the way revolt is linked with absurdity but rather the way the problem of absurdity and revolt is connected with the existence of legitimate murder. It is thus an introduction to a previous reflection of violence and murder that significantly changes the dynamics of the absurd–revolt connection. Camus is clearly conscious of the hermeneutical significance of this connection. The discussion of 1942 did negatively answer Camus's question regarding the possibility of the absurd having a consequence in suicide. But the question of murder – especially a murder founded on a philosophical conclusion[35] – makes it impossible to rely on the absurd itself in the search for the limitation of murder and violence. In 1949 Camus openly states that the feeling of the absurd leads to indifference toward murder and that such indifference makes murder at least a possibility for the human subject.[36] We may observe here an especially interesting element in Camus's argument: it is a feeling (which causes human suffering) that leads to indifference (toward human suffering). The harm that is experienced leads to indifference toward pain, which has, as Camus suggests, the consequence of the possibility of murder. I believe there is something significantly different in this position when compared with the problem of suicide. In suicide, our feeling of suffering leads us to an idea, which is that the end of suffering is achievable by means of death. The suffering of having experienced the absurd is so severe that the natural fear of death (and possibly the pain accompanying the act of suicide) is considered inferior to the consequences of the act. In the case of murder, however, the action caused by the suffering is directed against another living subject. Why? In what way does another agent's death relieve my pain of existence? It is certainly not an act of empathy – delivering somebody else from suffering – as we cannot be sure whether he or she is experiencing the absurdity in the same way as we do. Why, then, do we kill another human being after having experienced the absurd? Camus's answer in 1949 was that the absurd makes murder indifferent,[37] but that does not

---

35 Interestingly, in 1949 Camus wrote about "Bourreaux philosophes" (OC III, p. 345). In 1951, the same passage is about "l'assassin" (OC III, p. 65). The author clearly combined both subjects with the belief that in the absurd world everything is possible and that there is no value which would limit the action of the individual.

36 Compare variations of the aforementioned passage which shows many corrections in Camus's manuscripts: OC III, p. 65, 345, 1240. The whole argument regarding the foundation of the feeling of the absurd on human reflection and decision relates clearly to Camus's observation on the feeling of absurdity from 1942; see: OC I, p. 238.

37 OC III, p. 345.

make murder desirable or purposeful. In effect, I believe that he makes the following claim here: the absurd (considered as a feeling, a reaction to the experience of absurdity) does lead to the possibility of killing another human being (like in the case of Meursault), but it does not have any grounds for being a source of making killing purposeful. It is when the absurd gets reflected upon, and considered not only as a feeling but also as a foundation for any "moral" conduct (although nihilistic in its nature), which does not lead to affirmative and compassionate kind of revolt, Camus claims, that possibilities arise, opening contemporary moral philosophy to the problem of the legitimization of another agent's death.[38] Camus's main argument for the reconsideration of the absurd/revolt dynamic is that, although the absurd position does allow, on an individual level, a person to battle against the logic of suicide, the same reasoning, when applied to the social world where murder is possible, results in a paradox. On the one hand, in the experience of the absurd and its impossibility of finding a reliable (and reasonable) source of values, one admits that murder is possible. This stance – without a clear limitation of murder – leads to a shift from the possibility of killing to a practice of killing, in the struggle for domination, which instantly follows the approval of the rule, stating that in the absurd world everything is possible. On the other hand, Camus claims in 1949, the same reasoning cannot reject self-killing and approve of the possibility of murder (indifference toward murder makes murder possible). It is in this argument, I believe, that the progression of Camus's thought between 1942 and 1949 is most visible. Although Camus did consciously avoid connecting the early revolt with a value, stressing the negative aspect of escaping from the absurd condition by death, which leads nowhere, his conclusions, shaped between 1943 and 1949, clearly lead him to the following statement: the decision to remain alive after the experience of the absurd, which is formed on the position of revolt of saying "No" to suicide, to false hope and to the faith-based construction of meaning, makes life valuable.[39] When he considered revolt in

[38] Camus's main argument about the direction of action from the experience of absurdity toward murder is that, deprived of the belief in a higher principle, the absurd man or woman resorts to the only value remaining after the nihilistic experience, that of direct efficacy (see: OC III, p. 345).

[39] In the 1949 version of the essay, Camus considers that absurd experience is founded on contradiction, shaped by indifference toward life and (as a consequence of rejecting suicide) making life a "seule valeur de fait" (OC III, p. 346). In 1951 he changed the description of life to "bien nécessaire" (OC III, p. 66). I believe that his later avoidance of calling life a value resulted from the author's intention to make the essay coherent with the chapter that followed, in which Camus considered the value found in revolt more important than the life of the rebel itself (OC III, p. 72–73), which clearly means that life cannot be the only end of revolt.

the 1942 essay, Camus did limit the description of the consequences to the individual (existential) level. In 1949, following his numerous reflections on the necessity of reflecting on solidarity of revolt, he writes:

> Dès l'instant où cette valeur de fait [that is: life; M.K.] est reconnue, elle se généralise à tous les hommes. On ne peut donner une cohérence au meurtre si on la refuse au suicide.[40]

How compelling is Camus's argument? He considers the decision of preserving one's life as having a consequence in making life valuable. Consequently, this decision of rejecting suicide makes any decision regarding murder illegitimate as long as we do not reject the value of our own life as well (Camus calls such situation "absolute nihilism"). However, there is a debatable difference between suicide and murder: the decision to end my own life on the basis of a philosophical reflection on absurdity may be perceived as being made in agreement with the subject's will, whose life is threatened – a person who kills him – or herself agrees to his or her own death. Murder, in contrast, is clearly a deprivation of the life of a subject who does not want his or her life to end and is a violation of the subject's right to live with a conscious disregard of his or her will. It may therefore be debatable whether the decision, formed on basis of one's conviction that one should maintain one's own life, results in a direct condemnation of murder, because there is a specific difference between the decision to kill oneself willingly and to deprive a subject of life against his or her own will.[41] This difference leads to the possibility of imagining a person who is morally against murder but not against suicide. We may also consider that it is possible for a person to separate the value of his or her own life from the value of somebody else's life, leading to a decision to kill, if the subject rejects the idea of community with other human beings, which itself may be, as I believe, the result of absurd experience, given its enumerated expressions from MS.[42] These dilemmas aside, we may clearly see that for Camus, such considerations were, at least in 1949, manageable only by a firm rejection of both murder and suicide on the basis

---

[40] See: OC III, p. 346. In a further part of the essay (p. 347), Camus develops the argument by stating that one cannot preserve one's own life and accept others to sacrifice the life of someone else.

[41] For a brief and analytic summary of contemporary arguments in the ethical debate concerning murder, see: S. Luper, *The Philosophy of Death*, Cambridge University Press, Cambridge, 2009, p. 143–170. For the debate concerning the possibility of the decision for suicide being rational, refer to p. 178–180.

[42] See: OC I, p. 229

of the valorization and affirmation of the life of all human beings, following the absurd experience. Camus claims, that the absurd position he proposed in 1942 did not make this statement, requiring him to develop the stance of revolt toward value affirmation. Camus considers the absurd position contradictory and provisional, not leading unequivocally to a value-affirming stance,[43] and presents the situation of absurd reasoning as an impasse. This, as far as I am concerned, does not mean that the whole reflection concerning absurdity was futile nor that the observed contradiction of the absurd stance necessitates a fundamental change in thought. On the contrary, Camus clearly returns to the subject of absurdity and considers the initial discovery of revolt an essential aspect of reasoning that requires both further development and a rethinking given the change of context in the philosophical climate.[44] In one of the versions of the aforementioned essay, we may find the aspect of continuity between the essays described in a more direct way than is found in the final conclusion from HR. In the final version, Camus considers the absurd experience a moment that leaves the human being in a state of "tabula rasa," without any guidance as to the limit or direction of action in the world. He adds, however, that this state may lead to new research.[45] In an earlier version of the essay, however, Camus clearly admits that this new study is rather a development, not a revolution:

> Le miroir birsé, il reste une évidence qui est la protestation même conenue dans l'absurde, c'est-à-dire la révolte.[46]

It is in the consequent changes of the 1949 essay that the distance between "Sisyphus" and "Prometheus" deepens (leading many commentators to

---

43 See: OC III, 349. More precisely, I believe Camus claims that the absurd position leads both toward the affirmation of values and indifference toward any valorization of life, making the nihilistic cult of efficacy an emerging possibility.

44 The moment of presenting revolt as an important element that requires further development may be considered the goal of the whole essay from 1949. It is important to remark here that the first version of the essay did in fact describe revolt, arising from and beyond the experience of absurdity as "La premiére et la seule valeur" (OC III, p. 350). Aligning the essay with the conclusion of his essay on revolt, modified for the purpose of HR, Camus changed the description of revolt: "La premiére et la seule evidence" (OC III, p. 69).

45 OC III, p. 69.

46 OC III, p. 1242. In later revisions, the quoted sentence changes, increasing, as I interpret these lines, the distance between MS and HR. In 1949, Camus wrote: "Le miroir birsé, il ne reste rien qui puisse nous servir pour repondre aux questions du siècle," (OC III, p. 350). The same sentence appears in HR (see: OC III, p. 70).

confirm a split, or discontinuity between Camus's thinking between the cycle of absurd and the cycle of revolt), but given the aforementioned importance of revolt in MS, we may note that there is a strong interpretative background for seeing the 1942 and 1949 reflections on absurd and revolt as a continuity.[47] There are, however, as I strongly believe, important differences that make any categorical statement about the continuity or discontinuity between the MS and HR much more complex. Camus not only considers revolt a source of value but also finds the human protest, as depicted in MS, open for dangerous effects in human activity, once the reflective stance becomes an active position. The fragments of the argument in the final version of the text refer to the symbol of the mirror, which, in an earlier version of the essay, was more openly related to the situation of Caligula, representing Camus's vision of murderous, destructive revolt.[48] In the version of the aforementioned essay from 1949, the author explained in much greater detail the problem of revolt that related to the experience, without a clear reference to value and to other human beings. He wrote that human protest in the face of the absurd brings back meaning and unity, contrasting with the content of the absurd experience itself. Camus acknowledges, however, that this feeling of unity coincides with the memory of "l'aspect impossible de la réalité."[49] Our recognition of unity, founded on the protest against absurdity and replying to our call for coherence, clashes with the lucidity of the discovery that such unification is unachievable. This longer description, eliminated from the later version, makes the metaphor of breaking the mirror, as I believe, much more meaningful. Camus follows it with a statement that the absurd position is ambiguous and that such ambiguity may result in complaisance. The revolt, considered as a solitary act, could have, as I understand from Camus's comments, resulted in a state in which the protest ends in something that could be seen as coherence within incoherence, a pleasure of discovering one's own unity in protest against absurdity, without transgression of the discovery, with an act that would force the absurdity to lessen its grip on the relation of man and the world. Alternatively, the revolt ends in asceticism and poverty, a voluntary Nietzschean exile suitable for poets and writers.[50]

47 This proposal has been developed and defended recently in the excellent book by John Foley, *Albert Camus from the absurd to revolt*, Durham, Acumen Publishing, 2008.

48 See: OC III, p. 1242: "il faut, avec Caligula, briser les jeux fixes du miroir et entrer dans le mouvement vécu où l'absurde se depasse lui méme."

49 OC III, p. 348–349.

50 Camus's conclusion, which ended with a quote of Arthur Rimbaud's final words: "J'irai sous la terre et, toi, tu marcheras dans le soleil!" (OC III, p. 68), is certainly open for interpretation as

In conclusion we may observe that the newly proposed focus on revolt (as presented in 1949) is clearly not based on apprehension of former considerations nor on a direct continuation of the idea of revolt, as presented in 1942. Camus not only considered the absurd as an unavoidable point of departure, from which the reflection (and rebellion) must start. Given the objective and troubling historical change, the harm-seeking forms of nihilism based upon the same source of the absurd, he aims at developing the content of the rebellious act. Revolt, as formed in the context of absurdity, may have made individual life bearable and meaningful. But living in constant tension and refusal, together with the desire for unity and coherence, seems to have become unbearable for many, who like their literary presentations: Caligula and Martha, direct their protest and desire against others. As the description of Camus's archetypical revolt would show, in the chapter following Camus's consideration of the newly considered dynamics between absurdity and revolt, the protest against absurdity and injustice may lead to a discovery (or creation)[51] of human value, affirming human nature and allowing the protest to embrace others, leading Camus to his famous statement: "I rebel, therefore we exist" – an element evidently not explicitly considered in Camus's earlier description of the solitary revolt of Sisyphus.

BIBLIOGRAPHY

Bowker, M.H., *Albert Camus and the Political Philosophy of the Absurd*, Lanham, Lexington Books, 2013.

Camus, A., *Letter to Roland Barthes on The Plague* [in:] *Lyrical and Critical Essays*, New York, Vintage Books, 1970.

Camus, A., *Œuvres complètes*, toms I, II and III, Paris, Gallimard, Bibliothèque de La Pléiade, 2006–2008.

to his judgement of such a position. We may, however, observe that the statement shows that the decision to remain in solitude, when confronted with death, results in a despair and nostalgia for life that would encompass suffering and pleasure, solitary creation and solidarity with others, not just constant refusal.

51 Camus uses in his depictions of value in revolt the verbs *créer* and *trouver*. In the final version of the essay on revolt (OC III, p. 73), heads a paragraph about the pre-existence of value, which precedes any action and is linked with the concept of human nature, changing the context from 1945, in which value was related to the human condition, not nature. This addition, however, does not completely eliminate the ambiguity, as the later statement of the final version of the essay from 1951 (OC III, p. 78, 79) contains statements that value is born out of revolt and that revolt itself is the foundation of value.

Camus, A., Grenier, J., *Correspondence, 1932–1960*, Lincoln, University of Nebraska Press, 2003.

Cruickshank, J., *Albert Camus and the Literature of Revolt*, London, Oxford University Press, 1959.

Duff, R.A., Marshall, S.E., *Camus and Rebellion: From Solipsism to Morality*, "Philosophical Investigations" 1982, vol. 5, no. 2.

Guvritch, M., *Les tendances actuelles de la philosophie allemande. E. Husserl – M. Scheler – E. Lask – M. Heidegger*, Paris, Vrin, 1930.

Heffernan, G., *Absurdity, Creativity, and Constitution: Critical Observations on Camus's Critique of Husserl's Phenomenology in The Myth of Sisyphus*, "Journal of Camus Studies" 2014, vol. 4.

Hochberg, H., *Albert Camus and the Ethics of Absurdity*, "Ethics" 1965, vol. 75, no. 2.

Luper, S., *The Philosophy of Death*, Cambridge University Press, Cambridge, 2009.

Pölzler, T., *Absurdism as Self-Help: Resolving an Essential Inconsistency in Camus's Early Philosophy*, "Journal of Camus Studies" 2014, vol. 4.

Sagi, A., *Albert Camus and the Philosophy of Absurd*, Amsterdam–New York, Rodopi, 2002.

Part Two:
Camus's Revolt in Contemporary Analysis

L'éthique camusienne comme aliment de résilience

SOPHIE BASTIEN, EMMANUEL HABIMANA

Le point de départ de la présente réflexion concerne la fortune de l'œuvre camusienne, mais un aspect de cette fortune qui se situe hors des sphères savantes. Depuis une vingtaine d'années, nous avons souvent remarqué que Camus est cité dans des contextes non littéraire, philosophique ou politique. Certes, on voit couramment de grands auteurs cités sur des objets du quotidien, comme des agendas, mais ce que nous avons observé par rapport aux citations camusiennes relève d'un emploi plus ciblé : elles sont utilisées par des associations caritatives, des organismes communautaires, ou dans des documents liés à la thérapie personnelle et au dépassement de soi. Les exemples que nous avons glanés au fil des ans dégagent un objectif commun : ils se réfèrent à Camus pour dire la résilience.

Leur style varie cependant, et pour cette raison, nous les classerions en deux catégories. L'une d'elles se décline sur un registre individuel et introspectif. Sa phrase emblématique pourrait être celle-ci, tirée de « Retour à Tipasa » dans le recueil *L'Été*, et que nous avons maintes fois aperçue par hasard[1] : « Au milieu de l'hiver, j'apprenais enfin qu'il y avait en moi un été invincible ». Quoique cet autre passage du même essai soit aussi éloquent : « garder intactes en soi une fraîcheur, une source de joie, aimer le jour qui échappe à l'injustice, et retourner au combat avec cette lumière conquise » (OC III, 613).

La deuxième catégorie stylistique, plus impersonnelle et impérative, adopte la position debout comme métaphore. Cet alexandrin rythmé, avec une rime à l'hémistiche, la représente bien : « Plutôt mourir debout que de vivre à genoux » (OC III, 73). Tout comme la phrase emblématique précédente,

---

1 La reproduction la plus récente dont nous avons été témoins se trouve dans *Le Courage de changer*, Virginia, Al-Anon Family Group Headquarters, 1994, p. 13.

nous avons repéré cette antithèse dans divers documents[2]. Chaque fois, on l'attribue à Camus ; il n'en est peut-être pas l'inventeur[3] mais l'utilise avec brio dans *L'Homme révolté*, pour montrer que le révolté se tient debout malgré sa misère. Elle complète, en quelque sorte, un passage de *La Peste*, puisque pour le docteur Rieux, soigner les malades équivaut à « ne pas se mettre à genoux » (OC II, 125). La même métaphore revient avec une conviction renouvelée dans le « Message en faveur de la Hongrie » par rapport au camp soviétique : « rien n'abat, ni n'abattra jamais, cette force violente et pure qui pousse les hommes et les peuples à revendiquer l'honneur de vivre debout » (OC III, 1136).

En vue du colloque mettant l'accent sur la Révolte et dont provient le présent recueil, nous nous sommes demandé ce qui, chez Camus, justifie la récupération vulgarisatrice que nous avons observée, où il est évoqué tel un mentor dans le domaine personnel, par des associations d'individus éprouvés et leurs instances thérapeutiques. Quelles caractéristiques se trouvent dans le versant lumineux de son œuvre et seraient susceptibles d'alimenter le phénomène de la résilience ?

1. LE MOT ET LA CHOSE

Remarquons d'abord que la notion de résilience est très récente dans son acception psychologique, et encore plus en français qu'en anglais. Sa définition originelle concerne plutôt les sciences physiques. C'est la capacité d'un matériau à résister aux chocs et à reprendre sa forme ; et plus généralement, le fait de rebondir, de se redresser – ce qui apparente ce phénomène physique au champ lexical de la position debout, chère à Camus. En psychologie, la résilience devient objet de recherche dans les années 1950 chez les Anglo-Saxons[4], et prend un essor considérable dans les années quatre-vingts avec les travaux du pédopsychiatre britannique Michael Rutter, qui la définit

---

2 La reproduction la plus récente dont nous avons été témoins se trouve sur la page d'accueil du site internet de la Fondation québécoise de la déficience intellectuelle : http://www.lesupport.ca/ (consulté le 15 septembre 2015).

3 Elle serait dérivée d'une devise plus longue d'Emiliano Zapata, révolutionnaire mexicain très actif au début du XXe siècle : « Es mejor morir de pie que vivir toda una vida arrodillado. » Voir notamment J.F. Montero Medina, *Vivamos Nuestra Historia*, Quintana Roo, Municipio de Felipe Carrillo Puerto, 2011, p. 35.

4 S. Ionescu, *Origine et évolution du concept de résilience*, dans *Résilience. Connaissances de base*, éd. B. Cyrulnik, G. Jorland, Paris, Odile Jacob, 2012, p. 19, 29.

comme la capacité de résister aux épreuves sévères[5]. Mais ce n'est que dans la décennie quatre-vingt-dix qu'elle s'étend au monde universitaire francophone, grâce au psychiatre Boris Cyrulnik. Rescapé de la Shoah, ce dernier la définit comme l'aptitude à surmonter des situations traumatiques, à se développer et à se projeter dans l'avenir en dépit d'événements ou de conditions chroniques terribles[6]. Dans le langage courant, par contre, l'acception psychologique de la résilience tarde encore davantage à percer. À l'aube du XXIe siècle, elle ne se trouvait pas dans *Le petit Robert*[7]. En revanche, l'édition actuelle du dictionnaire encyclopédique *Le Trésor de la langue française* comporte ce sens « figuré » : « Force morale, qualité de quelqu'un qui ne se décourage pas, ne se laisse pas abattre »[8]. Ces dernières années, le concept de résilience a vite monté en popularité, autant chez les profanes que chez les spécialistes. Comme sujet d'étude scientifique, il est devenu de plus en plus fructueux, au point de susciter trois congrès internationaux en quatre ans, dans trois régions très différentes du monde occidental[9].

Nous croyons que si ce concept avait été connu plus tôt, la critique camusienne aurait déjà apprécié sa pertinence pour appréhender Camus – tant l'homme, le penseur que l'artiste. C'est ce que nous nous proposons de faire ici. À partir d'éléments biographiques et de morceaux choisis dans le vaste corpus camusien, nous relèverons quelques traits aptes à inspirer la résilience.

2. « FACTEURS DE RISQUE » ET TRANSPOSITION LITTÉRAIRE

Un fait préalable à souligner est que Camus a lui-même expérimenté la souffrance ; il a été exposé à des « facteurs de risque », selon l'expression consacrée des psychologues[10]. Sur le plan strictement personnel, par exemple, il venait d'avoir dix-sept ans quand il reçut un diagnostic de tuberculose. Cette

---

5 M. Rutter, *Resilience in the Face of Adversity: Protective Factors and Resistance to Psychiatric Disorder*, « British Journal of Psychiatry » 1985, vol. 147, no 6, p. 608.

6 B. Cyrulnik, *Un merveilleux malheur*, Paris, Odile Jacob, 1999.

7 *Le petit Robert*, rubrique « Résilience », Paris, Le Robert, 2000, p. 2188.

8 *Le Trésor de la langue française informatisé*, rubrique « Résilience » : http://atilf.atilf.fr/dendien/scripts/tlfiv5/advanced.exe?8;s=2356356315 (consulté le 9 septembre 2015).

9 Le premier, du 7 au 10 juin 2012 à Paris ; le second, du 8 au 10 mai 2014 à Timisoara en Roumanie ; le troisième, du 22 au 24 août 2016 à l'Université du Québec à Trois-Rivières (UQTR) au Canada.

10 Bien qu'elle existe depuis des siècles, l'expression « facteurs de risque » est devenue courante en psychologie après la parution en 1951 d'un ouvrage de référence de John Bowlby, *Maternal Care and Mental Health* (Genève, WHO).

« maladie métaphysique », comme il l'appelle[11], lui fait sentir la menace de la mort en pleine jeunesse et le rongera sa vie durant par épisodes sporadiques. Mais il y a aussi des épreuves d'envergure collective : « J'ai grandi, avec tous les hommes de mon âge, aux tambours de la Première Guerre et notre histoire, depuis, n'a pas cessé d'être meurtre, injustice ou violence » (OC III, 606). Orphelin d'un père tué à la Grande Guerre, il est interpelé par la Guerre d'Espagne, la Seconde Guerre mondiale, les dictatures franquiste, fascistes, communistes, et les guerres de décolonisation dont évidemment celle de son Algérie natale. Bref, en plus d'avoir côtoyé la souffrance, Camus l'a connue dans sa chair. C'est pourquoi sa plume découle du senti. Or, comme il l'affirme dans l'introduction de *L'Homme révolté*, « parler répare » (OC III, 68). D'éminents critiques camusiens, tels Raymond Gay-Crosier[12] et Maurice Weyembergh[13], sont frappés par cette formule aussi dense que succincte. Nous observons quant à nous que celle-ci cristallise un processus de rétablissement et que, du coup, elle résume exactement le principe fondateur de la psychothérapie.

Selon Weyembergh, par « le recours à l'imagination », par son « pouvoir d'évocation et d'empathie », la littérature permet de dire symboliquement même la pire souffrance[14]. Chez Camus, le dire de la souffrance possède cette acuité. D'une part, dans la production fictionnelle, il se caractérise par un lyrisme épuré et par la précision des mots qui circonscrivent leur objet – encore qu'il puisse emprunter un langage non verbal, sur la scène de théâtre. Il couvre également une variété de causes et de contextes, ce qui lui confère un spectre très riche. D'autre part, en dehors des textes de fiction, là aussi Camus évoque abondamment la souffrance, comme le montrent les travaux d'Ève Morisi[15]. Parfois, comme dans les *Discours de Suède* qui

---

11 H. Lottman, *Albert Camus*, Paris, Seuil, 1978, p. 58.

12 R. Gay-Crosier, *Exiled in a Spiritual Geography: Albert Camus's Road to Values* [dans :] *A Writer's Topography: Space and Place in the Life and Works of Albert Camus*, éd. J. Herbeck, V. Grégoire, Leiden–Boston, Brill–Rodopi, 2015, p. 20 ; *idem*, Les *enjeux de la pensée de midi*, dans *Albert Camus : Paradigmes de l'ironie – révolte et négation affirmative*, Toronto, Paratexte, 2000, p. 183–184.

13 M. Weyembergh, *Albert Camus ou la mémoire des origines*, Bruxelles, De Boeck, 1998, p. 13 ; *idem*, La *grâce, la justice et l'amour* [dans :] *Albert Camus : l'exigence morale*, éd. A. Spiquel, A. Schaffner, Paris, Le Manuscrit, 2006, p. 182.

14 M. Weyembergh, *Albert Camus. Guerre totale et philosophie de la mesure. Réflexions sur les bombardements des villes au travers de la littérature*, « Études camusiennes » 2011, no 10, p. 145.

15 Notons le titre révélateur de sa monographie : *Albert Camus, le souci des autres* (Paris, Classiques Garnier, 2013), et de son article : *Visages de 'l'art et la douleur' chez Camus* (dans *Camus, l'artiste*, éd. S. Bastien, A. Prouteau, A. Spiquel, Presses universitaires de Rennes, 2015, p. 235–246).

témoignent de la maturité de l'auteur, les allusions à la souffrance servent justement à indiquer, telle une prescription, le devoir empathique de la fiction.

3. COMBATIVITÉ ET REFUS DE L'INACCEPTABLE

En conséquence de la souffrance, il y a d'abord la lucidité indéfectible de Camus qui est inspirante, comme en fait foi cette citation dans un documentaire sur la résilience[16] : « Le grand courage, c'est encore de tenir les yeux ouverts sur la lumière comme sur la mort » (OC I, 71). Mais surtout, la réactivité très énergique de Camus avoisine la résilience. Devant l'adversité qui frappe opiniâtrement, loin d'être tenté par la fuite géographique, comme l'étaient nombre de ses contemporains autour de la Seconde Guerre mondiale, il adopte un comportement combatif : « Je suis du côté de la lutte. L'époque s'y prête », déclare-t-il (I, 279). Il ne faut pas cesser de « lutter » contre la cruauté qui la caractérise, poursuit-il (III, 606). Le paradigme de la « lutte » prend valeur de *leitmotiv* chez lui : ce terme exact, ses dérivés, son champ lexical sont très récurrents ; nous en verrons d'autres occurrences plus loin. Le refus viscéral de Camus par rapport aux situations qu'il juge inacceptables, est susceptible de nourrir la résilience – d'autant plus que celle-ci peut être considérée comme le fruit d'une révolte devant l'injustice, selon le psychiatre Michel Hanus[17]. Ce refus de l'injustice se trouve explicite dans de nombreux écrits civiques du corpus camusien. Nous en examinons deux ci-dessous, les *Lettres à un ami allemand* et « La Crise de l'Homme », parce que dans les deux cas, la résilience est suggérée non seulement par la dynamique de la lutte, mais aussi par une aspiration prometteuse sur laquelle l'auteur conclut.

Les quatre *Lettres à un ami allemand* ont la hardiesse de condamner âprement le nazisme ; et les deux premières, de paraître en pleine Seconde Guerre mondiale. À la fois ironique et métonymique, le titre joue la carte de l'amitié, quand l'« ami » au singulier sous-entend un adversaire pluriel (OC II, 1). Vu la forme épistolaire, le corps du texte interpelle directement un « vous » (OC II, 9–29), ce qui place le belligérant tortionnaire dans un rapport de vis-à-vis, et ce qui suppose l'insoumission du locuteur. Ces astuces rhétoriques permettent aussi de mêler le ton amical et l'objection catégorique. Elles recèlent néanmoins un espoir sincère et un effort pacifiste, qui se manifestent avec

---

16 L. Marcotte, M. Chartrand, *De l'ombre à la lumière*, série documentaire télévisuelle en cinq épisodes, Montréal, Lowik Média, 2011.

17 M. Hanus, *La Résilience à quel prix? Survivre et rebondir*, Paris, Maloine, 2002, p. 22, 32, 175.

persévérance : au début des deux premières lettres, quand l'auteur affirme une intention de transparence et d'ouverture ; au début de la quatrième lettre, quand il exprime sa compréhension pour son destinataire ; puis, quand il se dit « sans haine » contre lui (OC II, 28) ; enfin, quand il en appelle à un dialogue équitable. Au final, perce une aspiration à « créer du bonheur pour protester contre l'univers du malheur » (OC II, 26). …N'est-ce pas là une illustration possible de la résilience?

Au XXIe siècle, Michel Terestchenko, qui étudie la bienveillance et l'altruisme selon une approche psychosociale, apprécie que Camus proscrive la vengeance et incarne une attitude constructive. On dirait qu'il a assimilé les *Lettres à un ami allemand*, mais peut-être aussi bien « L'exil d'Hélène » ou *Les Justes*. Il synthétise également un autre message camusien : même inutile, la contribution d'un individu qui se dresse et qui résiste, a une signification absolue, puisqu'elle sous-entend que l'humanité n'est pas perdue[18]. Ce que Terestchenko retient de Camus rappelle le sens physique de la résilience et sa portée psychologique, qui prend ici une envergure métaphysique.

Notre deuxième exemple textuel où Camus manifeste une révolte devant l'inacceptable, est la conférence qu'il prononce à l'Université Columbia de New York en 1946. L'intitulé en est arboré comme un diagnostic incisif : « La Crise de l'Homme ». L'expression n'est pas exclusive à Camus[19], mais ce dernier met une majuscule aux deux substantifs pour appuyer la gravité de l'enjeu. « Une Crise de l'Homme » sévit, scande-t-il, « puisque la mort ou la torture d'un être peut […] être examinée avec un sentiment d'indifférence […] ou d'expérimentation […] ; être envisagée autrement qu'avec l'horreur et le scandale qu'elle devrait susciter » (OC II, 739). Après avoir exposé les symptômes de cette « Crise », l'auteur en dépiste la racine : « une perversion des valeurs » qui fausse le jugement (OC II, 740). Mais malgré son insistance à analyser la « Crise », Camus ouvre l'horizon vers une quête prometteuse – comme dans les *Lettres à un ami allemand*, et comme s'il indiquait de nouveau la direction de la résilience : Il faut créer des « valeurs positives » (OC II, 744) ; ce monde doit cesser d'être empoisonné

---

18 M. Terestchenko, *Banalité du mal, banalité du bien*, conférence prononcée le 1er juin 2007 dans le cadre d'un cycle de conférences organisé par l'association philosophique Agora à Orange (France), http://www.agorange.net/Conf_Terestchenko.pdf (recherche du 28 septembre 2015).

19 Le philosophe Emmanuel Mounier la dilue parmi d'autres expressions connexes : « la crise de la civilisation », « la crise du XXe siècle », « par-delà la crise »… (*Œuvres, vol. 1 : 1931–1939*, Paris, Seuil, 1961, p. 137 ; *Œuvres, vol. 3 : 1944–1950*, Paris, Seuil, 1962, p. 204, 207).

de violences, et devenir « celui de l'homme et de la femme, du travail fécond et du loisir réfléchi » (OC II, 746).

4. DES « FACTEURS DE PROTECTION » : LE BEAU, LA NATURE, L'AMOUR

Selon Camus, la recherche de l'équité s'arrime à un idéal de beauté, celui-ci étant tout aussi nécessaire que celle-là. Sans les deux principes helléniques que sont la mesure et la beauté, nul apaisement possible : « Il n'est pas de lutte qui, sans le frein de ces mêmes valeurs, ne s'étende indéfiniment » (OC III, 599). Camus reconnaît ces deux tendances chez son contemporain le poète René Char, héritier des Grecs lui aussi, mû par un besoin vital de justice autant que d'émotion esthétique. Camus lui voue donc une estime immense[20]. Quand il déplore le contexte de la guerre où l'homme, exsangue et appauvri, perd de vue « la beauté du monde et des visages » (OC II, 437), Camus admire Char qui, même les armes à la main, « aux prises [...] avec l'histoire la plus enchevêtrée, n'a pas craint d'y exalter la beauté dont l'histoire justement nous donnait une soif désespérée » (OC IV, 620).

Au risque de paraître anachronique, nous ajouterions que le prosateur de la résilience, qu'est Camus, a pour homologue le poète de la résilience, qu'est Char. Car ce dernier illustre précisément le phénomène de la résilience à l'aide d'images poétiques, entre autres dans les vers suivants :

> [...] rien ne fait naufrage ou ne se plaît aux cendres ;
> Et qui sait voir la terre aboutir à des fruits,
> Point ne l'émeut l'échec quoiqu'il ait tout perdu[21].

Ce que Camus puise dans la poésie de Char s'approche effectivement de la résilience, si l'on en croit les commentaires qu'il émet dans une émission radiophonique consacrée au poète : Avec cette « œuvre née de la Résistance », « au milieu de nos citadelles démantelées » et des « ténèbres », « la Beauté, enfin, s'élève » (OC II, 767). « Les paroles de guérison » « purifient l'ulcère du monde » et annoncent « les temps de la fertilité » (OC II, 764–765), une « grande chaleur fraternelle où l'homme produit ses meilleurs fruits ». Cette

---

20 « René Char est le plus grand événement dans la poésie française depuis Rimbaud » (OC III, 867) ; « je tiens René Char pour notre plus grand poète vivant » (OC IV, 618).

21 R. Char, *Redonnez-leur* [dans :] *Fureur et mystère*, *Œuvres complètes*, éd. J. Roudaut, coll. « Bibliothèque de la Pléiade », Paris, Gallimard, 1983, p. 242.

« voix [...] accompagne notre navigation difficile et nous parle sans relâche d'une Ithaque où nous aborderons [...] et où nous retrouverons enfin la simple joie d'être homme » (OC II, 767–768). Camus renchérit plus tard, dans sa préface aux *Poésies* de Char : Ce dernier « donne ses formules à notre malheur comme à notre renaissance », et procure un « secours ». Il « a jalonné une route » où « nous réapprenons à marcher » et où « la lumière point ». Il est « le poète de nos lendemains » (OC IV, 619–620). Cependant, dans une lettre à Char, c'est avec un style minimal que Camus cerne la résilience. Le ton de la confidence fait sentir l'impact intime de sa lecture : « Avec vous, le poème devient courage et fierté. On peut enfin s'en aider, pour vivre »[22].

Camus investit la beauté de propriétés psychologiques et spirituelles quasi thérapeutiques. Tantôt il la définit comme « vertu vivante » (OC III, 299) ; tantôt il l'appelle « l'amie, l'amante, la compagne de nos jours » ; tantôt il affirme qu'elle tient lieu « d'espérance » « face au nihilisme » (OC IV, 620). Il bénéficie de ce que les spécialistes de la résilience appellent un « facteur de protection ». Nous avons nommé plus haut des « facteurs de risque », selon l'expression qu'utilisent les psychologues ; les spécialistes de la résilience, quant à eux, cherchent plutôt des « facteurs de protection », qui favorisent la résilience[23]. Ainsi, la sensibilité esthétique de Camus en serait un.

Et il y en a d'autres, puisque Camus traite la nature, voire le cosmos, avec la même déférence qu'il traite le beau artistique, parce qu'elle lui fait ressentir un émerveillement similaire. Comme plusieurs de ses personnages, il tire une nourriture substantielle du contact avec la nature, que ce soit des phénomènes grandioses qui soulèvent un sentiment cosmique, ou des sensations plus fines. Il lui est même arrivé d'imaginer un personnage « guéri de ses déchirements par la seule et longue contemplation d'un paysage » (OC II, 1075) : l'effet salvateur reçoit ici un traitement hyperbolique. Dans la veine de la sensualité, il y a également les joies du corps et de l'amour, que Camus appelle « cette grande force » (OC III, 867) ; comme l'observe Gaëtan Brulotte, le lecteur accueille ce champ d'expériences comme libérateur[24]. Nous pouvons donc voir des « facteurs de protection » dans les vibrations fortifiantes que procurent à Camus la nature, la sensualité et l'émotion amoureuse.

---

22 Lettre datée du 21 septembre 1948 [dans :] A. Camus, R. Char, *Correspondance, 1946–1959*, éd. F. Planeille, Paris, Gallimard, 2007, p. 38.

23 Rutter a orienté l'étude de la résilience vers celle des « protective factors », comme l'expose le titre de cet article qui a fait date : *Resilience in the Face of Adversity: Protective Factors and Resistance to Psychiatric Disorder* (M. Rutter, *op.cit.*, p. 598).

24 G. Brulotte, *Survie d'Albert Camus*, « Liberté » 1994, vol. 36, no 6, p. 141.

5. LANGAGE ACCESSIBLE ET HUMILITÉ, MAIS MESSAGE EXIGEANT

Brulotte évoque la réception positive que récolte l'écriture sensuelle de Camus, mais en fait, le public est très accueillant à l'endroit de l'auteur en général. De plus, il provient de divers horizons et de toutes générations. Ce succès notoire s'avère une condition nécessaire à la récupération vulgarisatrice que nous avons relevée en introduction et qui a déclenché notre réflexion. Il y a alors lieu de se demander ce qui permet une telle popularité. Premièrement, Camus emploie le plus souvent un langage accessible aux gens ordinaires, une syntaxe claire, sans mots superflus. Certaines assertions ont un poids capital tout en étant des bijoux de simplicité. Des exemples convaincants se trouvent dans *Caligula*, avec le fameux constat du héros : « les hommes meurent et ils ne sont pas heureux » (OC I, 332) ; et la phrase de Cherea, symétrique dans son antinomie : « J'ai envie de vivre et d'être heureux » (OC I, 369). Outre la sobriété du style, les fondements de la pensée camusienne contribuent à l'accessibilité de l'auteur, parce qu'ils ne découlent pas de constructions intellectuelles, font moins appel aux ressources cérébrales qu'au sens commun. Ainsi, Camus dit convoquer la « notion d'*homme* », l'« *instinct* moral » (OC I, 934–935) et la « révolte la plus *instinctive* » (OC III, 299 ; ce sont nos italiques).

L'humilité contribue également à son accessibilité. Or, les psychiatres le soulignent, la résilience ne conduit pas à une impression d'invulnérabilité ; cette observation constitue maintenant une assise dans la théorie sur la résilience[25]. À l'abri de la surestimation, Camus sait que « tout effort humain est relatif » (OC II, 532). Il lui arrive même de ressentir avec bouleversement l'impuissance, comme dans sa « Lettre aux Japonais » (OC III, 869) ou dans sa « Réponse à un appel des intellectuels hongrois »[26] – mais il se ressaisit aussitôt en exprimant un vif encouragement. Par ailleurs, d'autres traits chez Camus impliquent une posture humble : Weyembergh mentionne la quête de sens[27] ; Alexis Lager, l'absence de mépris[28], puisque

---

25 Bien que la personne résiliente ait déjà été vue comme invulnérable (*The Invulnerable Child*, ed. J. Anthony, B. Cohler, New York–London, Guilford, 1987), aujourd'hui cette perception est contredite, sinon nuancée (voir M. Hanus, *op.cit.*, p. 167, 217).

26 A. Camus, *Écrits libertaires (1948–1960)*, éd. Lou Marin, Marseille, Égrégores Éditions, 2013 [2008], p. 202.

27 M. Weyembergh, *Albert Camus. Guerre totale et philosophie de la mesure. Réflexions sur les bombardements des villes au travers de la littérature*, « Études camusiennes » 2011, no 10, p. 144–145.

28 A. Lager, *Deux visages de l'artiste selon Camus : René Char et Roger Marin du Gard*, dans *Camus, l'artiste*, éd. S. Bastien, A. Prouteau, A. Spiquel, Presses universitaires de Rennes, 2015, p. 72.

Camus conseille de « lutter » contre les nihilistes sans pour autant s'ériger en juge (OC IV, 241).

Chez lui, l'accessibilité du langage et du contenu ne mène pas au laxisme, et la modestie n'empêche pas la fermeté. S'il se fait comprendre par la majorité, il ne veut pas de complaisance et réfute l'immobilisme – des attitudes d'ailleurs contraires à la résilience. Les expressions « instinct moral » et « notion d'homme » que nous avons citées, sont tirées d'un article dont le titre est déjà exigeant : « Au service de l'homme » (OC I, 933). Selon le corps de cet article, est moral ce qui *sert* l'homme « au lieu de le dégrader » (OC I, 935), ce qui porte « à être courageux et juste » (OC I, 933). Les prises de position de Camus ont le potentiel non seulement d'éveiller les consciences, mais aussi de les secouer avec tonus.

Dans l'immédiat après-guerre, Camus « ne se laisse pas emporter par l'immense cortège des morts […] et il reste debout », mentionne Thierry Fabre en reconduisant la métaphore physique de la résilience[29]. L'écrivain récuse l'apitoiement et le ressentiment (d'autres attitudes contraires à la résilience), choisit d'intituler « Espoir » la collection qu'il dirige chez Gallimard, pendant que ses éditoriaux dans *Combat* mettent vaillamment à l'avant-plan les responsabilités de la France afin qu'elle se relève et se rebâtisse. Quant à la conférence qu'il adresse aux chrétiens dans un couvent dominicain de Paris, au début il signale un point commun avec ses auditeurs : « Je partage avec vous la même horreur du Mal, confie-t-il, […] et je continue à lutter contre cet univers où des enfants souffrent et meurent » (OC II, 471). Mais par la suite, la rigueur de l'argumentation est de nature à provoquer une remise en question et à lancer un défi ; c'est encore pour faire avancer les choses. En somme, Camus atteint le plus grand nombre grâce à un langage simple, mais il ébranle le récepteur pour le faire cheminer ; voilà pourquoi on a pu le vulgariser comme modèle de résilience.

6. HUMANISME ET RESPONSABILITÉ SOCIALE

D'autres éléments sont en mesure de marquer les assoiffés de résilience parmi les lecteurs camusiens. L'humanisme, certainement. Jamais le désenchantement de Camus, si amer qu'il soit, n'annihile sa foi en l'homme ; et son amour de la vie persiste, même déchiré. Comme l'observe Jean-François

---

29 T. Favre, *La pensée de midi* [dans :] *Pourquoi Camus?*, éd. E. Castillo, Paris, Éditions Philippe Rey, 2013, p. 184.

Mattéi, « loin d'en vouloir au destin [...], il tira de l'injustice qu'il ressentait un amour plus puissant encore »[30]. À son image, le narrateur, dans *La Peste*, veut témoigner de la douleur humaine, mais aussi de ce qui suscite l'admiration. La conclusion de Rieux : « il y a dans les hommes plus de choses à admirer que de choses à mépriser » (OC II, 248), survient après une année extrêmement éprouvante. De surcroît, elle est reprise d'un article que Camus avait publié quelques temps auparavant (OC I, 935) : la conviction qu'elle renferme en est donc renforcée.

Elle correspond au plus haut niveau de résilience, c'est-à-dire la « croissance post-traumatique »[31]. Les recherches récentes établissent en effet différents niveaux possibles de résilience[32]. Le premier niveau équivaut au rétablissement, au bon fonctionnement de l'individu après une situation traumatique sévère. Le second donne lieu à une force accrue ; l'individu se trouve plus outillé, mieux armé pour d'autres épreuves éventuelles. Le troisième, enfin, est la croissance post-traumatique : l'individu en sort transformé, grandi, conduit plus loin qu'il ne serait allé sans la situation traumatique, parce qu'il y a reconfiguration interne de croyances et de cognitions, comme l'apprentissage d'une vision philosophique, d'un nouveau sens à la vie. C'est ce dont font preuve Camus dans la citation de Mattéi (« il tira de l'injustice qu'il ressentait un amour plus puissant encore ») et Rieux quand il conclut qu'il y a en l'homme davantage « à admirer » qu' « à mépriser ». C'est aussi ce dont fait preuve Joseph Grand après avoir réchappé de la peste : lui qui était inhibé par la timidité et l'échec sentimental, prend confiance et écrit sa lettre à Jeanne. L'écriture velléitaire de son roman aboutira, peut-on en déduire. Rétrospectivement, Camus met en relief ce phénomène selon lequel de graves difficultés apportent une sorte de gain : « Les souffrances et les luttes de cette époque [les années quarante] n'ont pas été absolument vaines pour ceux qui y ont survécu ; la nécessité même de ces épreuves était alors un enseignement »[33].

Rieux affirme envers et contre tout « l'exigence généreuse du bonheur » (OC II, 128), ce qu'il y a « de fier en chacun de nous » (OC II, 130). Camus

---

30 J.-F. Mattéi, *Sonate pour un homme bon* [dans :] *Pourquoi Camus?*, éd. E. Castillo, Paris, Éditions Philippe Rey, 2013, p. 62.

31 L. Calhoun, R. Tedeschi, *The Foundations of Posttraumatic Growth : New Considerations*, « Psychological Inquiry » 2004, vol. 15, no 1, p. 93–102.

32 S. Lepore, T. Revenson, *Resilience and Posttraumatic Growth : Recovery, Resistance and Reconfiguration*, dans *Handbook of Posttraumatic Growth. Research and Practice*, éd. L. Calhoun, R. Tedeschi, New York, Psychology Press, 2014 [2006], p. 24–46.

33 A. Camus, *Écrits libertaires (1948–1960)...*, p. 174–175.

écrira ailleurs : « ce qui, en l'homme, est toujours à défendre » (OC III, 77) et « refuse de mourir » (OC II, 495). Il postule ainsi une vitalité à préserver coûte que coûte. Aussi, en tant qu'essayiste et que journaliste, il clame la dignité de la personne et le droit au respect, d'autant plus fort qu'il se débat à contre-courant, dans un monde où ces valeurs sont dévastées.

Outre la pulsion de vie et la philanthropie authentique, une autre qualité fondamentale chez lui agit comme « facteur de protection », selon la terminologie des psychologues : la bonté[34]. Dans *La Peste*, elle a partie liée avec la figure du médecin, qui conjugue l'abnégation et l'attention à autrui. C'est avec sincérité que Rieux prend soin de ses patients. De plus, le personnage qu'il propose comme modèle d'héroïsme pendant l'épidémie, Grand, n'a à son actif que la « bonté » (OC II, 128) ; cette vertu s'en trouve hautement valorisée. Tarrou lui accorde même le pouvoir transcendant de contrer la maladie, quand il écrit au sujet de la mère Rieux : « un regard où se lisait tant de bonté serait toujours plus fort que la peste » (OC II, 113). En outre, Lager met en lumière une autre puissance réparatrice chez Camus : la capacité de pardon[35] – une faculté que possèdent les résilients, selon les spécialistes[36]. Mais quel que soit le chemin qu'elle emprunte, la bienfaisance incite à la résilience. À ce compte, Stepan, dans *Les Justes*, serait le parfait contre-exemple. Les années de bagne pendant lesquelles il a enduré des sévices corporels, ont laissé des séquelles psychologiques en plus des cicatrices : l'aigreur qui l'anime. Cet épisode traumatisant lui sert à justifier son absence de réserve face au terrorisme et au meurtre, au point que Stepan a l'effet d'un repoussoir, comparé à l'idéal pacifiant qu'exprime ailleurs Camus : « vous n'avez pas […] tiré prétexte du sacrifice de tant d'hommes pour hurler de nouvelles haines »[37].

Camus ne sépare pas l'épanouissement de l'individu et celui de la communauté, comme l'attestent de multiples écrits et interventions. Or, des travaux récents élargissent le concept de résilience à l'échelle collective[38]. En quoi le sens de la responsabilité sociale chez Camus est-il pertinent, dans

---

34 C'est ce qui frappe Mattéi, selon le titre de son essai : *Sonate pour un homme bon*, *op.cit.*, p. 56–57, 65.

35 A. Lager, *op.cit.*, p. 72.

36 L. Calhoun, R. Tedeschi, *The Foundations of Posttraumatic Growth : an Expanded Framework*, dans *Handbook of Posttraumatic Growth. Research and Practice*, New York, Psychology Press, 2014 [2006], p. 5–6.

37 A. Camus, *Écrits libertaires (1948–1960)…*, p. 176.

38 L. Calhoun, R. Tedeschi, *The Foundations of Posttraumatic Growth : New Considerations…*, p. 97; *idem*, The *Foundations of Posttraumatic Growth : an Expanded Framework…*, p. 12.

cette perspective? Il jette des bases sur lesquelles peut s'élever la résilience. Depuis le jeune reporter qu'il était en Algérie, le tribun libertaire mène de vigoureux combats en faveur des groupes sociaux déshérités. Quand il exhorte à « se dresse[r] devant l'oppression » (OC III, 986), il emploie le verbe inhérent à la définition physique de la résilience. On reconnaît aussi ce champ sémantique dans sa réponse à la question « Qu'est-ce que le peuple ? C'est ce qui dans une nation ne veut jamais s'agenouiller » (OC II, 520). C'est peut-être néanmoins dans la fiction que réside le meilleur enseignement de résilience sur le plan collectif : dans le roman *La Peste*. Devant l'épidémie destructrice, Rieux suscite une généreuse solidarité autour de lui, en l'incarnant lui-même ; à son instar, plusieurs personnes s'unissent et se dévouent, et la cohésion qui en résulte renforce la communauté dans le combat contre la peste.

VERS UNE CONCLUSION

Serge Doubrovsky, qui a fait carrière aux États-Unis, a détaché les trois points de l'œuvre camusienne les plus significatifs pour le lectorat nord-américain : le courage devant l'échec, l'amour des hommes tels qu'ils sont, et la confiance en l'homme[39]. Chacun de ces trois points nourrit la résilience, comme le montrent les experts[40], mais le courage devant l'échec est le plus à propos. Char, quant à lui, détecte une propriété contiguë : « l'œuvre de Camus est, sera infiniment *utile* aux êtres, en grand nombre, tournés vers une sorte d'entéléchie »[41]. Comme l'implique cette notion aristotélicienne d'entéléchie, l'œuvre camusienne permet la réalisation de soi, amène le lecteur à s'édifier. Pour Fabre, elle offre un « viatique »[42]. Pour Morisi, elle coupe court à l'omnipotence possible de la douleur[43]. En fin de compte, ces quelques témoignages

---

39 S. Doubrovsky, *Camus et l'Amérique*, dans *Parcours critique II (1959–1991)*, éd. I. Grell, Grenoble, Ellug, 2006, p. 45 [« La nouvelle revue française » 1961, no 98, p. 295].

40 K. Reivich, A. Shatté, *The Resilience Factor: 7 Keys to Finding your Inner Strength and Overcome Life's Hurdles*, New York, Broadway Books, 2002.

41 Lettre de Char à Gaston Gallimard, datée du 21 mai 1962, reproduite en 2009 sur le site internet *L'histoire de la Pléiade*, http://www.la-pleiade.fr/La-vie-de-la-Pleiade/L-histoire-de-la-Pleiade/Lettres-de-Rene-Char-a-Gaston-Gallimard-1962 (consulté le 15 décembre 2015). L'italique est de Char.

42 T. Favre, *op.cit.*, p. 184.

43 È. Morisi, *Visages de 'l'art et la douleur' chez Camus* [dans :] *Camus, l'artiste*, éd. S. Bastien, A. Prouteau, A. Spiquel, Presses universitaires de Rennes, 2015, p. 238.

laissent croire qu'elle fournit un antidote en sollicitant les ressources intérieures les plus profondes.

Elle y parvient grâce à ses visées éthiques et à une conscience existentielle aiguë, cet état d'esprit que cerne Camus par des oxymores : une « plénitude angoissée » (OC III, 597), un « optimisme tragique » (OC II, 764 ; OC IV, 618). On peut y voir une manière de dire la résilience avant la lettre. Le discours scientifique sur la résilience se caractérise en effet par des oxymores semblables, depuis le titre d'une monographie majeure de Cyrulnik, *Un merveilleux malheur*, dont l'intitulé d'un chapitre comprend l'expression *Soleil noir*[44]. C'est que le véritable résilient garde en lui « une souffrance insondable »[45]. Il n'évolue pas dans la candeur ou dans le déni du tragique, mais en en mesurant tout le poids – comme dans la phrase conclusive : « Il faut imaginer Sisyphe heureux » (OC I, 304).

Mais selon Lager, la personne de Camus autant que son œuvre « nous construisent, nous élèvent et nous révèlent à nous-mêmes »[46]. À propos de la personne, nous avons évoqué le défi que représente la tuberculose ; André Abbou examine de son côté le sentiment d'échec qui accable Camus dans les sphères familiale et professionnelle, à l'époque de la genèse de *La Peste*[47] puis de *La Chute*[48]. Mais selon Abbou, l'écrivain compense cet état dépressif par un travail énergétique et salutaire sur soi : la création littéraire. Quoi qu'il en soit, les morceaux – de l'œuvre, de la pensée ou de l'homme – que nous avons exposés ici, servent la démonstration, dans le champ littéraire, du concept psychologique de résilience, avec la sagesse régénératrice qui lui est propre. Camus l'héliotrope, qui se tourne vers le soleil, qui énonce « la postérité du soleil »[49], ressort comme un phare en matière de résilience.

---

44 B. Cyrulnik, *op.cit.*, p. 115.

45 M. Hanus, *op.cit.*, p. 11. Voir aussi B. Cyrulnik, *op.cit.*, p. 22–24.

46 A. Lager, *op.cit.*, p. 64.

47 A. Abbou, *Sous le soleil du père et de l'histoire. Dialogue avec un mythe personnel fondateur dans* La Peste, « Europe » 1999, no 846, p. 112–117.

48 A. Abbou, *Albert Camus entre les lignes*, Paris, Séguier, 2009, p. 16–17, 33–34, 51, 72, 83.

49 C'est le titre de son livre écrit avec Char (OC IV, 669). Notons aussi le titre de deux monographies dont l'antithèse rejoint les oxymores cités plus haut : *Albert Camus. Soleil et ombre* (R. Grenier, Paris, Gallimard, 1987) et *L'Ombre d'un homme qui marche au soleil. Réflexions sur Albert Camus* (M. Bay, préf. C. Camus, Montpellier, Éditions Chèvre-Feuille étoilée, 2004).

BIBLIOGRAPHIE

Œuvres d'Albert Camus

Écrits libertaires (1948–1960), éd. L. Marin, Marseille, Égrégores Éditions, 2013 [2008].

Dans la coll. « Bibliothèque de la Pléiade » chez Gallimard :

Œuvres complètes I : 1931–1944, éd. J. Lévi-Valensi, 2006 : *L'envers et l'endroit*, p. 69–72 ; *Le Mythe de Sisyphe*, p. 217–304 ; *Caligula*, p. 323–388 ; *Au service de l'homme*, p. 933–935.

Œuvres complètes II : 1944–1948, éd. J. Lévi-Valensi, 2006 : *Lettres à un ami allemand*, p. 1–19 ; *La Peste*, p. 31–248 ; *Le siècle de la peur*, p. 436–438 ; *L'incroyant et les chrétiens*, p. 470–474 ; *Le Témoin de la liberté*, p. 488–495 ; *Conférence au couvent de Latour-Maubourg*, p. 502–512 ; *Ils ne passeront pas*, p. 520–521 ; *Le Mouvement national de libération*, p. 531–532 ; *La Crise de l'Homme*, p. 737–748 ; *Ce soir le rideau se lève sur... René Char*, p. 764–768 ; *Carnets 1935–1948*, p. 793–1125.

Œuvres complètes III : 1949–1956, éd. R. Gay-Crosier, 2008 : *L'Homme révolté*, p. 61–324; *L'Été*, p. 565–623 ; *Interview au* Diário *de São Paulo*, p. 866–867 ; *Lettre aux Japonais*, p. 869 ; *Hommage à un journaliste exilé* », p. 982–988 ; *Message à de jeunes Français en faveur de la Hongrie*, p. 1135–1137.

Œuvres complètes IV : 1957–1959, éd. R. Gay-Crosier, 2008 : *Discours de Suède*, p. 235–265 ; *Préface à l'édition allemande des* Poésies *de René Char*, p. 617–620 ; *La Postérité du soleil*, p. 669–737.

Ouvrages consultés

Abbou, A., *Albert Camus, entre les lignes. 1955–1959 : Adieu à la littérature ou fausse sortie?*, Paris, Séguier, 2009.

Abbou, A., *Sous le soleil du père et de l'histoire. Dialogue avec un mythe personnel fondateur dans* La Peste, « Europe » 1999, no 846, p. 104–118.

Bay, M., *L'Ombre d'un homme qui marche au soleil. Réflexions sur Albert Camus*, préf. Camus, C., Montpellier, Éditions Chèvre-Feuille étoilée, 2004.

Bowlby, J., *Maternal Care and Mental Health*, Genève, World Health Organization, 1951.

Brulotte, G., *Survie d'Albert Camus*, « Liberté » 1994, vol. 36, no 6, p. 140–148.

Calhoun, L., Tedeschi R., *The Foundations of Posttraumatic Growth: an Expanded Framework* [dans :] *Handbook of Posttraumatic Growth. Research and Practice*, New York, Psychology Press, 2014 [2006], p. 2–23.

Calhoun, L., Tedeschi, R., *The Foundations of Posttraumatic Growth: New Considerations*, « Psychological Inquiry » 2004, vol. 15, no 1, p. 93–102.

Camus, A., Char, R., *Correspondance, 1946–1959*, éd. F. Planeille, Paris, Gallimard, 2007.

Char, R., Lettres à Gaston Gallimard, 1962, reproduites en 2009 sur le site internet *L'histoire de la Pléiade* : http://www.la-pleiade.fr/La-vie-de-la-Pleiade/L-histoire-de-la-Pleiade/Lettres-de-Rene-Char-a-Gaston-Gallimard-1962 (consulté le 15 décembre 2015).

Char, R., *Œuvres complètes*, éd. J. Roudaut, coll. « Bibliothèque de la Pléiade », Paris, Gallimard, 1983.

Char, R., *Redonnez-leur* [dans :] *Fureur et mystère, Œuvres complètes*, éd. J. Roudaut, coll. « Bibliothèque de la Pléiade », Paris, Gallimard, 1983.

Le Courage de changer, Virginia, Al-Anon Family Group Headquarters, 1994.

Cyrulnik, B., *Un merveilleux malheur*, Paris, Odile Jacob, 1999.

Doubrovsky, S., *Camus et l'Amérique* [dans :] *Parcours critique II (1959–1991)*, éd. I. Grell, Grenoble, Ellug, 2006, p. 43–46 [« La nouvelle revue française » 1961, no 98, p. 292–296].

Favre, T., *La pensée de midi* [dans :] *Pourquoi Camus?*, éd. E. Castillo, Paris, Éditions Philippe Rey, 2013, p. 183–190.

Fondation québécoise de la déficience intellectuelle, http://www.lesupport.ca/ (recherche du 15 septembre 2015).

Gay-Crosier, R., *Les enjeux de la pensée de midi*, dans *Albert Camus : Paradigmes de l'ironie – révolte et négation affirmative*, Toronto, Paratexte, 2000, p. 179–192.

Gay-Crosier, R., *Exiled in a Spiritual Geography: Albert Camus's Road to Values* [dans :] *A Writer's Topography: Space and Place in the Life and Works of Albert Camus*, éd. J. Herbeck, V. Grégoire, Leiden–Boston, Brill–Rodopi, 2015, p. 20–33.

Grenier, R., *Albert Camus. Soleil et ombre*, Paris, Gallimard, 1987.

Hanus, M., *La Résilience à quel prix? Survivre et rebondir*, Paris, Maloine, 2002.

Ionescu, S., *Origine et évolution du concept de résilience* [dans :] *Résilience. Connaissances de base*, éd. B. Cyrulnik, G. Jorland, Paris, Odile Jacob, 2012, p. 19–32.

Lager, A., *Deux visages de l'artiste selon Camus : René Char et Roger Marin du Gard* [dans :] *Camus, l'artiste*, éd. S. Bastien, A. Prouteau, A. Spiquel, Presses universitaires de Rennes, 2015, p. 63–73.

Lepore S., Revenson, T., *Resilience and Posttraumatic Growth: Recovery, Resistance and Reconfiguration*, dans *Handbook of Posttraumatic Growth. Research and Practice*, éd. L. Calhoun, R. Tedeschi, New York, Psychology Press, 2014 [2006], p. 24–46.

Lottman, H., *Albert Camus*, Paris, Seuil, 1978.

Marcotte, L., Chartrand, M., *De l'ombre à la lumière*, série documentaire télévisuelle en cinq épisodes, Montréal, Lowik Média, 2011.

Mattéi, J.-F., *Sonate pour un homme bon* [dans :] *Pourquoi Camus?*, éd. E. Castillo, Paris, Éditions Philippe Rey, 2013, p. 55–69.

Montero Medina, J.F., *Vivamos Nuestra Historia*, Quintana Roo, Municipio de Felipe Carrillo Puerto, 2011.

Morisi, È., *Albert Camus, le souci des autres*, Paris, Classiques Garnier, 2013.

Morisi, È., *Visages de « l'art et la douleur » chez Camus* [dans :] *Camus, l'artiste*, éd. S. Bastien, A. Prouteau, A. Spiquel, Presses universitaires de Rennes, 2015, p. 235–246.

Mounier, E., *Œuvres, vol. 1 : 1931–1939*, Paris, Seuil, 1961.

Mounier, E., *Œuvres, vol. 3 : 1944–1950*, Paris, Seuil, 1962.

Le petit Robert, Paris, Le Robert, 2000.

Reivich, K., Shatté, A., *The Resilience Factor: 7 Keys to Finding your Inner Strength and Overcome Life's Hurdles*, New York, Broadway Books, 2002.

Rutter, M., *Resilience in the Face of Adversity: Protective Factors and Resistance to Psychiatric Disorder*, « British Journal of Psychiatry » 1985, vol. 147, no 6, p. 598–611.

Terestchenko, T., *Banalité du mal, banalité du bien*, conférence prononcée le 1er juin 2007 dans le cadre d'un cycle de conférences organisé par l'association philosophique Agora à Orange, http://www.agorange.net/Conf_Terestchenko.pdf (recherche du 28 septembre 2015).

The Invulnerable Child, éd. J. Anthony, B. Cohler, New York–London, Guilford, 1987.

Le Trésor de la langue française informatisé, http://atilf.atilf.fr/ (recherche du 9 septembre 2015).

Weyembergh, M., *Albert Camus. Guerre totale et philosophie de la mesure. Réflexions sur les bombardements des villes au travers de la littérature*, « Études camusiennes » 2011, no 10, p. 136–150.

Weyembergh, M., *Albert Camus ou La mémoire des origines*, Bruxelles, De Boeck, 1998.

Weyembergh, M., *La grâce, la justice et l'amour* [dans :] *Albert Camus : l'exigence morale*, éd. A. Spiquel, et A. Schaffner, Paris, Le Manuscrit, 2006, p. 165–185.

Le droit et le devoir de tuer : sémantiques du meurtre dans *L'Homme révolté*

THÉODORE CAPONIS

LES MOTS DU MEURTRE

En avril 1946, à mi-chemin entre la publication du *Mythe de Sisyphe* et celle de *L'Homme révolté*, Camus écrit dans ses *Carnets* :

> Révolte. Commencement : « Le seul problème moral vraiment sérieux c'est le meurtre. Le reste vient après. Mais de savoir si je puis tuer cet autre devant moi, ou consentir à ce qu'il soit tué, savoir que je ne sais rien avant de savoir si je puis donner la mort, voilà ce qu'il faut apprendre »[1].

Après le seul problème philosophique vraiment sérieux du suicide traité dans le premier essai, le meurtre devient le seul problème moral vraiment sérieux dans le second. Camus définit *L'homme révolté* comme étant un effort pour comprendre son temps, celui du crime logique, et lui donne comme propos de « poursuivre, devant le meurtre et la révolte, une réflexion commencée autour du suicide et de la notion d'absurde »[2]. La progression de l'absurde vers la révolte passe donc par le meurtre, et le choix des titres en est une parfaite illustration : « L'absurde et le meurtre » pour l'introduction et « Révolte et meurtre » pour la première section du dernier chapitre. Également, le mot *meurtre* est un des plus récursifs de la table des matières, derrière ceux de *révolte* et de *terrorisme* ; et une simple analyse lexicométrique atteste les dires de Roger Grenier qui considère que « le véritable sujet de *L'Homme révolté*,

---

1 A. Camus, *Carnets II. Janvier 1942 – mars 1951*, Paris, Gallimard, 1964, 2013, p. 176.

2 A. Camus, *L'Homme révolté*, Paris, Gallimard, 1951, p. 17.

celui qui resurgit à chaque page, est comment l'homme, au nom de la révolte, s'accommode du crime »[3] : le mot *crime* est presque aussi récurrent dans le texte que les deux mots-pivots de l'œuvre : *homme* et *révolte* (respectivement 526, 539 et 578 occurrences).

En tant que lecteur – plutôt que commentateur – de Camus, ses mots m'intéressent autant que ses idées. En tout cas, ils en sont aussi importants. Camus se considère artiste plutôt que philosophe, justement parce qu'il dit penser « selon les mots et non selon les idées »[4]. On ne peut que constater en fait que les mots occupent une place bien particulière au sein de l'univers camusien. Dans *La Peste,* Tarrou considère que tout le malheur des hommes vient de « ce qu'ils ne tenaient pas un langage clair »[5] ; dans *Les Justes,* Kaliayev interdit à Skouratov d'employer le *mot* même d'assassinat ; et la logique de *L'Homme révolté* est celle de « s'efforcer au langage clair pour ne pas épaissir le mensonge universel »[6].

Afin d'essayer de comprendre la place du meurtre dans la dynamique du voyage philosophique de Camus de l'absurde vers la révolte, j'ai choisi donc d'en examiner les sémantiques dans *L'Homme révolté.* Pour cela, j'ai eu recours à la technique d'analyse des champs sémantiques développée par le Centre de lexicologie politique de Saint-Cloud telle que présentée par Régine Robin dans son ouvrage *Histoire et linguistique* (1973). Cette technique postule que la recherche du sens d'un mot donné, au sein d'un texte donné, nécessite la déstructuration de ce texte et sa recomposition selon une *lisibilité significative.* Ainsi, le texte est réordonné en différents réseaux qui sont en relation avec le mot étudié sous toutes ces déclinaisons :

- les réseaux des relations thématiques (*associations* et *oppositions*) ;
- le réseau des qualifications ;
- les réseaux verbaux (*fonctions de* et *fonctions sur*).

Malgré ses limites, cette méthode a parfaitement servi le but recherché[7]. L'examen des réseaux tissés par les mots qui entourent la notion de meurtre chez Camus m'a permis d'en identifier tous les aspects. Je les ai classés en différentes catégories sémantiques qui permettent de visualiser assez clairement

---

3 R. Grenier, *Albert Camus. Soleil et ombre*, Paris, Gallimard, 1987, p. 239.

4 A. Camus, *Carnets II*..., p. 150.

5 A. Camus, *La Peste*, Paris, Gallimard, 1947, p. 229.

6 A. Camus, *L'Homme révolté*..., p. 356.

7 Pour plus de détails sur cette technique de recherche, voir R. Robin, *Approches des champs sémantiques : les expériences du Centre de lexicologie politique de Saint-Cloud, Histoire et linguistique*, Paris, Armand Colin, 1973, p. 139–158.

son raisonnement face au meurtre. J'en rapporte les quatre principales dans le texte qui suit :

- les sources du meurtre ;
- les cibles du meurtre ;
- le meurtre dans sa relation avec l'absurde et la révolte ;
- et la dualité face au meurtre.

AUX SOURCES DU MEURTRE : DES HOMMES ET DES INSTANTS

Le réseau des associations se présente comme un vaste ensemble de connections, 506 en tout. Il montre notamment que Camus fait appel à un large éventail de personnalités littéraires, philosophiques et historiques afin de penser le meurtre. Ces personnages sont appréciés en fonction de leur rapport au meurtre : tuer ou non, justifier le meurtre ou non.

Du côté littéraire d'abord, on retrouve au sein de l'entourage sémantique du meurtre Dostoïevski et son héros Ivan Karamazov (18 connections), étranglé par la contradiction de haïr la peine de mort et admettre le crime ; le marquis de Sade (17), critiqué pour avoir pu vivre à l'aise dans cette même contradiction ; les surréalistes (10), pour qui « l'acte surréaliste le plus simple consistait à descendre dans la rue, revolver au poing, et à tirer au hasard dans la foule »[8] ; les romantiques (9), pour qui le meurtre devient *aimable* ; ainsi que Heathcliff, le héros des *Hauts de Hurlevent* (3), célébré parce qu'il n'aurait jamais eu l'idée de dire que son meurtre est « raisonnable ou justifié par le système »[9].

Du côté de la philosophie ensuite, c'est Nietzsche (12 connections) qui « n'a pas formé le projet de tuer Dieu » mais qui l'a « trouvé mort dans l'âme de son temps »[10] ; Stirner (8) et les nihilistes (8) qui « courent aux confins, ivres de destruction »[11] ; ainsi que Hegel (3) dont certains admirateurs n'ont retenu que le premier terme de son dilemme « tuer ou asservir »[12].

Du côté historique enfin, Camus associe principalement au meurtre les terroristes russes de 1905 (avec 29 connections), ces hommes et ces femmes qui ont, selon lui, « passé rapidement dans l'histoire »[13]. Il s'attarde longuement

---

8 A. Camus, *L'Homme révolté*..., p. 123

9 *Ibidem*, p. 15.

10 *Ibidem*, p. 94.

11 *Ibidem*, p. 91.

12 *Ibidem*, p. 181–182.

13 *Ibidem*, p. 214.

sur ces meurtriers délicats « qui ont vécu le destin révolté dans sa contradiction la plus extrême »[14], et qui considèrent la violence comme à la fois inévitable et injustifiable. On retrouve également des personnalités de la Révolution française (12) notamment Saint-Just (8) qui « démontre que ce sont les philosophes qui vont tuer le roi »[15] ; des personnages antiques (4) avec Spartacus qui mourra « sous les coups des mercenaires, esclaves comme lui, et qui tuent leur liberté avec la sienne »[16] ; ainsi que des personnalités contemporaines telles que Hitler (2), Marx, Bakounine, Tito et Trotski (une connection chacun).

Le réseau des associations du meurtre est également riche en indicateurs spatio-temporels. Quelques 32 connections situent le meurtre dans différentes époques de l'histoire telles que l'Antiquité, les temps anciens, le 19e siècle ou le 20e siècle ; et l'associent à des dates charnières de l'histoire, européenne bien sûr (1789), mais également russe (1905).

La réflexion camusienne autour du meurtre n'est donc pas isolée : elle s'inscrit dans un contexte particulièrement rigoureux. On note surtout que ce sont des individus, plutôt que des courants de pensée, qui sont associés au meurtre. Camus semble ainsi vouloir souligner la part de responsabilité *individuelle* face au meurtre. Il semble se préoccuper d'abord de l'homme qui se donne le droit de tuer – et qui tue – plus que du principe meurtrier qui lui prescrit un tel choix et qui transforme ce droit en devoir. Mais l'homme n'est pas uniquement interprète et auteur du meurtre, il en est également une des victimes.

LES CIBLES DU MEURTRE : DES HOMMES ET DES DIEUX

Le réseau des qualifications (282 connections) indique principalement les cibles du meurtre dans *L'Homme révolté*. Il s'agit :

- du meurtre de Dieu (10 connections) ;
- du meurtre de l'homme, qui peut être le dirigeant (24), le semblable (30) ou le gouverné (6) ;
- et du meurtre total (12).

Le meurtre chez Camus est donc hiérarchique ; et c'est à tous les échelons que l'on voit se tisser la relation entre le meurtre, l'absurde et la révolte.

---

14 *Ibidem*, p. 217.

15 *Ibidem*, p. 149.

16 *Ibidem*, p. 145.

Dieu est tué à plusieurs reprises dans *L'Homme révolté*. Camus revient sur le meurtre divin dans l'histoire depuis la fin du monde antique. Convoquant les héros grecs désireux de devenir des dieux, « mais en même temps que les dieux déjà existants »[17], il remonte à l'homme de Lucrèce qui procède à une révolution en niant les dieux indignes et criminels et en prenant lui-même leur place ; et parviens à la révolution du 20e siècle qui « tue ce qui reste de Dieu dans les principes »[18], des principes mis en place un siècle plus tôt, lorsque Dieu fut tué dans la personne de son représentant. Le meurtre de ce dernier symbolise ici la désacralisation de l'histoire et la désincarnation du dieu chrétien.

Camus commence par montrer comment, en tuant Dieu, l'homme se retrouve en plein dans l'absurde. Il écrit : « On nie Dieu au nom de la justice, mais l'idée de justice se comprend-elle sans l'idée de Dieu ? »[19] Camus explique ensuite comment l'homme dépasse cette absurdité en tuant « la morale des principes où se retrouve encore le souvenir de Dieu »[20]. L'homme, installé dans l'absurde par le meurtre de Dieu, commence à progresser vers la révolte par un autre meurtre, celui de son représentant. Mais celle-ci n'est pas un aboutissement et le mouvement ne fait que commencer. « Tuer Dieu et bâtir une Église »[21], c'est ainsi que Camus décrit le mouvement constant et contradictoire de la révolte.

Camus revient sur la période entre 1878 et 1905 qui couronnent le 19e siècle de meurtres. Il retrace la longue série d'assassinats politiques qui ont lieu un peu partout en Occident et en Russie, avec comme aboutissement l'assassinat du grand duc Serge par Ivan Kaliayev. On connaît ici la position de Camus : cette date marque pour lui « le plus haut sommet de l'élan révolutionnaire »[22] à partir duquel commence la déchéance.

La révolte atteint ici son point culminant également à travers un meurtre, celui de l'homme par l'homme, un meurtre à la fois nécessaire et inexcusable. Mais à partir de cet instant, Camus évoque deux races d'hommes. Jusque-là l'homme tue l'homme « une seule fois et paie de sa vie » ; à partir de là il « justifie des milliers de crimes et accepte de se payer d'honneurs »[23]. D'une culpabilité raisonnable qui le plaçait au-dessus de l'histoire, l'homme passe à une culpabilité définitive qui le jette en-dessous.

---

17 *Ibidem*, p. 51.

18 *Ibidem*, p. 307.

19 *Ibidem*, p. 87.

20 *Ibidem*, p. 176.

21 *Ibidem*, p. 134.

22 *Ibidem*, p. 220.

23 *Ibidem*, p. 221.

Ce passage s'effectue quand la révolution, obéissant au nihilisme, se retourne contre ses origines révoltées. L'idée de meurtre total est récurrente dans *L'Homme révolté.* Camus y parle de meurtres « multipliés à l'infini », « universel », « de tout et de tous », il y est question de tuer « la terre entière », de tuer « tout le monde », d'assassiner « sept millions de Juifs, sept millions d'Européens ». Le meurtre de Dieu et de son représentant désacralisent l'histoire, le meurtre total la resacralise. L'homme trahit sa révolte également à travers le meurtre, celui de tous les hommes, un meurtre devenu ici total et excusable.

En somme, le réseau des qualifications nous montre que c'est un meurtre fondateur qui marque chaque étape dans le mouvement de l'absurde vers la révolte. Cet agencement n'est pas sans rappeler la centralité du meurtre dans les structures romanesque et théâtrale chez Camus. Dans *La Mort heureuse*, *L'Étranger* et dans *Les Justes*, c'est aussi un meurtre qui marque la transition entre les deux parties : le meurtre de Zagreus par Mersault, le meurtre de l'Arabe par Meursault et le meurtre du grand duc par Yanek (acte troisième d'une pièce en cinq actes).

Le réseau des qualifications positionne donc le meurtre dans le mouvement de l'absurde vers la révolte. L'examen du réseau des liaisons thématiques permet d'approfondir encore plus la lecture de cette relation : l'absurde et la révolte sont en effet étroitement liés au meurtre d'un point de vue sémantique.

RAISONNER LE MEURTRE : DE LA CONTRADICTION AU DÉCHIREMENT

Le réseau des liaisons thématiques (associations et oppositions) situe clairement le meurtre au sein même de l'absurde et de la révolte. Ainsi, reviennent régulièrement dans l'entourage sémantique du meurtre en tant qu'associations : l'absurde (11 connections), le suicide (12), le sacrifice (18), la révolution (9), et la révolte (51). Cette dernière y surgit également – et là réside toute la différence – en tant qu'opposition (12 connections).

Le lien sémantique entre l'absurde, le suicide et le meurtre est très fort dans l'introduction (intitulée d'ailleurs, on le rappelle, « L'absurde et le meurtre »). Camus considère que la notion d'absurde apporte une contradiction en ce qui concerne le meurtre. Il dit: « Le sentiment de l'absurde, quand on prétend d'abord en tirer une règle d'action, rend le meurtre au moins indifférent et, par conséquent, possible »[24].

---

[24] *Ibidem*, p. 17.

Mais, après avoir rendu le meurtre possible, l'analyse absurde le rend tout autant impossible. Camus avait déjà démontré dans *Le Mythe de Sisyphe* que la conclusion dernière du raisonnement absurde est le rejet du suicide. Il en déduit que « si l'on refuse ses raisons au suicide, il n'est pas possible d'en donner au meurtre »[25]. Suicide et meurtre coïncident donc dans l'absurde (le lien sémantique associatif entre les deux est d'ailleurs assez fort). Le raisonnement absurde nous abandonne dans la contradiction : rien n'empêche le meurtre et rien ne le légitime. Mais le raisonnement se poursuit quand le révolté tente de sortir de cette contradiction.

Camus démontre comment le meurtre devient déchirement au niveau de la révolte. Le lien sémantique entre la révolte et le meurtre (63 connections) est particulièrement fort dans la première partie du dernier chapitre (dont le titre, on le rappelle, est « Révolte et meurtre »). Camus y écrit :

> S'il y a révolte, c'est que le mensonge, l'injustice et la violence font, en partie, la condition du révolté. Il ne peut dont prétendre absolument à ne point tuer ni mentir sans renoncer à sa révolte, et accepter une fois pour toutes le meurtre et le mal. Mais il ne peut non plus accepter de tuer et mentir, puisque le mouvement inverse qui légitimerait meurtre et violence détruirait aussi les raisons de son insurrection[26].

Le révolté doit donc se réconcilier avec son acte meurtrier ; et il n'y a qu'une seule façon de le faire : accepter sa propre mort et le sacrifice. Meurtre et suicide coïncident de nouveau, mais cette fois à travers la révolte. Face au meurtre, le révolté sort de la contradiction dictée par l'absurde à travers un déchirement stipulé par la révolte. *Forcé* d'accepter le meurtre, il *choisit* d'accepter sa propre mort afin de dépasser ce déchirement et d'éviter de faire face de nouveau à la contradiction en légitimant le meurtre et en trahissant sa révolte. C'est comme ca que le meurtre devient la limite « qu'on ne peut atteindre qu'une fois et après laquelle il faut mourir »[27], faute de quoi on retomberait dans la contradiction et le nihilisme.

Ces deux idées de déchirement et de limite reviennent dans tous les réseaux sémantiques qui entourent le meurtre (avec un total de 169 connections).

---

25 *Ibidem*, p. 20.

26 *Ibidem*, p. 356.

27 *Ibidem*, p. 352.

DÉPASSER LE DÉCHIREMENT : LE MEURTRE COMME LIMITE

Plusieurs emplois sémantiques du mot meurtre le montre sous un angle négatif. On retrouve plusieurs attributs dépréciatifs (7 connections) parmi les qualifications comme : meurtre immoral, aveugle ou ignoble. On retrouve également des allégories de la mort dévalorisantes (8) telles que le « crâne des ennemis », le sang qui « n'éclabousse pas assez haut le visage de nos pharisiens », ou encore les « sanctuaires divins gonflés des cadavres accusateurs de la peste ».

Le réseau des associations place aussi le meurtre au sein d'un large champ lexical relatif à la violence (67 connections). L'acte de tuer est associé à ceux d'asservir, de déporter, de frapper. Le meurtre est encore associé à un champ lexical plus petit, celui du mensonge (10 connections) : « le mensonge perpétuel », « accepter de tuer et mentir ». Il est également opposé aux notions de vertu (9 connections), de vie (7), d'art (5) et d'innocence (4). Le meurtre porte donc bien une connotation dépréciative dans le langage camusien.

Mais en même temps, le réseau des qualifications montre que la plupart des attributs du mot *meurtre* constituent des couples antonymiques (17 connections doubles), il est à la fois : possible et impossible, direct et indirect, exceptionnel et universel ; le meurtrier est à la fois coupable et innocent. De même, on retrouve deux situations antithétiques parmi les qualifications du meurtre (25 connections) : celle du consentement et celle du refus. Le meurtre a « ses justifications », il a « ses raisons » ; en même temps, il se trouve proscrit, il « n'est pas systématique » et « ne peut être utilisé ».

Le réseau verbal montre lui également deux positions contraires : accepter le meurtre (47) et le refuser (17). Ainsi, il s'agit d'universaliser le meurtre, de le transfigurer, de l'admettre, d'y consentir. D'un autre côté, il s'agit de le condamner, de le haïr, de l'empêcher. Également, l'acte de tuer est antithétique en lui-même puisqu'il s'agit à la fois de tuer (24 connections) et de ne pas tuer (8). Sur le plan des fonctions du meurtre enfin, la majorité des fonctions répertoriées relèvent de la même contradiction (27 connections). Camus le dit d'ailleurs :

> Ces meurtriers délicats ont vécu le destin révolté dans sa contradiction la plus extrême. On peut croire qu'eux aussi, tout en reconnaissant le caractère inévitable de la violence, avouaient cependant qu'elle est injustifiée[28].

---

28 *Ibidem*, p. 217.

Finalement, l'analyse des champs sémantiques du meurtre chez Camus montre que ce dernier, comme ses meurtriers préférés, est déchiré face au meurtre. Ses mots sont en quelque sorte un reflet de lui-même : Camus *est* son langage.

Le meurtre ressort du réseau des qualifications comme étant à la fois une liberté absolue (12 connections) et une limite (11). Tuer c'est « dire oui à tout », c'est « quand tout est permis », le meurtrier c'est « celui qui nie tout et s'autorise à tuer ». Mais, le meurtre a également un « air d'effraction » et il est « une exception désespérée ». En parallèle, dans le réseau des associations (41 connections), le meurtre se retrouve lié en même temps à « l'irrationnel triomphant » et à « la vertu toute pure », au « oui absolu » et au « non absolu ». Face à ce déchirement, Camus trouve donc la limite dans le meurtre lui-même, et la pose comme mesure. Il formule ainsi l'attitude du révolté : « Il tue et meurt pour qu'il soit clair que le meurtre est impossible »[29].

On peut conclure que le meurtre est un des liens entre les trois cycles camusiens – qui ne sont pas parfaitement distincts – de l'absurde, de la révolte et de la mesure ; Sisyphe, Prométhée et Némésis sont, pour ainsi dire, liés entre autre par le meurtre.

LES MAUX DU MEURTRE

En septembre 1949, Camus écrit dans ses *Carnets* : « Pour finir, revaloriser le meurtre pour l'opposer à la destruction anonyme et froide, et abstraite. L'apologie du meurtre d'homme à homme est une des étapes sur le chemin de la révolte »[30]. Ces mots raisonnent particulièrement fort dans le monde d'aujourd'hui, plus particulièrement dans le monde arabe. Entre le fracas des bombes barils et les cous tranchés en sourdine, on est en plein dans la démesure. Les meurtriers délicats se cachaient pour mourir, voilà que les meurtriers ignobles se cachent pour tuer. Et quand ils meurent, ils le font au grand jour et dans un décor macabre, ensemble avec leurs victimes. La théâtralisation de la violence l'a rendu encore plus confortable que ne l'avait constaté Camus en 1947. On s'est accommodé au meurtre en acceptant le statut de victime et en concédant celui de bourreau. De son célèbre appel *Ni victimes ni bourreaux*, on est passé à *Et victimes et bourreaux*.

---

[29] *Ibidem*, p. 352.

[30] A. Camus, *Carnets II*..., p. 282.

Le juste milieu que Camus avait trouvé dans le meurtre est le résultat d'une tension et d'une contradiction continues entre deux pôles extrêmes : le oui absolu et le non absolu. Mais maintenir la balance n'est pas chose aisée ; face au confort de la violence, Camus prône l'inconfort de l'équilibre. Actuellement, c'est le premier qui fait légion. Notre tâche est d'œuvrer dans le sens de cet inconfort.

BIBLIOGRAPHIE

Camus, A., *Carnets II. Janvier 1942 – mars 1951*, Paris, Gallimard, 1964, 2013.

Camus, A., *L'Homme révolté*, Paris, Gallimard, 1951.

Camus, A., *La Peste*, Paris, Gallimard, 1947.

Camus, A., *Le Mythe de Sisyphe*, Paris, Gallimard, 1942.

Camus, A., *Les Justes*, Paris, Gallimard, 1950. 1977.

Camus, A., *Ni victimes ni bourreaux, Actuelles. Ecrits politiques*, Paris, Gallimard, 1950.

Grenier, R., *Albert Camus. Soleil et ombre*, Paris, Gallimard, 1987.

Robin, R., *Approches des champs sémantiques : les expériences du Centre de lexicologie politique de Saint-Cloud, Histoire et linguistique*, Paris, Armand Colin, 1973.

A "Culpabilité Raisonnable." Camusian Revolt as Modern Morality

TOMMASO VISONE

> – Après tout, reprit le docteur, et il hésita encore, regardant Tarrou avec attention, c'est une chose qu'un homme comme vous peut comprendre, n'est-ce pas, mais puisque l'ordre du monde est réglé par la mort, peut-être vaut-il mieux pour Dieu qu'on ne croie pas en lui et qu'on lutte de toutes ses forces contre la mort, sans lever les yeux vers ce ciel où il se tait.
> – Oui, approuva Tarrou, je peux comprendre. Mais vos victoires seront toujours provisoires, voilà tout.
> Rieux parut s'assombrir.
> – Toujours, je le sais. Ce n'est pas une raison pour cesser de lutter.
>
> Albert Camus, *La peste*, Paris, Gallimard, 1947

> L'homme est la seule créature qui refuse d'être ce qu'elle est. La question est de savoir si ce refus ne peut l'amener qu'à la destruction des autres et de lui-même, si toute révolte doit s'achever en justification du meurtre universel, ou si, au contraire, sans prétention à une impossible innocence, elle peut découvrir le principe d'une culpabilité raisonnable.
>
> Albert Camus, *L'homme révolté*, Paris, Gallimard, 1951

The purpose of this paper is to deepen the relationship between modernity, morality and Revolt in the thought of Camus, beginning from the critical consideration that he stressed in relation to the return of absolute values and theological positions, in 20th century ideologies. In particular I will focus on *The Rebel*, a book highlighting how "il ne peut y avoir pour un esprit humain que deux univers possibles, celui du sacré (ou, pour parler le langage chrétien, de la grâce), et celui de la révolte."[1] The study of the relation between these two

[1] A. Camus, *L'homme révolté*, Paris, Gallimard, 1951, p. 36.

universes is, according to Camus, fundamental in order to catch the ruinous contradiction of his epoch and understand "comment s'y conduire" within it.

1. As Mattew Sharpe recently wrote, "Camus' criticism of Nietzscheanism, fascism and revolutionary Marxism begins at the exact moment when these modern forms of thought come (unnecessarily and illegitimately, as he sees things) to reoccupy theological positions."[2] In *The Rebel* Camus argued that at the origins of contemporary nihilism – the second part of the Forties – there is the "divinisation de l'histoire" and the maxim "homo homini deus."[3] The fundamental source of this returning deification, in Camus' opinion, is in the philosophy of Hegel and of Hegelians who focused on the master-servant dilemma: "tuer ou asservir." In effect of this position, terrorists or cynics and murderous masters were convinced to find "God" in the historical future or in the historical "reality" ("Le vainqueur a toujours raison").[4] But this is not the only source of such nihilism. Another comes from Rousseau's thought that established a "new god," sovereign people, and a new religion of "holy humanity."[5] The same logic animates the "Revolution" described by Camus as follows: "Il s'agit de deifier l'espèce comme Nietzsche et de prendre en charge son ideal de surhumanité a fin d'assurer le salut de tous..." Thus, in his opinion, Revolution is "une croisade métaphysique démesurée."[6] Exactly such a return of God in the realm of immanence transforms "la révolte historique" into the victory of nihilism.[7] From this point of view it is interesting to stress how, according to Camus, this return to theological is unnecessary and illegitimate because of the direction

---

2 M. Sharpe, *Camus Philosophe. To Return to Our Beginnings*, Leiden, Brill, 2015, p. 137.

3 A. Camus, *L'homme révolté...*, p. 189.

4 *Ibidem*, p. 177. Here it is possible to underline how much Camus' Hegel is conceived through Kojeve's interpretation (directly quoted by Camus in *The Rebel* with the one of Hyppolite). According to Kojève, "what is good is what exists, to the extent that it exists. All action, since it negates existing givens, is thus bad: a sin. But sin can be pardoned. How? Through its success. Success absolves crime, because success is a new reality that exists." This is exactly what Camus firmly refused, the idea that success (or better history) could absolve crime. See: A. Kojève, *Introduction à la lecture de Hegel*, Paris, Gallimard, 1968, p. 95 and, about the Camusian critique of Kojève: P. Sabot, *Les mésaventures de la dialectique. Camus critique de Kojève dans L'Homme révolté* [in:] L. David (éd.), *Albert Camus contemporain*, Villeneuve d'Ascq, , Villeneuve d'Ascq, Presses Universitaires du Septentrion, 2009, p. 45–60.

5 A. Camus, *L'homme révolté...*, p. 153. But Camus also said that "Rousseau... avait bien vu que la societé du Contrat ne convenait qu'à des dieux. Ses successeurs l'ont pris au mot et ont taché de fonder la divinité de l'homme," *ibidem*, p. 168.

6 *Ibidem*, p. 142.

7 See: *ibidem*, p. 189–191.

originally taken by modern revolt[8] – "metaphysical revolt" – which must be interpreted as a claim, a challenge, for "unity:"

> La révolte métaphysique est le mouvement par lequel un homme se dresse contre sa condition et la création tout entière. Elle est métaphysique parce qu'elle conteste les fins de l'homme et de la création. L'esclave proteste contre la condition qui lui est faite à l'intérieur de son état; le révolté métaphysique contre la condition qui lui est faite en tant qu'homme... L'esclave dressé contre son maître ne se préoccupe pas, remarquons-le, de nier ce maître en tant qu'être. Il le nie en tant que maître. Il nie qu'il ait le droit de le nier, lui, esclave, en tant qu'exigence. Le maître est déchu dans la mesure même où il ne répond pas à une exigence qu'il néglige. Si les hommes ne peuvent pas se référer à une valeur commune, reconnue par tous en chacun, alors l'homme est incompréhensible à l'homme. Le rebelle exige que cette valeur soit clairement reconnue en lui-même parce qu'il soupçonne ou sait que, sans ce principe, le désordre et le crime régneraient sur le monde. Le mouvement de révolte apparaît chez lui comme une revendication de clarté et d'unité. La rébellion la plus élémentaire exprime, paradoxalement, l'aspiration à un ordre... L'histoire de la révolte métaphysique ne peut donc se confondre avec celle de l'athéisme. Sous un certain angle, elle se confond même avec l'histoire contemporaine du sentiment religieux. Le révolté défie plus qu'il ne nie. Primitivement, au moins, il ne supprime pas Dieu, il lui parle simplement de égal à égal. Mais il ne s'agit pas d'un dialogue courtois. Il s'agit d'une polémique qu'anime le désir de vaincre...[9]

Thus the original problem of such a revolt is to affirm a "common value," denounce a contradiction, and not to impose a new god. The rebel, in the beginning, looks for justice, not supremacy.

2. The horizon under consideration could not be comprehended through the "secularization thesis:"[10] there is no man who, originally, tries to usurp the place of God (of a master) or reply, at a "secular level," to the same God; there is no will to repeat the previous injustice. On the contrary, the idea

8 Among the numerous essays and publications on the Camusian concept of revolt see J. Foley, *Albert Camus: From the Absurd to Revolt*, Oxon, Routledge, 2014, and Giangiacomo Valle, *Rivolta e rivoluzione, misura e dismisura nel pensiero di Albert Camus* [in:] *Archivio Storico del Sannio*, A. VIII, n. 1–2, 2013, p. 11–40.

9 *Ibidem*, p. 43.

10 Regarding the "secularization thesis" – modern thought consists of usurped, corrupted or repeated religious matter – see H. Blumemberg, *Die Legitimität der Neuezeit*, Frankfurt am Main, Suhrkamp Verlag, 1974, and M. Scattola, *Teologia Politica*, Bologna, Il Mulino, 2007, p. 157–193.

is to create a different relationship among men and God. It is a challenge through which the human being hopes to find on a different basis – without "masters" – a new order that will allow him to grasp unity and justice. Modern thought is thus an "agnostic affair" and does not "intrinsically need to answer the question of Christian theology."[11] Such a thought, with its distance from a religious dimension, finds references in all Camusian work. A very famous example – out of an historical dimension – can be found in *The Plague.* One of the famous lines of dialogue occurs when Paneloux says to Rieux, on the subject of Grace, "you too are working for the salvation of human kind." Rieux replies: "Salvation is too big a word for me. I don't go that far. What interests me is man's health, his health first of all."[12] The difference between the concepts of "salvation" and "health" is a good example of the incommensurability of the two ways of thought that cannot simply be inferred as one from the other (being often opposed).[13]

3. In order to understand such a fundamental distinction, it is still more interesting to consider the double evaluation of Karl Marx's thought undertaken by Camus in *The Rebel.* In fact Camus, on the one hand, considers Marx to be a brilliant and fundamental critic of man's alienation, a defender of "man's quality." He writes:

> La liberté que rêverait M. Thiers était une liberté du privilège consolidée par la police; la famille exaltée par les journaux conservateurs se maintenait sur un état social où femmes et hommes étaient descendus dans la mine, à demi nus, attachés à la même corde; la morale prospérait sur la prostitution ouvrière. Que les exigences de l'honnêteté et de l'intelligence aient été colonisées à des fins égoïstes par l'hypocrisie d'une société médiocre et cupide, c'est là un malheur que Marx, déniaiseur incomparable, a dénoncé avec une force inconnue avant lui.[14]

And:

> Nous lui devons cette idée qui fait le désespoir de notre temps – mais ici le désespoir vaut mieux que tout espoir – que lorsque le travail est une déchéance, il n'est pas la vie, bien qu'il couvre tout le temps de la vie. Qui, malgré les

---

11 See: M. Sharpe, *op.cit.*, p. 136.

12 A. Camus, *The Plague*, New York, The Modern Library, 1948, p. 202.

13 In effect the fundamental character of Rieux in *The Plague* is defined by his fight "against creation." See B. Alluin, *Rieux Berard* [in:] J. Guérin (ed.), *Dictionnaire Albert Camus*, Paris, Laffont, 2009.

14 A. Camus, *L'homme révolté...*, p. 254.

> prétentions de cette société, peut y dormir en paix, sachant désormais qu'elle tire ses jouissances médiocres du travail de millions d'âmes mortes? Exigeant pour le travailleur la vraie richesse, qui n'est pas celle de l'argent, mais celle du loisir ou de la création, il a réclamé, malgré les apparences, la qualité de l'homme. Ce faisant, on peut le dire avec force, il n'a pas voulu la dégradation supplémentaire qu'en son nom on a imposé à l'homme. Une phrase de lui, pour une fois claire et coupante, refuse à jamais à ses disciples triomphants la grandeur et l'humanité qui étaient les siennes: "Un but qui a besoin de moyens injustes n'est pas un but juste."[15]

Thus Marx, as a critic and enemy of the inhuman condition of the proletariat, was well-considered and esteemed by Camus. He found in the German philosopher a fundamental ally and companion against injustice. But, on the other hand, there is another aspect of Marxian thought that was fiercely opposed and criticized by the Franco-Algerian writer. The aspect in question is directly connected with Christian and Jewish theology.

4. In fact, for Camus, Marx – and even more Marxism – must be blamed precisely for his "utopic messianism," his prophetic attitude.[16] And here the criticism is directed at the continuity among Christian philosophy of history and that of Marxism, a continuity that is thought of as being in direct opposition to the Greek world:

> En opposition au monde antique, l'unité du monde chrétien et du monde marxiste est frappante. Les deux doctrines ont, en commun, une vision du monde qui les sépare de l'attitude grecque. Jaspers la définit très bien: "C'est une pensée chrétienne que de considérer l'histoire des hommes comme strictement unique." Les chrétiens ont, les premiers, considéré la vie humaine, et la suite des événements, comme une histoire qui se déroule à partir d'une origine vers une fin, au cours de laquelle l'homme gagne son salut ou mérite son châtiment. La philosophie de l'histoire est née d'une représentation chrétienne, surprenante pour un esprit grec. La notion grecque du devenir n'a rien de commun avec notre idée de l'évolution historique. La différence entre les deux est celle qui sépare un cercle d'une ligne droite. Les Grecs se représentaient le monde comme cyclique. Aristote, pour donner un exemple précis, ne se croyait pas postérieur à la guerre de Troie. Le christianisme a été obligé, pour s'étendre dans le monde méditerranéen, de s'helléniser et sa doctrine s'est du

15 *Ibidem*, p. 264.

16 See M. Sharpe, *op.cit.*, p. 113.

> même coup assouplie. Mais son originalité est d'introduire dans le monde antique deux notions jamais liées jusque-là, celles d'histoire et de châtiment. Par l'idée de médiation, le christianisme est grec. Par la notion d'historicité, il est judaïque et se retrouvera dans l'idéologie allemande. On aperçoit mieux cette coupure en soulignant l'hostilité des pensées historiques à l'égard de la nature, considérée par elles comme un objet, non de contemplation, mais de transformation. Pour les chrétiens comme pour les marxistes, il faut maîtriser la nature. Les Grecs sont d'avis qu'il vaut mieux lui obéir.[17]

According to Camus, the consequences of this relationship between Marxism and Christianity are terrible. In fact, the "messianism"[18] of the latter united with German ideology caused the resurrection of several aspect of the Judaic world:

> Le dieu implacable des armées règne à nouveau, toute beauté est insultée comme source de jouissances oisives, la nature elle-même est asservie. Marx, de ce point de vue, est le Jérémie du dieu historique et le saint Augustin de la révolution.[19]

5. Marx is, precisely for these reasons, compared to Saint Augustine and Joseph de Maistre.[20] The German philosopher is considered – for his return to theological thesis regarding the final end of evil on earth or the deification of man – as a reactionary thinker. The reference to Saint Augustine is even more important. As Camus presented in his thesis about Christian metaphysics and Neoplatonism (1936), Augustine was the author of what he calls a "second revelation" that transformed the history of Christianity, creating a theory of "teodicea:" the explanation of evil – natural and human – as the "inherited punishment of human beings for the sin of the first man;" necessary "in order for the Greater Providential Good to manifest itself."[21]

---

17 A. Camus, *L'homme révolté...*, p. 241–242.

18 According to Camus, it is fundamental to introduce political thought "dèlivrée de tout messianisme." A. Camus, *Ni victime ni bourreaux. Sauver les corps* in *Combat*, 20 November1946 [in:] *idem*, *À Combat*, Paris, Gallimard, 2002, p. 644. Also on this point, see T. Visone, *International Dictatorship or International Democracy. A Discussion of Albert Camus' 1946 Considerations*, "Perspective on Federalism" 2015, vol. 7, issue 2, p. 120–121.

19 A. Camus, *L'homme révolté*, *op. cit.*, p. 242.

20 On such aspect of Camus' thought see also L. Pellicani, *La lezione di Camus* [in:] *Archivio storico del Sannio*, A. XVIII, n. 1/2, 2013, p. 61–64.

21 See: M. Sharpe, *op. cit.*, p. 116–117.

For this reason Camus considered Christianity a "religion of injustice"[22] and the Marxist revolution – as far as it returns to this position – as a way towards a general slavery.[23]

6. The aforementioned arguments of Camus – as presented by Sharpe in polemics with Srigley[24] – anticipated some of the thesis of the famous book *The legitimacy of modern age* (1966) by Hans Blumenberg. According to Blumenberg, there is no unbroken continuity between medieval and modern times (there is a moment in which a "sufficient rationality" emerges, e.g. Descartes) and no necessary need to reoccupy theological position, that is exactly what, for both Blumenberg and Camus, happened in late modernity.[25] Therefore in both authors modernity is characterised by creative "self-assertion" – "la conscience vient au jour avec la révolte"[26] – with its weight ("tension," according to the Franco-Algerian writer) and, thus its possibility, but not necessity, to reoccupy the theological framework of question. Camus, in contrast to Blumenberg, was more interested in the political effect of this theological position in the contemporary world which, he said, signifies the triumph of totality over unity; the myth over the rationality; revolution – as he often interpreted it – over revolt; a closed world of defined "answers and commentaries" over an open one; and an absolute power legitimated by a new absolute truth over the tension of measure.

7. Starting from the aforementioned distinction, it is possible to improve the understanding of Camus' position regarding modernity. In fact, he shows how modernity is characterised by revolt with its different manifestations originating from the contrast with the idea of a master (Christian God, Sovereign, etc.) who can legitimate the absurd condition of man. Revolt, he suggested, is agnostic; it represents a creative break with the theological heritage. But the latter is not fully destroyed by this break: it can return ("l'homme révolté est l'homme situé **avant** ou après le sacré"). In fact, following the paradoxes initiated by Revolt and trying to give absolute and total answer to these, the

---

22 See: A. Camus, *Justice et liberté* [in:] *Combat*, 8 September 1944, in: *idem*, A.Camus, *À Combat*..., p. 188–189.

23 See: A. Camus, *L'homme révolté*..., p. 292–293.

24 See: M. Sharpe, "*A Just Judgement? Considerations on Ronald Srigley's Camus' Critique of Modernity*,"Thesis Eleven" 2014, vol. 120, issue 1, 2014, p. 51–52.

25 It is interesting to note how starting from a very similar interpretation of the relationship between Augustine and gnostic thought, Blumenberg arrives to demonstrate how, for 18th-century philosophers (engaged, from other point of view, with the problem of the evil), God became a superfluous hypothesis more than a reality to be denied. See: H. Blumenberg, *op. cit.*, p. 68–69.

26 A. Camus, *L'homme révolté*..., p. 29.

human being ends in affirmation of himself and domination of other men, criminalising and subjugating them in the name of the new god. Thus the return of theological logic within modernity – in late modernity or contemporary times – is destructive because it is, with its limitless attitude, nihilistic.[27]

One important and paradoxical consequence of this return of god in the name of absolute human innocence – the system must be destroyed because it brings man to evil, there is an extra-human fault – is the final general criminalisation of man (as highlighted in Camus' depiction of Marxism).[28] This aspect caused an essential perversion of revolution:

> Au terme de cette longue insurrection au nom de l'innocence humaine, surgit, par une perversion essentielle, l'affirmation de la culpabilité générale. Tout homme est un criminel qui s'ignore. Le criminel objectif est celui qui, justement, croyait être innocent. Son action, il la jugeait subjectivement inoffensive, ou même favorable à l'avenir de la justice. Mais on lui démontre qu'objectivement elle a nui à cet avenir. S'agit-il d'une objectivité scientifique? Non, mais historique.[29]

Such is, wrote Camus, the closure of a circle that ends with the psychological and physical destruction of man by refusing to accept the existence of a limit, a measure, which was implicit in the "early modern revolt."

8. Against such a terrible danger/reality Camus affirmed the necessity of a "measure" based on Greek/Mediterranean thought and early modern revolt.[30] A measure that can manifest itself only fighting inside history:

---

27 On Camusian criticism of the religious forms taken by revolutionaries, see also T. Judt, *The Burden of Responsibility. Blum, Camus, Aron and the French Twentieth Century*, Chicago, University of Chicago Press, 1998, p. 93–96.

28 "Toute pensée purement historique, cependant, s'ouvre sur ces abîmes. Dans la mesure où Marx prédisait l'accomplissement inévitable de la cité sans classes, dans la mesure où il établissait ainsi la bonne volonté de l'histoire, tout retard dans la marche libératrice devait être imputé à la mauvaise volonté de l'homme. Marx a réintroduit dans le monde déchristianisé la faute et le châtiment, mais en face de l'histoire. Le marxisme, sous un de ses aspects, est une doctrine de culpabilité quant à l'homme, d'innocence quant à l'histoire. Loin du pouvoir, sa traduction historique était la violence révolutionnaire; au sommet du pouvoir, elle risquait d'être la violence légale, c'est-à-dire la terreur et le procès," A. Camus, *L'homme révolté...*, p. 301.

29 *Ibidem*, p. 303.

30 As has been underlined before, speaking about the Methaphysic Revolt: "Si les hommes ne peuvent pas se référer à une valeur commune, reconnue par tous en chacun, alors l'homme est incompréhensible à l'homme. Le rebelle exige que cette valeur soit clairement reconnue en lui-même parce qu'il soupçonne ou sait que, sans ce principe, le désordre et le crime régneraient sur le

> La mesure n'est pas le contraire de la révolte. C'est la révolte qui est la mesure, qui l'ordonne, la défend et la recrée à travers l'histoire et ses désordres. L'origine même de cette valeur nous garantit qu'elle ne peut être que déchirée. La mesure, née de la révolte, ne peut se vivre que par la révolte. Elle est un conflit constant, perpétuellement suscité et maîtrisé par l'intelligence. Elle ne triomphe ni de l'impossible ni de l'abîme. Elle s'équilibre à eux. Quoi que nous fassions, la démesure gardera toujours sa place dans le coeur de l'homme, à l'endroit de la solitude. Nous portons tous en nous nos bagnes, nos crimes et nos ravages. Mais notre tâche n'est pas de les déchaîner à travers le monde; elle est de les combattre en nous-mêmes et dans les autres.[31]

The aim of such a revolt is to fight "dans l'histoire pur préserver de l'histoire cette part de l'homme qui ne lui appartient pas."[32] It struggles for the preservation of human unity from new challenges that are continuously transforming. Thus, being such a measure/revolt, a rational answer to late modern excesses (*démesure*), it affirms the reality of a reasonable culpability against the specular couple absolute innocence/absolute culpability:

> La révolution du XXe siècle décrète que les valeurs sont mêlées au mouvement de l'histoire et sa raison historique justifie une nouvelle mystification. La mesure, face à ce dérèglement, nous apprend qu'il faut une part de réalisme à toute morale: la vertu toute pure est meurtrière; et qu'il faut une part de morale à tout réalisme: le cynisme est meurtrier. C'est pourquoi le verbiage humanitaire n'est pas plus fondé que la provocation cynique. L'homme enfin n'est pas entièrement coupable, il n'a pas commencé l'histoire; ni tout à fait innocent puisqu'il la continue. Ceux qui passent cette limite et affirment son innocence totale finissent dans la rage de la culpabilité définitive. La révolte nous met au contraire sur le chemin d'une culpabilité calculée.[33]

---

monde. Le mouvement de révolte apparaît chez lui comme une revendication de clarté et d'unité. La rébellion la plus élémentaire exprime, paradoxalement, l'aspiration à un ordre." And: "Mais l'absolutisme historique, malgré ses triomphes, n'a jamais cessé de se heurter à une exigence invincible de la nature humaine dont la Méditerranée, où l'intelligence est sœur de la dure lumière, garde le secret. Les pensées révoltées, celles de la Commune ou du syndicalisme révolutionnaire, n'ont cessé de crier cette exigence à la face du nihilisme bourgeois comme à celle du socialisme césarien." *Ibidem*, p. 374.

31 *Ibidem*, p. 376.

32 A. Camus, *Ni victimes ni bourreaux. Vers le dialogue* [in:] *Combat* 30 November 1946 [in:] *idem*, *À Combat*..., p. 670.

33 A. Camus, *L'homme révolté*..., p. 370.

9. Such idea of a "rational culpability," the modern fight that Camus sought to start against the "absolute culpability of man," is the other side of the reflection on the continuous attempt to reduce injustice inside history that goes to the origins of modern revolt. Camus' idea was that humans – being the only beings who need to give a meaning to life against the absurdity of the mere existence[34] – fight continuously inside history to creatively build such a meaning.[35] However, learning from what is taught by modernity, they can obtain only a "victoire provisoire" because in the moment in which they renounce the "intransigeance extènuante de la mesure," the tension of a unity that is not totality, they return to a sacred dimension that represents the negation of human rationality and human life. That message could, at the very end, be at the core of such a "moralité moderne" that Camus sought during that period of his life.[36] Far from being just a "moral" discover, it implies a political engagement and attitude: that of Revolt. In effect : "…la révolte, sans prétendre à tout résoudre, peut au moins faire face."[37]

BIBLIOGRAPHY

Alluin, B., *Rieux Berard* [in:] J. Guérin (ed.), *Dictionnaire Albert Camus*, Paris, Laffont, 2009.

Blumemberg, H., *Die Legitimität der Neuezeit*, Frankfurt am Main, Suhrkamp Verlag, 1974.

Camus, A., *À Combat*, Paris, Gallimard, 2002.

Camus, A., *L'homme révolté*, Paris, Gallimard, 1951.

Camus, A., *Œuvres*, Paris, Gallimard, 2013.

Camus, A., *The Plague*, New York, The Modern Library, 1948.

---

34 As Diego answered in *L'État de siège* to La Peste who asked him to accept her advice in order to save his life: "Ma vie n'est rien. Ce qui compte, ce sont le raisons de ma vie. Je ne suis pas un chien." A. Camus, *L'État de siege*, 1948, [in:] *idem*, *Œuvres*, Paris, Gallimard, 2013, p. 766. The same point is underlined inside the *Lettres à un ami allemande* where Camus said: "Je continue à croire que ce monde n'a pas de sens supérieur. Mais je sais que quelque chose en lui a du sens et c'est l'homme, parce qu'il est le seul être à exiger d'en avoir. Ce monde a du moins la vérité de l'homme et notre tâche est de lui donner ses raisons contre le destin lui-même." A. Camus, *Lettres à un ami allemand*, 1945, [in:] *idem*, *Œuvres…*, p. 484.

35 Thinking, according to Camus, "is, above all else, the desire to create a world." S. Novello, *Albert Camus as Political Thinker: Nihilism and the Politics of Contempt*, London, Palgrave Macmillan, 2010, p. 4.

36 As he wrote to Jean Grenier on 15th January 1949: "c'est une tentative –[he spoke about the *État de siege*] – pour faire une sorte de «moralité moderne»." See: A. Camus, J. Grenier, *Correspondance 1932–1960*, Paris, Gallimard, 1981, p. 152. For an introduction about Camus life, see the classic O. Todd, *Albert Camus une vie*, Paris, Gallimard, 1996.

37 A. Camus, *L'homme révolté…*, p. 380.

Camus, A., Grenier, J., *Correspondance 1932–1960*, Paris, Gallimard, 1981.

Foley, J., *Albert Camus: From the Absurd to Revolt*, Oxon, Routledge, 2014.

Judt, T., *The Burden of Responsibility. Blum, Camus, Aron and the French Twentieth Century*, Chicago, University of Chicago Press, 1998.

Kojève, A., *Introduction à la lecture de Hegel*, Paris, Gallimard, 1968.

Novello, S., *Albert Camus as Political Thinker: Nihilism and the Politics of Contempt*, London, Palgrave Macmillan, 2010.

Pellicani, L., *La lezione di Camus* [in:] *Archivio storico del Sannio*, A. XVIII, n. 1/2, 2013.

Sabot, P., *Les mésaventures de la dialectique. Camus critique de Kojève dans L'Homme révolté* [in:] L. David (éd.), *Albert Camus contemporain*, Villeneuve d'Ascq, Villeneuve d'Ascq, Presses Universitaires du Septentrion, 2009.

Scattola, M., *Teologia Politica*, Bologna, Il Mulino, 2007.

Sharpe, M., *A Just Judgement? Considerations on Ronald Srigley's Camus' Critique of Modernity*, "Thesis Eleven" 2014, vol. 120, issue 1.

Sharpe, M., *Camus Philosophe. To Return to Our Beginnings*, Leiden, Brill, 2015.

Todd, O., *Albert Camus une vie*, Paris, Gallimard, 1996.

Valle, G., *Rivolta e rivoluzione, misura e dismisura nel pensiero di Albert Camus* [in:] *Archivio Storico del Sannio*, A. VIII, n. 1–2, 2013.

Visone, T., *International Dictatorship or International Democracy. A Discussion of Albert Camus' 1946 Considerations*, "Perspective on Federalism" 2015, vol. 7, issue 2.

Timeliness Forms of Revolt by Albert Camus

IGNACY S. FIUT

The literature and philosophical thought of Albert Camus includes descriptions and analyses of the different forms of revolt against the contemporary human condition in the world. Camus opposes the colonial, wartime and occupational forms of oppression, as well as racial and cultural ones, in the name of the "Cosmic Idea of Man." These problems are also valid nowadays in the globalized world and therefore the categories of revolt developed by the French thinker are still pertinent. We can say even that they are currently more expressive and have a larger scale.[1]

1. INTRODUCTORY REMARKS

The situation of European Thought has changed radically in the modern period, mainly as a result of the anthropological and cognitive ideas created by René Descartes and John Locke. The social ground for acceptance of this way of thinking was prepared, on the one hand, by the social experience of the Reformation, on the other hand, by the Enlightenment and the Thought associated with the progressive process of democratization of the social texture of life. A special impetus to influence the widespread areas of these changes was given by the French Revolution and the Napoleonic wars that had spread the ideas, promoting individualization of human life in Europe, and after the Civil War, in North America.

The most decisive experiences for the development of the personalist and existential doctrines were the dramatic wartime events in the 20th century

[1] O. Todd, *Albert Camus. Biografia*, Warszawa, Wydawnictwo W.A.B., 2009, p. 472–489.

and the genocide and Holocaust, in the result of which millions of innocent victims died. Many nations and social groups have experienced the reversal and mishap in which the development of science and technology (intended for the improvement of the human condition in the world) contributed to the mass killing of people; following the ideologically founded objectification and deprivation of the right to dignity, leading to treatment worse than that of the proverbial wild animals or livestock. The trauma resulting from these experiences, especially in the dimension of mass, created a spiritual space to present a new question: "What is man?" In this context of the spontaneously developing mass society, aimed at social globalization, the question concerning the meaning of human existence was brought to the for ground with great force. In the period of the dawn of the 20th century, the ground for such an attitude of thought and philosophical reflection was prepared undoubtedly by the phenomenological method of Edmund Husserl, as well as Marxist and Neo-Marxist thought, based on the description and analysis of the individual human existence. In this context, the existential and philosophical reflection of the French novelist, playwright and essayist – Albert Camus, who along with his family and loved ones was involved in the complex historical experiences of the 20th century related to the two World Wars, is certainly worth analysing.[2] His questions concerning the meaning of human existence, rejecting formerly discredited results of essentialist anthropology, represent an important voice for the development of modern anthropological and philosophical reflection, on a global scale. Camus observed the dramatic enhancement of the processes of globalization in a culturally diverse world and civilization. His literary achievements were undoubtedly important sources, influencing the expansion of this type of awareness to the worldwide extent. They were also prolegomena for the development of philosophy and postmodern culture, both in terms of form and content. The heroes of his short stories, novels and philosophical essays were the people brought up in different cultures that have left their marks on their individual identities. However, the description of the fate of individuals and their experiences, from the perspective of existential analysis, shown through intellectual insight, led the author of *The Stranger* to the conclusion that,

[2] I.S. Fiut, *Człowiek według Alberta Camusa. Studium antropologii egzystencjalnej*, Kraków, Wydawnictwo KKL-A, 1993, see especially chapter I: "Artist, his work and epoch," p. 7–14; J. Daniel, "Le combat pour 'Combat'," P-H. Simon, "Le combat contre les mandarins," J. Roy, "La tragédie algérienne" [in:] R-M. Albérès *et al.*, *Camus*, Collection Genies Réalités, Paris, Hachette, 1964, p. 77–156 and 199–216.

concerning the meaning of their existence, the individual always refers to universal human problems. This discovery transcends all boundaries defined by the religious, cultural, racial, or class patterns. Human beings become relative reference systems for the specific understanding of their own identity and personal fate. The historical situation of human reflection is formed by myths, by means of which one is not deprived of hope for a meaningful existence in the changing and diverse world. This approach proved that the myths in question operate in different cultures. Examples of their functioning in Europe are ancient myths, describing the heroic period of the formation of humanity. Their internal structure presents the specifics of the social situation of an ethnic group that always includes a universal moment.[3] They relate to essential themes of death, killing or suicide. In each of these myths, the human being is commonly presented as originating from God and striving to return to the deity.

In a deep, analytical assessment of the French writer, on the level of individual existence of the man, the creative forces are the values of love and friendship, contrasted with hate and hostility, expressing that original solidarity of the human species. These values should dominate in interactions between individuals, as well as in social groups (primary and secondary), forming ever-wider nations and their federations. They should already prepare people for the emerging globalization changes. They require adequate, universalist axiology and the resulting patterns of co-existence in adequate cultural, economic and political conditions primordially related with the typical human primary form of solidarity of species. Every living human being is a human being by the fact of birth (the appearance in the order of existence) and should be regarded as such by other people, regardless of his or her ethnic differences in the formation of culture.[4] It was an important reminder to *The Myth of Sisyphus* by Camus, showing his universal message and it's extraction from fundamental consequences, symbolized by Sisyphus in the face of the absurd fate of the human species, leading to the conclusion: "I rebel, therefore we are." Rebellion was shown as the centre of the humanity that not only liberated the intellect from animal-like life, but also a consistent attitude towards other people and their place in the world. This attitude gives meaning to every individual human existence and at the same time is the centre of human species' being, embracing opposition and active rebellion

---

3 W. Szydłowska, *Camus*, Seria: Myśli i Ludzie, Warszawa, Wiedza Powszechna, 2002, p. 36–37.

4 *Ibidem*, p. 135–138 and 141–143.

in defence of another member of our species.[5] Thanks to this rebellion the man existed, exists and shall exist forever.

In this way of thinking we can see components of the Cartesian method of doubt, which leads to the "undeniable thing:" my thinking and what is thought; what is discovered and what it illusory. It discovers the absurd that is my reified existence, as opposed to my personal being – a case of *res extensa*. A person reified is an effect of a deceitful move away from the source of man's own authenticity. The revolt directed against it is an expression of opposition against such a reified being; the existential situation of the rebel is like a return of thought to itself – to *res cogitans*. He not only leads the rebellion to an act of rejection of this reification (e.g. in the case of an actor), but also expresses opposition to the treatment of another human being in such a reifying manner, in which the individual is thrown beyond the limit of the species' organic solidarity. The rebellion's aim is to restore and adapt the human being to the return to the "human family" in which he or she was treated as a human being – a typically personal being, and not a thing in relation to which one cannot reasonably harbour a sense of moral obligation with all its existential consequences.

2. TRADITIONAL AND NEW UNIVERSALISM

Contemporary universalist approach to human beings encounters several difficulties that arise from the increasing number of divisions among people, at the basis of which there are cultural, economic and political differences. A group of thinkers, defined as the new left, appears to evaluate this situation pertinently. The work of Etienne Balibar – a French philosopher of Marxist orientation, takes an important place in the analysis of this situation. He sees the sources of the crisis severing the contemporary Europe from its historical heritage, which it imposed upon itself, but also upon the other areas of the world in the processes of colonization. It originates from a strategy of dividing and conflicting the parties concerned, according to the principle: *divide et impera*. The effects of this policy were the divisions of the world into the spheres of the colonizer's influence, which involved the construction and reconstruction of borders. These borders did not reflect the natural ethnic divisions between people, not only in Europe but also throughout the world. The conceptual output of Balibar and his multicultural knowledge enriches

5 *Ibidem*, p. 36–37.

the theoretical tools of contemporary historical materialism and can be useful for the evaluation and diagnosis of integrating Europe and globalizing world. Balibar also shows the need of creating a new discourse, e.g. in the sphere of universalism, whose current program is purely hypocritical in practice, as it leads to further divisions among people, instead of integrating them. This program supports numerous forms of particularism of the white and wealthy people of the West, and shows its violent character. Balibar does not propose to change this universalism and its components dividing people. However, as it harms the universal understanding of man in the contemporary postmodern and multicultural world, a new, multicultural universalism should arise at its base, leading to a universal attitude of the individual, which would increase by the pursuit of a universal understanding of contemporary humanity on the planet.[6] It should put up with the racist and nationalist attitudes as well as blurred identities, and in place of false universalistic contents discover and constitute new ones, more open to contemporary social situations, arising from the enormous acceleration of life and mobility of people in the contemporary world. This process leads the vast majority of societies to take shape of a mosaic character, which is made up both of indigenous people and immigrants. The content of the new universalism should belong to the category of the citizen of a given state, and not the one of national origin or religious affiliation. This must also apply to the dominant ideology of the ruling classes, which legitimizes these particularisms and is the source of false consciousness, dividing people. This prevailing false content in the social consciousness leads to a hegemonic divide and subordinates the world today to being a community in conflict. This situation applies nowadays in a significant way, after the unification of Europe, because it influences the framework of the existing universalism, e.g. in the development of "the Europe of different speeds," etc. A derivation of universalism from the ancient sources – Athens, Rome, Jerusalem – is also ineffective, because it applies only to the origins of southern Europe. Camus understood this issue of division of Europe, envisioned as "the warm South" and "the cold North," where immigrants are seen as foreigners. It is worth mentioning that the origin of the name of Europe also derives from a Phoenician word – "Erbe" (darkness, evening). The ancient Greeks saw themselves as "people inside," thrown between Asians and Europeans; their role was a constant "investigation into

6 E. Balibar, I. Wallerstein, *Race, Nation, Class. Ambiguous Identities*, London–New York, Verso, 1991, p. 44–46.

universalism," but not its petrification.[7] Balibar observes the problem in relation to the currently growing issue of proliferation of borders in Europe. These divisions are, in his opinion, without reasonable grounds.[8] This also is the source of the fundamental crisis in Europe and the world undergoing Europeanization. This crisis of borders is also the source of the changes in the concept of citizenship, as well as the wrong understanding of decolonization, which doesn't allow the citizens of former colonies to receive citizenship in the withdrawing metropolis. These processes are transferred to the issues of labour market and common currency, and their source is the economic neo-liberalism, awakening the demons of nationalism, racism and classism that appear in the analysis of the situation in contemporary Europe as seen today through the eyes of Balibar,[9] and were similarly perceived in the 20th century by Camus.

The new universalism, accepting the principle of multicultural coexistence of people – according to "left" researchers – should be based on ethnicity of diverse groups of people in the global world. Each group seeks to universalize their norms and cultural values of ethnic origin. In intercultural communication, there is a possibility of obtaining a dynamic consensus regarding the preferred universal values. At the same time it can also keep dissent, emphasizing the ethnic origins of all the values currently considered universal.[10] However, it should move away from the "western universalism," which is the source of "post-racism" and "neo-racism" proclaimed by rightist political centres in the name of "purity of cultural monolith" in the societies of the rich West.[11] "White universalism" generates existential and economic exclusion of people, and undermines the moral arguments of affluent societies, that the economic position is enriched both by the operation of natives as well as immigrants and refugees. These negative social processes are explained and justified by the "white ideology" presented as universalist and hegemonic. Thus only a new form of universalism, built on ethnic particularism, can create opportunities for resolving social conflicts in the contemporary and postmodern world. The present-day societies are even bound to create forms of "open societies," in which all the people, both natives and immigrants, will

7 R. Gasche, *Europe, or the Infinite Task. A Study of Philosophical Concept*, Stanford, Stanford University Press, 2009.

8 E. Balibar, *Trwoga mas. Polityka i filozofia przed Marksem i po Marksie*, Warszawa, Dialog, 2007, p. 289–300.

9 *Ibidem*, p. 369–371.

10 E. Balibar, I. Wallerstein, *op.cit.*, p. 56–59.

11 *Ibidem*, p. 17–28.

have their rights secured. However, the contemporary "postmodern man," by becoming an economic and cultural nomad, by losing consciousness of his original conception of nationality and his religious and cultural heritage, will weaken this distinction.[12]

3. STRUCTURE AND GENESIS OF EXISTENTIAL REFLECTION OF FRENCH INTELLECTUAL

The protest against the absurdity of human condition in the world, leading up to the rebellion, as understood by Camus, appeared relatively early in his life, because he did not agree with the conditions of existence of the poor district of Algiers, where he was raised. Therefore, he engaged in creative activities (sports and theatre), which provided social emancipation, but also created an opportunity to help other people remaining in a similar situation. Here the model for him was primarily his teacher, L. Germaine. The outbreak of World War II and the experience of terror in occupied France led Camus to political struggle with German occupiers. As a journalist and writer he also fought against oppression and military society in his native Algeria, and finally, as a theatre artist (actor, director) and a writer he started raising awareness of the human condition among the general public, who experienced the loss of dignity and freedom in thought and action. The creative tool of rebellion was for him the unconditional love to another human being, which knows no limits when it comes to being neighbours. Not only did he oppose totalitarian, government policies based on Nazi ideology or Marxism, but also the philosophical phenomenology of Edmund Husserl and the Catholic existential philosophy and religion. In the phenomenology of Husserl he saw structures in the area of idealistic collective consciousness of the transcendental ego – the last entity of the human reality in the world, which, in his opinion, was to offer the final contents of the universal sense of the world and point to the meaning of individual human existence. Camus described this type of consciousness as an "absurd wall" that blocks the development of the existential nature of man, leading to totalizing attempts of imposing it by transcendent ideas. This was not consistent with his understanding of the spirit of the Sartrean concept of man, as the one who "is what he is not, and is not what he is." He was rather closer to the

---

[12] J. Butler, E. Laclau, S. Žižek, *Przygodność, hegemonia, uniwersalność: współczesna debata na lewicy*, Warszawa, Krytyka Polityczna, 2014.

existential phenomenology (analytics) of Martin Heidegger, who perceived the man as *Dasein* – a specific being, conscious (aware) of its existence in the world – which is constantly "projected into the future" (*Einwurft für Zukunft*). He was standing in the clearance (*das Lichtung*), bringing concepts through entities that make up his world, extracted from his being and through which he became "shepherd of being of the beings" (*der Hirter des Seins den Seineden*). So the man, as a conscious being, by its psychophysical nature is set for the future; he is burdened by the choices and courses of actions, which create his essence and give him meaning and ends of his personal existence. As such, he is held responsible for his own existence, but also for that of other people's, as well as for the world and the whole society. If for Jaen-Paul Sartre and Martin Heidegger it was a tragic situation, resulting from the experience of one's own absurdity in the world, for Camus this tragedy of individual existence, and thus life filled with passion to create, has an optimistic dimension. Especially when he can make a rational justification of his passion for existence, exceeding (overstepping) the absurdity of human life. This belief has become for him a source premise, forming the basis of the whole philosophical culture of man and above all its metaphors – as contained in the ancient myth of Sisyphus – exceeding the human existential trauma. The passion of existence in the opinion of Camus has been recognized as a new way of creative rebirth of freedom in human beings. It was supported, on an emotional level, by a discovery and transformation of the ancient myth and its justification of both active opposition and existential rebellion, expressed positively in the creation and development of their individual and collective human aspects – i.e. being through a variety of works of creativity, typically existential (e.g. a style of life), but also to artistic activity. The objection and rebellion should be directed against the current, unnatural human condition in the world, created by the economic and the psychosocial mechanisms (condemning an entity to objectification, alienation from society and the world, in practice the marginalization in social life and the loss of their personal dignity as well as the dignity of other people), which limit the horizon of possibility of existential discovery of one's own meaning of life.[13] Camus, therefore, did not agree with radical models (mainly politico-ideological and religious), imposing limitations on people's choices and their attempts at making sense of their own existence. He denounced them in his short stories, novels, dramas and essays, revealing their dark sides in the context of their influence, not only on existential

---

13 I.S. Fiut, *op.cit.*, p. 49–52.

experience, but also on social conditions in cases of historical rebellions of the human being and social revolutions resulting from them. This was well illustrated in the case of the Emperor Caligula,[14] and descriptions of social revolutions, which – in accordance with a known rule of the fate of revolutionaries – "ate their own children."

Camus also denounced religion, seeing it as a tool of alienation of man from the world and from others; giving, in exchange, eternal care of God both in this life and the afterlife. As a result, he rejected the idealistic religious philosophy, which justified the dogmas of the Christian faith, leading to this type of attitudes. In its place, he began to look for something different, that could, in future, discover the universal end of human action, conferring it meaning. But this meaning should consider the aspects of individual existence, which is entangled in this aporetics and filled with existential contradictions and conflicts with the world, in which there are scorn and devastation of human dignity, performed frequently on behalf of the nation, humanity, or in the name of existence of God and the Church. Religions and ideologies exploit and oppose the people, frequently because of family ties.

Apart from the order of his philosophical essays, we should mention at least three notions, which are the body of his philosophy of absurdity and rebellion, i.e., *The Myth of Sisyphus*, *The Absurd Man* and *The Man in Revolt*. They are all in the core of Camus's philosophical reflection, abstracted from the thoughts of ancients, seeking a universal solution, compatible with the nature of human existence, which was suggested by the movement of the existentialist philosophy of the 20th century.

In the first period of his literary career, Camus made reconciliation with the world of human sensuality and exhibited a specific natural value of human life, while simultaneously discovering gaps in, being the source of human loneliness. In addition to describing this source, he referred to its functioning in society and religion. He came to the conclusion, that although in certain critical existential situations it may be better to choose death as a way of reconciliation with the world, suicide can never be justified in any moral perspective, because it always disavows human dignity. Suicide negates life itself, which is considered as an absolute value, being at the base of all other human values.

---

14 M. Kałuża, *Elementy filozofii absurdu w dramaturgii Alberta Camusa*, Kraków, Wydawnictwo Libron, 2016, p. 23–24.

Accompanying individual human existence is the feeling of the absurd, which led Camus to considerations in the essays known as depictions of "Absurd Man". These visions of existential human beings in the proverbial Actor, Don Juan, and Conqueror present people filled only with the passion for action. They do not lead – in the opinion of Camus – to the solution of his existential dilemmas, and their exhibited "ethics of quantity" does not give a qualitatively new ethic of human life. It rather deepens isolation of the human individual because the "consciousness of absurdity" of human existence cannot be, in these forms, helpful in the life of contradictions and the constant threat of death.[15] Not having full awareness of the consequences of the "consciousness of the absurd," being involved in the remnants of consciousness is quintessential to losing importance, and such a man becomes a "stranger to ourselves and the world." Such a situation leads to alienation, that is, "losing oneself" and the world, rather than leading to a renewal of the sense of his existence. Creative attitude should be, after all, essential for one's existential nature. Referring to the ancient myth of Sisyphus, Camus makes a transition from its traditional meaning, as a metaphor of human existence, to reading it in the contemporary existential perspective. In the case of "mythical Sisyphus," he sees now that there is room for substantial optimism – provided that human experience makes us realize the real meaning of our existence, as well as the need for notorious objection to the destructive forces directed against human dignity. Therefore, the philosopher states that "we can imagine Sisyphus happy" nowadays. This state of consciousness may therefore represent a further stage of development of individual consciousness of people, on which we can responsibly develop a "consciousness of rebellion;" the need for causal and proactive action against the forces and mechanisms, which disavow value and dignity of every human being. In the *Man in Revolt* Camus expresses this principle of restoration of the rebel, who rediscovers the meaning of existence, that is, the need for active solidarity with others. The author concludes the essay with an important conclusion: "I rebel, therefore we exist." This would mean that only if we become fully human we are able to actively oppose situations which disavow dignity and the absolute value of the Second man, that is defend absolutely his and our "is" in being the people in the world.[16] At that time we discover

15 A. Camus, *Mit Syzyfa. Rozumowanie absurdalne* [in:] *idem*, *Eseje*, wydanie drugie, Warszawa, PIW, 1974, p. 112–114.

16 A. Camus, *Człowiek zbuntowany* [in:] *idem*, *Eseje*..., p. 273–275, and: F. Estrade, *Człowiek i twórca: Albert Camus*, Warszawa, MUZA SA, 2008, p. 137–139.

that we are actually free as well as fully aware of our own existence, in order to co-exist with Others.

4. *THE FIRST MAN* – A FUTURE PROJECT OF THE HUMAN CONDITION IN THE WORLD ACCORDING TO CAMUS

Camus, an analyst of the phenomenon of human existence, was well aware that by his or her very nature, the human being, holding awareness of the intentional, is doomed by the fact of the incessant transcending towards the world and to the future (not only his or her own, but also of the human species in general). He was also aware that his proposals and analysis of the human condition are incomplete and that many of the phenomena of existence cannot be fully explained nor understood. We're guessing that's why he took on the next literary work, which was a novel – *The First Man*.[17] In it, he outlined the "Cosmic Idea of Man," a set of values, which must be constantly and consistently aimed at, if the human being wants to make his or her conscious revolt. This idea should have an important and universal character in all cultures, but also in the timeless, existential context, to protect the ability to sense the existence of human beings in the future and global dimensions. It could not be – of course – a product of a purely ideal and closed imposition from outside, limiting human freedom and one's ability to choose for oneself and the world.[18] For the human being, as a species and as an individual – of which the French existentialist was fully aware – is still developing and evolving in the globalized world and must take risks to live in different cultures (which was also a personal experience of Camus himself). This idea could not, cannot be now and in the future alien to the people throughout the world. Therefore, people should constantly create it, convert it within the limits that do not transgress the essence of humanity, so that they do not become the "slaves of history."

---

17 A. Camus, *Pierwszy człowiek*, Warszawa, PIW, 1994. Camus writes in this book of his own experience resulting from the lack of authority of the father in the family. This inhibited the development of his mature personality. He also splits experience with attempts to build a self-creative personality, approaching its existential situation to "a pupil of Socrates" after the death of the master who created it, "the tutelary spirit" – the internal censor. Camus's work developed in the soul of author's prototype of this "cosmic idea of man." It helped him through life itself and to choose their own way of life based on the physical and metaphysical revolt. In this book Camus shared this idea with his readers.

18 *Ibidem*, p. 81–98.

5. THE REVOLT AS THE TOOL TO DEFEND AND PROMOTE MEANINGFUL HUMAN EXISTENCE

In Camus's philosophical reflection we can distinguish two forms of revolt: the physical (existential and artistic) and the metaphysical revolt, with particular emphasis on the causative and created values. The physical revolt, without the former metaphysical revolt, is usually transformed into rape and violence, which confirms the tendency that reveals itself in all activities of revolutionaries, and so it is also present in the public consciousness: the majority of rebels seem as criminals in the immediate experience. Not accidentally revolutions and counter-revolutions "ate their own children." This mechanism consists of the fact that the new awareness of the rebellious fighting changes the perception of the man in the current "socio-awareness," proposing at the same time its new form, which justifies both the objection and the revolt in the context of existing essentialist patterns. They define who exactly should be the man, given our context of social awareness. The rebels, who challenge the existing essentialist models in the context of existential analysis, strengthen their acts of dissent and revolt and propose a new vision of the essential, metaphysical human nature. In the light of the facts of rape and violence, in which the rebels are living their own lives, they are not criminals, but creative heroes. Their rebellion stems from the love of other people, and its aim is to fight for their dignity without exception. The other people, by the fact of non-participation in opposition and rebellion, will be regarded as reactionary and counter-revolutionary. This fact explains the mechanism of the "social machine" in the case of counter-revolution eating revolution's "own children" – according to the known principle: "who is not with us, is against us."

This iconic physical revolt is frequently called the "the Spartacus model," referring to a historical rebellion against the slave conditions in the Roman Empire, which did not propose any solution of social improvement for the people other than pushing their earlier adversaries and opponents into slavery, leading consequently to their defeat. It can therefore be assumed that Camus understood this axiological mechanism of earlier historical rebellions and revolutions and wanted to propose a new solution for an axiological dimension of revolt, exposing primarily the metaphysical revolt on the level of collective consciousness, which would exclude and minimize bloody rape, violence, genocide and suicide. They accompany such rapid social changes of the physical nature of the revolt, which takes the form of mass revolutions and the accompanying axiological deprivation of values of the human dignity through "the active revolutionary rebels."

According to Camus, in the perspective of the historical experience of people, the metaphysical revolt is more valuable, being directed by the existential analysis of the current human condition and its associated axiological contexts against "the current idea of man." This revolt must be strictly universal, exposing mainly the primary, axiological value of human freedom and practically "solidarity in freedom." It has thus secured, without exception, the worth of life of every individual, but does not give any axiological justification to neither death, nor different forms of marginalization, murder and genocide.[19] This revolt also weakens the passion of individual consciousness and social attitudes to adopt physical revolt, because it allows them peacefully to correct and limit action, to trigger social protests and so-called attitudes of "passive resistance," which incidentally can lead to murder or suicide. In this perspective, metaphysical and universal revolt "in itself" becomes the value of formative and encouraging attempts to create new values. As a positive value, revolt prevents the absolutization of values and their idealistic essentialization, by including the existential concept of being a background for the human being in social consciousness of his or her ethnic. On the basis of this discovery, and rational justification and proposal for solving the antithetical nature of the human being, created in the context of his world, seems to count, in the future value of the thoughts of the French existentialist, which includes his philosophical and literary achievement.

BIBLIOGRAPHY

Albérès, R-M., *et al.*, *Camus*, Collection Genies Réalités, Paris, Hachette, 1964.

Balibar, E., *Trwoga mas. Polityka i filozofia przed Marksem i po Marksie*, Warszawa, Dialog, 2007.

Balibar, E., Wallerstein, I., *Race, Nation, Class. Ambiguous Identities*, London–New York, Verso, 1991.

Butler, J., Laclau, E., Žižek, S., *Przygodność, hegemonia, uniwersalność: współczesna debata na lewicy*, Warszawa, Krytyka Polityczna, 2014.

Camus, A., *Człowiek zbuntowany* [in:] A. Camus, *Eseje*, wydanie drugie, Warszawa, PIW, 1974.

Camus, A., *Eseje*, wydanie drugie, Warszawa, PIW, 1974.

Camus, A., *Pierwszy człowiek*, Warszawa, PIW, 1994.

Estrade, F., *Człowiek i twórca: Albert Camus*, Warszawa, MUZA SA, 2008.

[19] W. Natanson, *Szczęście Syzyfa*, Kraków, Wydawnictwo Literackie, 1980.

Fiut, I.S., *Człowiek według Alberta Camusa. Studium antropologii egzystencjalnej*, Kraków, Wydawnictwo KKL-A, 1993.

Gasche, R., *Europe, or the Infinite Task. A Study of Philosophical Concept*, Stanford, Stanford University Press, 2009.

Kałuża, M., *Elementy filozofii absurdu w dramaturgii Alberta Camusa*, Kraków, Wydawnictwo LIBRON, 2016.

Natanson, W., *Szczęście Syzyfa*, Kraków, Wydawnictwo Literackie, 1980.

Szydłowska, W., *Camus*, Seria: Myśli i Ludzie, Warszawa, Wiedza Powszechna, 2002.

Todd, O., *Albert Camus. Biografia*, Warszawa, Wydawnictwo W.A.B., 2009.

Does Justice Require Victims?
Reflections on Albert Camus's Thought

EWA ŚREDNICKA

INTRODUCTION

> Democracy – real democracy – remains to be constructed.
> And we will do so in an orderly society – a truly orderly society.[1]

The trials of Nazi collaborators, which took place after the liberation of Paris from the grips of occupants, proved it necessary to redefine the definitions of primary values such as freedom, justice and equality. As Maurice Merleau-Ponty noticed, people who collaborated with the Nazi camp were proclaimed "traitors" not by means of criteria which could be set objectively, but due to the fact that the resistance movement had won.[2] In an alternative course of events, they would have been introduced as heroes, whose heroic attitude would have been inscribed on the pages of history forever. This shows only the evanescence of ideals, which can be easily manipulated when considered in the context of one prevailing concept. Czesław Miłosz in *The Captive Mind* captured this process most accurately. The writer managed to pinpoint the strength with which one dominant thought

---

1 A. Camus, the editorial of September 2nd, 1944 [in:] *Camus at Combat: Writing 1944–1947*, trans. A Goldhammer, ed. J. Levi-Valensi, Princeton and Oxford, Princeton University Press, 2006, p. 27.

2 See: M. Merleau-Ponty, *Humanizm i terror*, trans. J. Migasiński [in:] *Marksizm XX wieku: antologia tekstów*, cz. 1–3, ed. J. Dobieszewski, M.J. Siemek, Warszawa, Wydawnictwo Uniwersytetu Warszawskiego, 1990.

infiltrated the considerations of many minds of the post-war intellectual world. He also pointed out the consequences that occurred in the wake of the fleeting blindness which affected people's view of reality and impaired their ability to look critically at events.[3] Even among the most sapient minds, the lack of unambiguous definitions of fundamental categories entails the danger of becoming lost when faced with the need for decision-making, and uttering distinct and unpopular judgments. However, events which took place in post-occupation France showed that the discourse regarding intuitively comprehended values gains significance when standing on the verge of inevitable fatalism.

The liberation became an impulse to discuss the fate of collaborators who, during the Second World War, did not cooperate with enemies actively, but encouraged such cooperation or criticized the State of Vichy for its passive participation in creating state politics.[4] Such collaborators often provided arguments for the ultimate and official alliance with the aggressor. Among these collaborators were those who were known and acknowledged in the public eye and had a major impact on opinions within French society. Making use of their position, they tried to persuade as many people as possible to agree with their beliefs and, as a result, to weaken the influence of the resistance movement on the society. Such actions, however, in reference to the French Penal Code, which was officially valid at that time, could not be acknowledged as treason and qualified as a crime. The 75th article which regulated that issue defined particular premises of criminal liability, i.e. bearing arms against France, maintaining relations with a foreign power, committing to undertake hostilities against France, providing means to facilitate the entry of foreign forces into French territory, entering the service of a foreign power, and maintaining relations with a foreign power in order to encourage actions of this power against France.[5] The lack of a premise which would allow people who were guilty of supporting the policy of occupants to be criminally responsible led to an extension in the interpretation of the phrase "maintaining relations with a foreign power." Strong voices were heard arguing that pro-Nazi agitation was also eligible to be qualified as a crime due to the contest of the article mentioned

3 See: Cz. Miłosz, *Zniewolony umysł*, Kraków, KAW, 1990.

4 See: T. Judt, *Historia niedokończona. Francuscy intelektualiści 1944–1956*, trans. P. Marczewski, Warszawa, Krytyka Polityczna, 2012.

5 The full text of the article is available at: http://www.cdvfe-divisioncharlemagne.com/upload/Article%2075.pdf [access: 22.09.2015].

before, even though an explicit base did not exist. Such an understanding of the article would have enabled as many supporters of the Third Reich as possible to be held criminally responsible, without the need for adjusting the law[6] (which *nota bene* would not have been possible without breaching one of the most important elements of the rule of law: that law must not be applied retroactively, i.e. it is wrong to judge actions which happened before the law was enacted[7]).

The problem was the justification of many trials which relied on an ambiguous and equivocal legal basis. It raised doubts regarding the existence of the ideals of the rule of law, which the French Republic after the war was supposed to respect. The purge trials were conducted promptly, often without allowing witnesses to testify or evidence to be presented. The accused were also often sentenced to death.[8] The purges brought about a division among prominent French intellectuals into two camps: those who raised critical questions about the trials and those who provided arguments for the endorsement of the trials. The head of the first group was Francois Mauriac, who tried to remind *Le Figaro*'s readers of the issue of mercy. The second group was led by Albert Camus, who referred in the editorials of *Combat*[9] to the issue of justice as the ground for the justification of the controversial trials.[10]

In this essay, only the *Combat* editorials which relate to the problem of justice will be taken into account. *Combat* was a newspaper established by the United Movements of Resistance, and Camus was the editor-in-chief in the period of 1944–1947.[11] We will attempt to unveil how Camus harnessed the concept of justice in order to justify the purge trials, and how the ambiguity of justice resulted in difficulties when considered in relation to the problem of the purges. The reasoning will lead us to the significant concept

---

6 See: T. Judt, *Powojnie. Historia Europy od roku 1945*, trans. R. Bartołd, Poznań, Rebis, 2013, p. 59–65.

7 See: L.L. Fuller, *The Morality of Law: Revised Edition*, New Haven–London, Yale University Press, 1964, p. 51–63.

8 See: T. Judt, *Historia niedokończona...*, p. 67.

9 It is worth noting that even if Camus wasn't the direct author of some of the editorials, he had a major impact on creating them – the editorials were at first profoundly discussed by the whole editorial board of *Combat* (which *nota bene* were composed only of Camus, Henri Frederic, Albert Olliver and Pascal Pia) and published exclusively if each member accepted them (see: O. Todd, *Albert Camus. Biografia*, trans. J. Kortas, Warszawa, Wydawnictwo W.A.B., 2009, p. 375).

10 See: R. Drai, *Camus i Mauriac. Spór o miłosierdzie*, trans. S. Kowalski, „Gazeta Wyborcza", 9th August 2014.

11 See: J. Levi-Valensi, *Introduction* [in:] *Camus at Combat: Writing 1944–1947...*, p. xxxi.

of revolution provided by Camus. Subsequently, *The Just Assassins* will be taken into consideration to provide us with deep insight into the relationship between justice and terror. Finally, the set of editorials titled *Neither Victims nor Executioners* will be discussed in regard to Camus's answers to the issues raised before. Our thesis is as follows: Camus sees the way out of the contradiction resulting from the concept of justice as provided in the *Combat* editorials in the rejection of the ideological thinking leading to absolutization of justice.

JUSTICE AND REVOLUTION

As Camus wrote in September 1944: "The difficult and prodigious task we face is to establish justice in the most unjust of worlds."[12] This is just one of many claims from the beginning of the post-occupation purge. He referred to the idea of justice as the most desired value needed for the foundation of the restoration process in France. In the same editorial, Camus explained how justice can be understood: "Justice for all means that the personality of the individual must be subordinated to the collective good."[13] Later on, he added: "Whenever we deal with a social issue, we need to think about the individual, and whenever the individual claims our attention, we need to consider the good of all."[14] Camus believed that social order required equilibrium between the government and the people it governed. And this harmony could be achieved on the basis of justice. As he put it directly: "There is no order without justice, and the ideal order lies in the happiness of people."[15]

For Camus, the common good demanded vengeance for the victims of the occupation. Their death was brought about by people, many of whom remained unpunished after the liberation. However, such a lack of compensation leads directly to the division of the society into those whose relatives have not been avenged and those whose actions have led to the death of others. In Camus's eyes, such a situation immediately causes the rise of hatred. In the long term it would also lead to the destabilization of the whole

---

12 *Camus at Combat: Writing 1944–1947...*, p. 257.

13 A. Camus, the editorial of September 8th, 1944 [in:] *Camus at Combat: Writing 1944–1947...*, p. 31.

14 Ibidem, p. 32.

15 A. Camus, the editorial of October 12th, 1944 [in:] *Camus at Combat: Writing 1944–1947...*, p. 69.

nation. Therefore, in order to avoid internal disintegration, the society must face the problem of the embodiment of justice in the post-liberation system. In this context, Camus says:

> We know full well that on the day the first death sentence is carried out in Paris, we will feel repugnance. At that moment we will need to remember the countless other death sentences imposed on men who were pure and will have to recall so many cherished faces now buried in the ground and so many hands we once loved to shake.[16]

Moreover, Camus had a negative opinion on the issue of divine justice. To put it simply, he claimed that there was no faith in divine justice anymore. Consequently, people have to turn themselves to human justice "with its terrible imperfections."[17] One of the negative sides of human justice is the necessity of making choices and accepting the consequences of one's decisions. In the age of war, a human being becomes an arbiter and faces all the difficulties entailed by the new role. Otherwise, depending only on divine justice, society would not be able to rid itself of postwar dilemmas. As Camus says: "One doesn't have to be a Christian to believe that sacrifices for justice are necessary."[18] He adds in the same editorial:

> We invite Mr. Mauriac to consider the dilemma of those to whom the notion of divine judgment is foreign yet who retain a taste for man and hope for its grandeur. They must either hold their peace forever or become converts to human justice. This cannot take place without distress. But after four years of collective suffering in the wake of twenty-five years of mediocrity, doubt is no longer possible. And we have chosen to embrace human justice with its terrible imperfections.[19]

The principle of justice is therefore coupled with the problem of responsibility, which can be considered at two levels. The first one is related to the responsibility of the judges, the second one refers to the criminals who committed

---

16 A. Camus, the editorial of October 21th, 1944 [in:] *Camus at Combat: Writing 1944–1947...*, p. 82.

17 A. Camus, the editorial of October 25th, 1944 [in:] *Camus at Combat: Writing 1944–1947...*, p. 90.

18 A. Camus, the editorial of October 25th, 1944 [in:] *Camus at Combat: Writing 1944–1947...*, p. 89.

19 *Ibidem*.

crimes during the war. When it comes to the latter, the responsibility of wrongdoers, Camus relates it to the concept of "proportional responsibility." Responsibility did not concern only evident acts from the people criminally liable under the 75th article of the French Penal Code that was binding after the Second World War. Those who contributed indirectly to the criminal acts, such as industrialists and opinion-makers, were also considered responsible. That is why, according to Camus, an amendment of the Penal Code was needed. The crimes of the prominent politicians of the Vichy regime could be judged on the basis of the 75th article which determined that people who collaborated with the enemy should be judged. However, the post-liberation dilemma applied mostly to people who could not be judged on the grounds of this article, for example journalists or writers, whose fault had been to persuade others to collaborate with the Nazi occupants. For this reason, Camus postulated introducing a new type of crime: "consorting with the enemy,"[20] that would have had retroactive power. However, such a type of crime would have made the law unpredictable and vulnerable to change by the ruling regime. Camus seemed to recognize this problem when stating:

> The notion of "consorting with the enemy" is useful. Or, rather, it must be put to use. Furthermore, if it is indeed the case that the application of this higher moral law involves the assertion of principles of punishment incompatible with the spirit of democracy, a corrective is nevertheless available.[21]

We come therefore to the first type of responsibility – responsibility of the judges of the actions from the occupation period. To consider this issue, we will appeal to the concept of revolution, as delivered by Camus. According to him – from the period of the *Combat* editorials – revolution is the use of force against the life of individuals in order to embody justice in reality. Camus wrote:

> Nor can we forget that in both cases the lives of Frenchmen are at stake: the best of us will have to die in the war, and we will have to destroy the worst of us in the revolution.[22]

---

20 A. Camus, the editorial of September 28th, 1944 [in:] *Camus at Combat: Writing 1944–1947...*, p. 50.

21 A. Camus, the editorial of October 18th, 1944 [in:] *Camus at Combat: Writing 1944–1947...*, p. 77.

22 A. Camus, the editorial of October 21th, 1944 [in:] *Camus at Combat: Writing 1944–1947...*, p. 82.

And also:

> Regardless of our desires and reactions, there can be no doubt that France has a revolution to make as well as a war. That is indeed the drama it faces.[23]

Revolution therefore is a tool held in the hands of the guards of the new order. It is the necessary step towards the restoration of social harmony. As was shown before, in Camus's eyes, justice demands vengeance for the pointless deaths of many victims. And revolution is the tool to cope with this issue. For Camus, revolution is inevitable for the same reason as in the case of war. Revolution is just the necessary corollary of the actions of people from the period of occupation, which enables sins to be judged. It helps with the restoration of social order, trust and the authority of the new power. Weaknesses will not pass unnoticed. Responsibility should be taken even after considering the fact that the choices were made in the extreme circumstance of occupation. Revolution is also the tool to restore the spirit of the nation, which will not break again under the influence of external forces. And, ultimately, revolution makes it possible to face hesitations that inevitably arise after each conflict, stifling the society.

> We cannot escape from this drama by evading the question it raises. We can escape only by enduring it to the bitter end and drawing from it whatever truth it contains.[24]

Revolution therefore strengthens bonds between members of the society. It enables a sense of security to be restored and harm to be redressed, building grounds for a liberated society. It is the tool embodying the pure concept of justice in the real world.

One of the problems with the concept of revolution is that revolution does not have to be legal. Camus says this explicitly. By postulating the *post factum* amendment of the law, he falls into a trap, which, when recognized, leads to his later reconsiderations. The winners of the war are allowed to build the post-conflict order on their own and no one is strong enough to stand up against them. And they can do it on behalf of justice. They are allowed to judge anyone anytime they find necessary, even if they have no grounds in the law

[23] A. Camus, the editorial of October 20th, 1944 [in:] *Camus at Combat: Writing 1944–1947...*, p. 81.

[24] *Ibidem.*

to do this. Such actions are allowed therefore to be arbitrary and judges are permitted to sentence anyone to death or to prison, if they find it beneficial for social order. Actions that are performed on behalf of justice are justified. The post-Hobbesian question remains: What is the difference between a state in which the winners are in control of other people's lives and a state of war?

The other problem with the concept of revolution in the shape that Camus provides is that the post-war time is defined by disorder. There are no new institutions created yet. It is hard to find judges whose opinions would not have been distorted by an occupation that caused emotional biases and who would consequently be able to defend themselves against the pressure imposed on them by the divided society. Society wants a quick punishment and that is the perfect field for abuse. People who were victims during the war, now turn into the judges of those who hurt them or their relatives. War provides two categories of people: occupants and victims. But when victims win the war, they get the power to judge the occupants. And if their means are unrestricted, then this can cause an overuse of power. Therefore, the revolution that was supposed to be carried out on behalf of justice can become an alibi for new tyrants.

Thus, starting with justice, Camus comes to the idea against which he fights shortly afterwards: that the pure concept of justice requires the division of the world into two categories and can provide justification for violence. This is what happened in France after the occupation: trials from the purge period were conducted promptly and often without allowing evidence or witnesses.[25] Their legal base was the amendment to the Penal Code implemented after the liberation, which was retroactively binding. The guilt of the collaborators was therefore often prejudged. This made the trials far from just, if justice is understood in terms of the rule of law. The concept of revolution that Camus provided, which was supposed to be applied in the context of the purges, leads to the idea of the division of society into two opposite camps and to the justification of the use of violence. Very promptly, however, Camus recognizes the failure of the purges:

> We beg the reader's indulgence if we begin today with a basic fact: there can no longer be any doubt that the postwar purge has not only failed in France but is now completely discredited. The word "purge" itself was already rather distressing. [...] It seems that the straight path of justice is not easy to find amid

[25] See: T. Judt, *Powojnie...*, p. 59–65.

> the cries of hatred coming from one side and special pleading of guilty consciences coming from the other. In any case, the failure is complete.[26]

Camus had to deal with this issue of the purge trails on three different levels: (1) the issue of people who committed war crimes; (2) the issue of people who committed treason, but were acting according to the law as the authorities of the Vichy State; and (3) the issue of people who were urging others to leave the values of pre-war France and to turn towards Nazi occupants. And he seems to be aware of the complexity of this issue. The government officials of the Vichy regime tried to present themselves as heroes who were protecting the homeland. Their actions were not supposed to be considered as collaboration with the enemy, but as an appeal to the instinct of self-preservation.[27] The attempt of reconciling two different attitudes was not successful either for the left or for the right side. In this context, it is worth mentioning the case of Robert Brasillach – a critic of the government of Vichy, who was a well-known and respected writer in France at that time and an editor-in-chief of the pro-fascist magazine *Je suis partout*. On the pages of the magazine, he preached the need to transform cooperation with the Nazis into "a level of social friendship."[28] He criticized the government for the lack of involvement in rebuilding the grandeur of France in accordance with the Nazi ideology and for throwing France into the arms of Bolshevism.[29] The trials of such people resonated strongly in intellectuals' minds after the war and polarized society. A good illustration of this division was the petition in favor of mercy for Brasillach, who was sentenced to death before evidence was provided during the trial. More importantly for us, Camus eventually signed the petition. However, in a letter to Marcel Ayme, he explained that his reasons for doing so were related to his moral turn against the concept of the capital punishment.[30]

Camus's primary faith in justice, as expressed in early *Combat* editorials, was seriously reconsidered, leading the author to divide society into two categories: people who were allowed to make executions and those who could

---

26 A. Camus, the editorial of August 30th, 1945 [in:] *Camus at Combat: Writing 1944–1947...*, p. 249–250.

27 See: P. Klamann, *Między realizmem a oportunizmem. Rzecz o Francji Vichy*, „Folia Historica Cracoviensia" 2012, no. XVIII, p. 310. See: R.O. Praxton, *Francja Vichy. Stara gwardia i nowy ład 1940–1944*, trans. J. Lang, Wrocław, Bukowy Las, 2011.

28 J. Bartyzel, *Robert Brasillach*, http://www.legitymizm.org/ebp-robert-brasilach [access: 11.01.2015].

29 See: *ibidem*.

30 See: T. Judt, *Brzemię odpowiedzialności. Blum, Camus, Aron i francuski wiek dwudziesty*, trans. M. Filipczuk, Warszawa, Krytyka Polityczna, 2013, p. 146.

be judged out of the law system. The reason for this was war, which brutally destroyed the order of the nation. And defending the trials led Camus to the justification of violence. Having realized the consequences and the coherence between his former propositions and the effects of the purge, however, he confessed his aberration very quickly and put all his effort into pointing out the mistakes he had made in his previous reasoning.

JUSTICE AND TERROR

> – With whom to talk about murder if not with a murderer?
> – What murder? I remind myself only of an act of justice.[31]

The concept of the justification of violence occurs throughout Camus's later work. Mark Orme, the author of a detailed analysis of Camus's concept of justice, asserts even that the experience of the purge trials was a turning point in the writer's life, without which there would be no Camus that we know now.[32] The thesis can be disputed – we need to remember that Camus took his stand in the dispute on the purge trials after having written *Caligula*, *The Myth of Sisyphus* and *The Stranger*, in all of which he tried to develop his own attitude to the crucial problem of the death of a single man. It was however in 1949, in the play titled *The Just Assassins*, where the writer dealt directly with the issue of the mechanism at the foundation of the legitimization of murder. For the purpose of this essay, the play is especially interesting for two reasons: firstly, there is much dispute concerning the meaning of the play, and secondly, it depicts many ways in which violence could be justified, but ultimately rejects all of them.

In *The Just Assassins*, Camus portrays a group of young people who decide to murder the Grand Duke for a higher purpose, i.e. in order to liberate the whole of society from the power of tyranny.[33] In the name of freedom they decide to kill their ruler, and this action is subsequently supposed to bring prosperity to the next generations. However, many more justifications for their

---

31 "– Z kim mówić o zbrodni, jeśli nie ze zbrodniarzem? – Jakiej zbrodni? Przypominam sobie tylko akt sprawiedliwości." A. Camus, *Sprawiedliwi*, trans. J. Błoński [in:] A. Camus, *Dramaty*, trans. W. Natanson, M. Leśniewska, W. Błońska, J. Błoński, Kraków, Wydawnictwo Literackie, 1987, p. 274. All the quotes which appear in the essay were translated by the author.

32 See: M. Orme, *The Development of Albert Camus' Concern for Social and Political Justice*, Madison and Teaneck, Fairleigh Dickinson University Press, 2007, p. 127–152.

33 A. Camus, *Sprawiedliwi*..., p. 229.

deed emerge from the pages of *The Just Assassins*. For Kaliayev, taking the life of the despotic ruler seems to be the only possible way that would allow a world where "no one would ever kill"[34] to arise. His romantic soul longs for beauty and joy, which can be embodied exclusively in a society deprived of violence. He understands revolution, therefore, in the way that it is an action carried out due to the faith in the opportunity to realize the vision of a just world in which no unjustified death would occur:[35]

> I am preparing the revolution, because I love life. (...) The revolution for life in order to give it a chance. (...) Besides, we are killing to build the world.[36]

Annenkov – Kaliayev's companion – decides to take part in the assassination due to his belief in the possibility of liberating society from the power of the tyrant. He is a sensitive man of honor, who regards the temporary violence solely as a means to prevent any future terror.[37] Dora – Kaliayev's beloved – perceives murder as a terrifying necessity imposed by the demand for justice. She believes that the death penalty which will be later imposed on the perpetrator provides absolution for the sin. Death suffered on behalf of fulfilling one's beliefs means that the murderers who died for their ideas will arise as heroes:

> To perform the attack and then to go to the gallows – it's giving your life twice. We will pay more than we owe.[38]

Dora seems to recognize the evil to which she and her colleagues contribute, but her feeling appears to be blurred by the conviction that one day, evil itself will disappear. In the world surrounding the revolutionaries there is no place for such emotions as mercy or love – justice has engulfed them all, demanding full dedication and commitment.[39]

Vojnov – another of Kaliayev's companions – perceives the justification for murdering the Grand Duke in taking the decision to renounce lies. Justice

---

34 *Ibidem*, p. 238.

35 *Ibidem*.

36 "Dlatego przygotowuję rewolucję, że kocham życie. (...) Rewolucja dla życia, aby dać życiu szansę. (...) A zresztą zabijamy, żeby budować świat." *Ibidem*, p. 236–238.

37 *Ibidem*, p. 229.

38 "Ale dokonać zamachu, a później iść na szubienicę, to oddać życie dwa razy. Zapłacimy więcej niż jesteśmy winni." *Ibidem*, p. 239.

39 *Ibidem*, p. 259.

needs words – silence is exclusively another way of bearing the responsibility for injustice.[40] The sole means which can lead to liberation from this dilemma is an open fight, justified by one's beliefs. That is the only way to live in coherence with one's conscience, dictating the moral obligation of resisting evil.[41] Such a position is essentially different from the attitude of Stepan, for whom the highest justification of murder is the idea of revolution itself.[42] For him, the sacrifice of life is pointless, because one loses the chance to devote oneself to the revolution in the future.[43] Absolute justice requires obedience rather than exalted attitudes (which may lead solely to a stupor in the face of the need for real action[44]):

> I don't love life but justice, which is above life. (...) I came here to kill the man, not to love him or respect his distinctiveness.[45]

The fight with tyranny requires toughness – only then can it be accomplished with success.[46] Thereby, according to Stepan, everything which serves the revolution is allowed. Stepan feels responsible not just for the freedom of society in general but also for the freedom of each man separately, which positions him beyond all moral principles.[47] In a world where God is dead, someone has to take God's duties on their shoulders. Although not a ruler-tyrant, justice has to be given to someone who feels strong enough for this task:

> For us who don't believe in God, there's no choice: either full justice or despair.[48]

However, in the face of human feelings and hesitations, the revolutionaries prove to be powerless. The perseverance of their ideals is examined when they reach the inevitable adversities. Kaliayev requires an explicit order to be given in order to gain the strength to overcome them and to regain moral composure, getting rid of the dilemma concerning the responsibility for his actions.

---

40 *Ibidem*, p. 232.

41 *Ibidem*.

42 *Ibidem*, p. 251.

43 *Ibidem*, p. 236.

44 *Ibidem*.

45 "Ja nie kocham życia, ale sprawiedliwość, która jest ponad życiem. [...] Przyszedłem tu, aby zabić człowieka, nie po to, by go kochać czy uszanować jego odrębność." *Ibidem*.

46 *Ibidem*, p. 248.

47 *Ibidem*, p. 250.

48 "Dla nas, niewierzących w Boga, nie ma wyboru: albo pełna sprawiedliwość albo rozpacz." *Ibidem*, p. 263.

Annenkov recalls the principles of honor, which would aid him as a leader drawing an unambiguous line between morally right and wrong actions. Dora demands love in order to sacrifice her life to the revolution ultimately. The impulse forcing her to such devotion is the death of beloved Kaliayev, which results in the idea of perfect victory justifying the committed murder and prompting her to volunteer for another terrorist act.

According to some critics, Camus in *The Just Assassins* allows murder to be justified under certain conditions which all need to be fulfilled. John Foley, in his recent book addressing the issue, lists them all: (1) the victim is a tyrant; (2) the act must be discriminate; (3) the assassination is committed by a rebel in close proximity to his victim and the assassin must accept full responsibility for his individual action; (4) there is no less violent alternative to assassination.[49] It remains unnoticed, however, that the justification of murder can be considered at two different levels: the first one is the murder of a tyrant and the second one – the murder of a human. Despite the fact that killing the tyrant seems to become legitimate under some conditions, it automatically entails taking the life of a single man and, when perceiving the issue in compliance with Camus, justification for such an aspect of liberation from tyranny can never be provided. The death of an unjust ruler causes the death of a husband, a father and a friend as well.[50] "Murderers don't know about that. If they knew, how could they inflict death?,"[51] the Grand Duchess asks in her final dialogue with Kaliayev. The bomb thrown at tyranny also implies the death of a single human, which seems to be expressed by Camus in the play. And when we forget about this, we can describe ourselves as already lost and subordinated solely to our theoretical considerations.

Compelling is the scene when Kaliayev meets Foka – a prisoner who hangs convicts based on orders that have been issued to him. However, when Kaliayev calls him explicitly "an executioner,"[52] Foka's answer appears quickly: "But aren't you one as well?"[53] The same concept is manifested in the conversation with Skouratov – a member of the secret police who visits Kaliayev in prison. "The bomb wasn't thrown by me at the man, but at tyranny,"[54] Kaliayev insists. "You shouldn't pretend that you forgot about the head of the Grand Duke. But if you had taken it into account, your idea wouldn't

49 See: J. Foley, *From the Absurd to Revolt*, Stocksfield, Acumen, 2008, p. 93–96.

50 See: A. Camus, *Sprawiedliwi…*, p. 274.

51 *Ibidem.*

52 "To ty jesteś katem?" *Ibidem*, p. 269.

53 "A ty, barin, to nie?" *Ibidem*

54 "Bombę rzuciłem nie na człowieka, ale na tyranię." *Ibidem*, p. 271.

have been useful. For instance, what you have done would bring disgust not pride,"[55] Skouratov notes.

Camus asserts that any idea (including the idea of justice) can justify the murder of a man. The Grand Duchess recalls the Grand Duke sleeping in his armchair two hours before the assassination. "Many things die with one man,"[56] she notes. He wasn't only a tyrant, but also a man, whom his relatives needed, who was giving support and who had his own habits. The revolutionaries backed away from the murder of children, drawing here a clear line for their actions. But one question was raised by Camus's character: "If the idea cannot kill a child, is it worth killing the Grand Duke?"[57] There is no difference between these two types of homicide. No matter if one victim is a child and the other not – both are humans. A murder committed on a despotic ruler for the sake of the liberation of society remains always a violent act performed against someone. Therefore, it cannot be justified.

It has to be underlined that Kaliayev did not abandon his task easily, still being ready to sacrifice children in order to implement the pure idea into reality:

> Here's what I propose. If you decide the children have to be killed, I'll wait outside and throw the bomb alone. I know I won't miss. Just make the decision, I'll be obedient to the Organization.[58]

So was Stepan, who gave the most extreme arguments and had the most revolutionary attitude. Dora, in turn, took into account the authority and influence of the Organization which could be lost.[59] For Annenkov, the death of children was simply unnecessary.[60] One issue, however, remained forgotten by the revolutionaries: the murder of children would contradict the rule of justice, on behalf of which they committed their actions. If one draws a strict border between permissible and impermissible murder and distinguishes

---

55 "(...) nie powinien pan udawać. Udawać, że zapomniał pan o głowie wielkiego księcia. Gdyby wziął ją pan pod uwagę, na nic by się panu nie przydała idea. Tak na przykład to, co pan zrobił, budziłoby w panu nie dumę, ale wstyd." *Ibidem*, p. 272.

56 "Wiele rzeczy umiera wraz z jednym człowiekiem." *Ibidem*, p. 274.

57 "Nasuwa się więc pytanie: jeśli idea nie potrafi zabić dziecka, czy zasługuje na to, a by zabić dla niej wielkiego księcia?" *Ibidem*, p. 273.

58 "Oto, co proponuję. Jeśli postanowicie, że te dzieci mają zginąć, zaczekam przy wyjściu i rzucę bombę sam. Wiem, że nie chybię. Postanówcie tylko, będę posłuszny Organizacji." *Ibidem*, p. 246.

59 *Ibidem*, p. 248.

60 *Ibidem*, p. 251.

one from the other, the existence of the justification of "permissible" violence must be admitted.

Such a conclusion offers a substantial insight into Camus's thought: he finds himself far from the condemnation of murder in general, but his ambition is to disclose the contradiction contained in the considerations and actions of the revolutionaries. The author does not aim to create a tone of moral correctness, but to draw the reader's attention to the obvious fact: placing any theoretical idea at the beginning of one's deliberations can lead to contradictory conclusions. The revolutionaries could have been right about the permissibility of the homicide of the Grand Duke, but they only considered it at an abstract level – when implemented in reality, it came down to the obvious, physical act of killing a specific man, which can never be morally justifiable. However, it needs to be underlined that Camus seems to believe that murder is not always unambiguously morally wrong – nonetheless, it is in each case one-sided, which results in rejecting the possibility to provide justification for killing – even for an exceptional one. Otherwise, a protest against violence would end up violently as well. The question could be raised, however, whether a murder, even if not justified, can be in some instances inevitable. And to this dilemma Camus seems to answer positively. But this issue requires a completely distinct deliberation.[61]

VICTIM AND EXECUTIONER

> I would never count myself among people of whatever stripe who are willing to countenance murder.[62]

Any attempt to accept certain acts of permissible killing ends up in failure. Justice comprehended abstractly requires advocating one of two sides: victims or executioners. Nevertheless, there is a considerable remedy to be given and Camus provides it explicitly in his set of essays titled *Neither Victims nor Executioners*. The essays appeared in *Combat* before *The Just Assassins* was published, but they can be considered as an answer to the problems identified in the play. Such a view seems to be questionable, but grounds for it can be seen when perceiving *The Just Assassins* as an endeavor to look closer at the

---

61 For deliberations on the inevitability of murder in Camus' thinking see: J. Foley, *op.cit.*, p. 96–100.

62 A. Camus, the editorial of November 30th, 1946 [in:] *Camus at Combat: Writing 1944–1947...*, p. 274.

pure mechanism of reaching the intellectual allowance for killing and at the dilemmas which accompany it. Only then does it appear that Camus, in *The Just Assassins*, set his goal in taking into consideration different ways of possible justification, instead of focusing on giving an answer to the basic question: Do actions completed on behalf of justice always require the occurrence of executioners and victims, as was the case during the purge trials and in the situation presented in *The Just Assassins*? In order to take a stance, thus, some of Camus's arguments and assertions from *Neither Victims nor Executioners* need to be presented:

1. Murder can never be legitimized.[63] Camus claims that if one rejects that fact, he or she must inevitably agree to replace one form of terror with another. Only by refusing the legitimization for the justification of violence would it be possible to "create the conditions for a just philosophy and for a provisional accord among those of us unwilling to be either victims or executioners."[64]
2. There is no way of persuading the representative of an ideology,[65] i.e. someone who is filled with ideological ideas will not be able to look critically at his standpoint. "In order to escape from this terror, we need to be able to think and to act on the basis of our thoughts,"[66] Camus asserts.
3. The end can never justify the means.[67] Another attitude leads directly to implementing nihilism into the world. However, it is important to note that giving unprecedented priority to moral issues is also an end that cannot be justified by any means.[68]
4. The idea of a unified world order cannot be implemented without war,[69] i.e. each attempt to embody an order based on any value leads to failure – it entails murder, which is then legitimized by the value itself. According to Camus, such a situation can never take place. Murder cannot be justified.

---

63 A. Camus, the editorial of November 20th, 1946 [in:] *Camus at Combat: Writing 1944–1947...*, s. 260.

64 *Ibidem*, p. 261.

65 A. Camus, the editorial of November 19th, 1946 [in:] *Camus at Combat: Writing 1944–1947...*, p. 258.

66 *Ibidem*, p. 259.

67 A. Camus, the editorial of November 21th, 1946 [in:] *Camus at Combat: Writing 1944–1947...*, p. 262.

68 *Ibidem*, p. 263.

69 A. Camus, the editorial of November 26th, 1946 [in:] *Camus at Combat: Writing 1944–1947...*, p. 267.

5. A world order must be based on dialogue.[70] For Camus, the dialogue is a state in which no value has been given a superior merit. Only then is it possible to open one's mind to the diversity of the world of morality.

Absolute justice requires an affirming answer to the following basic questions: "Yes or no, directly or indirectly, do you want to be killed and assaulted? Yes or no, directly or indirectly, do you want to kill or assault?"[71] Each man who wishes to answer positively needs to come back to the beginning of their deliberations and get rid of the uncritical faith in abstractly comprehended moral values. Only the rejection of an ideological division into good and evil is able to safeguard an individual from the trap of a series of justifications for their actions. Only when the premise of the lack of possibility regarding the existence of justification for murder is set can real order based on justice be built. Camus seems to warn here against the sacrifice of one's life for the sake of a supreme principle, which can lead to its own contradiction when comprehended abstractly and perceived solely theoretically.

In the set of essays *Neither Victims nor Executioners*, Camus states ultimately that each attempt to unify the world poses a danger of violence being implemented – someone always proves to be stronger.[72] Such danger can be avoided only by dialogue held between contradictory sides of the dispute, which makes it possible to avoid the vicious circle of such reasoning that can reflect upon overuses. The pure concept of justice demands power, victims and executioners for its existence. The only remedy for such a condition is to divert justice from its absolute understanding, leading to the possibility of saving human life.

CONCLUSIONS

Abstract considerations regarding justice have led to the philosophical justification of violence, which Camus discerned in the pro-Marxist attitude of the intellectuals of post-liberation France.[73] The critics of deliberations encompassed

---

70 A. Camus, the editorial of November 29th, 1946 [in:] *Camus at Combat: Writing 1944–1947...*, s. 271.

71 A. Camus, the editorial of November 19th, 1946 [in:] *Camus at Combat: Writing 1944–1947...*, p. 259.

72 A. Camus, the editorial of November 26th, 1946 [in:] *Camus at Combat: Writing 1944–1947...*, p. 267.

73 See: R. Aronson, *Camus and Sartre, The story of a friendship and the quarrel that ended it*, Chicago, University of Chicago Press 2005, p. 115–127.

in such works as *Humanism and Terror* by Merleau-Ponty or *Materialism and Revolution* by Sartre enabled Camus to pay close attention to the crucial aspect of the problem of justice: its absolute form can entail the justification of murder. Each attempt to draw any limit ends up in automatically placing someone in the role of an arbiter, who would impose such a border authoritatively. However, who is going to be that judge? And what if a mistake is made? Camus seems to remind us in *Neither Victims nor Executioners* of such fundamental questions which simply cannot be answered. Each person who performs such a role contravenes the assumptions of justice, which needs, above all, dialogue for its existence. But only the construction of a discourse deprived of any previous emotional biases is able to lead to distinct conclusions.

A query thus emerges: it is viable to leave emotions aside in the face of extreme events? The history of post-occupation France reveals the answer: it is highly difficult. Camus urges therefore putting another value on a pedestal which would be, firstly, free from such emotional attitude and secondly, would have clear and obvious borders. Only then would grounds for the elimination of all overuses would be given. This value would be the life of a person.

BIBLIOGRAPHY

Aronson, R., *Camus and Sartre: The Story of a Friendship and the Quarrel that Ended It*, Chicago, University of Chicago Press, 2005.

Bartyzel, J., *Robert Brasillach*, http://www.legitymizm.org/ebp-robert-brasilach [access: 11.01.2015].

Camus, A., *Camus at Combat: Writing 1944–1947*, trans. A. Goldhammer, ed. J. Levi-Valensi, Princeton–Oxford, Princeton University Press, 2007.

Camus, A., *Człowiek zbuntowany*, trans. J. Guze, Warszawa, Warszawskie Wydawnictwo Literackie MUZA SA, 1998.

Camus, A., *Neither Victims nor Executioners* [in:] *Camus at Combat: Writing 1944–1947*, trans. A. Goldhammer, ed. J. Levi-Valensi, Princeton–Oxford, Princeton University Press, 2007.

Camus, A., *Sprawiedliwi*, trans. J. Błoński [in:] A. Camus, *Dramaty*, trans. W. Natanson, M. Leśniewska, W. Błońska, J. Błoński, Kraków, Wydawnictwo Literackie, 1987.

Caroll, D., *Albert Camus – Political Journalist: Democracy in an Age of Terror* [in:] *Camus at Combat: Writing 1944–1947*, trans. A. Goldhammer, ed. J. Levi-Valesi, Princeton–Oxford, Princeton University Press, 2007.

Cielecki, P., *Bunt metafizyczny jako reakcja na doświadczenie nicości w filozofii Alberta Camus*, „Nowa Krytyka" 2010, no. 24–25.

Drai, R., *Camus i Mauriac. Spór o miłosierdzie*, trans. S. Kowalski, „Gazeta Wyborcza" 9th August 2014.

Foley, J., *From the Absurd to Revolt*, Stocksfield, Acumen, 2008.

Fuller L.L., *The Morality of Law: Revised Edition*, New Haven–London, Yale University Press, 1964.

Judt, T., *Brzemię odpowiedzialności. Blum, Camus, Aron i francuski wiek dwudziesty*, trans. M. Filipczuk, Warszawa, Krytyka Polityczna, 2013.

Judt, T., *Historia niedokończona. Francuscy intelektualiści 1944–1956*, trans. P. Marczewski, Warszawa, Krytyka Polityczna, 2012.

Judt, T., *Powojnie. Historia Europy od roku 1945*, trans. R. Bartołd, Poznań, Rebis, 2013.

Kaplan, A., *The Collaborator: The Trial and Execution of Robert Brasillach*, Chicago, University of Chicago Press, 2014.

Klamann, P., *Między realizmem a oportunizmem. Rzecz o Francji Vichy*, „Folia Historica Cracoviensia" 2012, no. XVIII.

Levi-Valensi, J., *Introduction* [in:] *Camus at Combat: Writing 1944–1947*, trans. A. Goldhammer, ed. J. Levi-Valesi, Princeton and Oxford, Princeton University Press, 2007.

Merleau-Ponty, M., *Humanizm i terror*, trans. J. Migasiński [in:] *Marksizm XX wieku: Antologia tekstów*, cz. 1–3, ed. J. Dobieszewski, M.J. Siemek, Warszawa, Wydawnictwo Uniwersytetu Warszawskiego, 1990.

Miłosz, Cz., *Zniewolony umysł*, Kraków, KAW, 1990.

Orme, M., *The Development of Albert Camus' Concern for Social and Political Justice*, Madison–Teaneck, Fairleigh Dickinson University Press, 2007.

Praxton, R.O., *Francja Vichy. Stara gwardia i nowy ład 1940–1944*, trans. J. Lang, Wrocław, Bukowy Las, 2011.

Santoni, R.E., *Sartre on Violence: Curiously Ambivalent*, Pennsylvania, The Pennsylvania State University Press, 2013.

Sartre J.-P., *Materialism and Revolution* [in:] *Literary and Philosophical Essays*, trans. A. Michelson, New York, Collier Books, 1967.

Todd O., *Albert Camus. Biografia*, trans. J. Kortas, Warszawa, Wydawnictwo W.A.B., 2009.

Part Three:
Camus's Revolt in Comparatistic Studies

"I Hope This Ireland We're Fighting for is Worth It": Camus' *L'Homme Révolté* through Ken Loach's *The Wind That Shakes the Barley*

GIOVANNI GAETANI

THREE METHODOLOGICAL PREMISES

a) The wide(r) boundaries of Philosophy

One of the presupposed methodological principles implied in Camus' intellectual activity is the conviction that the boundaries of philosophy are wider than the ones set by the Western tradition in its two and a half millennia of history. In this regard, Camus has been quite clear in many passages of his works and notebooks,[1] but among them one in particular is worth quoting here:

> On ne saurait trop insister sur l'arbitraire de l'ancienne opposition entre art et philosophie. Si on veut l'entendre dans un sens trop précis, à coup sûr elle est fausse. Si l'on veut seulement dire que ces deux disciplines ont chacune leur climat particulier, cela sans doute est vrai, mais dans le vague. [...] Au surplus, rien n'est plus vain que ces distinctions selon les méthodes et les objets pour qui se persuade de l'unité de but de l'esprit. Il n'y a pas de frontières entre les

1 For all the quotes from Camus, I will use the abbreviation "OC" (followed by the number of the tome and the page), referring to A. Camus, *Œuvres Complètes*, Paris, Gallimard, 2006–2008. OC II, p. 659: "Les sentiments, les images multiplient la philosophie par dix." OC II, p. 800: "On ne pense que par image. Si tu veux être philosophe, écris des romans."

> disciplines que l'homme se propose pour comprendre et aimer. Elles s'interpénètrent et la même angoisse les confond.[2]

Since I personally share this of Camus' convictions, in this paper I will analyse one of his books, *L'Homme Révolté*, through a film on the Irish revolution of 1916, *The Wind That Shakes the Barley*, made in 2006 by a well-known Irish film-maker Ken Loach, and awarded with the Palme d'Or at the 2006 Cannes Film Festival.

b) A novel rather than a documentary

The intent of this paper is not to discuss the political legitimacy of the Irish revolution or the historical accuracy of the film. In regard to this last point, Loach's perspective may not be fully impartial, given his nationality and his leftist political view, as Simon Lea has pointed out during my conference presentation in Cracow.[3] Anyway, for the purpose of this paper, I am going to put this aspect in brackets as a precaution, focusing my attention on the narrated story (treating the film as a novel) rather than on the historical facts (as if the film was a documentary instead).

c) Is there an historical revolt which is not already a revolution?

L'Homme Révolté is a quite complex and dense book which analyses the concepts of both revolt and revolution in all their different declinations – metaphysical

---

2 OC I, p. 285–286.

3 Indeed, many other film critics have pointed out this weakness of Loach's, like for example Peter Bradshaw for *The Guardian* (23 June 2006): "It is fatuous and tiresome to wonder if Loach and Laverty should have been less severe in their portrayal of the Black and Tans, in the interests of broadsheet brow 'balance' [...]. Loach is not interested in splitting the difference between historical realities and lenient liberal scruple. In any case, the point of the film lies elsewhere, in the agony of what happened after 1922." Even harsher, if not exaggerated, was the invective of Christopher Tookey for the *Daily Mail Online* (23 June 2006): "A columnist for *The Times* recently compared Ken Loach with Hitler's favourite director, Leni Riefenstahl. That strike's me as harsh. Riefenstahl was far more visually talented. [...] Loach has no use for light and shade, no room for facts that don't fit his hardline Marxist dialectic." Tookey is referring here to Tim Luckhurst's article for *The Times* (31 May 2006), where he calls Loach's film "a poisonously anti-British corruption of the history of the war of Irish independence." Finally, also Dominic Lawson for the *Independent* (30 May 2006) wrote an article ("A hard-line Marxist distortion of history") where he says, "I don't mean to suggest that Ken Loach's film can be dismissed simply because of his political opinions, but it is my observation that hard-line Marxists see historical truth as merely a convenient weapon in the class war. In Loach's socialist realism, the IRA represent the victims of class struggle and are therefore all heroes, while the British soldiers represent the ruling elite and are therefore all brutes. Real history is much more complicated – and much more interesting."

or historical, individual or collective, affirmative or negative, aesthetic, political, moral, etc. In this paper, however, my attention will be focused entirely on one particular kind of revolt: the *historical revolt*, which can be considered a synonym of *revolution*, if my interpretation is correct.

Indeed, affirming that "La révolution n'est que la suite logique de la révolte métaphysique,"[4] and, similarly, "L'insertion de l'idée dans l'expérience historique,"[5] Camus seems to leave no room for a historical revolt which is not already revolutionary – and we know that, for Camus, the revolutionary approach is always despicable, not only for its historical-empirical failures to reach the Utopia without murdering, but rather *in itself*, given its totalitarian goals and its essential "ontological impatience," as Maurice Weyembergh calls it.[6]

L'Homme Révolté is nothing but a description of an insurmountable tragedy. If it were not for the last part of the book, "La Pensée de Midi," we should consider it a fully nihilistic and fatalistic work. The core of this tragedy is the desperate search of a fruitful and loyal revolt far both from the sterility of the metaphysical rebel's dreams and from the bloodied hands of the revolutionary. Ken Loach's film describes exactly the same tragedy, although, and in contrast to Camus, without any final message of hope. Let us see why.

THE FOUR ACTS OF A TRAGEDY NAMED "REVOLUTION"

a) "To engage or not to engage?": Damien's and Rambert's dilemma

In the film, Damien O'Donovan (Cillian Murphy) is a young Irish student who is about to leave his native village in order to go practise medicine in a London hospital. His brother, Teddy (Pádraic Delaney), is the commandant of the local flying column of the Irish Republican Army. It is important to pay attention to the change in the relationship between the two brothers, as they actually represent two different political approaches to the Irish revolution: the idealistic and intransigent revolt of Damien, and the strategic and realistic fight of Teddy, "a man of action."[7]

---

4 OC III, p. 151.

5 OC III, p. 152.

6 M. Weyembergh, *Albert Camus ou la mémoire des origines*, Paris–Bruxelles, De Boeck université, 1998, p. 29–40.

7 It is Damien himself that uses these words to describe his brother, while he is in prison.

At the beginning of the film, while everyone is wishing good-bye to Damien, a squad of the British Black and Tans[8] kills one of his young friends, Micheál, who refused to say his name in English. The day after, some hours before Damien's planned departure, everyone is asking him not to leave. He refuses, arguing that the British soldiers are too many (and too well-equipped); he decides to leave, because the revolution will never succeed – what one can call the "efficacy argument." Accused by his companions of cowardice, Damien goes straight to the train station with his luggage, ready to leave. Here, he will be a witness to the umpteenth act of injustice of the Black and Tans, this time directed against the station master and the train driver, who refuse to let the soldiers get on the train, following the orders of their rail company. It is at this point that Damien realizes that he has to stay – the train leaves without him, while he swears allegiance to the Government of the Irish Republic. He is now part of his brother's IRA brigade.

It is essential to stress that Damien's choice is not a matter of rational evaluation – the "efficacy argument" is still valid in fact – but rather the sudden empathic comprehension of the fact that he would never reach happiness alone in London while his companions are fighting for freedom in his motherland. Even if Damien does not say it explicitly, the reason why he decides to stay is the same as that of Rambert in *La Peste*. The French journalist, who tries to escape from Oran by all possible means in order to go back to his beloved, decides to join the medical units of Rieux and Tarrou the same day of his clandestine departure. To Rieux, who remarks that "il n'y a pas de honte à préférer le bonheur," he replies: "Oui, […] mais il peut y avoir de la honte à être heureux tout seul."[9]

The stories of Damien and Rambert are extremely similar. The only major difference between them is that, in the first case, the reluctance to join is genuinely *political*, while in the second case it is rather *humanitarian* – or even *metaphysical*, if we consider the plague as a representation of the natural evil.[10] Anyway, the two characters at issue have at least six traits in common:

---

8 Officially the Royal Irish Constabulary Special Reserve, the Black and Tans were a force of Temporary Constables recruited to assist the Royal Irish Constabulary (RIC) during the Irish War of Independence. The nickname "Black and Tans" arose from the colours of the improvised uniforms they initially wore, composed of mixed khaki British Army and rifle green RIC uniform parts.

9 OC II, p. 178.

10 In this regard cf. Marie-Thérèse Blondeau, *La Peste*, roman de la résistance ? [in:] "Albert Camus 22: Camus et l'Histoire", 2009, 22, Raymond Gay-Crosier et Philippe Vanney (eds.), Caen, Lettres

1. they both feel "strangers" to the resistance;
2. they do not consider themselves cowards;
3. they dislike heroism;
4. they are ready to leave, in order to pursue their personal idea of happiness;
5. they decide to stay on the day of their departure;
6. they feel ashamed "to be happy all alone."

Damien himself, in particular, could have pronounced one part of Rambert's speech:

> J'ai toujours pensé que j'étais étranger à cette ville et que je n'avais rien à faire avec vous. Mais maintenant que j'ai vu ce que j'ai vu, je sais que je suis d'ici, que je le veuille ou non. Cette histoire nous concerne tous.[11]

At this point, what both the novel and the film show is that the beginning of the revolt – that is, the choice of engagement – does not derive from a rational and consequential reasoning about the actual *efficacy* of the revolt, but rather from a *moral commitment* to fight against what is (or seems to be) unjust *a priori*. For the moment, the discussion about the goals and the means of the revolt is set aside: what matters now is the position of a frontier, which is not merely *axiological* ("this is allowed, this is forbidden"), but rather *temporal-axiological* ("*from now on*, I will not accept it any more"). The "frontière" described by Camus is like a watershed that divides the history in two – *before* and *after* the revolt. A passage of the book may help us to better understand this nuance:

> Un esclave, qui a reçu des ordres toute sa vie, juge soudain inacceptable un nouveau commandement. Quel est le contenu de ce "non" ? Il signifie, par exemple, "les choses ont trop duré", "jusque-là oui, au-delà non", "vous allez trop loin", et encore, "il y a une limite que vous ne dépasserez pas". En somme, ce non affirme l'existence d'une frontière.[12]

Modernes Minard. Cf. also Camus' *Lettre à Roland Barthes* [in:] OC II, p. 285–287. Finally, really important is Camus' letter reported in O. Todd, *Albert Camus. Une vie*, Paris, Gallimard, 1996, p. 454: "On peut lire *La Peste* de trois façons différentes. Elle est à la fois le récit d'une épidémie, le symbole de l'occupation nazie (et d'ailleurs la préfiguration de tout régime totalitaire quel qu'il soit) et en troisième lieu l'illustration concrète d'un problème métaphysique, celui du mal."

[11] OC II, p. 178.

[12] OC III, p. 71.

For this reason, it is possible that the same act that the rebel now firmly condemns was before tolerated, accepted, or even justified. What changes now, then, is not the external state of affairs: the revolt is always an inner change in the human will. It is the passage from the *factual* plan to the *idealist* one – "un passage du fait au droit"[13] – and from the patience to the impatience, as we read in *L'Homme Révolté*:

> Toutes les exactions antérieures au mouvement d'insurrection, l'esclave les souffrait. Souvent même, il avait reçu sans réagir des ordres plus révoltants que celui qui déclenche son refus. Il y apportait de la patience, les rejetant peut-être en lui-même, mais, puisqu'il se taisait, plus soucieux de son intérêt immédiat que conscient encore de son droit. Avec la perte de la patience, avec l'impatience, commence au contraire un mouvement qui peut s'étendre à tout ce qui, auparavant, était accepté. Cet élan est presque toujours rétroactif.[14]

Damien's revolt follows exactly this dynamic: he has been patient for long, he has stood many manifest injustices with the excuse that he was impossible to fight against them, given the disproportion in strength between their clandestine organization and the British army. Suddenly, he revolts, preferring to pursue a bigger ideal than his individual happiness:

> I do solemnly swear that to the best of my ability I will support and defend the Government of the Irish Republic, which is Dail Eireann,[15] against all enemies, foreign and domestic, and I will bear true faith and allegiance to the same, and I take this obligation freely, without any mental reservation or purpose of evasion. So help me, God.

---

13 OC III, p. 73: "Le passage au droit est manifeste, nous l'avons vu, dans la révolte. De même le passage du «il faudrait que cela fût», au «je veux que cela soit». Mais plus encore, peut-être, cette notion du dépassement de l'individu dans un bien désormais commun. Le surgissement du Tout ou Rien montre que la révolte, contrairement à l'opinion courante, et bien qu'elle naisse dans ce que l'homme a de plus strictement individuel, met en cause la notion même d'individu. Si l'individu, en effet, accepte de mourir, et meurt à l'occasion, dans le mouvement de sa révolte, il montre par là qu'il se sacrifie au bénéfice d'un bien dont il estime qu'il déborde sa propre destinée."

14 OC III, p. 326.

15 Dail Eireann is the lower house, and principal chamber, of the *Oireachtas* (Irish legislature), which also includes the President of Ireland and *Seanad Éireann* (the upper house).

b) "To kill or not to kill?": crossing the line between revolt and revolution

Enrolled in the IRA's brigade, Damien starts his clandestine fight together with his brother and his friends. They drill in the mountains, preparing their military strategies. One night, they assault a barrack of the Black and Tans in order to steal weapons from the armoury. The day after, they kill four soldiers in a pub, stealing their weapons. Up to this point, Damien and his companions are not touched by any moral issue: their clandestine actions and their murders appear legitimate, since they are all directed against a well-defined enemy: the Black and Tans, who represent the invaders, the oppressors, in short: the evil.

The retaliation of the British army is almost immediate: Sir John Hamilton, an English landlord, denounces a young IRA member, Chris Reilly, to the Brits, coercing him to reveal the position of his companions. In the night, the whole brigade is arrested. Teddy is tortured, the soldiers pull out his fingernails, but he will not confess anything. All of a sudden, a British soldier of Irish descent opens the prison cells: Damien, Teddy and all the others escape, except for three prisoners that will be tortured and killed some days after. Meanwhile, the order from the IRA central organization is clear: "execute the spies."

It is here that the first moral problem arises for Damien and his friends: while considering the murder of British soldiers legitimate from every perspective, what about the execution of a) an English civilian and b) an Irish friend who betrayed? The discussion about their destinies is agitated: Dan suggests that they could order Sir Hamilton to leave the country for Congo; that they have to forgive Chris, since he is "a young fella, one of our own;" but Steady Boy argues that they cannot but kill Chris, because he is "a traitor" and because "they are in war."[16] It is at this point, in my opinion, that the film reaches its first dramatic peak. Damien loads his gun, staring into space. His speech is dramatically meaningful:

> I studied anatomy for five years, Dan. And now I'm going to shoot this man in the head. I have known Chris Reilly since he was a child. I hope this Ireland we're fighting for is worth it.

Damien shoots both Sir Hamilton and Chris, with two clean blows straight to the heart. Like the conclusion of *L'Étranger*'s first part, where Meursault

[16] By the way, Steady Boy is the same who, way after this execution, will refuse to fight against the Free-Staters since "they are our own lads."

describes the four shots as "quatre coups brefs que je frappais sur la porte du malheur,"[17] also in the film the sound of bullets signs a dramatic turning point: Damien has crossed the line. In this regard, it is Damien himself who uses this expression in a fundamental dialogue with his beloved Sinead:

> We buried him [Chris] in this chapel in the mountains. And I went down and I told his mother. His mother who has cooked meals for me and her son. And when I told her she... she just looked at me. And then she went in and she put on her shoes. And she came out and she said: "Take me to my child." And we walked for six hours and she didn't say one word. Then we got to the chapel. And I showed her the grave. And I'd put a cross and some flowers on it. And she turned to me and she said: "I never want to see your face again." I've crossed the line now, Sinead.

"Crossing the line" means here that Damien is forced by the same fatal act to pursue his ideal "jusqu'au bout" until the end: indeed, from the moment of execution on, he can never go back. His hands are red. That blood is indelible. The moment he pulled the trigger against Chris, he divided the world in two: those who are with us, those who are against us; no possibility of a third choice. But he also divided the time in two: before the shot, he could still give up, cleaning his hands like nothing ever happened and getting back to his life; after the shot, he has to go straight to the end, in order to be loyal to his almost-brother Chris, killed in the name of the Irish revolution. "I hope this Ireland we're fighting for is worth it," he said minutes before shooting. A passage of the book is extremely meaningful in this regard, because it describes exactly what happens when the rebel authorizes himself to kill in the name of his ideal:

> Dès qu'il frappe, le révolté coupe le monde en deux. Il se dressait au nom de l'identité de l'homme avec l'homme et il sacrifie l'identité en consacrant, dans le sang, la différence. Son seul être, au cœur de la misère et de l'oppression, était dans cette identité. Le même mouvement, qui visait à l'affirmer, le fait donc cesser d'être. Il peut dire que quelques-uns, ou même presque tous, sont avec lui. Mais, qu'il manque un seul être au monde irremplaçable de la fraternité, et le voilà dépeuplé.[18]

Chris is this "single human being missing in the irreplaceable world of fraternity:" with his killing, the revolt has now become a revolution.

---

[17] OC I, p. 176.

[18] OC III, p. 302.

c) "Intransigence or compromise?": Damien versus Teddy

A little recap of the history of the Irish Revolution is obligatory here, in order to properly understand the events described in the film:

- Easter 1916. The Irish rebels proclaim the Irish Republic during the "Easter Rising," a revolt that will last five days, ending with the execution of 15 rebels and many imprisonments;
- 1916–1920. Constitution of the IRA (Irish Republican Army) and resistance to the bitter end against the Brits; the 21th June 1920 is the first Bloody Sunday;
- 6 December 1921. Sign of the Anglo-Irish Treaty that proclaims the birth of the "Irish Free State," which still remains a dominion of the Commonwealth under the king of England;
- 1922. The IRA splits in two: the Republicans on the one side, the Free-Staters on the other side; it is the beginning of the Irish civil war, which will result in more Irish victims of the Independence war.

In the film, O'Donovan brothers, now separated again, represent the two sides of the civil war. Damien considers the Treaty "a betrayal of 1916," that is, the ideal of the Irish Republic for which many IRA's fighters died before, including Chris. At the cinema, during the showing of the Treaty's signature, he shouts twice at the screen: "Is this what we fought for, is it?," while Teddy sits silent in the back.

In the following scene, all the members of the IRA's brigade gather in order to discuss whether or not to sign the Treaty. The choice is hard, not only for the matter of divergent political ideals, but also (and above all) because England has threatened to launch "immediate and terrible war" if the IRA does not ratify the Treaty.

The principal positions are essentially two: on the one side, the *intransigence* of the Republicans, who want to stay loyal to the Easter Rising's declaration of 1916, to the Dáil Éireann's independence declaration of 1919, and to all their companions tortured and killed by the enemy during those years of resistance. On the other side, the *compromise* of the FreeStaters, who reject the hardline policy of the Republicans because they consider the Treaty the legitimate realization of their revolutionary expectations.

The exchange of accusations is heavy: Finbar, a Republican, accuses the FreeStaters of "spitting on the graves of our dead martyrs by swearing an oath of allegiance to the British Crown;" Teddy in turn accuses the Republicans of being "too stubborn" to understand that "if [they] really want to desecrate the graves of those boys" and "to insult their memories [they] go ahead and reject this treaty, because this is what they died for."

It is a tragic prelude of the civil war: while the British army finally leaves the country in parade, the Free-Staters, including Teddy, wear the new green uniforms, arming their new recruits with English weapons. The same revolutionaries who previously fought against the British soldiers have now taken their place, substituting the direct English domination with an indirect one: as Dan says, what changes is only "the accents of the powerful and the colour of the flag."

This aspect of the film sheds light on an important passage of *L'Homme Révolté*, where Camus underlines the inextricable contradiction between the original act of revolt and the subsequent revolutionary approach that pretends to be loyal to that source:

> La contradiction est, en réalité, plus serrée. Le révolutionnaire est en même temps révolté ou alors il n'est plus révolutionnaire, mais policier et fonctionnaire qui se tourne contre la révolte [like Teddy]. Mais s'il est révolté, il finit par se dresser contre la révolution [like Damien instead]. Si bien qu'il n'y a pas progrès d'une attitude à l'autre, mais simultanéité et contradiction sans cesse croissante. Tout révolutionnaire finit en oppresseur ou en hérétique. Dans l'univers purement historique qu'elles ont choisi, révolte et révolution débouchent dans le même dilemme: ou la police ou la folie.[19]

In the film, Teddy chooses the first alternative: he is the new oppressor, the policeman, the presumed orthodox who now wears the uniform of power, while Damien is, in Teddy's perspective, the heretic, the fool, the radical idealist who refuses any compromise and who will never recognize that uniform. The first calls the second "a dreamer," who in turn replies: "I am not a dreamer, I am a realist." Who is right?

If we judge them from an idealistic point of view, maybe Damien is right, because the establishment of the Irish Free State is actually a betrayal of the original ideal on which all IRA's members swore. Conversely, if we judge them from a practical point of view – the one of the political efficacy – maybe Teddy is right, because the Republicans' goals could seem too utopian and unobtainable, while such a political compromise is an actual progress.

The important point is that no one can resolve this contradiction, establishing once and for all that one character is *absolutely* right while the other

---

19 OC III, p. 275.

is *absolutely* wrong: we are not living in the artificial world of melodrama, where good and evil are always definable with certainty, but rather in the one of tragedy, where every force in the field is partly right, partly wrong, as Camus himself remarked in a conference speech in Athens:

> La tragédie diffère du drame ou du mélodrame. Voici quelle me paraît être la différence: les forces qui s'affrontent dans la tragédie sont également légitimes, également armées en raison. Dans le mélodrame ou le drame, au contraire, l'une seulement est légitime. Autrement dit, la tragédie est ambiguë, le drame simpliste. Dans la première, chaque force est en même temps bonne et mauvaise. Dans le second, l'une des forces est le bien, l'autre le mal (et c'est pourquoi de nos jours le théâtre de propagande n'est rien d'autre que la résurrection du mélodrame). Antigone a raison, mais Créon n'a pas tort. De même Prométhée est à la fois juste et injuste et Zeus qui l'opprime sans pitié est aussi dans son droit. La formule du mélodrame serait en somme: "Un seul est juste et justifiable" et la formule tragique par excellence "Tout sont justifiables, personne n'est juste"[20].

"Everyone is justifiable, no one is just" – this principle perfectly describes the tragic situation of the O'Donovan brothers, even if Loach's sympathies seem to be all with Damien. However, like in all greatest tragedies, the conclusion of the film will be bloodstained.

d) "Sacrifice or homicide?": Damien's and Kaliayev's acceptance of death

We have arrived at the tragic epilogue: Damien is in prison for an unsuccessful attempt of stealing weapons. I believe that the second true dramatic peak of the film is actually the last dialogue between Damien and Teddy, which symbolically takes place in the same cell where they were once imprisoned together: Teddy begs Damien ("heart and soul") to confess where the weapons and his friends are, because he is sure that "they will listen to him;" Damien's short but dense reply is clear: "You listen to me. I shot Chris Reilly in the heart. I did that. You know why. I'm not going to sell out." Damien is condemned to death by his own brother. During his last night, he will not confess, adding his own signature to his death sentence. At dawn, Teddy himself will pull the trigger.

[20] OC III, p. 1121.

I think that Damien's final reference to Chris's execution, after all the things that happened in the meantime, clearly gives the idea of how similar Damien's and Kaliayev's reasonings are. Indeed, their final speeches in the prison cell are quite comparable.

Damien refuses to "sell out" in order not to betray Chris, who was executed in the name of the Irish revolution by Damien himself – and we have to remember that he justified his act with the hope that "this Ireland we are fighting for is worth it." Selling out now, when he in turn is threatened to be killed for his loyalty to the same ideal, would mean to kill Chris twice. In particular, his execution would lose any moral and political legitimacy, becoming in this way a mere murder, a simple crime. Damien knows that he cannot say: "I was wrong, this Ireland we are fighting for was not worth Chris's execution, so he died in vain, it was all a mistake." No, Damien has to go until the end, because with that execution he "crossed the line" – reaching a point of no return. Now he has to accept his own death in order to be loyal to Chris and to not become a mere murderer. Between sacrifice and homicide,[21] he cannot but choose the first one.

Kaliayev refuses the pardon of the Grand Duchess exactly for the same reason: if he accepts – that is, if he "sells out" – he is going to become a murderer, making the assassination of the Grand Duke a mere crime,[22] not a necessary act of justice made in the name of a higher ideal – and indeed he says to the Grand Duchess: "Laissez-moi me préparer à mourir. Si je ne mourais pas, c'est alors que je serais un meurtrier."[23]

Both characters have now to decide between the personal sacrifice or the de-legitimization of their acts of justice. One passage of *L'Homme Révolté* can help us understand this issue:

> [Le meurtre] est la limite qu'on ne peut atteindre qu'une fois et après laquelle il faut mourir. Le révolté n'a qu'une manière de se réconcilier avec son acte meurtrier s'il s'y est laissé porter: accepter sa propre mort et le sacrifice. Il tue et meurt pour qu'il soit clair que le meurtre est impossible. Il montre alors qu'il préfère en réalité le *Nous sommes* au *Nous serons*.[24]

---

[21] OC III, p. 301: "Les révoltés qui, dressés contre la mort, voulaient bâtir sur l'espèce une farouche immortalité, s'effraient d'être obligés de tuer à leur tour. S'ils reculent pourtant, il leur faut accepter de mourir; s'ils avancent, de tuer. La révolte, détournée de ses origines et cyniquement travestie, oscille à tous les niveaux entre le sacrifice et le meurtre."

[22] Kaliayev remarks more than once on this aspect, like in OC III, p. 41: "Quel crime? Je ne me souviens que d'un acte de justice."

[23] OC III, p. 42.

[24] OC III, p. 302.

This analogy between Damien and Kaliayev is not the last of significant intersections between the film and the book. There is, for example, Damien's letter to Sinead. Already the *incipit* – "Dear Sinead. I tried not to get into this war. And did. And now try to get out. And can't." – reminds us of a brief passage of the *Lettres à un ami allemand*, where Camus writes that: "C'est beaucoup que de se battre en méprisant la guerre."[25] But there is one passage in particular that sheds light on the contradiction of revolt:

> Dan once told me something I've struggled with all this time. He said: "It's easy to know what you're against, quite another to know what you are for." I think now I know, and it gives me strength.

The true, unsolvable contradiction of the rebel is this incapacity to define the positive content of his revolt with the same clarity and determination of his original negation: at the end of his days, Damien realizes that the fight against an unjust oppression is easier and more spontaneous than the concrete establishment of a just society which would replace it.

Damien and his friends had initially a clear concept of who their enemy was. But during their fight this certainty vanished, day by day, and they eventually became their own enemies – friends against friends, brothers against brothers. If only they had the same certainty in saying "yes" as they originally had in saying "no," their rebellion would have been easy to carry on. But human beings are "strange creatures, even to [them]selves," as Damien writes. Their destiny is tragic.

In conclusion, both Loach and Camus seem quite pessimistic about the actual possibilities of the revolt, even if they feel it is a fundamental part of the human experience. Maybe the tragic epilogue of every revolt is already determined at the beginning by the essential darkness of the human heart – heart that no revolution will ever enlighten enough. But Damien's last words in the film, as well as Camus' ones in the book, are words of love – and it is here that we maybe have to stop. "Goodbye, Sinead. I love you now, and always will."

---

25 OC II, p. 10.

BIBLIOGRAPHY

Blondeau M.T, *La Peste*, roman de la résistance ? [in:] "Albert Camus 22: Camus et l'Histoire", 2009, 22.

Camus A., *Œuvres Complètes*, Paris, Gallimard, 2006–2008.

Weyembergh M., *Albert Camus ou la mémoire des origines*, Paris–Bruxelles, De Boeck université, 1998.

Vers le dialogue : Albert Camus et Leszek Kolakowski

RAPHAEL LUIZ DE ARAÚJO[1]

LES FONDEMENTS DE LA CRITIQUE DE LA RÉVOLTE

Une partie considérable des critiques négatives de *L'homme révolté* accusent la notion de révolte mesurée d'idéaliste et de conformiste. Nous relevons de tels reproches chez Jeason et Sartre dans la fameuse polémique de « Les temps modernes » ainsi qu'en lisant Breton dans la revue *Arts* et chez ses disciples surréalistes dans l'édition de la revue *La rue* de juin 1952[2]. Une remarque semblable se répète dans le cas des critiques négatives de *La peste*, comme chez Roland Barthes dans son texte « Annales d'une épidémie ou roman de la solitude ? », du début de 1955 lorsque le critique affirme que l'auteur du livre s'écarte des demandes de son époque, ignorant le matérialisme dialectique. Moins connu que ces polémiques, nous avons encore le cas de Dyonis Mascolo dans son livre *Le communisme : dialectique des valeurs et besoins*, de 1953. Parmi ces nombreuses critiques adressées à Camus, il n'est pas d'accord avec l'idée « que tout le malheur des hommes venait de ce qu'ils ne tenaient pas un langage clair » présente dans *La peste*, et qualifie la notion de mesure comme une demande naïve : « On aime comme tout un chacun la clarté, la modestie, la mesure, vertus que Camus met obstinément en avant comme

1 Doctorant au département de Lettres Modernes de l'Université de São Paulo et boursier de la Fondation d'Appui à la Recherche de l'État de São Paulo (Fapesp).

2 Sous le thème *Révolte sur mesure*, comme le montre Jean-Louis Meunier : *La révolte et la rue. En commune présence : Albert Camus & René Char. Rencontres méditerranéennes*, Bédée, Éditions Folle Avoine, 2003, p. 47–72.

principales. [...] Mais les événements manquent de mesure. L'histoire manque de modestie. La révolution manque de clarté »[3].

Les lecteurs les plus avisés sont peut-être familiers avec les réponses de Camus aux critiques les plus polémiques à l'exception des notes de lecture sur le livre de Mascolo, qui n'ont pas été publiées, mais que nous trouvons dans une sous-chemise du dossier « Némésis. Notes. Éléments » dans les Archives Camus[4]. Nous connaissons peut-être l'argument que définit la mesure en tant que nécessaire pour éviter que la révolte se tourne contre ses valeurs premières, la nécessité de s'opposer au nihilisme historique et aux meurtres rationnels et irrationnels du XXe siècle, dont l'expérience personnelle de l'écrivain a suscité l'écriture de l'essai central de son deuxième cycle d'œuvres. Néanmoins, l'occasion de cette rencontre autour de Camus à Cracovie m'a incité à prendre en compte le fait d'avoir trouvé dans ce même dossier pour Némésis deux articles de la revue « Les temps modernes » de mai-juin 1958 concernant la Pologne, qui touchent à des questions semblables à celles de ces polémiques. Le premier texte est d'un auteur peu connu, T.S. Karol, sous le titre « L'avenir reste ouvert en Pologne » et, le second, vient d'un philosophe, assez célèbre en Pologne, Leszek Kolakowski, ayant pour titre « Responsabilité et histoire ». Les pages des deux articles n'ont pas été rognées par Camus, ce qui suggère que, probablement, il ne les ait pas lues, mais j'ai trouvé opportun d'examiner comment ce « hasard » sur le chemin de ma recherche pourrait contribuer à amener à réfléchir sur les arguments qui défendent la révolte en dialogue avec le contexte polonais quelques années après l'apparition de *L'homme révolté*. En ce sens, tandis que le texte de T.S. Karol présente un panorama du débat entre les intellectuels et le parti communiste ainsi que l'importance du rôle du penseur révisionniste Leszek Kolakowski en Pologne, l'article « Responsabilité et histoire » propose, lui, une réflexion sur les stratégies discursives utilisées par les stéréotypes du clerc et de l'anti-clerc dans leur débat.

Historien des idées et également philosophe, Kolakowski s'attachait au christianisme et à la théologie et, à l'instar de Camus, il s'attaque au nihilisme. Sa critique du caractère hagiographique de la philosophie stalinienne fait partie de son positionnement à l'égard des dogmes religieux, le plaçant, de fait, dans une situation paradoxale vis-à-vis du Parti Communiste en

---

3 D. Mascolo, *Le communisme. Révolution et communication ou la dialectique des valeurs et des besoins*, Paris, Gallimard, 1953, p. 507.

4 Fonds Camus. Cote CMS2 Atl1 01.04 – Je remercie Catherine et à Jean Camus pour l'autorisation accordée de consulter ce dossier.

Pologne. T.S. Karol remarque qu'« il était à la fois un militant extrêmement apprécié et d'une fidélité à toute épreuve, véritable fierté du Parti, et déjà un petit hérétique qu'il fallait surveiller de près »[5].

Ainsi, dans la première partie de ce texte, on reprendra le panorama présenté par T.S. Karol pour introduire les trois éléments jugés importants pour le dialogue entre l'intellectuel et le politicien : le langage idéal, le réalisme et l'efficacité. Nous verrons alors que le texte de Kolakowski est fécond pour critiquer cette proposition, étant donné que ces notions sont construites selon les intérêts de celui qui les emploie dans le débat. Dans la deuxième partie, nous reviendrons à Camus pour montrer comment, lui aussi, a essayé de critiquer ces notions, reconnaissant les obstacles qu'elles peuvent constituer pour le dialogue. Ce rapprochement nous semble important pour réfléchir sur le rôle de la mesure dans la communication et son emploi dans une politique qui part de la pensée réformiste pour arriver aux idéaux libertaires.

LE DÉBAT DU CLERC ET DE L'ANTI-CLERC EN POLOGNE

Le texte de T.S. Karol pourrait être considéré comme une introduction à l'article de Kolakowski. Étant ami de jeunesse du philosophe polonais, l'auteur le présente comme un intellectuel de la génération des révisionnistes qui propose une pensée communiste vive et dynamique en opposition au bureaucratisme de la génération antérieure : « Leszek Kolakowski proposait un nouveau *modus vivendi* à l'intérieur du Parti communiste : les intellectuels n'ont plus à recevoir les ordres de la direction du PC et leur rôle n'est pas de fournir *a posteriori* des justifications théoriques à n'importe quelle décision »[6]. Karol fait une synthèse de la révolte de cette nouvelle génération moins soumise au stalinisme, défendant leur liberté de penser « en remettant en cause les dogmes les plus sacro-saints du monde soviétique »[7]. Dans le cadre de cette prolifération de jeunes révisionnistes, la plupart des prix littéraires commencent à avoir moins de 50 ans, le journal économiste le plus influent, « Życie Gospodarcze », appartient aux jeunes intellectuels et étudiants communistes ainsi

---

5 S. Karol, *L'avenir reste ouvert en Pologne*, « Les temps modernes » 1958, vol. XIII, no 147/148, p. 2030.

6 « La déstalinisation a permis à cette nouvelle élite de se frayer rapidement le chemin au premier plan de la vie polonaise. Sa qualité et son ardeur lui ont acquis aussitôt la sympathie de la gauche du monde entier », *ibidem*.

7 *Ibidem*, p. 2031.

que l'hebdomadaire « Po Prostu », devenu l'organe de presse le plus puissant et le plus lu de la Pologne avec un tirage de 150 000 exemplaires.

Cependant, cette nouvelle génération rencontre des difficultés pour dialoguer avec Wladyslaw Gomulka, le premier secrétaire général du Parti en Pologne, à partir d'octobre 1956. Selon Karol, le problème de la revue « Po Prostu » est qu'elle ne formule pas des théories sociales nouvelles et ne présente pas de solutions pour l'immédiat, son intervention se centrant surtout sur la critique du socialisme. Elle va donc souffrir une forte censure à partir de 1957, accusée de diffamation du socialisme et, finalement, sa publication sera interdite en octobre de la même année. Karol affirme que « Po Prostu » a dû être supprimé parce que personne, parmi les gomulkistes, n'a su dialoguer avec lui ni l'inciter à adopter une certaine ligne de conduite conforme aux intérêts immédiats du Parti »[8]. En revanche, il conclut que les économistes étaient ceux qui ont vraiment réussi à avoir une communication idéale avec le Parti. Dans leur revue « Polityka », les informations sont plus clairement diffusées, ils collaboraient efficacement avec le gouvernement et leurs critiques étaient accompagnées de solutions. En outre, ils employaient un « langage idéal » dans le dialogue et leurs interventions étaient plus « réalistes » que celles de « Po Prostu ».

Même faisant partie de cette nouvelle génération, dans son article « Responsabilité et histoire », Kolakowski cherche à problématiser les conditions de ce débat entre les intellectuels et le Parti à partir d'une analyse des arguments que nous relevons dans le dialogue typique marqué par des stéréotypes du clerc et de l'anti-clerc. Il observe que dans ces débats, les intellectuels sont qualifiés comme ceux qui mettent en danger l'avenir de la Pologne du fait de leur « philosophie de la non-action ». Ils jouent le rôle de juges gardiens des valeurs universelles et leur non-intervention est, en fait, un manque de responsabilité, car elle ouvrirait un vide qui peut être rempli par des actions violentes et brutales. Par ailleurs, l'anti-clerc est un personnage qui collabore avec le cours de l'histoire, mais qui n'est pas apte à voir la dimension de ses propres actions[9]. Il lui manque le sang-froid et la raison, nécessaires à la préservation de l'espèce humaine. Ainsi, le révolutionnaire est normalement défini comme un *réaliste*, car « il considère le monde du point de vue

---

8 *Ibidem*, p. 2044.

9 « L'individu engagé activement dans les grands conflits politiques ne parviendra jamais à s'élever à une hauteur intellectuelle d'où il puisse apprécier les limites de son propre camp et le caractère irrationnel des actions auxquelles il participe (...) », L. Kolakowski, *Responsabilité et histoire*, « Les temps modernes » 1958, vol. XIII, no 147/148, p. 2052.

de l'*être* – contrairement au clerc, qui le considère du point de vue du *devoir-être*, c'est-à-dire d'une fiction qu'il a forgée lui-même et veut imposer sans succès à la réalité »[10].

Kolakowski simule alors un dialogue de sept pages entre le clerc et l'anti-clerc. Le premier critique toujours la dialectique au nom de l'avenir qui guide les actions du deuxième et justifie ses actes criminels à partir d'un relativisme constant selon lequel on aime un dieu par jour. Il revendique ainsi un « crédit moral illimité » pour son engagement. En revanche, le clerc lui dit :

> Quel droit avez-vous, au nom de cette dialectique spéculant sur l'avenir, de renoncer en fait aux meilleures valeurs de l'existence humaine ? Or, jusqu'à présent, l'expérience ne confirme pas votre optimisme ; tout au contraire, elle enseigne que cet intérêt particulier, tel que vous le comprenez, se réalise fréquemment au détriment des valeurs communes à toute l'humanité[11].

Mais, le révolutionnaire lui répond en affirmant que les mandements sur l'amour universel du clerc ne peuvent rien face à la violence du monde, qu'une *belle âme*[12] face à la guerre ne sert à rien et que les valeurs ne sont pas capables de changer la réalité.

Le philosophe polonais propose alors une réflexion sur le rapport engagé de l'homme au réel selon lequel il faut distinguer des notions de réalité. En ce sens, le clerc voit le monde comme un humaniste, il projette les valeurs humaines sur les nécessités sociales qui apparaissent au cours de l'histoire : si une société développe le besoin de voler, le clerc doit dire : « Ne volez pas ! ». Sa conception de réalité évoque des valeurs supra-historiques car il n'est pas capable de trouver toutes ses références dans l'histoire telle qu'elle se présente à lui. Néanmoins, l'anti-clerc crée une conception de réalité basée sur la pensée historique qui risque d'avoir pour résultat le phénomène du sectarisme où « l'organisation politique est devenue un but en soi »[13] et ignorer les vrais besoins sociaux qui sont apparus – ce qui se rapproche un peu du raisonnement nihilo-marxiste que Camus critique dans *L'homme révolté*. Le stalinisme est devenu une religion dans laquelle tous sont athées, mais « il n'y a pas, à vrai dire, de différence entre ne pas croire

---

10 *Ibidem*, p. 2051.

11 *Ibidem*, p. 2053.

12 Cette expression, « belle âme », qui renvoie à Hegel, est très utilisée à l'époque dans ce genre de débat, étant présente dans le titre de la critique de Jeason concernant *L'homme révolté*.

13 L. Kolakowski, *Responsabilité et histoire...*, p. 2063.

aux miracles de saint Expédit et professer un athéisme complet »[14]. Cet athéisme manichéiste voit dieu dans le Parti et le diable dans le capitalisme, « (...) les cataclysmes semblaient être le monopole des pays capitalistes et donnaient l'impression de catastrophes propres au régime »[15]. Tous ceux qui critiquent le monologue de la secte deviennent des ennemis. Puisqu'elle n'a plus de conditions d'évoluer, n'importe quel changement peut signifier un déclin, ainsi des dissidents, comme Doriot, Trotski et Koestler se voient-ils qualifiés de renégats de la droite. Il en résulte le besoin d'une critique de la notion de « réalisme politique », car face à l'impossibilité de comprendre la réalité d'une manière absolue, le réalisme n'est plus qu'un « instrument servant à déverser des invectives sur ses adversaires »[16]. La notion de réalisme devrait naître d'une revendication sociale de ce qui peut être *réalisable*, ce qui se trouve à la croisée des chemins entre une limite contextuelle concrète et une demande utopique. Il n'y a pas de sens à débattre de la nécessité ou non de prendre en compte uniquement une vision de « réalité » telle que la conçoivent le clerc et l'anti-clerc. Il faudrait plutôt se poser la question autrement : « (...) est-il possible de parvenir à énoncer un principe très général permettant de régler les rapports entre notre connaissance des nécessités et le monde des valeurs ? Entre la réalité et le 'devoir-être' ? »[17]. Il s'agirait d'un principe que soutient le dialogue entre les conceptions de réalité idéale et de réalité historique, les hommes devant s'adapter aux pressions des conditions dans lesquelles ils se trouvent. La tension entre obéissance au monde existant et impératif moral prendra des formes différentes selon l'expérience historique vécue, l'homme va donc danser selon « la musique naturelle de l'histoire » et cette question devra être résolue pour chaque nouvelle situation historique[18].

Dans la deuxième moitié de l'article publié dans « Les temps modernes » de juillet 1958, Kolakowski maintient le refus de la critique pseudo-réaliste des utopies moralisatrices. En fait, la disproportion entre les exigences intellectuelles et les possibilités réalisables y figurent comme nécessaires pour mobiliser les efforts vers ce qu'il considère comme un progrès social. Il distingue également le jugement moral et le jugement historique. D'un côté, le jugement moral est inévitable et il est d'abord de l'ordre individuel, n'étant

[14] *Ibidem*, p. 2064.

[15] *Ibidem*.

[16] *Ibidem*, p. 2073.

[17] *Ibidem*, p. 2075.

[18] « [...] étant donné que chacune d'elles [...] ne saurait se répéter et qu'aucune ne se laisse analyser par seule référence aux analogies du passé », *ibidem*, p. 2090–2091.

pas un acte de « pure connaissance » où l'on reçoit passivement une vision des choses, mais « la formule verbale d'une attitude pratique, le début d'une action à l'égard de la situation qui est l'objet du jugement »[19]. D'un autre côté, le jugement historique constitué par un amoralisme considère la vie quotidienne comme l'illustration de catégories théoriques, les individus sont des exemplaires des idées qui ont pour but la réalisation du *Weltgeist*. En confrontant ainsi la conception de l'homme, en tant que maître de ses propres passions à partir de Descartes, au mouvement historique qui ignore les actes individuels chez Hegel, Kolakowski soutient qu'il n'est pas contradictoire qu'une action ne soit pas acceptée du point de vue moral, mais le soit du point de vue historique[20] car, en fin de compte, c'est l'individu qui doit répondre par la responsabilité de son choix. L'engagement politique est lui aussi de l'ordre d'un choix moral, non d'une nécessité théorique – personne ne lutterait par la révolution seulement par le fait d'avoir été convaincu théoriquement, mais plutôt selon ses principes. Et de ce point de vue ni l'affection, ni le conformisme, ni l'ordre d'un supérieur, ni les nécessités de l'histoire ne se superposent au pouvoir absolu du choix individuel.

Le grand danger, c'est quand l'individu se base moralement sur la philosophie de l'histoire. Les actions du visionnaire fanatique le mènent au sectarisme où le royaume promis semble être à portée de main et il peut tout se permettre pour l'atteindre. La philosophie de l'histoire justifie ses actes comme s'il n'avait pas de responsabilité par ses choix. On abandonne tout scepticisme et encourt l'erreur du messianisme prophétique qui veut prévoir l'avenir[21]. Ainsi, l'auteur termine-t-il son article sur la même critique qui est objet du chapitre « Le terrorisme d'État et la terreur rationnelle » de *L'homme révolté*, dans lequel Camus compare l'idéal de la cité communiste universelle de Marx au rêve de la cité de Dieu du penseur chrétien Joseph de Maistre. Ce danger se concrétise donc dans le terrorisme de l'État, lorsque les individus ignorent leur choix moral au nom de la philosophie de l'histoire : « La revendication de justice aboutit à l'injustice si elle n'est pas fondée d'abord

---

19 L. Kolakowski. *Responsabilité et histoire* (fin), « Les temps modernes » 1958, no 149, p. 264–297.

20 « Il en découle que les hypothèses énumérées ci-dessus acceptent comme non-contradictoire une situation (bien qu'elles ne l'entraînent pas logiquement) dans laquelle un comportement humain déterminé doit être apprécié négativement du point de vue moral, et positivement du point de vue de sa participation au procès historique – ou inversement », *ibidem*, p. 269.

21 « [...] ceux qui veulent, à partir de ses prédictions, organiser leur propre engagement dans des processus qui doivent survenir, ne sont que des touristes qui gravent leur nom sur les murs des cités mortes », *ibidem*, p. 297.

sur une justification éthique de la justice »[22]. La prophétie fait donc partie des mystifications utilisées par les gouvernements afin de se servir du prolétariat comme un moyen pour les ascètes révolutionnaires.

RÉVOLTE ET « RÉFORMISME INTRANSIGEANT »

L'un des événements qui a marqué l'apparition de la génération révisionniste en Pologne a été le massacre des ouvriers à Poznan en juin 1956, quelques mois avant l'ascension de Gomulka au pouvoir. Camus a préparé une allocution sur le sujet en juin-juillet de la même année dans laquelle il manifeste son indignation contre la répression des ouvriers à Varsovie sous le gouvernement Cyrankiewicz. Il signale que c'est dans la mort de ces martyrs que se manifeste la vérité de la condition du peuple, en opposition aux mythes créés par les régimes soviétiques, qui se présentent comme prolétariens, mais oppriment la classe ouvrière :

> Aujourd'hui la vérité, la terrible vérité éclate, le mythe vole en éclats. Mais nous savons que ce mythe pendant des années a perverti les consciences et les intelligences européennes. Même devant l'éclat du jour, ces aveugles diront encore qu'il fait nuit. Ils le diront plus malaisément aujourd'hui. Les ouvriers de Poznan viennent de porter le dernier coup à une mystification longtemps triomphante, longtemps cynique. Les feux de l'insurrection polonaise illuminent aux yeux de tous la déchéance et le malheur d'une révolution pervertie. Il ne peut plus y avoir d'aveugles ou de naïfs, aujourd'hui, autour de cette déchéance. Il ne peut plus y avoir que des complices[23].

L'écrivain signe, en outre, un texte de la revue *Kultura* dont le thème est, également, la révolte prolétarienne[24]. Cette revue est mentionnée par T.S. Karol comme l'un des médias les plus importants des révisionnistes polonais, ce qui met encore en évidence une certaine proximité d'esprit chez Camus à l'égard de ces jeunes intellectuels. À l'instar de leur lutte contre la limitation des libertés pour dialoguer avec le Parti et pour une révision constante des actions politiques à partir de la théorie – mises à part les différences entre le sens

---

22 A. Camus, *Œuvres complètes*, Tome III, Paris, Gallimard, 2008, p. 241.

23 *Ibidem*, p. 1139.

24 Dans l'édition de la Pléiade, Philippe Vanney remarque que Camus a signé « un texte préparé par la revue *Kultura* qui souligne justement ce caractère prolétarien de la révolte », *ibidem*, p. 1465.

plus général du réformisme et le révisionnisme centré plutôt sur la théorie marxiste en Union Soviétique –, Camus avait déjà rapproché la révolte en matière politique d'un « réformisme intransigeant » lorsqu'il écrit une note pour une éventuelle préface d'*Actuelles II* dans son sixième cahier, en 1949 :

> Préface. – Se dire révolutionnaire et refuser par ailleurs la peine de mort [...], la limitation des libertés, et les guerres, c'est ne rien dire. Il faut donc déclarer que l'on n'est pas révolutionnaire – mais plus modestement réformiste. Un réformisme intransigeant. Enfin, *et tout bien pesé*, on peut se dire révolté[25].

Le refus et la limitation ici démarquent l'étendue partagée par le réformisme et la mesure camusienne, c'est leur frontière à l'égard du nihilisme révolutionnaire, le résultat de l'action de la projection des valeurs à partir de règles. L'écrivain sympathise avec les syndicats réformistes des socialistes scandinaves et des travaillistes britanniques. Il publiait quelques articles réformistes dans « L'Express » et il avait déjà souhaité, en 1946, que les réformistes prennent le pouvoir au parti socialiste pour un vrai changement social[26]. Si l'idée de mesure dans *L'homme révolté* est souvent remise en question dans des monologues épineux, du fait de son rapport à une conception spécifique de réalisme – comme lorsque Breton dit que la mesure castre la révolte ou quand Jeason signale que l'écrivain ignore les infrastructures précédentes à une demande sociale –, la réforme se veut action politique *réalisable* comme nous l'avons vu chez Kolakowski dans la mesure où elle ne peut pas se passer de l'expérience d'un peuple. Elle s'oppose ainsi à la propagande d'un réalisme politique fondée sur « un romantisme de l'efficacité »[27] qui manipule l'individu à l'amour ou à la haine dans une logique destructive.

Demande qui accompagne souvent le réalisme, le souci d'efficacité peut rendre l'homme aveugle selon Camus. Dans l'article *L'artiste et son temps* (1952), il rapproche le sentiment de fascination de la force de l'efficacité, en ce qui concerne la droite d'avant la Seconde Guerre mondiale, et ce même

---

[25] *Ibidem*, p. 1005.

[26] « Il faut attendre de longues années après sa mort pour qu'un Jean-François Ravel développe le même argument, sans d'ailleurs se référer à Camus, à la fin des années 2000 pour que, tirant la leçon de ses échecs, la gauche socialiste française mette son discours en harmonie avec sa pratique et s'affirme réformiste. Le débat n'est plus entre réforme et révolution ; il est, comme il le pensait, entre la réforme et le *statu quo* », J. Guérin, *Réforme, Dictionnaire Albert Camus*, Paris, Robert Laffont, 2009, p. 763. Guérin soutient le réformisme de Camus surtout dans son livre remarquable *Albert Camus. Littérature et politique*, Paris, Champions Classiques Essais, 2013.

[27] A. Camus, *Œuvres complètes...*, p. 265.

sentiment au sein de la gauche soviétique : « Les premiers ont voulu être des nationalistes réalistes ; les seconds veulent être des socialistes réalistes. Finalement, ils trahissent également le nationalisme et le socialisme au nom d'un réalisme désormais sans contenu et adoré comme une pure et illusoire technique d'efficacité »[28].

Au-delà de la pensée réformiste, cette recherche d'une troisième voie chez l'écrivain, basée sur la confrontation entre théorie et expérience et illustrée par sa sympathie avec « le syndicalisme » présent dans le chapitre « La pensée de midi » de *L'homme révolté*, se manifeste aussi dans son affinité avec la pensée libertaire depuis 1940 grâce, surtout, à Rirette Maîtrejan, qui lui a présenté le milieu anarchise pendant l'exode du journal *Paris Soir* à Lyon et à Clermont-Ferrand. Les idées libertaires, telles que le refus de sacrifier la vie pour un avenir indéfini, la critique du nationalisme, la plaidoirie pour un parlement mondial, l'intervention sociale extra-parlementaire figurent dans l'activité journalistique de Camus déjà au début des années 1940, mais surtout dans les articles publiés dans la revue *Témoins* dans les années 1950, revue qui faisait elle-même preuve d'une capacité autocritique[29]. Et dans le texte posthume *Défense de L'homme révolté*, Camus revient à la critique du nihilisme historique en affirmant que « l'effort des mouvements libertaires et communautaires en Espagne ou en France sont les repères » auxquels il s'est référé pour illustrer ce qu'il y a de fécond dans la tension entre la révolte et la révolution[30].

Nous pourrions souligner encore sa proximité également avec les anarchistes espagnols auxquels il offre une partie de l'argent reçu du Prix Nobel ou ses articles réunis dans *Chroniques algériennes* qui illustrent son effort pour construire une Algérie plus juste au nom de l'autonomie des différentes communautés du pays contre la violence terroriste et les discours nationalistes. Ces quelques exemples, pourtant, peuvent nous donner déjà une idée de comment la mesure peut répondre à la demande d'un progrès historique à partir d'une éthique qui ne se laisse pas avaler par l'abstraction totalisatrice des discours révolutionnaires. Comme le confirme la phrase du livre d'Ernest Tanrez, dit Ernestan, *Le socialisme et la liberté*, citée par Camus dans *L'homme révolté* : « Si le socialisme, dit un essayiste libertaire, est un éternel

[28] A. Camus, *L'artiste et son temps* [dans:] *idem*, *Œuvres complètes*, Tome III..., p. 453.

[29] L. Marin, *Préface* [dans:] A. Camus, *Albert Camus et les libertaires*, Écrits rassemblés par Lou Marin, Marseille, Égrégores éditions, 2008. p. 49.

[30] A. Camus, *Œuvres complètes*, Tome III..., p. 371.

devenir, ses moyens sont sa fin »[31]. Devant cet aspect illogique de l'application d'un matérialisme dialectique selon lequel la fin justifie les moyens, l'écrivain circonscrit ses efforts pour concilier la justice et la liberté sur des problèmes concrets, ayant pour prémisse la capacité de dialoguer avec son adversaire.

VERS LE DIALOGUE

Ce renvoi au débat entre le clerc et l'anti-clerc de « Responsabilité et histoire » pour réfléchir sur les critiques autour de *L'homme révolté* n'a pas la finalité de cadrer Camus dans l'un de ces deux pôles. En effet, la mise-en-scène de ces deux stéréotypes, ainsi que leurs arguments concernant la morale, la philosophie de l'histoire et le réalisme, nous aide à mieux comprendre les caractéristiques du lieu d'énonciation où ils se trouvent au long de ce conflit entre la gauche indépendante et la gauche communisante[32]. Face aux raisonnements du clerc et de l'anti-clerc, Kolakowski soutient que si l'on arrive à maintenir le dialogue, la tension peut être politiquement féconde. Camus, de son côté, reconnaît que pour n'importe quel dialogue il faut chercher un rapport commun à ce réel à partir de quelques règles. Il est nécessaire de se repérer sur une notion de réalisme qui ne soit ni la proie de l'efficacité ni celle de l'abstention et éviter que l'argument ne se confonde avec l'insulte. La solidarité du révolté doit l'empêcher de laisser son semblable seul dans son discours, puisque la révolte met au premier rang « une complicité des hommes entre eux, une texture commune, la solidarité de la chaîne, une communication d'être à être qui rend les hommes ressemblants et ligués »[33].

Camus dénonce que dans les débats engagés après la publication de *L'homme révolté,* parfois le langage est manipulé de telle façon que les mots signifient leur contraire. Il rédige alors dans le texte posthume *Le Dialogue et le Vocabulaire* – une réponse à Georges Cogniot, après que celui-ci l'a qualifié de fasciste – que « La tactique se donne en somme pour but de remplir les mots mécaniquement d'un contenu opposé à celui qu'ils détenaient jusque-là. Le libéralisme, c'est le fascisme, le parti unique c'est la liberté, la vérité c'est le

---

31 *Ibidem*, p. 254.

32 « [Camus] protestait que le problème essentiel de 'notre mouvement' était aujourd'hui le conflit entre la gauche libre e la gauche dite progressiste, c'est-à-dire entre la gauche indépendante et la gauche communisante ». Citation de H. Lottman dans A. Camus, *Albert Camus et les libertaires…*, p. 51.

33 A. Camus, *Œuvres complètes*, Tome III..., p. 301.

mensonge, les généraux sont pacifistes »[34]. Le dialogue n'est donc pas possible si les interlocuteurs utilisent les mêmes mots pour parler de choses complètement différentes. Kolakowski fait le même constat dans son texte lorsqu'il affirme que « Nous nous mouvons dans un domaine où chaque point de vue construit sans mal, pour son propre usage, une façade verbale suggestive, ce qui prouve que la discussion s'efforce d'éviter les questions claires et univoques, en opérant à l'aide de rhétorique et non d'arguments »[35]. Les deux écrivains invitent ainsi à une analyse du discours censée séparer l'argumentation de la pure rhétorique dans les débats politiques afin de déconstruire les mythes qui transforment constamment l'interlocuteur en ennemi, le dialogue en monologue.

Camus a également réfléchi au dialogue dans ses pièces de théâtre, dans ses articles politiques, dans ses conférences[36]. Il admire la méthode socratique, selon laquelle le dialogue était un moyen de partir à la recherche d'une vérité inaccessible et de reconnaissance de notre propre ignorance. Kolakowski cherche aussi à libérer la pensée de sa prison discursive, à la rendre indépendante et plus proche de ce qui est *réalisable* sur une expérience politique spécifique. Mais nous ne saurons peut-être jamais si Camus utiliserait ou non les réflexions autour du contexte polonais dans la suite de la révolte. Sachant pourtant qu'il se sert d'une méthode de création en spirale[37], selon laquelle il revient à des questions formulées auparavant, les parcourant chaque fois d'une nouvelle manière, nous pouvons construire un déploiement possible à la révolte en relisant son œuvre. Le dossier *Némésis. Notes. Éléments*, dans lequel sont contenus les articles de la revue « Les temps modernes », riche aussi en matériel utilisé dans la rédaction de *L'homme révolté.*

À l'interprétation de l'homme révolté camusien, Kolakowski apporte donc l'homme révisionniste, mais nous pourrions dire que le choix éthique de Camus dépasse une idée de réforme centrée sur le progrès social étatique. Et si Jean-Yves Guérin affirme que, « [Camus] a été un non-conformiste des années 1950 en affirmant que le changement social ne peut se faire, en France, que selon la méthode réformiste »[38], la réforme n'était que le point de départ d'une politique libertaire qui se centrait sur la spécificité concrète de chaque situation mais qui pourrait également avoir des demandes plus ambitieuses,

---

34 *Ibidem*, p. 1106.

35 L. Kolakowski, *Responsabilité et Histoire...*, p. 2052.

36 À l'exemple de « Les temps des meurtriers », présentée à São Paulo en août 1949.

37 Dont il parle dans une lettre à M. Nicolas, assez citée par la critique camusienne. A. Camus, *Essais*, Paris, Gallimard, 2000, p. 1615.

38 J. Guérin, *op.cit.*, p. 763.

tels le fédéralisme en Algérie, l'antimilitarisme et l'établissement d'un parlement international.

Ainsi, face à la mélodie imprévisible de l'histoire, la mesure joue le rôle d'un métronome qui établit les limites du rythme sans empêcher que le musicien ait sa propre interprétation artistique, sans le contraindre pour autant dans sa créativité. La liberté du révolté, c'est la liberté de créer à partir d'une correction du monde, sa logique profonde partant de son choix politique devant l'histoire. Les propositions de Kolakowski peuvent servir donc comme une manière de traduire la matérialité de la mesure camusienne qui a été tellement critiquée par l'intelligentsia parisienne dans les années 1950.

BIBLIOGRAPHIE

Bober, W., *Leszek Kolakowski as moralist and moral philosopher,* « Dialogue and universalism » 2011, no 2, p. 85–91.

Camus, A., *Albert Camus et les libertaires*, Écrits rassemblés par Lou Marin, Marseille, Égrégores éditions, 2008.

Camus, A., *Essais*, Paris, Gallimard, 2000.

Camus, A., *Œuvres complètes*, Tome III, Paris, Gallimard, 2008.

Guérin, J., *Albert Camus. Littérature et politique*, Paris, Champions Classiques Essais, 2013.

Guérin, J., *Réforme, Dictionnaire Albert Camus*, Paris, Robert Laffont, 2009.

Karol, K., *L'avenir reste ouvert en Pologne*, « Les temps modernes » 1958, vol. XIII, no 147/148, Paris, Gallimard, p. 2026–2048.

Kolakowski, L., *Petite Philosophie de la vie quotidienne*, Monaco, Éditions du Rocher, 2001.

Kolakowski, L., *Responsabilité et Histoire*, 1958–05/06, vol. XIII, n°147/148, Paris, Gallimard, 1958.

Kolakowski, L., *Responsabilité et Histoire* (fin), « Les temps modernes » 1958–05/06, vol. XIII, no 147/148, Paris, Gallimard, 1958.

Mascolo D., *Le communisme. Révolution et communication ou la dialectique des valeurs et des besoins*, Paris, Gallimard, 1953.

Meunier, J.L., *La révolte et la rue. En commune présence : Albert Camus & René Char. Rencontres méditerranéennes*, Bédée, Éditions Folle Avoine, 2003.

Le rire de Sisyphe et la danse de Zarathoustra

BARBARA ZAULI

Il est souvent dit en présentant la pensée philosophique et l'œuvre littéraire d'Albert Camus que cette dernière se construit sur trois cycles de création: le cycle de l'absurde, celui de la révolte et enfin, inachevé, celui de l'amour. Or comme il a été souligné précédemment[1] ces trois cycles ne correspondent pas à quelque chose de l'ordre d'un système figé, refermé clôturant une période spécifique de la pensée camusienne, pensée qui est toujours en chantier[2], mais ils s'entremêlent, au contraire, l'un avec l'autre dans son écriture comme à remplir, chacun de sa touche personnelle, un même tableau. Nous lisons dans les *Carnets:* « Je peux en tout cas vous dire que tout écrivain se répète en même temps qu'il progresse, que l'évolution d'une pensée ne se fait pas en ligne droite, qu'elle soit ascendante ou non, mais selon une sorte de spirale, ou la pensée repasse par d'anciens chemins sans cesser de le surplomber » [3].

Il n'est pas difficile de constater comme dans le *cycle de l'absurde*, première partie de la production camusienne, celui de la révolte soit déjà présent pour le moins en puissance dans le héros absurde qui se révolte contre sa condition existentielle, celle qui lui a été attribuée par un destin qu'il n'a pas choisi. La dynamique de la révolte prend en effet ses racines dans la conscientisation de l'absurde. Dans cette perspective nous observons *Sisyphe* soulever l'énième rocher et défier les dieux de son rire moqueur, *Mersault* tuer *Zagreus* pour pouvoir enfin changer un destin qui est le sien et qu'il n'a pas choisi (la première partie du roman est fortement autobiographique et rappelle la jeunesse

---

[1] Notamment par Agnès Spiquel en occasion des rencontres méditerranéennes Albert Camus, 17–18 octobre 2015.

[2] K. Jaspers, *Nietzsche: introduction à sa philosophie*, Paris, Gallimard, 1978.

[3] A. Camus, *Essais*, «Bibliothèque de la Pléiade», Paris, Gallimard, 1965, p. 1614–1615.

pauvre d'Albert Camus), *Caligula* se révolter contre les dieux qui ont laissé mourir Drusilla (dans la première version du 1939) et contre la mort elle-même et enfin *Meursault* se révolter contre toute absolution juridique ou religieuse en acceptant sa condition de condamné à mort et en se souhaitant d'être accueilli lors de son exécution par des cris de haine.

Nous pouvons donc affirmer que la révolte est implicitement disséminée dans la mise en scène camusienne de l'absurde. Cependant c'est bien dans *Le Mythe de Sisyphe*, celui qui est définit explicitement par Camus comme un « Essai *sur*[4] l'absurde », que la révolte apparait thématisée pour la première fois.

ABSURDE ET NIHILISME, AUX SOURCES

Avant de rentrer dans le vif du sujet il me semble important d'ouvrir une brève parenthèse sur l'origine de la notion philosophique de l'absurde chez Camus. Cette dernière est indissociable du jeune Albert Camus lecteur de Nietzsche et de la construction nietzschéenne du nihilisme.

Petit rappel biographique. L'initiation du jeune Camus à la philosophie de celui qui sera son maître spirituel, Friedrich Nietzsche, qui l'accompagnera toute sa vie durant, jusqu'à sa mort[5], se fait en grand partie, à travers l'œuvre d'André Gide. Dans l'œuvre de Gide, pensons notamment à *L'Immoraliste*, Camus retrouve la vigueur et la fermeté d'une pensée philosophique lucide et audacieuse fortement résolue à détruire toutes sortes de doctrine méprisante la vie et à s'émanciper de toute morale grise et pétrifiée, je pense particulièrement au Christianisme. Son mémoire de licence, *Métaphysique chrétienne et néoplatonisme*, témoigne déjà de cette prématurée fascination de Camus pour Nietzsche. Camus, persuadé que « notre royaume appartient à ce monde »[6] est bien conscient de l'impossibilité tragique de pouvoir recréer l'idéal grec dans une époque, la sienne, particulièrement stérile et éminemment chrétienne et il regrette de ne pas pouvoir « aller à Delphes pour se faire initier »[7].

---

4 C'est moi qui souligne.

5 Sur la présence de Friedrich Nietzsche dans l'œuvre philosophique et dans la vie d'Albert Camus voir : M. Weyemberg, *Camus et Nietzsche. Evolution d'une affinité* [dans :] *Albert Camus ou la mémoire des origines*, Bruxelles, De Boek Université, 1998.

6 A. Camus, *Métaphysique chrétienne et Néoplatonisme* [dans :] *Essais* (1965) et : A. Camus, *Œuvres complètes*, Tome I, *1931–1944* (2006).

7 A. Camus, *Carnets II*, Janvier 1942–Mars 1951, Paris, Gallimard, 1964.

Il ne serait pas pertinent dans le cadre de cet article, de parcourir (comme nous l'avons fait ailleurs) la présence de Nietzsche dans l'œuvre et dans la vie d'Albert Camus. Je voudrais me limiter ici de rappeler que la lecture que Camus fait de l'œuvre de Nietzsche (et par conséquence celle du nihilisme de Nietzsche) est à contextualiser dans le vaste phénomène qui a été la réception-réhabilitation française du philosophe de Röcken et qui va des années 1930 jusqu'aux années 1960[8].

Revenons maintenant à l'origine du mot *absurde* et à sa proximité avec le terme *nihilisme.*

Absurde et *nihilisme*, bien que portant sur des significations analogues, ne correspondent pas. Le nihilisme, ayant une ampleur majeure, désigne chez Nietzsche une situation qui concerne l'histoire de la pensée occidentale et en particulier celle européenne. Du mot est considéré par Nietzsche comme « un système de pensée européen aussi bien que le kantisme et l'atomisme ». Nous retrouvons plusieurs significatives définitions nietzschéennes du mot nihilisme dans les *Fragments* de l'automne 1887. Nietzsche y écrit: « Le nihilisme est un état normal. Nihilisme: le but fait défaut; la réponse au pourquoi fait défaut. Que signifie le nihilisme ? Que les valeurs suprêmes se dévalorisent »[9].

Non seulement le mot nihilisme revêt pour le philosophe une signification multiforme de « pessimisme », « décadence », « mal radical », mais son équivocité est donnée par le fait que *le nihilisme* est tantôt considéré par Nietzsche comme symptôme tantôt comme cure, tantôt « en tant que signe de la puissance accrue de l'esprit: en tant que nihilisme actif »[10] tantôt « en tant que déclin et régression de la puissance de l'esprit: le nihilisme passif »[11].

Dans un fragment daté 1977 Nietzsche caractérise le *nihilisme* en tant que « forme typique de la décadence »[12]. Le philosophe-médecin avait en effet diagnostiqué chez les penseurs et les écrivains-poètes français de la décadence (notamment Bourget, Taine, puis Baudelaire) – qu'il lit avec fougue – une perte des repères qu'il jugeait comme étant indiscutablement liée à un vaste phénomène de déchristianisation. Nietzsche parle à ce propos de la perte d'un centre de gravité :

---

8 Pour approfondir une telle question se référer à l'ouvrage de P. Boudot, *Nietzsche et les écrivains français*, Paris, Union générale d'éditions, 1975.

9 F. Nietzsche, *Fragments posthumes*, OCXIII, 9 [35], p. 28.

10 F. Nietzsche, *Fragments posthumes*, FP, OCXIII, 9, [35] p. 28.

11 *Ibidem.*

12 F. Nietzsche, *Œuvres philosophiques complètes*, *Fragments posthumes*, t. XIV, W II, 5, 14, 1977, p. 78.

« Il manque dans leurs instincts le centre de gravité, le sens de la direction à prendre »[13].

Or un tel phénomène de désorientation assume chez les artistes de la *Décadence* l'envergure d'une expérience intime. Terriblement hantés par la recherche d'une signification autre à donner à leur existence ces penseurs se posent la question fondamentale : « Peut-on vivre sans rien croire ? ».

Camus, aussi tributaire de cette vision et sur le sillage de Nietzsche, définit l'absurde comme *un sentiment.* Nous pouvons définir l'absurde comme étant le sentiment éprouvé par l'homme qui vit dans le nihilisme.

Loin d'être interprété par Camus comme un concept métaphysique *l'absurde* est un *fait de cœur,* un 'expérience vécue intimement, une question de *sensibilité*[14]. Une même conception peut s'appliquer à la vision que Camus a de la philosophie que Camus décrit en début du *Mythe de Sisyphe.*

Camus y écrit que la tache fondamentale de la philosophie est de :

« Juger que la vie vaut ou ne vaut pas la peine d'être vécue ». Et il continue:

> Le reste, si le monde a trois dimensions, si l'esprit a neuf ou douze catégories, vient ensuite. Ce sont des jeux; il faut d'abord répondre. Et s'il est vrai, comme il le veut Nietzsche, qu'un philosophe pour être estimable doive prêcher d'exemple, on saisit l'importance de cette réponse puisqu'elle va précéder le geste définitif. Ce sont là des évidences sensibles au cœur, mais qu'il faut approfondir pour les rendre claires à l'esprit[15].

Camus démarque ici une fois de plus sa vision de la philosophie qui est tributaire de celle de Nietzsche, mais qui se révèle néanmoins socratique et présocratique (la philosophie était considérée comme un art de vivre[16]), de celle universitaire, issue de la scolastique médiévale et opérante un décrochage entre le savoir philosophique et le mode de vie du sujet. Le M*ythe* se pose donc la question fondamentale de la philosophie qui est une question assurément *vitale.* La vie que je mène vaut-elle la peine être vécue ? Peut-on vivre sans rien croire? Pouvons-nous les hommes vivre sans dieux, rongés par un sentiment d'absurdité, seuls devant un monde qui reste silencieux à nos appels et qui crie de toute sa force le silence de notre divorce ? Celui

---

13 *Ibidem.*

14 Camus écrit en avant-propos au *Mythe de Sisyphe* « Les pages qui suivent traitent d'une sensibilité absurde qu'on peut trouver éparse dans le siècle [...] » [dans :] *Œuvres Complètes d'Albert Camus*, Paris, Quarto Gallimard, 2013, p. 253.

15 A. Camus, *Le Mythe de Sisyphe...*, p. 255.

16 Voir : P. Hadot, *La philosophie comme manière de vivre*, Paris, Le livre de Poche, 2003.

du suicide est un thème très recourant par les auteurs de la *Décadence* chez lesquels Nietzsche trouve des rares et dignes copains de voyage et auxquels Camus semble se référer. Le suicide est considéré par ces penseurs comme le *dernier couac*[17], le dernier geste envisageable pour ne pas adhérer à cette nouvelle idéologie de l'impuissance, à cette asthénie de la volonté reconnue comme principal symptôme déclamateur du cancer du nihilisme. Indicatifs à un tel égard sont les mots choisis par Charles Baudelaire adressant, en juin 1845, une lettre de suicide à son ami Narcisse Ancelle, à qui il écrit : « Je me tue parce-que je ne puis plus vivre, que la fatigue de m'endormir et la fatigue de me réveiller me sont insupportables [...] »[18]. Loin de signifier un geste de renoncement, le suicide est considéré par Baudelaire et les décadents français, comme un des solutions envisageables par l'homme qui vit dans le nihilisme.

Or, bien que reconnaissant une telle solution comme une parmi les solutions possibles, ni Nietzsche, ni Camus ne sauraient s'arrêter là.

Nietzsche le philosophe-chirurgien ne se borne pas du diagnostic de ce stade intermédiaire de la maladie mais il entend surmonter le nihilisme, il veut aller au-delà de celui-ci. Il montre qu'exactement de la même manière que le corps repoussant sa maladie par les anticorps que celle-ci a déclenché, le nihilisme doit s'auto-dépasser, se surmonter par lui-même et devenir actif. C'est un tel sens qu'il faut attribuer aux mots de Nietzsche quand il affirme dans le *Fragments* de 1887 de vouloir devenir « le premier nihiliste parfait d'Europe » et de vouloir, à ce fin, accomplir l'autodépassement du nihilisme par lui-même et en lui-même.

Toutefois, que signifie-t-il autodépassement du nihilisme par lui-même et en lui-même? C'est là que l'activité de la conscience intervient. La conscience, ce mot capital pour Nietzche et qui donne la cadence au pas de la dynamique de l'absurde chez Camus, est l'antidote qui permet le passage d'un *nihilisme* malade, *passif*, pathologique au *nihilisme actif*, lucide et permettant à Camus de se déplacer du constat des *murs absurdes* pour atteindre le mouvement de *la révolte*. Expliquons-nous sur ce point.

---

17 Pour approfondir une telle perspective se référer aux *Actes du Colloque de Keele : Albert Camus, les extrêmes et l'équilibre* et en particulier à l'article d'Anne-Marie Amiot *Interférences Dada/ Camus*).

18 Ch. Baudelaire, *Lettre à Narcisse Ancelle*, 30 juin 1845, dans Isabelle Vieville Degeorges, Baudelaire clandestin de lui-même, Paris, Ed. Léo Scheer, 2015.

DU RÔLE DE LA CONSCIENCE OU DU RIRE DE SISYPHE ET DE LA DANSE DE ZARATHOUSTRA

Sisyphe est condamné par les dieux à pousser éternellement un rocher qui ne cesse, une fois atteint le sommet de la montagne, de retomber. Sa condamnation est éternelle et irrémédiable. C'est au nom de la vie que Sisyphe avait défié les dieux en déjouant Thanatos. D'après Homère, au moment de sa mort, Sisyphe avait réussi à enchaîner le dieu évitant ainsi d'être emporté aux enfers. Zeus s'apercevant bientôt de la ruse avait été le libérer. Sisyphe, obstiné, avait alors étudié une nouvelle ruse : en demandant à sa femme de lui organiser des funérailles inadéquates il avait obtenu de rester parmi les hommes le temps utile à préparer une cérémonie digne de ce nom, mais une fois des nouvelles funérailles organisées, Sisyphe refuse toujours de se rendre chez les morts. Thanatos, outragé d'avoir été obligé de venir le chercher, condamne Sisyphe à sa peine éternelle.

Les jours s'écoulent et Sisyphe répète incessamment son geste. Nous le voyons « tout l'effort d'un corps tendu pour soulever l'énorme pierre [...] le visage crispé, la joue collée contre la pierre »[19]. Il répète son geste conscient de l'absurdité qu'il recèle.

Or Camus souligne:

> « Si ce mythe est tragique c'est que son héros est conscient »[20].

Camus décrit ce moment décisif de la prise de conscience dans le chapitre du *Mythe* dédié aux murs absurdes. Un jour « arrive » – dit-il – « que les décors s'écroulent »[21]. Soudain, un bruit, une couleur, un regard, une rencontre, vient troubler le scander prévisible du quotidien. Les êtres humains vivent au jour le jour leur existence absurde, surmenés par les taches de la vie quotidienne, dans une routine plus ou moins confortable, rassurante. Et pourtant eux-mêmes sécrètent de l'absurde, de *l'inhumain*, mais ils en sont pour la plus part du temps inconscients. Seulement, « dans certains heures de lucidité, l'aspect mécanique de leur gestes, leur pantomime privée du sens rend stupide tous ce qui les entoure »[22].

---

19 A. Camus, *Le Mythe de Sisyphe*..., p. 326.

20 *Ibidem*, p. 326.

21 *Ibidem*, p. 260.

22 *Ibidem*, p. 262.

L'absurde, écrit Camus dans *L'Homme Révolté*, fait vivre l'homme devant un miroir.

Ce miroir rassemble bien à celui de l'enfant apparu en rêve à Zarathoustra et lui montrant son vrai visage : « la face grimaçant d'un démon ».

Marcel vit oisivement baignant dans le luxe de la noblesse, jusqu'au jour où la saveur d'une madeleine le fait tressaillir. Cet acte qui pourrait apparaître comme absolument dérisoire et qui assume pourtant la valeur d'une conversion existentielle. Belluca, l'employé comptable, protagoniste de la nouvelle de Pirandello, entend le sifflement d'un train et comprend soudain que sa vie ne pourra plus être la même. Marcel et Belluca partagent avec Sisyphe ce moment d'éveil de la conscience.

Les cloches sonnent désormais la mort de Dieu comme seule certitude. L'absurde hurle de toute sa voix le creux de son vide. La conscience[23], éveillée, se tient à son écoute.

Regardons-le alors ce *dernier homme*, qui a croisé le regard de Zarathoustra. Le nihilisme, « le plus inquiétant des hôtes » a toqué à sa porte. Que fait-il ?

Plusieurs scenarios se dessinent:

1. Il décide de répondre au regard et il décide d'en finir avec sa vie étant donné qu'elle n'a pas de sens. Pour amour de la vie il quitte la vie. Mais en fin des comptes nous explique Camus « le suicide, comme le saut », n'est que « l'acceptation à sa limite »[24]. Ces mots font échos à ceux de Nietzsche dans Zarathoustra : la Vie répond au prophète, désemparé et proche du geste définitif : « O Zarathoustra, tu ne m'es pas assez fidèle ! Tu es loin de m'aimer autant que tu les dis. Je sais que tu penses me quitter bientôt »[25].
2. Il tourne la tête et il recommence son existence maladive, il replonge dans le piège de son rituel inconscient, jusqu'au jour ou l'évidence de l'absurde croisera à nouveau son chemin, quand il recevra un télégramme disant : « Arrivo domani »[26].

---

23 Il me semble tout d'abord nécessaire de distinguer entre deux types de conscience. La conscience psychologique et la conscience morale. Car si avec la première Nietzsche évoque une présence à soi, un état d'éveil, de lucidité qui seul peut conduire l'homme à s'auto-dépasser et à apprendre à vivre dans le nihilisme, la deuxième héritière d'une quelque croyance représente pour lui la cause même du nihilisme dans sa phase négative, passive. « Pour autant que nous croyons à la morale, nous condamnons l'existence ».

24 A. Camus, *Le mythe de Sisyphe...*, p. 286.

25 F. Nietzsche, *Ainsi parlait Zarathoustra, L'autre chant de danse* [dans :] *Œuvres complètes de F. Nietzsche*, vol. 6, Paris, Gallimard, 1972.

26 Référence au roman puis film de P.P. Pasolini *Théorème* ou l'arrivé d'un hôte mystérieux bouleverse la vie des membres d'une famille bourgeoise du nord de l'Italie ainsi que de leur domestique.

3. Il accepte l'absurdité de son existence en poussant le raisonnement absurde jusqu'à ses conséquences ultimes, il fait de ceci l'emblème de sa révolte. C'est ainsi que: « Le déchirement initial risque alors de devenir confortable. La plaie qu'on gratte avec tant de sollicitude finit par donner du plaisir »[27].

A la négation *dernier homme*, qui a rencontré l'absurde et qui a renoncé à toute forme de *vouloir* s'ensuit l'affirmation du *surhomme* qui décide de *vouloir le rien* pour enfin vivre pleinement.

Cependant un tel renversement n'est possible chez Nietzsche uniquement qu'une fois le processus de déconstruction opéré par la généalogie, achevé : c'est seulement une fois que la tympanisation[28] des fausses croyances et des toutes valeurs préexistants (Dieux-morale-métaphysique-science) a été accomplie que l'homme, cet *esprit* devenu désormais *libre*, peut réaliser l'autodépassement du nihilisme, et célébrer la venue d'un nihilisme accompli, c'est-à-dire actif. C'est dans un tel accomplissement que nous retrouvons l'élan d'une première révolte. Cette dernière découle du refus radical de toute indulgence et de l'acceptation des nouvelles exigences dictées par l'*éthos* absurde. Le style de vie de l'homme absurde consistera alors en une sorte d'ascèse faite d'une alternance de « détachement et passion » celle-ci étant justifiée par la nécessité de maintenir la confrontation de l'être humain avec l'opacité du monde toujours éveillée.

Ceux qui réussissent un tel exploit, ces seuls grands aventuriers de l'absurde ne renversent pas pour détruire, mais pour créer.[29] La mort de Dieu décrète en quelque sorte le commencement du vouloir humain : aux prises avec cette nouvelle liberté désertique l'homme choisit de *vouloir le rien* (dans le but de plus pleinement vouloir) plutôt que de *rien vouloir* car –privé de Dieu – il n'est homme qu'à partir du moment il veut. C'est au point le plus extrême de cette volonté du néant que l'être humain déciderait donc de vouloir que sa vie se répète éternellement. En tant qu'origine du nihilisme, la mort de Dieu provoque la gaieté philosophique qui se retrouve dans la pensée de l'éternel retour, pensée éminemment révolté et provoquant une crise radicale à l'intérieur du nihilisme. À ce sens ce qui dépasse se confond donc avec ce qui va être dépassé. Zarathoustra se dépasse en dépassant sa volonté du néant, y compris son dégout envers une humanité voulant le néant, et va désirer, puis enseigner une vie qui se répète éternellement dans la totalité de ses expériences possibles.

Son arrivé est annoncé par un télégramme disant « Arrivo domani », « J'arrive demain ».

[27] A. Camus, *L'Homme révolté* [dans :] *Œuvres complètes d'Albert Camus...*, p. 851.

[28] Expression utilisée par Jacques Derrida notamment dans son ouvrage *Marges de la philosophie*.

[29] Distinction opérée par Camus dans *L'Homme Révolté*, sur la lignée de Nietzsche. Voir *op.cit.*, p. 851.

Zarathoustra muni de son bâton « dont la poignée est un serpent s'enroulant autour du soleil »[30] voit un jour un jeune berger se convulser, tordu de douleur avec un lourd serpent noir qui pend hors de sa bouche. Sur conseil du prophète le berger mord la tête noire du serpent – image déformée, *annihilée* du serpent de Zarathoustra – et la recrache loin de lui. C'est là que le jeune homme guéri, transformé, auréolé, se livre à un rire divin qui provoque à Zarathoustra une immense jouissance: « Non plus un pâtre, non plus un homme – un être transformé, transfiguré, un être qui *riait* ! Jamais encore sur terre n'a ri personne comme *il* riait ! »[31].

Zarathoustra le guérisseur n'est plus seul et son enseignement, enfin intériorisé par un homme, un berger, le plus commun des mortels, assume ici une valeur universelle. Ce moment d'ivresse fait vibrer le sens de cet *hymne à la vie* que Zarathoustra, avocat de Dieu, mais d'un dieu païen, ennemi de l'esprit de la lourdeur, avait chanté aux charmantes jeunes filles qui dansaient sur la verte prairie.

Nous avons laissé Sisyphe au sommet de sa montagne. Ce sommet qui représente pour lui l'image d'un fardeau qui se répète éternellement, d'une condamnation inutile qui lui a été injustement infligée, mais qui représente aussi le lieu d'une conquête toujours renouvelée. Le sommet de la montagne est le sommet du nihilisme, la limite exacte entre nihilisme actif et passif. Frontière, celle-ci marquée par l'éternel retour.

Sisyphe, tout près du ciel, regarde son énorme rocher dévaler, il descend et il retrouve toujours son fardeau. Mais c'est précisément au moment de cette énième descente que quelque chose arrive: Sisyphe appréhende que cette pierre qu'il porte dans ses bras est sa chose. La vie, pour amour de laquelle il avait osé défier les dieux s'identifie désormais avec cette descente éternellement identique. C'est là que Sisyphe comprend.

La prise de conscience du long, exténuante gaspillage de force se transforme alors en révolte de la chair. La révolte fait donc sa première apparition dans la chair de Sisyphe, ce premier révolté devenant, par l' acceptation inconditionnelle et lucide de sa condition existentielle, un seul avec son rocher, C'est par cette sorte de première *affirmation plastique*, ce « oui » de Sisyphe, le visage collé à la pierre que nous nous retrouvons au point les plus haut, à l'extrémité de la pensée de l'absurde.

En devenant un avec sa pierre, Sisyphe devient celui qu'il est . Regardons-le ce héros absurde, il a déjà vécu des milliers de vies identiques, il répète son

---

30 F. Nietzsche, *Ainsi parlait Zarathoustra, De la vision et de l'énigme, op.cit.*

31 *Ibidem.*

geste sans cesse, il arrive en bas et recommence sa montée, aucune hésitation serre son cœur.

Seulement parfois, une fois attentes les pieds de la montagne, au moment où il s'apprête à reprendre son chemin, notre héro s'arrête un instant, il regarde le ciel et sourit. Sisyphe *veut*[32] son absurde. « Il faut imaginer Sisyphe heureux »[33].

BIBLIOGRAPHIE SÉLECTIVE

Actes du Colloque de Keele, 25–27 Mars 1993, Albert Camus, *Les extrêmes et l'équilibre*, réunis et présentés par Davis H. Walker.

Baudelaire, Ch., *Fusées, mon cœur mis à nous et d'autres fragments*, Paris, Gallimard, 2016.

Boudot, *Nietzsche et les écrivains français*, Paris, Union générale d'éditions, 1975.

Camus, A., *Carnets II*, Janvier 1942–Mars 1951, Paris, Gallimard, 1964.

Camus, A., *Essais*, «Bibliothèque de la Pléiade», Paris, Gallimard, 1965.

Camus, A., *Le Mythe de Sisyphe* [dans :] A. Camus, *Œuvres Complètes*, Paris, Quarto Gallimard, 2013.

Camus, A., *L'Homme Révolté* [dans :] A. Camus, *Œuvres Complètes*, Paris, Quarto Gallimard, 2013.

Camus, A., *Métaphysique chrétienne et Néoplatonisme* [dans :] *Essais* (1965) et : A. Camus, *Œuvres complètes,* Tome I, *1931–1944* (2006).

Hadot, P., *La philosophie comme manière de vivre*, Paris, Le Livre de Poche, 1993.

Jaspers, K., *Nietzsche: introduction à sa philosophie*, Paris, Gallimard, 1978.

Nietzsche, F., *Ainsi parlait Zarathoustra* [dans :] *Œuvres Complètes philosophiques de F. Nietzsche,* vol. 6, Paris, Gallimard, 1978.

Nietzsche, F., *Fragments Posthumes* [dans :] *Œuvres philosophiques complètes de Friedrich Nietzsche*, Tome XIII, dir G. Collie, Mazzino Montinari, trad. A. Baatsch, P. Klossowski, Paris, Gallimard, 1976.

Weyemberg, M., *Camus et Nietzsche. Evolution d'une affinité* [dans :] *Albert Camus ou la mémoire des origines*, Bruxelles, De Boek Université, 1998.

32 C'est moi qui souligne.

33 A. Camus, *Le Mythe de Sisyphe...*, p. 328.

Is a Rebel an Outsider?
Rebellion in the Interpretation of Colin Wilson

MARCIN URBANIAK

Colin Wilson, an English writer, philosopher and novelist, nowadays seems to be a somewhat forgotten thinker in the area of contemporary philosophy that emphasizes individual existence, freedom and choice. Nonetheless, his main work, *The Outsider*, together with some reflections and conclusions included therein, still remains a valuable source of inspiring ideas for subsequent generations of humanists. Considerations comprised in *The Outsider* oscillate around such problems, as: social alienation; possibilities to live free; nihilism and a negation of reality; relation between ideal world and material world; identity and social masks or a problem of effective expression of oneself. The main aim of the article is to compare the idea of Camus' "rebel" with Wilson's idea of an "outsider" and to answer two questions:

1) what are the functions of the phenomenon of rebellion according to both thinkers?

2) are these functions of rebellion similar?

Colin Wilson named his philosophical conception "new and optimistic existentialism" and "phenomenological existentialism." He wrote: "I have attempted to outline a 'new existentialism' that will possess what is so notably lacking in Heidegger and Sartre – the possibility of future development. [...] I have preferred to speak of a 'new existentialism' rather than a 'phenomenological existentialism' because it is less of a mouthful; but later the two terms are used as interchangeable."[1] In his project of phenomenological existentialism Wilson made a few crucial assumptions, which were already seen in his

[1] C. Wilson, *Introduction to the New Existentialism*, Boston, Houghton Mifflin, 1967, p. 9.

main work *The Outsider*: (1) metaphysical dualism (an outsider lives between the reality of thoughts or mind and the reality of empirical experience); (2) the sphere of thoughts is ruled by hardly discovered spiritual laws; (3) the sphere of thoughts can directly be accessible by phenomenological reduction (*Einklammerung*) or so-called instant mysticism and some psychoactive substances; (4) freedom exists and is possible to experience through a limit situation (*Grenzsituation*) or crisis. It is worth reminding that, in his work, Wilson distinguishes many types of outsider due to the kind of their activity, temperament and the way of expression. There are the following types of outsider:

- romantic outsider is a man whose "thoughts are mainly absorbed by the fact that his surroundings are not able to satisfy his desires completely" (trans. M. U.)[2] – it concerns for example some characters from the works by Novalis, Gérard de Nerval, Ugo Foscolo, Johann Goethe or Friedrich Schiller;
- emotional outsider "of great emotional discipline, but lacking body and intellect control" (trans. M. U.);[3] the cultural example of this type of outsider is Vincent van Gogh;
- intellectual outsider, who thinks too much to enjoy his life; it is a man "of great mind discipline, but he controls neither his body, nor his emotions" (trans. M. U.),[4] like for example the literary protagonists Stephen Dedalus and Antoine Roquentin, or the writers Herbert George Wells and David Herbert Lawrence;
- outsider-mystic "uses techniques like meditation and prayer to still his 'energy-stealing emotions' in order to «steadily increase his supply of surplus vital power,»"[5] for example William Blake, George Fox and Ramakrishna;
- spiritual outsider is characterized by "a mixture of peculiar religious despair and primal, intrinsic mysticism" (trans. M. U.),[6] for example Søren Kierkegaard, Thomas Ernest Hulme or Thomas Stearns Eliot;
- physical outsider "of great body discipline, but he controls neither his emotions nor his intellect;" a personification of this type was Vaslav Nijinsky;

---

2 C. Wilson, *Outsider* (*The Outsider*), trans. M. Traczewska, Kraków, Wydawnictwo Literackie, 1959, p. 34.

3 *Ibidem*, p. 4.

4 *Ibidem*.

5 *Around the Outsider: Essays Presented to Colin Wilson on the Occasion of his 80*th *Birthday*, ed. C. Stanley, Winchester/Washington, O-Books, 2011, p. 85.

6 C. Wilson, *Outsider* (*The Outsider*)..., p. 24.

- criminal outsider, for example Marquis de Sade or Jean Genet;
- "weak" outsider, whose attitude is characteristic for such characters as Hamlet, Prince of Denmark and Jay Gatsby, and for such real-life people as Paul Verlaine or other poètes maudits.

Despite the smaller or bigger differences mentioned, every type of outsider has got one characteristic base, common to them all. They are individuals with unusual sensitivity and extraordinary self-awareness, having their "sense of existence" sharpened. This outstanding ability to perceive existence, on the one hand causes obsessive concentration on some problems of human condition, but on the other hand excludes individuals from the sphere of society. The society is understood here as the thoughtless mass; the crowd of "One-Dimensional" consumers and embodied *Das Man* or "The They." In short, regardless of the type, each outsider is an anonymous Person from the Outside, that is, someone outside the norms, rules and social conventions. It is a person who rebels against the general attitude of opportunism and affirmation of the mindless life. "Outsider is always a man who is not in thrall to ubiquitous enthusiasm" (trans. M. U.).[7] He stays away from the society and observes everyday existence like through a metaphorical hole in the wall. A flawless representation of all types of outsider is the unnamed narrator of Henri Barbusse's novel entitled *The Inferno* – the main character spies on the inhabitants of the next room through a hole in the wall of his hotel room, uncovering some secrets of human condition and "the whole spiritual tragedy of life."[8] Both the unnamed outsider-voyeur from *The Inferno* and each outsider in Wilson's meaning observe the humanity in all its perspectives – from the most private moments and secret activities to the most spurious attitudes and masks. Howard F. Dossor wrote about the outsider in this way: "The Outsider is not an oddity. He is a composite of a host of individuals, living, breathing, agonizing their way through contemporary culture with its dehumanizing processes, its insensitive organization and its rationalized mayhem."[9] Wilson compares this mindless state to a disease known as inauthentic existence. The opposite of an outsider is a philistine referred to as an insider, who is characterized mainly by the lack of sensitivity and consideration as to his limitations. Insiders are engrossed in everyday bustle, petty things completely attracting their attention, which prevents them

7 *Ibidem*, p. 33.

8 E.J. O'Brien, *Introduction* [in:] H. Barbusse, *The Inferno*, trans. E.J. O'Brien, The Floating Press, 2009, p. 8.

9 H.F. Dossor, *Colin Wilson: The Man and His Mind*, Shaftesbury, Element Books, 1991, p. 55.

from living authentically – in a non-conformist, creative and critical manner. However, when an insider has experienced doubt, or has ever been in a borderline situation, then a intuitive anxiety appears, and the world ceases to be easily explained by the widespread opinions, stereotypes and conventions.

Outsiders turn away – they are opposed to being enslaved by conventions and stereotypes, rejecting the state of mindless compromise. This is due to one's aversion to indifference and hypocrisy, which stems from a deep awareness of inauthentic, insincere, hypocritical existence, but also from a sense of absurd and the indifference of the world. The sense of the absurd gives rise to despair at first, only to turn into self-conscious rebellion. It is a rebellion against the universal escape from freedom and authenticity that ultimately casts the rebel away, outside of society.

According to Colin Wilson, no ideology can arbitrarily impose on people the concept of rebellion in the name of freedom. Neither political ideologies, nor academic theories solve the problem of human freedom, as the issue of freedom is not a social issue, but a metaphysical one. Theories and ideologies create an unreal illusion, a facade of illusions that disguise the real world. As Colin Wilson stated, the desire for authenticity and freedom must be inspired by a radical stimulus, such as a widely understood borderline experience, which would allow an individual to see the world stripped of social masks and courtesy.

As Wilson wrote, an outsider is excessively sensitive, which puts him on the sideline of the social world due to him noticing the temporariness and instability of every type of order. The world is not rational and free – it enslaves creative individuals, and behind lofty ideals of humanism, hides uniformity and chaos. The facade of harmony veils the real world, ruled by atavistic instincts and coincidences. An outsider assumes that the customs, conventions, sets of rules and doctrines are intended to confer an appearance of rationality and refinement to our barbarous behavior and irrational impulses. Love seems impossible, and the theses about the perfection of man are false, since they are defied by the harsh facts such as wars and suffering, as well as the commonly encountered ordinariness and mediocrity. Staying on the margins of society, an outsider sees people stripped of their masks and appearances, and hence is able to reach the deeper layers of humanity – primitive instincts. Seeing subsurface instincts that determine social behavior evokes a sense of dread, while the sight of people masking their drives using arbitrary conventions or rational theories makes an outsider realize the illusion of the power of culture. An outsider cannot live in a comfortable, ordered world of naive rules, because such a life is much like a dream.

The reaction of an outsider is to put oneself in opposition to the norms and customs without violating them. This attitude of discord and rebellion against the existing world manifests itself in two ways: the first may involve falling into apathy, and the other – actively revealing the human nature through literature and art. Colin Wilson not only presupposes the existence of human nature, but he also believes that this nature is ill. However, to recognize the symptoms of the illness and to make a diagnosis regarding the human condition, one must remain outside the society – he must become an outsider. The conclusion is the following: the main function of outsider rebellion is an attempt to raise awareness that the state of our environment is pathological. This pathology manifests itself in phenomena that Heidegger collectively defined as "the dictatorship of *Das Man*" – an inauthentic mode of existence and amorphous part of social life. The second function of rebellion is to protect individualism, that is, self-realization and creative self--expression. In other words, rebellion allows to preserve the authentic identity and individual freedom. Unfortunately, however, the protest of an outsider is egocentric, focused around the individuals themselves. The third primary function of rebellion is the ability to look soberly at the surrounding society as an unreal realm, which at its foundation is conditioned by chance, indifference, human stupidity, low desires and instincts. This diagnosis prevents dialogue with the outside world – an outsider is not seeking an agreement with their environment, but a better understanding of themselves.

In Camus's thought, we have a similar situation only to some extent. In his view, the world does not satisfy the human need for sense, which is why there is a contrast between a person's aspirations and the actual realization of these aspirations. A rebel feels oppressed by the existing order, to which he says "no!" He therefore moves to the sidelines of society, instinctively rejecting and rebelling against the everyday reality, thus becoming an outsider. Initially, an individual is lonesome in their rebellion when they reach the clarity of vision of the absurd world. However, in contrast to Colin Wilson, a protest of a rebel is also an affirmation of positive values in society. The revolt against metaphysical ideas and political dogmas affirms the freedom and creativity of the whole community. It is not a negation of the diseased human condition, but faith in humanity and the values that are realized through humanity. In other words, according to Camus, rebellion does not lead to loneliness, individualism or relativism, but overcomes them effectively.

The attitude of rebellion – according to both Camus and Wilson – is a response to the disappointment with the world, the experience of randomness and indifference of the world. However, in contrast to Wilson, Camus believes the function of the rebellion to exceed the individuality of existence in the name of collective values, such as dignity, happiness, friendship, brotherhood, humility, dialogue, or justice. Rebellion also allows evaluating human actions: it is possible to criticize suicide as escapism; criticize war, genocide and the death penalty as a triumph of the absurd; criticize revolutions as a triumph of nihilism. Outsiders in the view of both Camus and Wilson rebel against reality, and so their rebellions have a common source. However, their consequences are completely different – as far as Colin Wilson applauds an outsider's isolation from society, in Camus's opinion a rebel believes in other individuals and defends the common human dignity. If there is no metaphysical goal, then humanity itself – negated by an outsider – is the goal of a rebel. Thus, a rebel goes beyond the simple outsider-insider division, which seems to be a personification of the "to be" and "to have" attitudes. In the context of Camus's consideration, an outsider stopped halfway between the passivity of philistinism and the activity of a rebel. Now, I am going to develop this thesis.

To this end, I shall compare the function of rebellion, which is typical of an outsider and a rebel. Surely, both are particularly highly sensitive to social issues. With that sensitivity, they notice indifference, poverty, suffering or despair of individuals. However, only in Camus's view rebellion is an attitude of disagreement with the suffering of others. Wilson stops at the outsider's own misfortune. The sensitivity of Camus's rebel makes him sensitive to the manifestations of the plague. Only cowards are indifferent, as are despicable people or madmen – they cannot rebel, but merely passively watch the society from the outside. Thus, sensitivity through rebellion opens us up to others, to the You aspect of human nature.

In Camus's view, the function of rebellion is to transcend selfishness in the name of the common good. Furthermore – if rebellion make us focus on someone else's suffering, which we refuse to agree to, and which we prevent, then the function of rebellion is to implement social justice. Rebellion turns out to be a strategy of pulling individuals from their loneliness by identifying the social reasons for action. Negation of the society's indifference and negation of the passivity of some outsiders allows the rebel to get involved and indicate a higher sense of existence. In this way, the function of rebellion is to save man. Rebellion is a way to save another human being, because it protects dignity, brotherhood and justice. Perhaps the function of rebellion is to witness universal values – truth and kindness. What I am referring to is the truth and kindness that do not need any form of transcendence – neither sacrum, nor the world of ideas. It only takes a common place where people are willing to join the community – this place requires protection, and this is the role of a rebel. Not an outsider, but a rebel protects their neighbor, giving evidence to human solidarity; rebellion itself is insomuch creative that it reveals the existence of universal values. Rebellion would thus be the medium through which the collective kindness and truth are made manifest. Consequently, responsibility should also be universal, and then in case of evil, we are also all collectively responsible for it.

Going back to Wilson's idea, the outsider's sensitivity is directed egocentrically, referring only to Me. Wilson goes straight to the point, stating that outsiders remain selfish, because the issue of their own identity bothers them too much to be able to focus on someone else. The society is only a backdrop for the contemplation of their own frustration. The outsider's entire activity comes down to a critical observation of the world and learning about himself. Thus, while the outsider longs for harmony and happiness supporting their isolation from people, the rebel is the key to full self-realization, opening to the society. A rebel surpasses an outsider by finding a solution to his problem – the secret to fullness and self-realization is an active involvement in the world. Here Albert Camus refers to *Meditations* by Marcus Aurelius and *Essais* by Michel de Montaigne. As we remember, Aurelius in almost every book of his *Meditations* recalls the moral obligation of social involvement of a citizen in public affairs, for example: "(...) carefully observe all things necessary to the government, and keep an account of the common expenses" (The First Book, part XIII); "Spend not the remnant of thy days in thoughts and fancies concerning other men, when it is not in relation to some common good" (The Third Book, part IV); "If the whole city be not hurt by this, neither am I certainly. And if the whole be not, why should I make it my private grievance? consider rather what it is wherein he is overseen that is thought to have done the wrong" (The Fifth Book, part XIX); "wouldst think him a happy citizen, whose constant study and practice were for the good and benefit of his fellow citizens, and the carriage of the city such towards him, that he were well pleased with it" (The Tenth Book, part VI); and so on.[10] And Michel de Montaigne wrote likewise, for example: "Well-governed corporations take care to assemble their citizens, not only to the solemn duties of devotion, but also to sports and spectacles. They find society and friendship augmented by it" (Book The First, Chapter XXV); "he who confers a benefit on any one, loves him better than he is beloved by him again, (...) every artificer is fonder of his work, than, if that work had sense, it would be of him, (...) it is dear to us to be, and to be

[10] Marcus Aurelius, *Meditations*, trans. G. Hays, New York, Modern Library, 2003.

consists in movement and action. He who confers a benefit exercises a fine and honest action" (Book The Second, Chapter VIII).[11]

Going back to Colin Wilson, an outsider cannot achieve harmony because he is focused on being, and the philistine he criticizes cannot achieve it because he is focused on having. A rebel exceeds both being and having and chooses to act. Action as a remedy still boils down to overcoming one's destiny and reconciliation with existence. We can therefore conclude that Wilson's outsider continues to live in the illusion of an authentic existence. He has merely made the first step to wake up and see the actual reality, which involves unpredictability, risk, absurd. However, the final step to authentic existence belongs to Prometheus, who can move from his own good to the common good. In Camus's interpretation, the person of Prometheus symbolizes mostly action in the name of human community – as he wrote, "Prometheus was that hero who loved man sufficiently to give him fire and freedom, technology and art at the same time" (trans. M. U.).[12] Promethean activity seems to be completely strange for Wilson's outsider. Paradoxically, however, in Wilson's opinion the first outsider was not somebody from the modern or early modern period of human history – the very first outsider appeared already in ancient myths and his name was Prometheus. The problem is that between the idea of Prometheus in Camus's and Aeschylus's reflection, and the idea of Wilson's outsider, there is an impassable abyss, for Wilson's outsider appears to be the exact opposite of Camus's Prometheus. First of all, the outsider is not a person, who – as Prometheus does – "implants blind hope into a heart of a man" – hope that, in a manner of speaking, shapes humanity fundamentally. Secondly, the outsider is not capable of Promethean solidarity with people, enabling the continuity of society. The only common attribute that connects the idea of Camus's Prometheus with the idea of Wilson's outsider is the ability to cast a more penetrating and profound glance into human nature. This is something that Camus called the "clarity of vision." Thanks to it both Prometheus and the outsider have the knowledge about human condition, which makes them suffer. But the consequences of their suffering are different – when the outsider withdraws from society, Prometheus comes out to the people and teaches them to rebel and to transcend themselves to live authentically. In brief, Prometheus does not agree to human suffering – he rebels and teaches us how to rebel in order to transform our

---

11 M. de Montaigne, *The Complete Essays*, trans. M.A. Screech, London, Penguin Books, 2003.

12 A. Camus, *Prometeusz w piekle* [in:] A. Camus, *Zaślubiny; Lato* (*Noces*, suivi de *L'été*), trans. M. Leśniewska, Kraków, Wydawnictwo Literackie, 1981, p. 83.

world into a better one, to improve and rearrange our existence. In contrast, the outsider is indifferent to injustice and the suffering of others – he is only interested in himself and his own suffering.

Summing up my considerations regarding the existential functions of rebellion, the act of rebellion in Camus's view brings the individual out of his loneliness and exceeds individuality itself. Meanwhile, the outsider remains alone to the end. Camus wrote that: "In the absurd experience, suffering is individual. But from the moment when the movement of rebellion begins, suffering is seen as a collective experience" (trans. M. U.).[13] Therefore, an outsider appears as an alienated individual who only came close to rebellion, but has not acknowledged yet that they share their alienation with others. In all his insight, an outsider does not see that he constantly participates in the sense of alienation from other people, "that the human reality suffers as a result of man's distance to himself and to the world." For this reason, the outsider says "I rebel; therefore I exist," but is unable to repeat after Camus "I rebel; therefore we exist."[14] Rebellion in the name of community confirms the existence of certain limits and values beyond those limits, which must be protected. These values are common to all people. They are the forgotten common good, the warmth of the human heart. Wilson's outsider keeps neglecting the common good. The rebel stands up in defense of what the oppressed and the oppressors have in common, above all differences; of what is shared by those who live authentically and inauthentically. If we agree with the concept of André Malraux,[15] that the individual is not only entirely dependent on the course of history, but is also powerless and alone in the collision with history, then Camus found the a how to overcome this powerlessness and solitude. It can be said that for Camus action, understood as rebel action, is a countermeasure discarding man's loneliness. Differently than in Malraux's concept, however, a rebel is no longer alone in the heat of action – there is solidarity with others, which motivates individuals to cooperation. If characters from Malraux's novels find brotherhood only in the very moment of agony, then characters created by Camus are their antagonists – to realize brotherhood, we have to live and act. The transcendence of individual loneliness is not the main aim here, as Malraux liked, but an additional effect of the realization of common, panhuman values. The rebellion appears to be a symbolic

---

13 A. Camus, *Człowiek zbuntowany* [in:] A. Camus, *Eseje* (*Essais*), trans. J. Guze, Warszawa, PIW, 1974, p. 282.

14 *Ibidem.*

15 See: M. Malraux, *Man's Fate*, trans. H.M. Chevalier, New York, Vintage, 1990.

action – it is a courageous challenge we make in the absurdity of the world, in the fatalism of history, in the bad conditions of human nature, and also in the withdrawn attitude of an antisocial outsider. The outsider cannot see human warmth and solidarity beyond the facade of masks and conventions, because he only sees the heart of darkness there – the lowest instincts, desires and impulses. For this reason, the outsider is unable to defend a higher value, instead shying away from society. As Wilson wrote, "the instinct of brotherhood with people in general, the herd instinct; an outsider most strongly feels the sense of brotherhood with something other than man" (trans. M. U.).[16] An outsider sees himself as a prophet above and beyond the community rather than a fighter for the values representing the community. Nonetheless, thinking about oneself as a prophet suggests either infantile megalomania, or a narcissistic personality. From the perspective of the so-called humanistic psychiatry, which was developed in Poland among others by Antoni Kępiński, Wilson's outsider fits the definition of an individual who can be diagnosed with narcissistic personality disorder. Kępiński wrote: "A consolidation of narcissistic attitude (prevalence of 'I take' over 'I give') makes a man unhappy mainly because he becomes unable to love; such a man cannot come out fully to the surrounding world, his feelings are centered on themselves" (trans. M. U.).[17] It sounds as probably the best characteristic of an outsider, especially the romantic type. What is more, in Kępiński's opinion, a narcissistic person is not in love with themselves, but feels ambivalent emotions towards himself or herself. This description perfectly corresponds to Wilson's thesis that the two main problems of an outsider are: to find my very own identity, and how to express myself in the most adequate way. Wilson disregarded the psychological perspective which explains why a narcissist has problems with self-identification. This arises from an ambivalent relation to oneself. An outsider, as a "narcissistic person, due to focusing his/her feelings on himself/herself, cannot develop the image of himself/herself in a proper way" (trans. M. U.).[18] The problem of the impossibility to develop self-identity and the expression of this identity is discussed thoroughly and precisely by Wilson throughout over 300 pages of the book. Different types of outsider struggle against these problems in different ways, searching for and trying out different strategies, like rational analysis, art, mysticism, even crime. In the meantime, considering an outsider's behavior as a disorder,

---

16 C. Wilson, *Outsider* (*The Outsider*)..., p. 90.

17 A. Kępiński, *Melancholia*, Kraków, Wydawnictwo Literackie, 2001, p. 121.

18 *Ibidem*, p. 122.

the psychiatric diagnosis grasps the problem within about two pages plus recommendations. I would like to emphasize yet another issue. If we take into consideration the fact that narcissistic outsider, as Wilson was proving, is a main character in the majority of great European literary works of the 19th and 20th century, then the question arises: what kind of culture, or what stage of civilization development holds up as a model and focuses around narcissistic behaviors? Perhaps Wilson's analyses indicate a deeper cultural phenomenon, which is our actual life in the time of common (digital) narcissism. Perhaps narcissism became the general pattern of behavior nowadays.

There is an anecdote told by Wilson about his meeting with Camus and why Camus disagreed, when Wilson suggested that a mystical experience might unite us in a higher meaning instead of a rebellion.[19] Concluding the chapter, let me remind you that the function of an outsider's rebellion is the isolation from society and focusing on themselves. Contrary to that, Prometheus's rebellion brings people together, making them close and similar to one another. Such a rebellion is a form of communicating collective values, and also of defending dignity and dialogue. It effectively delivers us not only from individual loneliness, but also from the world of the absurd. The value of rebellion in Camus's and Wilson's view is best illustrated by the consequence of that rebellion; in the case of the symbolic Prometheus, rebellion leads to heroism, cooperation and progress, and in the case of the outsider, rebellion results in loneliness, despair and madness. There is a third possibility, when rebellion leads to irony, as we know thanks to the works by Beckett, Ionesco or Pinter, but that is a topic for another day.

BIBLIOGRAPHY

Around the Outsider: Essays Presented to Colin Wilson on the Occasion of His 80th Birthday, ed. C. Stanley, Winchester–Washington, O-Books, 2011.

Barbusse, H., *The Inferno*, trans. E.J. O'Brien, The Floating Press, 2009.

Camus, A., *Człowiek zbuntowany* [in:] A. Camus, *Eseje* (*Essais*), trans. J. Guze, Warszawa, PIW, 1974.

Camus, A., *Zaślubiny; Lato* (*Noces,* suivi de *L'été*), trans. M. Leśniewska, Kraków, Wydawnictwo Literackie, 1981.

Dossor, H.F., *Colin Wilson: The Man and His Mind*, Shaftesbury, Element Books, 1991.

Kępiński, A., *Melancholia*, Kraków, Wydawnictwo Literackie, 2001.

---

19 See: S. Woodward, *Understanding Nietzscheanism,* Routledge, New York 2014, p. 47.

Malraux, M., *Man's Fate*, trans. H.M. Chevalier, New York, Vintage, 1990.

Marcus Aurelius, *Meditations*, trans. G. Hays, New York, Modern Library, 2003.

Montaigne, M. de, *The Complete Essays*, trans. M.A. Screech, London, Penguin Books, 2003.

Wilson, C., *Introduction to the New Existentialism*, Boston, Houghton Mifflin, 1967.

Wilson, C., *Outsider* (*The Outsider*), trans. M. Traczewska, Kraków, Wydawnictwo Literackie, 1959.

Woodward, A., *Understanding Nietzscheanism*, New York, Routledge, 2014.

Il faut sauver les jeunes filles qui se précipitent d'un pont : pour un renouvellement de la lecture de *L'Envol* de J. Iwaszkiewicz (1957)[1]

JUSTYNA GAMBERT

L'Envol de Jaroslaw Iwaszkiewicz (1957)[2], nouvelle-monologue qui s'affirme comme l'un des textes les plus significatifs de la littérature polonaise de son époque, offre une réponse intertextuelle à *La chute* d'Albert Camus.

L'œuvre de Camus fut découverte en Pologne à la faveur du bouleversement de 1956 qui marque un appel d'air et de liberté devant une culture et une société asphyxiées par douze années de stalinisme. Dans le sillage du XX Congrès du P.C. de l'U.R.S.S. qui révèle les crimes staliniens, germe en Pologne un ample mouvement de révolte populaire, emblématisé par les manifestations ouvrières à Poznan, en juin 1956, quand cent mille manifestants pour le pain et la liberté sont écrasés par quatre cent chars de combat des forces armées de l'état communiste, téléguidées de Moscou. On assiste alors, au sein de la société polonaise, aux premières étincelles d'une fermentation qui déclenchera un mouvement de résistance contre le stalinisme. Ce mouvement aboutira au VIII Congrès du Parti Ouvrier Polonais Unifié, en octobre 1956, qui jettera les bases d'une politique réformiste, définie par l'aspiration

1 Notre communication s'accompagne d'une présentation en ligne, composée d'un diaporama Power Point, d'une part, et, d'autre part, d'un site internet. Ces deux composantes sont reliées par un réseau d'hyperliens. Voir https://docs.google.com/presentation/d/1AajjUPciURaEzp-C0AYvRjyddKRfDQxNNL-NAsrPNEHQ/edit#slide=id.p; https://editor.wix.com/html/editor/web/renderer/edit/ea2d9a6e-8e51-4ac4-b571-94db4dc57a2e?metaSiteId=c8b86db9-5f28-4d44-8748-e72104bb6f1a&editorSessionId=EB87BEF8-C041-4B6F-AFDE-EBA495BCF0C9.

2 J. Iwaszkiewicz, *Wzlot*, « Twórczość » 1957, no 12, p. 11–38.

à un communisme national. Les glaces totalitaires se mettent à fondre, un peu. On parle de dégel[3].

Or, dans le domaine culturel et littéraire, le dégel polonais apporte une explosion de la liberté. En effet, après des années de léthargie, quand la littérature polonaise se trouvait muselée par le carcan idéologique de la doctrine socréaliste, imposée comme seule esthétique admise, on rejette désormais le socréalisme, la vie littéraire s'éveillant et revendiquant davantage d'autonomie[4]. La production littéraire s'enrichit au contact des littératures occidentales, car l'Octobre ouvre les frontières et les œuvres de Beckett, de Ionesco, de Sartre ou encore de Camus sont traduites, avec quelques années de décalage. Le courant qui domine dans la prose est celui de la littérature dite « littérature des règlements de comptes » : il s'agit désormais de régler ses comptes avec le passé stalinien[5].

Certes, le cadre de la révolte est balisé. En effet, s'il est désormais possible de critiquer le stalinisme comme « période des erreurs et des errements », les intellectuels polonais n'imaginent même pas s'attaquer au complexe idéologique plus ample qu'est le communisme marxiste : la censure, également la censure intérieure, oblige. En 1956, personne n'ose ni ne peut dénoncer ouvertement le marxisme[6].

Mais le vent de la liberté a soufflé. Ce système idéologique, brutalement imposé par l'occupant soviétique, en 1945, ne peut être qu'instinctivement repoussé par une société qui de toute son histoire a fait de la liberté politique et spirituelle sa raison d'être.

On sait que la littérature est un vecteur de l'inconscient collectif, l'auteur, lui- un sismographe qui perçoit et traduit, grâce à cette mystérieuse alchimie qu'est la transposition artistique, les signes les plus infimes que renvoie le réel,

---

3 N. Davies, *Histoire de la Pologne*, trad. fr. D. Meunier, Paris, Fayard, 1984, p. 30–37 ; *cf.* T. Drewnowski, *Literatura polska 1944–1989. Próba scalenia*, Kraków, Universitas, 2004, p. 140–154.

4 J. Smulski, *Pękanie lodów. Krótkie formy narracyjne w literaturze polskiej lat 1945–1955*, chap. 1 « Symptomy « odwilży » w życiu literackim pierwszej połowy lat siedemdziesiątych », Toruń, UMK 1995, p. 11–26 ; Z. Jarosinski, *Literatura lat 1945–1975*, Warszawa, Wydawnictwo Naukowe PWN, 1996, p. 123–131 ; M. Januszkiewicz, *Tropami egzystencjalizmu w literaturze polskiej XX-go wieku*, Poznań, Poznańskie Studia Polonistyczne. Seria literacka, 1998, p. 28–31 ; T. Drewnowski, *op.cit.*, p. 140–171 ; S. Burkot, *Literatura polska po 1939 roku*, Warszawa, PWN, 2006, p. 188.

5 I. Wachlowska, *Przekłady z literatur zachodnio-europejskich w Polsce Ludowej*, « Kwartalnik Neofilologiczny » 1956, no 1–2, p. 68–71 ; M. Głowiński, *Narracja jako monolog wypowiedziany* [dans :] *idem*, *Gry powieściowe*, Warszawa, PWN, 1973, p. 106–148 ; J. Smulski, *op.cit.*, p. 11–26; Z. Jarosinski, *op.cit.*, 1996, p. 123–131 ; M. Januszkiewicz, *op.cit.*, p. 28–31 ; T. Drewnowski, *op.cit.*, p. 140–171. S. Burkot, *op.cit.*, p. 188.

6 N. Davies, *op.cit.*, p. 150.

pour les soumettre à un travail esthétique révélateur et purificateur. C'est ce qui se passe, à nos yeux, dans *L'Envol* de Jaroslaw Iwaszkiewicz.

Nous nous attacherons à montrer, en effet, que ce texte orchestre un ample procès de l'idéologie marxiste dans ce qu'elle a de limitatif, d'aliénant pour une sensibilité individuelle. C'est voir dans *L'Envol* un texte des plus contestataires, texte qui déconstruit, de façon extrêmement subtile, les schèmes marxistes. Or, cette déconstruction est possible grâce à la rencontre intertextuelle avec *La chute* de Camus.

Après un retour contextuel sur la réception de *La chute* et de *L'Envol* par la critique polonaise, nous montrerons les procédures textuelles, grâce auxquelles certains postulats essentiels du marxisme, repérables et vérifiables, sont déconstruits à travers la valeur illocutoire du texte iwaszkiewiczien, pour postuler, enfin, un renouvellement de la lecture de *L'Envol*.

Dans notre étude, nous mobiliserons les instruments analytiques très performants élaborés par l'esthétique de la réception, essentiellement la théorie de l'effet esthétique de Wolfgang Iser[7] et la rhétorique de la fiction de Wayne Booth[8].

I. LA RÉCEPTION CRITIQUE DE *LA CHUTE* D'A. CAMUS ET DE *L'ENVOL* DE J. IWASZKIEWICZ EN POLOGNE, EN 1957

La critique polonaise des années cinquante et soixante accrédite la thèse de la visée polémique du monologue iwaszkiewiczien. Ce dernier est interprété comme l'expression d'une remise en question des valeurs éthiques dont débat le narrateur de *La chute*, tenues pour inadéquates, voire dérisoires, en Pologne de l'après-guerre. Quelles sont ces valeurs ?

Dans *la chute,* Camus pose le problème de savoir comment réagir face à la peste, face au Mal. Et nous savons que l'auteur de *L'Homme révolté* prône la révolte comme seule réaction possible. Dans cet essai, il préconise, comme dans le roman *La Peste*, cette morale pragmatique qui pousse le révolté à agir au nom de « cette part de lui-même qu'il voulait faire respecter, (qu'il) met alors au-dessus du reste et la proclame préférable à tout, même à la vie. Elle

---

7 W. Iser, *L'acte de lecture. Théorie de l'effet esthétique*, trad. fr. E. Sznycer, deuxième édition coll. Philosophie et langage, Liège, éd. Mardaga, 1973 ; H-R. Jauss, *Pour une esthétique de la réception*, trad. fr. C. Maillard, coll. Tel, Paris, Gallimard, 1988 (1990) ; H.-R. Jauss, *Pour une herméneutique littéraire*, trad. fr. M. Jacob, Paris, Gallimard, NRF, 1988.

8 W.C. Booth, *The Rhetoric of Fiction*, Chicago, University of Chicago Press 1963.

devient pour lui le bien suprême »[9]. Or, *La chute* pose ce même problème, mais à travers un écran d'ironie[10].

Il nous faut donc, pour commencer, mettre en perspective l'accueil respectif de chacun des deux textes, en Pologne, en 1957.

I.A. La réception de *La chute* d'A. Camus en Pologne

La traduction de *La chute* par Joanna Guze est publiée dans la revue Twórczość en mars 1957. Le récit suscite beaucoup d'intérêt. Cependant, les voix critiques qui se lèvent portent souvent l'empreinte de la distorsion idéologique qui marque les esprits de cette époque. L'idée conductrice est la suivante : dans une situation historique difficile, comme celle où se trouve la Pologne en 1957, les « questions morales » soulevées par Clamence dans *La chute* n'ont aucun sens.

Ainsi, le ton est donné par l'article de Ryszard Przybylski, paru dans la revue politique et sociale *Polityka*. L'auteur tente d'établir un parallèle entre le monologue camusien et les *Notes d'un souterrain* de F. Dostoïewski. A ses yeux, Camus, en marchant dans les pas de Dostoïevski, dénonce le « tunnel individualiste du XX- ème siècle ». Mais la lecture se révèle clairement infléchie par les présupposés marxistes:

> Le point de départ commun de *La Chute* et des *Notes d'un souterrain* a partie liée avec une volonté d'illustrer le *fiasco* d'une éthique individuelle [...] selon laquelle c'est l'individu, seul et voué à la destruction, qui serait appelé à statuer de la justice, du bien et du mal, individu pour qui les catégories telles que la société, la nation, la classe, l'humanité n'ont aucune valeur. C'est le charabia de l'existentialisme du XXème siècle qui en a assez du baragouin sur l'absurde cosmique [...] qui a démasqué la platitude d'un Beckett-tragédien[11].

Et Przybylski, fort des dogmes de l'historicisme marxiste, de démolir la morale décadente de Clamence. Le personnage camusien se trouve ainsi « démystifié » en tant que « Je cartésien », taxé de « mépris de l'action historique des hommes »[12].

---

9 A. Camus, *L'Homme révolté* [dans :] idem *Œuvres Complètes III : 1949–1956*, dir. R. Gay-Crosier, coll. Bibliothèque de la Pléiade, Paris, Gallimard, 2008, p. 72.

10 Voir R. Gay-Crosier, *Les codes ironiques dans* La Chute : *un humanisme à rebours* [dans :] *Pour un humanisme Romanesque*, dir. G. Phillipe, A. Spiquel, Paris, SEDES, 1999, p. 227–235.

11 R. Przybylski, *Camus i Dostoïevski nad Upadkiem*, « Polityka » 1957, année 1, no 23, p. 4.

12 *Ibidem.*

D'autres lectures critiques suivent. Certains iront jusqu'à stigmatiser Camus comme « le représentant-type de la dégénérescence du monde bourgeois et de sa culture »[13].

I.B. La réception de *L'Envol* de Jaroslaw Iwaszkiewicz

Quand, dans le sillage de cet accueil des plus mitigés, Iwaszkiewicz publiera sa réponse intertextuelle à *La chute*, sous le titre de *L'Envol*, en 1957[14], la critique polonaise s'adonnera à cœur joie aux facilités d'une prétendue opposition binaire entre les deux textes.

Selon les auteurs des recensions, les atermoiements d'un Clamence, belle âme qui connaît le luxe de l'introspection et qui s'emploie à couper un cheveu en quatre, regrettant, par exemple, de ne pas avoir sauvé la jeune fille qui se jette d'un pont de la Seine – ne sont que chimère de la conscience occidentale et suprême dérision. Dès lors, *L'Envol* serait une réponse polémique à *La chute*. Certains soutiennent l'idée d'une dichotomie entre le « jardin français », d'une part, et, d'autre part, la « jungle sauvage » locale qui échappe totalement aux valeurs de la morale et de la culture[15].

Or, cette vision qui déprécie la position de l'auteur occidental, au profit de celle qu'on attribue, *a contrario*, à son homologue polonais, fixe une grille de lecture qui fera long feu. En 1998 encore, G. Ritz continue de voir, dans *L'Envol*, une prétendue dévaluation de la philosophie de Camus, qualifiée approximativement d'« existentialiste », face à la sanction transcendante de l'Histoire du XXème siècle[16]. Enfin, en 2004, pour T. Drewnowski, les

---

13 K. Morawski, *Książka o mieszczańskim świecie*, « Dziś i Jutro » 1956, no 5, p. 3 (pour la citation). Voir aussi Z. Dolecki, *Proces wieku*, « Kierunki » 1957, no 35, p. 5, 11 ; J. Kolera, *Od ślepoty do kapitulacji*, « Nowe Sygnały » 1957, no 32, p. 4–7 ; M. Liklaszewska, *Upadek Camusa, czyli strzeżmy sie ludzi niewinnych*, « Prawo i Życie » 1957, no 15, p. 6 ; W. Sadkowski, *Camus i Gascar*, « Trybuna Ludu » 1957, no 217, p. 6 ; C. Skoluda, *Uwięzieni w człowieku*, « Tygodnik Zachodni » 1957, no 36, p. 5 ; Ariel, *Zamiast przeglądu prasy. Wzlot i Upadek*, « Życie i Myśl » 1958, no 1–2, p. 195–200.

14 J. Iwaszkiewicz, *op.cit.*, p. 11–38.

15 H. Bereza, *Demonizm przewrotny*, « Twórczość » 1968 no 10, p. 121–124.

16 « La philosophie existentialiste de Camus, transposée dans l'histoire polonaise contemporaine, subit une transformation radicale. Elle perd son caractère philosophique [...] ». En réalité, A. Camus n''a de cesse de réfuter la thèse de son appartenance à l'école existentialiste: « Non, je ne suis pas existentialiste. Sartre et moi nous étonnons toujours de voir nos deux noms associés. [...] Sartre est existentialiste, et le seul livre d'idées que j'ai publié, *Le Mythe de Sisyphe*, était dirigé contre les philosophies dits existentialistes ». A. Camus, *Le 15 novembre 1945* [dans :] A. Camus, OCI, *Biographie*, par R. Quilliot, *op.cit.*, p. XXXIII–XXXIV. G. Ritz, *Jarosław Iwaszkiewicz. Pogranicza nowoczesności*, trad. A. Kopacki, Kraków, Universitas 1998, p. 242 *sq*.

interrogations morales de Camus ne font pas le poids, face aux « murs » qui encerclent le sujet à une époque « post- apocalyptique et post- métaphysique »[17].

I.C. Le problème de l'impératif moral

Or, il semble essentiel de souligner que la tension problématique cruciale qui est en jeu entre les deux textes réside dans la réponse au problème de l'impératif catégorique, posé par Clamence dans *La chute* et repris, *mutatis mutandis*, par le narrateur de *L'Envol* qui se prénomme Romek. Ce dernier est un jeune voyou somme toute sympathique, pilier du bar de Zielonka où il se livre à des confidences alcoolisées, à l'instar de Clamence, même si ce n'est pas du gingembre qu'il boit. Romek lit à ses heures perdues. C'est ainsi qu'il découvre *La chute* de Camus. Or, il n'adhère pas aux « questions morales » soulevées par ce roman : « il faut bien vivre, il faut bien exister, et il ne faut pas chercher à sauver les jeunes filles qui se précipitent d'un pont »[18].

Il apparaît donc que les critiques polonais, en s'attachant à accréditer cette même thèse, suivent, en réalité, à la lettre la valeur sémantique du discours narratif. Or, ce faisant, ne tombent-ils pas, avec le personnage, dans le piège de la *doxa* marxiste du *Primum Vivere* qui postule que la vie détermine la conscience et qui évacue la dimension éthique comme « formelle » et illusoire ?[19]

A contrario, nous proposons à présent de tenir à distance la valeur sémantique des propos du narrateur de *L'Envol*. En nous inscrivant dans la perspective de l'Esthétique de la Réception, nous soutenons, en effet, ce dernier est un narrateur « non fiable », un narrateur auquel on ne peut pas faire confiance[20].

---

17 « Si, dans le passé, les cas d'indifférence et de cruauté, les meurtres et les suicides, étaient encore considérés comme des malheurs exceptionnels, l'état d'esprit de l'homme d'aujourd'hui a partie liée avec le caractère de l'époque contemporaine. La primauté du mal dans le monde emporte les habitants de ce dernier, en effaçant la frontière claire entre les bons et le mauvais ». T. Drewnowski, *op.cit.*, p. 220.

18 J. Iwaszkiewicz, *op.cit.*, p. 21.

19 G. Claeys, *Encyclopedia of Nineteenth-century Thought*, London – New York, Taylor & Francis, 2005, p. 265 *sq*. *Cf.* P. Ricoeur, *Marx: L'idéologie allemande (1)* [dans :] *idem*, *L'idéologie et l'utopie*, coll. Essais, Paris, Seuil, 1997, p. 118 *sq*.

20 Nous empruntons ce concept à Wayne Booth. En effet, conformément aux postulats de l'Esthétique de la Réception, il apparaît que nous sommes ici en présence d'une « subdivision » de l'horizon textuel en deux perspectives dissociées contradictoires. W. Booth indique ici, d'une part, la perspective de « l'auteur implicite » (*implied author*), et, d'autre part, celle d'un « personnage auquel on ne peut pas faire confiance » (*unreliable narrator*). W.C. Booth, *op.cit.*, p. 211 *sq*. et 339 *sq*.; cité par W. Iser, *op.cit.*, p. 354 (en italique dans le texte).

L'esthétique de la réception considère l'œuvre comme un ensemble de perspectives qui s'éclairent mutuellement, dont la perspective narratrice, certes, mais aussi les perspectives de l'espace, de la temporalité, du lecteur implicite ou encore de l'auteur implicite. C'est bien l'interaction entre ces perspectives qui forme cet ensemble esthétique qu'est l'œuvre[21]. Ceci induit une approche critique du discours narratif. Ce dernier n'est pas envisagé dans sa valeur sémantique, mais bien dans sa valeur pragmatique et illocutoire : ce n'est pas ce qui est dit qui nous intéresse, mais comment c'est dit[22].

Nous nous attacherons dès lors à vérifier, dans la deuxième partie de notre étude, l'hypothèse suivante : le rapport entre la perspective de l'auteur implicite et celle du narrateur, dans *L'Envol*, n'est ni simple, ni immédiat, ni harmonieux. Il s'agit, au contraire, d'un rapport ironique de mise à distance. L'enjeu de cette démonstration sera donc de démontrer que, loin de la positivité sémantique du discours narratif empreint des *doxas* marxistes, Iwaszkiewicz dit, avec Camus : « il faut chercher à sauver les jeunes filles qui se précipitent d'un pont ». Ne pouvant le dire ouvertement – la censure, dont intérieure, oblige ! – l'auteur élabore une savante dynamique textuelle, travaillant à déstabiliser les dogmes marxistes qui collent à la peau. Ceux-ci apparaissent comme délétères, une fois révélées leurs conséquences virtuelles aberrantes sur le psychisme d'un sujet individuel.

II. LA THÉMATISATION DE L'IMPACT DESTRUCTEUR DES SCHÈMES DU MARXISME SUR UNE PSYCHÉ ALIÉNÉE

Faire le procès de l'idéologie marxiste, c'est, dans *l'Envol*, d'abord décrire un sujet emblématique, un sujet mutilé par certains schèmes de cette idéologie.

II.A. Ruptures tonales et décrochages énonciatifs

Considérons, d'abord, l'emblématique énoncé du narrateur iwaszkiewiczien, s'employant à nier l'impératif éthique qui sous-tend le dilemme de Clamence :

---

21 En se situant dans une perspective plus large, W. Kajtoch souligne, dans tout texte, la prégnance lexicale, syntaxique et pragmatique d'une vision du monde qui préside à l'économie discursive du texte. Cette vision souterraine s'avère attribuable à une instance qui semble coïncider, dans le domaine du texte narratif, avec le concept de l'auteur implicite, forgé par W. Iser. Voir W. Kajtoch, *Językowe obrazy świata i człowieka w prasie młodzieżowej i alternatywnej*, t. 1 i t. 2, Kraków, Wydawnictwo Uniwersytetu Jagiellońskiego, 2008, t. 1, p. 14–15.

22 W. Iser, *op.cit.*, p. 128–131.

« [...] il faut bien vivre, il faut bien exister, et il ne faut pas chercher à sauver les jeunes filles qui se précipitent d'un pont »[23].

Ne sommes-nous pas surpris ici par le décalage entre la gravité de la thématique qui reprend le motif central de *La Chute*, le suicide d'une jeune femme sur le Pont Royal, d'une part, et, d'autre part, la tonalité burlesque du propos ? Pourquoi Romek profère-t-il des jugements si ouvertement cyniques qu'ils semblent relever de l'antiphrase ?

Nous sommes, d'évidence, face à une anomalie au regard des règles pragmatiques de l'usage de la langue[24]. Or, cette anomalie apparaît comme l'indice d'une subjectivité narratoriale pathologique. En effet, c'est parce que le narrateur présente une mentalité destructurée qu'il est incapable de saisir la problématique morale soulevée par Camus.

Nous tâcherons à présent de comprendre le pourquoi de cette pathologie de la subjectivité narratrice.

On pourrait penser que c'est la réalité historique de la Pologne de l'époque qui est à l'origine de cette dernière. Certes, les drames de la guerre et de l'après-guerre éprouvent l'individu et placent l'éthique d'A. Camus de la révolte dans un éclairage particulier. En même temps, cependant, la révolte camusienne offre une proposition efficiente, permettant précisément de ne pas sombrer dans l'absurde de l'Histoire. Or, Romek, lui, n'a pas été formé par la lecture de Camus, en raison de la fermeture des frontières. En revanche, il a grandi dans un pays totalitaire où une seule et unique idéologie était admise d'office : le marxisme.

C'est une idéologie qui prône le relativisme moral et qui justifie la peste. Nous pensons et nous montrerons que c'est bien cette idéologie qui est à l'origine de la pathologie du narrateur et que c'est elle qui constitue donc l'obstacle empêchant ce dernier de comprendre l'humanisme de Camus.

Ainsi, le fameux discours de méthode de Romek, interprété par la critique polonaise comme l'expression d'une polémique avec l'auteur de *La peste*, ne fait que thématiser les postulats essentiels du jeune Marx, qui seront confortés par les derniers écrits.

Ainsi, P. Ricoeur a magistralement montré que la doctrine marxiste élimine la dimension éthique, qualifiée, avec la religion, la métaphysique ou encore la réflexion philosophique, d'« idéologique », « formelle » et « dépourvue de toute autonomie ». En effet, pour Marx, la morale n'existe pas, elle n'est

[23] « Jakoś trzeba żyć, jakoś trzeba istnieć, a dziewczynek, co się z mostu rzucają, nie trzeba ratować ». Voir J. Iwaszkiewicz, *op.cit.*, p. 21.

[24] D. Wilson, D. Sperber, *L'interprétation des énoncés*, « Communications » 1979, vol. 30, p. 80–94.

que projection chimérique d'une conscience individuelle[25]. Ayant évacué la morale, le marxisme fait de la vie la seule valeur : « Ce n'est pas la conscience qui détermine la vie, mais la vie qui détermine la conscience »[26].

Qui est à l'école de Marx ne peut pas lire Camus. Un tel constat motive possiblement la genèse *L'Envol*. Qu'advient-il de la sensibilité morale d'un sujet, pour qu'il dise, comme Romek : « [...] il faut bien vivre, il faut bien exister, et il ne faut pas chercher à sauver les jeunes filles qui se précipitent d'un pont » ?

Il semble plausible, en effet, que c'est bien cette cuisante question que l'auteur polonais se voit amené à poser à sa collectivité nationale, soumise à l'impact d'une formation idéologique délétère. Dans cette perspective, Iwaszkiewicz n'écrit pas *L'Envol* pour engager une polémique avec Camus, mais bien pour faire le procès de l'idéologie marxiste. Celle-ci domine le répertoire[27] du lecteur polonais de 1957, mais elle le menace aussi lui-même, dans le monde qui l'entoure et au fond de lui-même.

II.B. Une subjectivité parlante déstructurée

Qui est Romek?

Pour tenter de cerner la source de la pathologie du narrateur de *L'Envol*, nous nous attacherons à passer au crible certaines structures de son discours, en exploitant les ressources de la linguistique. La linguistique, depuis les grammairiens du Pont Royal jusqu'aux représentants actuels des sciences du discours, comme G. E. Sarfati ou O. Galatanu, considèrent que dans les structures du discours s'est déposée l'empreinte de la subjectivité fondatrice et que l'étude du discours est apte à nous en fournir les clés.

A l'intérieur de ce dispositif d'investigations, on peut facilement constater que le discours du narrateur du monologue d'Iwaszkiewicz présente une série

---

25 « [...] la morale, la religion, la métaphysique et tout le reste de l'idéologie, ainsi que les formes de conscience qui leur correspondent, perdent aussitôt toute apparence d'autonomie. Elles n'ont pas d'histoire, elles n'ont pas de développement, ce sont, au contraire, les hommes qui, en développant leur production matérielle et leurs rapports matériels, transforment, avec cette réalité qui leur est propre, et leur pensée et les produits de leur pensée ». In K. Marx, *L'idéologie allemande*, p. 36–37 ; cité par P. Ricoeur, *Marx...* , p. 118.

26 « Ce n'est pas la conscience qui détermine la vie, mais la vie qui détermine la conscience. C'est une proposition classique du marxisme. Si nous appelons ' conscience ' non pas simplement l'attention, mais la capacité de projeter des objets, alors cela désigne le monde objectif de Kant et de Hegel, la constitution d'un monde objectif par la représentation. Il s'agit de tout le monde phénoménal, en tant qu'il est mentalement interprété ». P. Ricoeur, *Marx...*

27 Voir W. Iser, *op.cit.*, p. 128 *sq.*

de particularités ou d'anomalies au regard de la norme langagière. Ces anomalies sont plausiblement dues à l'impact destructeur de certains schèmes de l'idéologie marxiste repérables et vérifiables. Nous pourrons relever ici trois faits linguistiques, relatifs respectivement à la *deixis*, aux structures modales du discours, enfin à la circulation des isotopies sémantiques.

Les distorsions de l'organisation pronominale du discours au regard des modèles canoniques de la subjectivité parlante

Commençons par examiner le fonctionnement des pronoms personnels, pour vérifier la place que notre narrateur s'assigne dans la réalité qui l'entoure. Des anomalies notables pourront être relevées.

Le système classique de l'énonciation s'articule normalement, depuis E. Benveniste, autour du Je locuteur[28]. Or, ce n'est pas le cas dans le discours narratif de *L'Envol*. En effet, on trouve peu d'occurrences du pronom personnel de la P1 en position de sujet d'une phrase, en particulier d'une phrase de sémantisme actif. Le sujet ne se pose pas donc pas comme un sujet agissant (« Je »). En revanche, sont légion les constructions où il se présente comme un objet grammatical-objet passif (« me »).

Qu'en est-il, dès lors, de l'emplacement syntaxique dominant de sujet de la phrase ? Fait significatif, on note un nombre très important de phrases où cette fonction syntaxique est remplie par le pronom pluriel « Ils ». Le plus souvent, il s'agit d'un sujet indéfini et anonyme :

1. « […] **ils** m'ont accusé, et je ne sais même pas qui »[29] ;
2. « […] **ils** ne me cherchaient plus […] »[30] ;
3. « […] et si, Dieu m'en garde, ils s'en rappelaient, **ils** m'y colleraient encore »[31] ;
4. « **ils** m'ont laissé dormir, et puis **ils** m'ont libéré […] »[32] ;
5. « […] **ils** ne savaient même pas »[33] ;
6. « […] **ils** m'avaient tout de suite libéré de la tôle »[34] ;

---

28 E. Benveniste, *Problèmes de linguistique générale*, chapitre XX « La nature des pronoms », coll. Tel, Paris, Gallimard, 1966, p. 251–257.

29 « (...) a oni mi wypomnieli, bo nawet nie wiem kto ». J. Iwaszkiwicz, *op.cit.*, p. 36.

30 « (...) powiedziała, że już mnie nie szukają (...) ». *Ibidem*, p. 20.

31 « A jakby, broń Boże, sobie jeszcze przypomnieli o tym, to by mnie jeszcze przyskrzynili ». *Ibidem*, p. 29.

32 « Dali mi się wyspać i wypuścili (...) ». *Ibidem*, p. 34.

33 « (...) nawet się tego nie spodziewali ». *Ibidem*, p. 35.

34 « (...) z tego mamra mnie wydalili ». *Ibidem*.

7. « [...] **ils** m'ont accusé [...] »[35] ;
8. « [...] s'**ils** te condamnent à quinze ans [...] »[36] ;
9. « [...] quelques semaines plus tard, **ils** sont venus nous chercher [...] »[37] ;
10. « [...] **ils** m'ont accusé, et je ne sais même pas qui »[38] ;
11. « Et, en plus, **ils** veulent que je construise la Pologne populaire [...] »[39] ;
12. « A Varsovie, oui, **ils** ne me connaissent pas, mais va savoir, ils ont leurs tuyaux »[40] ;
13. « **Ils** ne m'auront pas, **ils** n'auront pas ma tête, ni cette foutue Marysia, ni cette tante béate, ni cette putain varsovienne, ni tous ces *ubek*'s qui m'ont supplicié, ni tous ceux qui m'ont fait voir le sang »[41].

Le patron syntaxique actualisé dans cet échantillon non exhaustif d'exemples textuels s'avère très largement dominant, dans *L'Envol*. Les « ils » monopolisent ainsi la position forte de sujet de la phrase, en saturant le discours narratif des marques de la présence envahissante de l'Autre. L'Autre, d'autant plus menaçant qu'indéfini, obsède le narrateur qui, quant à lui, se perçoit comme victime.

Il est à noter que dans les séquences relatives à la guerre de 1939–1945, l'Autre réfère aux Nazis. Mais dans celles qui dépeignent la réalité d'après-guerre (voir les exemples ci-dessus), le pronom « ils » continue de monopoliser la position de sujet. Il apparaît donc que nous sommes ici face à une sorte de *Big Brother* orwellien qui se fond insidieusement dans les structures de l'Etat communiste.

Les « Ils » se révèlent attachés à l'espace central de la capitale, mais leurs tentacules peuvent à tout moment atteindre le narrateur, positivement piégé: « A Varsovie, oui, ils ne me connaissent pas, mais va savoir, ils ont leurs tuyaux »[42].

La position dominante de ce sujet pluriel anonyme, détenteur du pouvoir est souvent, comme ici, mise en relief par des répétitions, le narrateur, lui, se

[35] « (...) mi zarzucają (...) ». *Ibidem*.

[36] « (...) pietnaście lat mi dają (...) ». *Ibidem*.

[37] « (...) w parę tygodni potem przyjechali po nas ». *Ibidem*, p. 17.

[38] « (...) a oni mi wypomnieli, bo nawet nie wiem kto ». *Ibidem*, p. 36.

[39] « A jeszcze chcą, żebym ja Polskę budował ». *Ibidem*.

[40] « W Warszawie to mnie nie znają, choć kto ich tam wie, mają i oni swoje jakieś rozeznanie ». *Ibidem*.

[41] « A niedoczekanie im wszystkim, na złość im wszystkim, i tej zasranej Marysi, i tej cioci rozanielonej, i tej babie warszawskiej rozpierdolonej i tym wszystkim ubekom, co mnie męczyli, i tym wszystkim, co mi kazali patrzeć na krew... ». *Ibidem*, p. 37.

[42] « W Warszawie to mnie nie znają, choć kto ich tam wie, mają i oni swoje jakieś rozeznanie ». *Ibidem*, p. 36.

trouvant toujours objectivé dans des emplacements syntaxiques subalternes (« me »). Nous sommes donc en présence d'un Je positivement aliéné, car incapable de se poser en sujet, de dire Je.

Comment expliquer cette aliénation ? Il semble plausible qu'elle ait partie liée avec l'un des postulats essentiels du marxisme. On sait que le marxisme nie les subjectivités individuelles, au profit de l'affirmation de la suprématie de l'Histoire. Celle-ci se conçoit, selon cette idéologie, comme la seule et unique subjectivité. En se référant au cadre conceptuel forgé par Hegel, posant que c'est dans le mouvement de l'Histoire que s'incarne l'immanence de l'Esprit[43], Marx affirme, en effet, le caractère absolu du devenir historique, ce dernier étant censé organiser le champ ontologique, sous forme de la *praxis*[44]. P. Ricoeur montre très bien que cet axiome marxiste de suprématie de l'Histoire s'accompagne de l'instrumentalisation de l'individu humain, considéré comme moyen[45].

Dans le système interprétatif surdéterminé par l'idéologie marxiste, le Je individuel n'est donc ni le sujet ni l'acteur de son propre destin. P.Ricoeur souligne, en effet, le déplacement, chez Marx, de l'instance de subjectivité de l'individu vers la *praxis* historique qui instaure les conditions de possibilité de « libération » du Je de son statut de sujet. Ce déplacement est esquissé chez le jeune Marx et conforté, sous la forme la plus aboutie, par les *Manuscrits de 44* et par les *Principes de la philosophie du droit*[46]. C'est l'un des thèmes fondateurs du marxisme.

Ces distorsions manifestes au regard des modèles classiques de l'énonciation, dans le discours du narrateur de *L'Envol,* distorsions plausiblement motivées par les postulats marxistes, révèlent donc un Je parlant mutilé dont l'autonomie subjective s'avère défaillante.

Examinons à présent rapidement les structures modales du discours qui elles aussi font apparaître des déformations signifiantes.

---

[43] « L'Histoire universelle est la manifestation du processus divin absolu de l'Esprit dans ses plus hautes figures ». G.W.F. Hegel, *La raison dans l'histoire,* trad. K. Papaioannou, Paris, Plon, 1965, p. 97. Sur ce sujet, on consultera également G.W.F. Hegel, *La phénoménologie de l'Esprit,* section B « Conscience de soi », texte traduit et établi par J. Hyppolite, coll. Philosophies de l'Esprit, Paris, Aubier, 1977, p. 145–167.

[44] P. Ricoeur, *Le Marx de Michel Henry, Approches de la personne* [dans :] *idem*, *Lectures 2,* coll. Essais, Paris, Seuil, 1999, p. 289.

[45] *Ibidem.*

[46] K. Marx, *Principes de la philosophie du droit,* paragraphe 149, *cf.* P. Ricoeur, Marx..., p. 107 *sq.*, p. 115–119 ; *cf.* D. Julia, *Dictionnaire de la philosophie,* Paris, Larousse, 1964, p. 174.

Le Verbe : l'étude des modalités du discours, révélatrices d'une subjectivité destructurée

On note, dans le discours narratif de *l'Envol,* des anomalies affectant les structures modales du syntagme verbal.

La modalité épistémique

On observe, tout d'abord, un déficit de verbes de modalité épistémique, celle-ci dénotant les opérations intellectuelles et cognitives, conjugués à la première personne. Ainsi, les verbes comme « savoir » sont toujours de forme négative, laissant apparaître un sujet qui *ne sait pas* octroyer du sens aux choses : « je ne sais pas »[47]. « je ne comprends pas »[48].

Parallèlement, l'absence de verbes d'opinion témoigne d'une cognition déformée et incapable de structurer significativement le réel. On soulignera l'absence générale du verbe transitif « penser à /de... » (myśleć (o ...)) à la première personne et à la voix active. Son paronyme « réfléchir » (rozmyślać) est représenté[49], mais à travers un emploi intransitif qui semble substituer à une opération cognitive, centrée sur une réalité précise, une méditation apparemment dépourvue d'objet concret.

Cette déficience de verbes dénotant une opération intellectuelle s'avère compensée par la surreprésentation des constructions impersonnelles à sujet grammatical: « il semble » (zdaje się), « il me semble » (wydaje mi się)[50] ou encore de constructions lexicales dénotant la perception involontaire: « j'ai l'impression/ l'illusion » (mam wrażenie/złudzenie)[51]. Tout se passe donc comme si l'idée s'imposait seule à la cognition.

Le caractère compulsif de la mémoire est mis en avant, perceptible dans les expressions du type: « [...] l'enterrement me trottait dans la tête »[52]. La résurgence erratique des souvenirs semble, en effet, échapper au contrôle de la subjectivité parlante, en transformant le narrateur en siège passif du processus remémoratif.

Le flot mental advient donc à cette conscience d'une manière anarchique, antérieure à la conceptualisation. Ceci pourrait être motivé par un autre postulat marxiste, celui de la prééminence du « flux du réel pré- réfléchi »

---

47 J. Iwaszkiewicz, *op.cit.*, p. 15, 17, 21, 29, 35.

48 *Ibidem*, p. 21.

49 *Ibidem*, p. 12.

50 *Ibidem*, p. 12–13, 16, 31.

51 *Ibidem*, p. 13, 32.

52 « (...) tak mi ten pogrzeb chodził po głowie ». *Ibidem*, p. 18.

sur la réflexion, celle-ci étant considérée comme « spéculative » donc inférieure[53].

Mais cette incapacité du narrateur à organiser sa propre pensée, donc à dissiper l'opacité du monde qui l'entoure, dans une réalité ambiante inspirée par les postulats marxistes, génère, à son tour, une inhibition de la capacité à agir. Ceci motive la carence, dans le discours narratif de *L'Envol*, de la modalité aléthique, manifeste à travers l'absence du verbe « pouvoir » à la première personne du singulier.

Modalité aléthique

A contrario, on trouvera plusieurs occurrences du verbe « pouvoir » soumises à la modalité négative. Il est à noter que cet aveu d'impuissance porte sur deux types de prédicats: la cognition d'une part et l'activité sexuelle d'autre part.

Ainsi, les fonctions intellectuelles sont relativisées: « on **ne peut rien** savoir »[54] ; « viennent à nous alors tous les assassinés et nous **ne pouvons rien** leur dire »[55].

Mais les aveux d'impuissance portent souvent sur la relation sexuelle: « [...] je **ne peux pas** regarder ton corps! »[56], « [...] **je ne supporte pas** le corps d'une femme nue! »[57], « **Je ne peux pas** avec les bonnes femmes »[58] ; « Eh bien, **j'en peux plus**! J'en ai assez de ces bonnes femmes. »[59] ; « [...] elle m'attire au lit, et moi, mon cher monsieur, **je n'en peux plus**, ce n'est **pas que je ne puisse pas** physiquement, mais, pour ainsi dire, moralement. **Je ne peux pas**, c'est tout »[60].

« Je ne peux pas », cet aveu d'impuissance sexuelle s'avère donc contemporain de l'incapacité à se penser, à se saisir dans une perspective signifiante, chez notre Je narratorial mutilé, aux structures cognitives déformées.

Mais cette difficulté à réfléchir et à agir demeure inextricablement liée à l'absence de l'impératif moral qui induit un déficit de la modalité déontique. Dire « je dois », c'est difficile, en effet, pour Romek.

---

53 P. Ricoeur, *Marx...*, p.107 *sq.*, p. 115–119.

54 « (...) nic nie możemy wiedzieć ». J. Iwaszkiewicz, *op.cit.*, p. 11.

55 « (...) przychodzą do nas wszyscy zabici i nic nie możemy im odpowiedzieć ». *Ibidem*, p. 31.

56 « (...) patrzeć na twoje cielsko nie mogę ». *Ibidem*, p. 15.

57 « Gołego ciała babskiego nie mogę ». *Ibidem*, p. 13.

58 « [...] z babami nie mogę ». *Ibidem*, p. 11.

59 « Nie mogę! Mam już dosyć tych bab ». *Ibidem*.

60 « Zaraz do łóżka ciągnie, a ja, panie drogi, już nie mogę, nie to, że fizycznie nie mogę, ale, że tak powiem, moralnie. Nie mogę i już! ». *Ibidem*.

Modalité déontique

On note ainsi la carence du verbe « devoir » et celle des autres verbes du même champ sémantique. Parallèlement, on observe l'absence de la locution impersonnelle normative « il faut », sauf dans une occurrence à laquelle nous reviendrons. Ce manque est interprétable comme traduction de la déficience, chez le narrateur iwaszkiewiczien, de l'impératif moral au sens kantien du terme[61]. Nous sommes donc en présence d'un Je incapable de fixer des impératifs éthiques et des impératifs d'action.

Or, la seule formule normative, présente dans le texte, est la fameuse phrase qui marque une référence d'intertextualité à *La Chute* d'Albert Camus: « [...] il faut bien vivre, il faut exister, et il ne faut pas chercher à sauver les jeunes filles qui se précipitent d'un pont »[62].

Mais cette règle de conduite, énoncée avec une assurance surprenante, surtout devant la carence constatée de la modalité déontique dans l'ensemble du discours, apporte une formulation transparente de la *doxa* marxiste du *Primum Vivere*. Selon l'auteur du *Capital*, la vie biologique, vie matérielle constitue, en effet, l'unique valeur[63]. La morale dite « formelle », est, quant à elle, stigmatisée par Marx comme le produit chimérique d'une conscience contemplant ses propres projections[64] : « Eh, monsieur, ne me faites pas peur avec des questions [...] morales. Mon école, c'était une vraie école. Ma vie, c'est la vie »[65], dit encore Romek.

Vivre plutôt que moraliser, n'est-ce pas le *credo* de l'homme marxiste dont Iwaszkiewicz nous offre, à travers son narrateur, une traduction fictionnelle impitoyable ?

Quoi d'étonnant à ce que l'isotopie de la vie se constitue en isotopie sémantique dominante, dans *L'Envol* ? Ceci semble paradoxal, dans un monologue narratif qui devrait génériquement apporter un retour réflexif sur l'expérience existentielle du sujet. Mais, en même temps, cette dominante lexicale s'avère on ne peut plus motivée par l'aliénation idéologique du narrateur.

---

61 E. Kant, *Critique de la raison pratique*, *cf. Dictionnaire de philosophie*, dir. G. Durozoi, A. Roussel, *op.cit.*, p. 216–219.

62 « Jakoś trzeba żyć, jakoś trzeba istnieć, a dziewczynek, co się z mostu rzucają, nie trzeba ratować ». J. Iwaszkiewicz, *op.cit.*, p. 11.

63 P. Ricoeur, *Le « Marx »...*, p. 285 *sq*.

64 La doxa marxiste du *Primum Vivere* qui stipule que la vie détermine la conscience s'associe au postulat de négation de l'impératif moral, ce dernier requérant l'autonomie du sujet. Voir P. Ricoeur, *Marx...*, p.118 *sq*.

65 « Ach, panie, niech mnie pan nie straszy zagadnieniami, jak to wy tam teraz nazywacie... Pan jest nauczyciel czy inżynier, już mi się poplątało... Zagadnieniami moralnymi. Moja szkoła, to była szkoła co się zowie. Moje życie, to jest życie ». J. Iwaszkiewicz, *op.cit.*, p. 21.

L'isotopie sémantique dominante : isotopie de la Vie

On note la surreprésentation du paradigme du verbe « vivre » dont les nombreuses occurrences émaillent les pages[66].

L'isotopie de la vie se diversifie ainsi en une pluralité de termes relatifs aux conditions matérielles de subsistance. Le verbe « manger » revient inlassablement[67], de même que la « vie », saisie dans une acception purement matérielle[68]. On parle également de « vivres »[69].

On peut établir, enfin, une liste détaillée des différentes denrées alimentaires dont l'importance est soulignée: le beurre[70], les œufs[71], et surtout la viande, dans la variété de ses hyponymes[72], sans oublier les médicaments[73], le thé[74], les cigarettes[75] et, bien sûr, l'alcool[76].

L'organisation pronominale, modale et lexicale du discours narratif témoigne donc de l'impact pathogène des schèmes de l'idéologie marxiste sur le profil discursif du locuteur-narrateur. Les distorsions de ce profil au regard des modèles canoniques de la subjectivité parlante s'avèrent à l'origine de la difficulté d'appréhension du concept éthique, chez ce Je aliéné. C'est bien ce qui motive son rejet ironique de *La chute* de Camus.

II. C. Vers une interprétation renouvelée du discours narratif de *L'Envol*

Certes, le narrateur de *L'Envol* engage une polémique avec les thèses humanistes de Camus. Or, encore faut-il considérer qui est ce narrateur. On ne saurait, en effet, oublier la pathologie des structures mentales qui affecte ce dernier, pathologie portant, comme nous venons de le voir, sur ses foyers de valorisation morale et de construction signifiante. Il est significatif que cette pathologie s'avère motivée par l'atteinte destructrice des schèmes marxistes.

Par conséquent, si le narrateur de *L'Envol* ne peut pas accéder aux problématiques éthiques soulevées par Camus, dans *La chute*, ce n'est pas parce que

---

66 *Ibidem*, p. 12, 14, 16, 19, 35, 36, 37.

67 *Ibidem*, p. 13–14.

68 *Ibidem*, p. 14, 28, 37.

69 *Ibidem*, p. 25.

70 *Ibidem*, p. 13–14.

71 *Ibidem*, p. 12.

72 *Ibidem*, p. 12 : six occurrences ; « viande » trois occurrences : *ibidem*, p. 6.

73 *Ibidem*, p. 27, 37.

74 *Ibidem*, p. 31.

75 *Ibidem*, p. 20, 27.

76 *Ibidem*, p. 13, p. 14, 19, 20–21, 29–33, 36–37.

ces problématiques perdraient leur sens, dans une réalité historique radicale, mais bien parce que lui-même n'est pas un sujet structuré. En effet, l'impératif moral n'ayant de réalité que pour une subjectivité individuelle, les circonstances extérieures ne sauraient l'invalider. Elles peuvent, en revanche, mettre en échec le critère d'autonomie subjective qui en fixe les conditions de possibilité[77]. C'est bien ce que semble nous montrer Iwaszkiewicz, dans *L'Envol.*

En effet, si le narrateur de ce texte déroutant refuse la révolte camusienne, c'est bien parce que, pour soutenir l'effort de la révolte, il faut être un sujet, c'est-à-dire, au sens kantien du terme, celui qui « existe comme fin en soi, et non pas simplement comme moyen dont telle ou telle volonté puisse user à son gré »[78]. Or, cette condition préalable n'est pas remplie dans le cas de Romek. Et ceci d'une part, certes, en raison de son parcours existentiel chaotique, mais aussi, d'autre part, en raison des principes délétères de l'idéologie marxiste dont il est imprégné.

Force est donc de postuler un renouvellement de l'interprétation du discours narratif de *L'Envol.* Ce discours, nous ne l'envisageons pas comme l'expression d'une remise en cause des thèses humanistes d'A. Camus, ainsi que le donne à croire une lecture critique limitée à l'aspect sémantique de ce discours, mais bien, *a contrario,* comme une mise en procès de l'idéologie marxiste. Cette mise en procès opère en filigrane, à travers la visée illocutoire et pragmatique du discours narratif.

C'est bien cette visée, orientée vers la description d'une subjectivité parlante bien problématique, dans ses conditionnements idéologiques, qui éclaire, à nos yeux, la signifiance du texte d'Iwaszkiewicz. Loin de prendre le contrepied de Camus, Iwaszkiewicz orchestre ainsi, dans *L'Envol*, un ample procès de l'idéologie marxiste, éprouvée comme un construit aliénant pour une subjectivité individuelle. Romek apparaît, en ce sens, comme une sorte de repoussoir qui incarne, en forçant le trait, les implications virtuelles aberrantes de cette idéologie sur le psychisme d'un Je.

Or, nous soutenons que c'est grâce à sa rencontre avec *La chute* que l'auteur polonais parvient à identifier comme néfastes les schèmes marxistes qui le guettent, pour les déconstruire, dans *L'Envol,* avant qu'ils ne l'atteignent lui-même, avant que lui-même ne dise, comme Romek : « Arrêtez

77 E. Kant, *Critique de la raison pure*, cité par P. Ricoeur, *Soi-même comme un autre*, coll. Folio Essais, Seuil, 1990, p. 245 *sq.*

78 « [...] l'homme, et en général tout être raisonnable existe comme fin en soi, et non pas simplement comme moyen dont telle ou telle volonté puisse user à son gré ». E. Kant, *Ecrits IV*, cité par P. Ricoeur, *Soi-même...*, p. 262.

de m'ennuyer avec, comment vous appelez ça, [...]. Avec vos questions morales »[79].

Dès lors, *L'Envol* a, peut-être, été écrit pour conjurer l'aliénation idéologique qui le menace et qui menace, plus largement, le lecteur polonais de l'époque. Ce lecteur, porteur, comme tout Polonais cultivé, de l'héritage spirituel d'un Norwid et d'un Słowacki, ne peut réellement adhérer aux *doxas* marxistes, aussi intrusives soient-elles. Il entend résonner, en effet, aux tréfonds de la mémoire collective qui l'a formée, tels vers du poète romantique :

> Ceux, pour qui oui, c'est oui
> Et non, c'est non
> Sans clair-obscur
> Ils me manquent, Seigneur[80].

Tant il est vrai que le carcan idéologique ne pèse rien, face à la prévalence de l'impératif catégorique, tant camusien qu'iwaszkiewiczien, au fond, car ancré dans le paradigme romantique, constitutif de la polonité.

Dès lors, c'est bien la rencontre entre le livre emblématique du moraliste français et le lecteur polonais de l'époque qui offre, à nos yeux, la motivation profonde de la genèse de *L'Envol*. Cette rencontre est difficile, le lecteur sentant qu'une barrière de nature idéologique l'empêche de lire ce livre. Mais cette rencontre est, en même temps, susceptible de libérer l'énergie d'un bouleversement cathartique, en ce qu'elle génère un retour réflexif réparateur, porté par l'éthos de l'Octobre 1956, mais portant plus loin encore.

***

Ces investigations nous conduisent donc à souligner que l'absence de pertinence des thèses camusiennes, dans un contexte de référence totalitaire, ne tient pas à des facteurs objectifs. Au contraire, la source de la difficulté d'appréhension de l'éthique camusienne est à chercher à l'intérieur même du sujet.

Ainsi, dans *L'Envol*, force est d'expliquer l'imperméabilité du narrateur à l'humanisme de l'auteur de *La Peste* par la pathologie affectant les structures

---

79 « [...] niech pan mnie nie straszy zagadnieniami, jak to wy tam teraz nazywacie... zagadnieniami moralnymi. J. Iwaszkiewicz, *op.cit.*, p. 21.

80 « Do tych, co mają tak za tak – nie za nie – Bez światło-cienia...Tęskno mi, Panie... ». C.K. Norwid, *Moja piosnka* (1865) [dans :] C.K. Norwid, *Pisma zebrane*, édition établie par Z. Przesmycki, Warszawa, 1911.

conceptuelles et les capacités de valorisation morale de ce Je, mutilé par une idéologie qui virtualise justement la dimension intellectuelle et éthique.

En jetant, grâce aux instruments critiques de l'Esthétique de la Réception, un nouvel éclairage sur le discours narratif *non crédible* du monologue iwaszkiewiczien, nous avons donc mis au jour certaines procédures textuelles travaillant à déconstruire les schèmes marxistes. Cette déconstruction est contemporaine d'un rapprochement entre l'horizon de l'auteur implicite de *L'Envol* et celui de *La chute*.

Il reste à explorer d'autres perspectives de ce texte vertigineux, comme la perspective de l'action, de l'espace, du temps, ou encore celle du lecteur implicite, pour mettre en lumière l'ampleur du processus esthétique de subversion qui, à l'œuvre par excellence dans *L'Envol*, confère, plus largement, à la littérature sa capacité à secouer les totalitarismes.

BIBLIOGRAPHIE

Ariel, *Zamiast przeglądu prasy. Wzlot i Upadek*, « Życie i Myśl » 1958, no 1–2.

Benveniste, E., *Problèmes de linguistique générale*, chapitre XX « La nature des pronoms », coll. Tel, Paris, Gallimard, 1966.

Bereza, H., *Demonizm przewrotny*, « Twórczość » 1968, no 10.

Booth, W.C., *The Rhetoric of Fiction*, Chicago, University of Chicago Press, 1963.

Burkot, S., *Literatura polska po 1939 roku*, Warszawa, PWN, 2006.

Camus, A., *L'Homme révolté* [dans :] A. Camus, *Œuvres Complètes III : 1949–1956*, dir. R. Gay-Crosier, coll. Bibliothèque de la Pléiade, Paris, Gallimard, 2008.

Claeys, G., *Encyclopedia of Nineteenth-century Thought*, London – New York, Taylor & Francis, 2005.

Davies, N., *Histoire de la Pologne*, trad. fr. D. Meunier, Paris, Fayard, 1984.

Dolecki, Z., *Proces wieku*, « Kierunki » 1957, no 35.

Drewnowski, T., *Literatura polska 1944–1989. Próba scalenia*, Kraków, Universitas, 2004.

Gay-Crosier, R., *Les codes ironiques dans* La Chute *: un humanisme à rebours* [in :] *Pour un humanisme Romanesque*, dir. G. Phillipe, A. Spiquel, Paris, SEDES, 1999

Głowiński, M., *Narracja jako monolog wypowiedziany* [dans :] M. Głowiński, *Gry powieściowe*, Warszawa, PWN, 1973.

Hegel, G.W.F., *La phénoménologie de l'Esprit*, texte traduit et établi par J. Hyppolite, coll. Philosophies de l'Esprit, Paris, Aubier, 1977.

Hegel, G.W.F., *La raison dans l'histoire*, trad. K. Papaioannou, Paris, Plon, 1965.

Iser, W., *L'acte de lecture. Théorie de l'effet esthétique*, trad. fr. E. Sznycer, deuxième édition coll. Philosophie et langage, Liège, éd. Mardaga, 1973.

Iwaszkiewicz, J., *Wzlot*, « Twórczość » 1957, no 12.

Januszkiewicz, M., *Tropami egzystencjalizmu w literaturze polskiej XX-go wieku*, Poznań, Poznańskie Studia Polonistyczne. Seria literacka, 1998.

Jarosinski, Z., *Literatura lat 1945–1975*, Warszawa, Wydawnictwo Naukowe PWN, 1996.

Jauss, H.-R., *Pour une esthétique de la réception*, trad. fr. C. Maillard, coll. Tel, Paris, Gallimard, 1988 (1990).

Jauss, H.-R., *Pour une herméneutique littéraire*, trad. fr. M. Jacob, Paris, Gallimard, NRF, 1988.

Julia, D., *Dictionnaire de la philosophie*, Paris, Larousse, 1964.

Kajtoch, W., *Językowe obrazy świata i człowieka w prasie młodzieżowej i alternatywnej*, t. 1 i t. 2, Kraków, Wydawnictwo Uniwersytetu Jagiellońskiego, 2008.

Kant, E., *Critique de la raison pure*, cité par P. Ricoeur, *Soi-même comme un autre*, coll. Folio Essais, Seuil, 1990.

Kant, E., *Ecrits IV*, cité par P. Ricoeur, *Soi-même...*

Kolera, J., *Od ślepoty do kapitulacji*, « Nowe Sygnały » 1957, no 32.

Marx, K., *L'idéologie allemande*, p. 36–37 ; cité par P. Ricoeur, *Marx...*

Morawski, K., *Książka o mieszczańskim świecie*, « Dziś i Jutro » 1956, no 5.

Norwid, C.K., *Moja piosnka* (1865) [dans :] C.K. Norwid, *Pisma zebrane*, édition établie par Z. Przesmycki, Warszawa, 1911.

Liklaszewska, M., *Upadek Camusa, czyli strzeżmy sie ludzi niewinnych*, « Prawo i Życie » 1957, no 15.

Przybylski, R., *Camus i Dostoïevski nad Upadkiem*, « Polityka » 1957, année 1, no 23.

Ricoeur P., *Le Marx de Michel Henry, Approches de la personne* [dans :] P. Ricoeur, *Lectures 2*, coll. Essais, Paris, Seuil, 1999.

Ricoeur, P., *Marx: L'idéologie allemande (1)* [dans :] P. Ricoeur, *L'idéologie et l''utopie*, coll. Essais, Paris, Seuil, 1997.

Ritz, G., *Jarosław Iwaszkiewicz. Pogranicza nowoczesności*, trad. A. Kopacki, Kraków, Universitas 1998.

Sadkowski, W., *Camus i Gascar*, « Trybuna Ludu » 1957, no 217.

Skoluda, C., *Uwięzieni w człowieku*, « Tygodnik Zachodni » 1957, no 36.

Ricoeur, P., *Soi-même comme un autre*, coll. Folio Essais, Seuil, 1990.

Smulski, J., *Pękanie lodów. Krótkie formy narracyjne w literaturze polskiej lat 1945–1955*, Toruń, UMK, 1995.

Wachlowska, I., *Przekłady z literatur zachodnio-europejskich w Polsce Ludowej*, « Kwartalnik Neofilologiczny » 1956, no 1–2.

Wilson, D., Sperber, D., *L'interprétation des énoncés*, « Communications » 1979, vol. 30.

Camus and Dostoyevsky's Philosophical Challenge – a Strange Spiritual Affinity

REMIGIUSZ KRÓL, PIOTR MRÓZ

The world of ideas is like a poker game or, to resort to existentialist terminology, appears to be deeply imbued with the illusive yet tangible atmosphere of *contingence*. Both Camus and Sartre were interested in world literature, both were avid readers of novels depicting the *conditio humana*, and did not limit themselves in their reading activities to French, contemporary and classic literary output but included in their perusals works scarcely known as well as those popular at the time (the thirties and early forties of the last century) among a wider public – such literary figures as Tolstoy and Dostoyevsky, Shestov or Merezhkovsky – Russian masters of the 19th and 20th century. But first and foremost it was Camus who seems to have followed and symphatized with the unique spirit of the Russian soul with its sense of ensuing absurdity and overwhelming blind chance. The following is a juxtaposition of Camus's understanding of the Russian giant of literature and ideas which were paradoxically close to his understanding and feeling – the views of a Polish Catholic existentialist (Camus's contemporary) Father Woroniecki. Such a "venue" of world views and opinions – irrespective of their ideological and religious foundations – is only possible in the meta-reality of the world of universal (*catholon*) culture. We shall make some references to the works of Merezhkovsky, Shestov and Evdokimov as close intellectual and spiritual allies of Camus.

On the basis of his numerous treaties, we can view Dostoyevsky as an expert on difficult and complicated philosophical-theological problems on the one hand, and on the other – the voice of a priest-tutor, a teacher-patriot constantly caring for and providing appropriate development to the vast masses of the faithful exposed to nefarious influences over many centuries, the faithful succumbing to degenerate fashion or harmful habits (e.g. sentimentalism, miscomprehended romanticism, relativist attitudes, eudemonistical or materialist stands) which take one far from the authentic dimension of faith. (All these are sings of inauthentic existence in existentialism.)

Many fragments of *Katolicka Etyka* (*Catholic Ethics*)[1] allude directly to the "beyond academic" threads, life situations or even personal recollections, various literary traditions: Romanticism, the Medieval Literature and the modern prose and drama, and are proof of the tremendous sensitivity of the author of *Katolicka Etyka*.

Like Camus, Jacek Woroniecki is deeply interested in the Russian culture, the spiritual impact of Orthodox Church and its practices and rituals. Woroniecki writes: "Dostoyevsky did not quarrel with the Orthodox Church as Tolstoy did. Just the opposite, he was attached to it in a way, as to the mainstay of social order against the gusts of revolution."[2] In the fragment discussed we do concentrate on a model, a picture of an individual, just as Woroniecki finds it in the critically presented, but highly evaluated literary *oeuvre* of the Russian writer. As Woroniecki notices, Dostoyevsky's works denounce a background of literary achievements of Catholic writers, Mauriac's and Bernanos's, and a well-known philosopher and theologian – Guardini. It is obvious that the author of *Katolicka Etyka* is deeply aware of the doctrinal differences in strictly religious issues. Knowing perfectly well Dostoyevsky's extensive literary *oeuvre*, our philosopher presents in a pertinent and interesting way (what is more, in a way still topical in our times) the manners of interpreting that complicated, heterogeneous and dramatic interpretation of man's paths, that human condition in the confrontation with history and other people, in the struggle with one's weaknesses and dreams of power and might, which are presented in Dostoyevsky's works. As far as we are concerned, Woroniecki (as an unusually erudite person) must have acquainted himself with the classical interpretations of the Russian writer's works presented by the two religious thinkers of the so-called pre-revolution "spirituality." We mean the works by Merezhkovsky and Shestov,[3] published first in Russian (Woroniecki was excellent at Russian), which later (in the thirties) had many translations

---

1 See: J. Woroniecki, *Katolicka etyka wychowawcza*, vols. 1, 2, Lublin, KUL, 2000.

2 J. Woroniecki, *Chrześcijanizm powieści Dostojewskiego i Mauriaca*, "Tygodnik Powszechny" 1947, nr 40, s. 4.

3 L. Szestow, *Dostojewski i Nietzsche – filozofia tragedii*, trans. H. Paprocki, Warszawa, Czytelnik, 1994.

into other European languages. It should be mentioned here that the interpretation of Dostoyevsky's literary *oeuvre* is not less of an achievement than the above-mentioned thinkers' *oeuvres*; what is more, it is Woroniecki who focuses on the undiscovered motives in the *oeuvre* of the Russian genius's – the motives which have fascinated many since then, to the present day.

The author of *Katolickość Tomizmu* emphasizes the fact that when it comes to Dostoyevsky as a person and his works, we do undoubtedly deal with a deeply Christian artist, an artist who in an almost visionary way presents his own independent concept of man and his relations with the world and God, achieved thanks to the artistic and theoretical means. The truth is that Woroniecki does not use the word "poliphony" (though his critical texts indicate it explicitly), a term bluntly reflecting human nature captured by the writer. In other words, the protagonists of *The Devils* are all human beings, but of an overturned balance, beings tinged with a certain ambiguity. In the greatest and most everlasting novels by Dosotoyevsky we do discern "sick" individuals, knocked out, as it were, of the existence, the people of the underground: reasoning, presenting their (sometimes unclear and irrational) motives of actions, but most of all, we do make out people who hurt themselves and others and experience existential pain.[4]

The criterion that Woroniecki uses in the analysis of human nature is balance, the evenness of a human being which comes from the ontological cooperation of the "elements" man is made of. A man, as we know, in Thomists' view is a being of special significance, a being bearing the duty to strive for certain aims, to fulfill certain tasks (according to Evdokimov,[5] these are defined tasks, transcendental aspirations). In other words, there are some determined implications of conduct and organizing one's life (on individual as well as on social grounds) arising from the fact of being a compound (an indissoluble one). According to Woroniecki, the disruption, the lack of balance of Dostoyevsky's man (inspired by most virtuous intentions) is caused in many cases by a dramatic negative experience: the loss of freedom or faith, the death of someone close, the incapability of fulfillment in love, loneliness, poverty, and impotence as far as the realization of certain ideals and far-reaching aims is concerned. It all leads to the previously mentioned

4 F. Dostoyevsky, *Biesy*, trans. Z. Podgórzec, T. Zagórski, Warszawa, PWN, 1993. See also: *idem*, *Zbrodnia i kara*, *Bracia Karamazow*, *Skrzywdzeni i Poniżeni*, trans. Z. Podgórzec, T. Zagórski, Warszawa, PWN, 1993.

5 P. Endokimov, *Gogol i Dostojewski*, trans. A. Kunka, Bydgoszcz, Homini, 2002.

feeling of bitterness, senselessness and existential emptiness, typical of many characters encountered in the novels of the Russian writer.

Analyzing the works of this greatest psychologist of world literature, Woroniecki concentrates on chosen individuals. The motive that we will focus on will be that obvious thing, the disruption of human unity, as well as the doomed-to-failure attempt to restore it. In other words, Woroniecki, being consistent in his Thomistic tenets, interprets Dostoyevsky's message in categories of undisturbed substantiality of faculties (human powers), showing – as it is in the case of the novels' protagonists – that relying on one "force," one side of human nature, leads to disastrous consequences. Let us follow this trail of interpretation. Let us commence from the rational aspect. Woroniecki calls purely rational stands intellectual moralizing. It is the full surrender to the power of *ratio* at the cost of free will, feelings and emotions (e.g. love, compassion). We do discover three classic examples of such an attitude in the rich gallery of Dostoyevsky's moralizing figures. The first stand, presented in the type of novel entitled *Crime and Punishment*, is shown in the existence of Rodion Raskolnikov. This sensitive young man (like other characters in the novels by the author of *The Devils*) deeply experiences the evil of the world. He wants to accomplish something unusual in his life, to act in the name of good for the society, complete law studies, help his family (especially his sister) – in other words, he firmly strives for his goals. However, we have to remember that this is a picture of the tsarist Russia of the second half of the 19th century. Rodion experiences impotence, powerlessness and immense obstacles in achieving his goals. In none of Dostoyevsky's other works can there be found examples of such apt, adequate descriptions of poverty and utter degradation as in the Petersburg presented in *Crime and Punishment*, all that demonstrated in bitter scenes of humiliation of those who have been destined to suffer eternal privations, destined for the lack of any possibilities whatsoever of changing their difficult situations. A brilliant – as well as analytical – interpretation of Raskolnikov reveals itself fully in the article published by the protagonist himself. Rodion presents there a concept of a strong and ruthless individual (an evident anticipation of the Nietzschean superman). This individual is equipped with laws (or he usurps those laws) to decide on the most significant matters (the typical "sacred problems," as Dostoyevsky suggests in one note in *The Diary of the Writer*). Let us then specify this theme by presenting (the seemingly virtuous) reasoning. Raskolnikov comes to the conclusion that a valuable, virtuous individual who strives for certain ideals has got the right, or even obligation, to remove all the obstacles which prevent his self-realization. If one is deprived of the essentials, if he has to beg the world and his widowed mother for the money he needs, and his penniless sister sacrifices herself by marring a despicable man, the moral world must be out of order. If, as Dostoyevsky's protagonist understands it, there are people who have been equipped by fate or coincidence with goods which they do not deserve, then one has the ethical permission to take them all away from them. In this manner one can help not only himself but also the others who are in the same situation. Dostoyevsky presents such mercenary moralizing in a superb way. It is the intellect, being at the peak of its power, that views the situation and decides. Not listening to the voice of conscience, killing the elementary emotions, the mind weighs precisely all the arguments for and against the intended action. The conclusion is "stunningly" easy: eliminate in the name of some "good" those social "nits" which cling tightly to the body of the Russian society. Just kill. In the end, then, we do learn about a deliberate crime committed against a usurer and an accidental murder of her sister. Rodion trusted the powers of the reason absolutely: he "balanced" the reasons and made a choice, like a demiurge who decides over life and death. By joining the mind with unlimited freedom, the main character created a rule of proceeding: those who constitute certain obstacles for our or the others' development can be eliminated. The narrative structure of the novel – and Dostoyevsky is a master of constructing such structures – does not bear vacuum, however. Element "A" evokes element "B." In other words, a reasoning is set off against some other one. Thus, Rodion encounters an equal (in the sense of the rational method employed) partner: someone different in essence, composed, equally "moralizing," and using reliable methods of logical exploration. Porfiry – the criminal investigator and prosecutor – does not resort to compulsion nor threats (his image differs from the stereotype notion of a tsarist policeman); he is intelligent, "delicate," subtle, but resolute and consistent. He assumes, stating that people like Rodion are weak by the weakness of those who lost their faith in the sense of existence, in social order, in truths coming from religion or faith. What is more, there is no such a degenerated and spoiled individual that would be devoid of the remnants of conscience. Porfiry's investigations are supported by coincidence: when an innocent man is captured – a fact about which Raskolnikov learns during the process of investigation as a formal witness to the crime – a kind of transformation takes place. If intellect appeared to be so cruel and ruthless (it led to a murder, a senseless crime, a murder which did not solve any problems), then another human power reveals itself to be stronger: the power of self-catharsis, a moral feeling manifested in the pangs of remorse. Dostoyevsky would not have been such an excellent psychologist, if he had not shown the impact of this power. Raskolnikov belongs to a group of people marked by the disease of being internally torn apart. He will never (after such an action) reach balance, neither physical nor psychological. Suffering, he immerses himself into the gloomy abyss of his visions, delusions, and hallucinations, which are accompanied by the attacks of epilepsy. Raskolnikov is scared as only a man who perceives in full the absurdity of the misdeed he committed can be scared. He would want to get rid of that burden, make a confession, but he cannot find enough strength of will to act. The protagonist cannot do that on his own. According to Dostoyevsky's artistic-moral message, Raskolnikov is an example of a total loss of orientation of the world: the loss of values, truths, emotions and human achievements. Moreover, he is a lonely and alienated individual, waiting for help and rejecting it at the same time – but up to a certain point in his life. In the extensive structure of the presented world, the author of *Crime and Punishment* finds a place for a special kind of help. It is the intervention from the outside, a type of an intervention which plays an extremely significant role in the work in question. The encounter of Rodion and Sonya (a daughter of a lower-rank clerk, an "iconic" alcoholic) seems to be an evident sign of the forthcoming help. Sonya Marmeladova is a woman (whom the society of that time treated as "fallen") cast away to the deepest levels of the "classless." This prostitute could have had – as Dostoyevsky suggested – all reasons to abandon the Catholic faith, to give up following the message of caritas. But she does not despise the society that doomed her and her family to incomprehensible poverty and degradation. Nevertheless, Sonya is the exact opposite of that: she does not moralize, she experiences all evil and suffering for the sake of others and her family (especially for her farher) and then for the one who does absolutely need help – the accidentally encountered Raskolnikov. Like the evangelical Mary Magdalene, Sonya believes unconditionally that Christ has not forsaken her and will forgive and finally save her. But not only her. Everything that Sonya does (by breaking down the resistance of the society and her family) is achieved in the name of one's neighbor. To our mind, Woroniecki discerns some deeper reason of moral actions in the character of Sonya. The author of *Katolickość Tomizmu* undoubtedly approves of the attitude of spotless and undisturbed faith. Believing in God – Christ – though deprived of such drastic moments as Kierkegaard's leap into the abyss, is said to be, according to our philosopher, supported by the rational reasoning. Despite the fact that Sonya is not an educated person, she has a great respect for knowledge, which is manifested in her acceptance of the permanence and inviolability of ordinary principles, and she respects the principles which sustain her decent existence even in the gutter. In an act of love and sympathy for Raskolnikov – a murderer, as well as a man who lost his way – she shows him a path of penance and redemption. A very moving scene with the medallion – the image of a saint icon – is mainly interpreted according to the categories of the order to return to the source: God's soil, in front of which one should bow and kiss it. Only in this way – irrational, one would think – a man can retrieve the lost balance, can recover and give up that ambiguous personality so deeply spoiled by the bad attitude of reason, intellect. And though Woroniecki, a follower of Thomas Aquinas's, in many of his works decidedly rejects that superficial sentimentalism and irrational attitude as far as faith is concerned, we can observe on the basis of Dostoyevsky's works discussed here that it is the feeling that is most important (the co-experiencing), not the clear and cool calculation of reason. To put it differently, the consequences of badly applied rationality can be the worst offence against the holiness of life. In this way a man or a woman loses irretrievably his or her being given by God. If Raskolnikov is lost through the wrong perception, characteristic of the "strong," demanding, self-made man, then another of Dostoyevsky's protagonists, Ivan Karamazov, falls into even heavier sin – the sin of excessive pride, which inevitably leads to atheism. It is a highly complicated problem when it comes to the socio-cultural aspect of the 19th-century Russia. If we were to consider atheism with reference to morality and ethics (and that is, according to Woroniecki, of Dostoyevsky's interest), then the denial of the existence of God leads to incalculable consequences. In other words, atheism propagated in Russia among some intellectual, liberal circles eliminates authentic compassion and love. Ivan is the best example of this. If there is no God, then everything is allowed. And in spite of the fact that the protagonist of *The Brothers Karamazov* is a sensitive man – sensitive to the issues of evil, harm and suffering – it is the cool rational calculation that leads him astray. The existence of God cannot be proved; for Ivan the evidence is unobtainable and impossible to grasp with a human mind. And if – as Ivan comprehends it – evil exists, children are starving, wars break out, innocent people are murdered, then there must exist some other premise allowing to confirm oneself in faithlessness: evil, which has spread all over the world so overtly. Dostoyevsky takes issue with what he recognizes as the source of such dangerous convictions. The blame falls on certain degradations of the Church, which had been enslaved by the spirit of rationality and calculation. In a significant fragment of *The Brothers Karamazov* – a story about the Great Inquisitor – we do find a literary interpretation of those difficult and urgent problems. It is not an accident that

Dostoyevsky makes Ivan the creator of that legend, and his brother – Alyosha Karamazov, a young practicing monk – the listener. According to Dostoyevsky (as the legend is a kind of exposition of the author's views), human society can be deluded by various temptations. Christ did not succumb to them (when put to the test), but overpowered those who strove to rule, to gain knowledge and prosperity, thus usurping the right to exercise power over believers. In other words, as this is actually what the parable is about, the man has concentrated on a few mundane aspects of life and lost the power to believe in a pure way. In addition to this, the human being gave freedom away and trusted Satan's message – following the wrong path to sheer power. The symbolic sword, bread and miracles are supposed to substitute real faith, give a poor semblance of happiness and peace. By doing that the man "closes" the path to salvation: he rejects Christ and goes over to evil's side. So, a comprehensively educated liberal, a "western" intellectual, which Ivan surely is, understands the importance of these problems, but is not able to apply this knowledge and help men to regain the lost balance, to wit, combine intellectual and spiritual powers. A different attitude towards the issues of God, faith, salvation and happiness can be found in Alyosha, who exemplifies the model of a lay saint (an ideal of Camus). Young Karamazov is an embodiment of what Woroniecki calls the religious emotion. And though it is not enough to secure full happiness, this authentic side of the human being is approved by Woroniecki. God is alive, present in the world revealing himself in the act of faith. A foster child and a favourite of the holy old man (*staryec*) Zosima, Alyosha is respected by the religious society he is a part of. He is a pure, though inexperienced individual. Zosima, who suffered a lot of evil, who turned away from a worthless life, attempts to spare Alyosha such dramatic experiences. The knowledge the old man gives to the young neophyte concerns the inner harmony of life, as well as the understanding of the others. That is where the saint's attitude – *caritas* – comes from: the love of the neighbor through the love for God. This simple but clear truth becomes powerful when, after his death, Zosima makes his appearance while Alyosha is dreaming about the Wedding at Cana. That symbolic summoning of the young man to the circle of the ones chosen by Christ is an evident sign that the feeling of love (love grounded in faith) is capable of solving the fundamental existential problems. And though Woroniecki cannot (as a Thomist) fully share the same interpretation of an individual's conception, this feeling (strengthened by the evangelical stand) eliminates the mock and self-righteous stand of a moralizer. A cool, calculating mind can lead to terrible mistakes, just as pure, atavistic vitality and impetuousness can, a vitality which is exemplified in the attitude of the third character of *The Brothers Karamazov*: Dmitri. The eldest of all the brothers, like Kierkegaard's man of esthetics, immerses himself in the abyss of sensual experiences, that sensual directness of experiencing things, elements of passion and unabashed lust of physical love. Nevertheless, such a way of acting is totally destructive. It results in the deepening of that internal state of being torn apart, making the individual a fragile and unstable object which can concentrate only on primeval instincts. The infatuation with a woman's physical beauty (Grushenka), the unlimited desire may lead to the heaviest crimes. Nevertheless, Dmitri, when compared with Ivan, bears much more of a resemblance to a human being: his directness, sincerity, ability to show sympathy for those who have been harmed by life to a greater extent (a dream during the trial), proves undoubtedly similar to experiences of the author of the novel himself. Following this interpretative trail can produce the temptation that the primeval stage of fascination with the element of sheer sensuality can lead to God's forgiveness towards mankind. That is the reason for the existence of the developmental dialectics of an individual (from sensuality through the mind to Christian love) which allows us to think that for Dostoyevsky – a moralist and psychologist – the question of a subject, human being is not only unsolved, but open in the sense that a man is a living hope. This exaggerated pathology of the novel's characters plays, according to Woroniecki, a pedagogical role. Unpredictable, torn, tragic individuals presented in such a brilliant manner are meant to teach us that human existence, exposed to so many perils and dangers, is a task, a moral challenge. In other words, a man has to gain balance of the powers and balance of the goals, emotionally and rationally strive for the height of feelings, cognition, comprehension and action. Strictly speaking, a man has to gain that balance characteristic of a real humanity. Raskolnikov, a man of the underground, Myshkin, Dmitri, Alyosha, and even Stavrogin and Verkhovensky, according to Woroniecki, have the chance to rebuild the human world. They will not create it on the life stage, however, on the stage they are "at this the earthly moment." They have to undergo a kind of conversion, a sudden transformation, a metamorphosis, a re-birth or a moral redemption.

The author of *Katolickość Tomizmu* is a sensitive recipient of that literary message. Despite the evident and unremovable differences in portraying the world as well as in the religious outlook on life, Woroniecki recognizes Dostoyevsky's tragic pessimism mostly as far as the category of a warning is concerned. The discrepancies between the eastern and the western doctrine of the Church are not so vital. In the work of the Russian author Woroniecki discerns a message based on the Gospel which teaches love and understanding.

In one of Dostoyevsky's notes we find a sentence in which the author claims that if he were given the choice between the truth and Christ, he would choose God's Son. This is the only direction which makes human existence meaningful. That is why the reader is so often appalled by the scenes in which lost, blaspheming individuals refer to God. In many dramatic scenes (the conversations between Kirillov and Stavrogin, Rogozhin and Nastasya Filipovna, Sonya and Raskolnikov) the main protagonist assumes the icon that, becomes a sign of unity between what is terrestrial (then prone to evil coming from people and their world) and what is divine. The visual sign of God's presence is addressed even to those who outspokenly negate His existence. For Dostoyevsky, human pride, the will to substitute God by some ideas, desires to be supermen, a strive for absolute freedom, all lead to a fall to "degradation," which means the disappearance of that supernatural element – the Absolute. The dread and drama of human existence, which constitute an integral part of the author's novels, have their counterbalance in the hope of the Re-birth of the individual, in the return to the source for those who got lost, went through the inferno of passions and comprehended in the end that God (hidden among the smallest of this world) has not left them to their own fate.

Although Camus is an atheist – his philosophy of man having been grounded in a specific kind of individualism and heroic humanism – he is far from denouncing all forms of moral transcendentalism. Human condition – *hic et nunc* – is tinged, marked with insoluble, intransigent and intrinsic absurdity. So, in the absence of God, man must resort to the values of his/her invention – the values we are responsible for. But humankind from times immemorial has committed grave mistakes – proposing false solutions and "ways out." According to the French writer, all attempts at overcoming our fate – aesthetic, political or economic – are doomed to failure. It is the overpowering nihilism that is a real threat and menace. But it is the reality where the man tries to replace the other's freedom irrespective of his/her humanity that makes Camus feel enraged. In this vision of the Russian master, especially in *The Devils*, Camus sees the true anticipation of the world to come. He openly states in his famous *The Rebel* that "the totalitarian theocrats of the twentieth century and state terrorism are thus announced. The new aristocracy and the Grand Inquisitors reign to day."[6] Those nihilistic, oppressive powers (antihuman) insidiously take advantage of the only "positive" power inherent in absurd men: the unity ensuing from the solidarity of saying no, to wit, of rebellion. They (the oppressive powers) make "use of the rebellion

6 See: A. Camus, *The Rebel*, trans. A. Bower, London, Penguin Books, 1973, p. 144.

of the oppressed, over one part of your history. Their reign is cruel, but they excuse their cruelty, like the Satan of the romantics, by claiming that it is hard for then to bear (...)."[7] But humanity, irrespective of the varying status – social, economic, educational – of particular individuals, is facing the same fate. We are all in the same boat, underlines Camus at one point. Thus, the oppressors make a horrible mistake; by trying to replace God they are not able to eliminate the inalienable elements of human condition – the lack of essence and freedom, the absurdity in a human situation, total responsibility. All these make us equal in the perspective of human eternity. "A new and somewhat hideous race of martyrs is now born. Their martyrdom consists of consenting to inflict suffering on others, they become the slaves of their own domination. For man to become God, the victim must bow down before the executioner. That is why both victim and executioner are equally despairing. Neither slavery nor power will any longer coincide with happiness, the masters will be morose and the slaves sullen."[8]

BIBLIOGRAPHY

Camus, A., *The Rebel*, trans. A. Bower, London, Penguin Books, 1973.

Dostoyevsky, F., *Biesy*, trans. Z. Podgórzec, T. Zagórski, Warszawa, PWN, 1993.

Dostoyevsky, F., *Zbrodnia i kara*, *Bracia Karamazow*, *Skrzywdzeni i poniżeni*, trans. Z. Podgórzec, T. Zagórski, Warszawa, PWN, 1993.

Endokimov, P., *Gogol i Dostojewski*, trans. A. Kunka, Bydgoszcz, Homini, 2002.

Szestow L., *Dostojewski i Nietzsche – filozofia tragedii*, trans. H. Paprocki, Warszawa, Czytelnik, 1994.

Woroniecki J., *Chrześcijanizm powieści Dostojewskiego i Mauriaca*, Tygodnik Powszechny, nr 40, 1947.

Woroniecki J., *Katolicka etyka wychowawcza*, vols. 1, 2, Lublin, KUL, 2000.

7 *Ibidem*, p. 144.

8 *Ibidem*.

EDITOR-IN-CHIEF
Agnieszka Stęplewska

TECHNICAL EDITORS
Agnieszka Stęplewska
Paulina Tumidajewicz

TECHNICAL PROOFREADER
Magdalena Jankosz

TYPESETTER
Marta Jaszczuk

Jagiellonian University Press
Editorial Offices: ul. Michałowskiego 9/2, 31-126 Kraków
Phone: +48 12 663 23 80, +48 12 663 23 82, Fax: +48 12 663 23 83